Destruction of Jewish Kovno
(Kaunas, Lithuania)

Translation of
Umkum fun der Yidisher Kovne

Original Book Edited by: Joseph Gar

Originally published in Munich 1948

A Publication of JewishGen,
Edmond J. Safra Plaza, 36 Battery Place, New York, NY 10280
646.494.2972 | info@JewishGen.org | www.jewishgen.org

©JewishGen, 2024. All Rights Reserved.
JewishGen is the Genealogical Research Division of the
Museum of Jewish Heritage – A Living Memorial to the Holocaust

Destruction of Jewish Kovno (Kaunas, Lithuania)
Translation of *Umkum fun der Yidisher Kovne*

Copyright © 2024 by JewishGen. All rights reserved.
First Printing: October 2023, Cheshvan 5784
Second Printing: March 2024, Adar II 5784
Editor of Original Yizkor Book: Joseph Gar
Translator and Project Coordinator: Ettie Zilber
Cover Design: Rachel Kolokoff Hopper
Layout: Jonathan Wind
Name Indexing: Stefanie Holzman

This book may not be reproduced, in whole or in part, including illustrations in any form (beyond that copying permitted by Sections 107 and 108 of the U.S. Copyright Law and except by reviewers for public press), without written permission from the publisher.

JewishGen is not responsible for inaccuracies or omissions in the original work and makes no representations regarding the accuracy of this translation. Digital images of the original book's contents can be seen online at the New York Public Library website or the Yiddish Book Center website.

Library of Congress Control Number (LCCN): 2022950714

ISBN: 978-1-954176-65-2 (hard cover: 308 pages, alk. paper)

About JewishGen.org

JewishGen, an affiliate of the Museum of Jewish Heritage - A Living Memorial to the Holocaust, serves as the global home for Jewish genealogy.

Featuring unparalleled access to 30+ million records, it offers unique search tools, along with opportunities for researchers to connect with others who share similar interests. Award winning resources such as the Family Finder, Discussion Groups, and ViewMate, are relied upon by thousands each day.

In addition, JewishGen's extensive informational, educational and historical offerings, such as the Jewish Communities Database, Yizkor Book translations, InfoFiles, Family Tree of the Jewish People, and KehilaLinks, provide critical insights, first-hand accounts, and context about Jewish communal and familial life throughout the world.

Offered as a free resource, JewishGen.org has facilitated thousands of family connections and success stories, and is currently engaged in an intensive expansion effort that will bring many more records, tools, and resources to its collections.

Please visit https://www.jewishgen.org/ to learn more.

Executive Director: Avraham Groll

About the JewishGen Yizkor Book Project

Yizkor Books (Memorial Books) were traditionally written to memorialize the names of departed family and martyrs during holiday services in the synagogue (a practice that still exists in many synagogues today).

Over the centuries, as a result of countless persecutions and horrific atrocities committed against the Jews, Yizkor Books (Sefer Zikaron in Hebrew) were expanded to include more historical information, such as biographical sketches of famous personalities and descriptions of daily town life.

Following the Holocaust, the idea of remembrance and learning took on an urgent and crucial importance. Survivors of the Holocaust sought out other surviving residents of their former towns to memorialize and document the names and way of life of those who were ruthlessly murdered by the Nazis. These remembrances were documented in Yizkor Books, hundreds of which were published in the first decades after the Holocaust.

Most of these books were published privately, or through Landsmanshaftn (social organizations comprised of members originating from the same European town or region) that still existed, and were often distributed free of charge. The languages used to document these crucial histories and links to our past were Yiddish and Hebrew.

JewishGen has undertaken the sacred responsibility of translating these books into English so that the culture and way of life of these communities will be preserved and transmitted to future generations.

In 1986, a group of farsighted JewishGenners started a project to pool their efforts together in groups based upon their ancestors from each town and raise funds to get the Yizkor books of their ancestral towns translated into English. As the translated material became available, it was made accessible for free at www.JewishGen.org/Yizkor. Hardcover copies can be purchased by visiting https://www.jewishgen.org/Yizkor/ybip.html (see below).

It is our hope that the translation of these books into English (and other languages) will assist the countless Jewish family researchers who are so desperately seeking to forge a connection with their heritage.

Director of JewishGen Yizkor Book Project: Lance Ackerfeld

About JewishGen Press

JewishGen Press (formerly the Yizkor Books-in-Print Project) is the publishing division of JewishGen.org, and provides a venue for the publication of non-fiction books pertaining to Jewish genealogy, history, culture, and heritage.

In addition to the Yizkor Book category, publications in the other categories978-1-954176-65-2 include Shoah memoirs and research, genealogical research, collections of genealogical and historical materials, biographies, diaries and letters, studies of Jewish experience and cultural life in the past, academic theses, and other books of interest to the Jewish community.

Please visit https://www.jewishgen.org/Yizkor/ybip.html to learn more.

Director of JewishGen Press: Joel Alpert
Managing Editor - Jessica Feinstein
Publications Manager - Susan Rosin

Notes to the Reader

The images in the original book were reproduced from photographs from the time of the first edition. These reproductions were already of poor quality, being pre-war and at least 30 or more years old. As a result, the images in the book are the best achievable.
A reader can view the original scans of the book on the websites listed below.

The original book can be seen online at the Yiddish Book Center website:

https://www.yiddishbookcenter.org/collections/yiddish-books/spb-nybc200549/gar-joseph-umkum-fun-der-yidisher-kovne

To obtain a list of Shoah victims from Kovno (Kaunas, Lithuania), the reader should access the Yad Vashem web site listed below; one can also search for specific family names using family name option. These lists are continually updated by Yad Vashem, so it is worthwhile to search them periodically.
There is more valuable information (including the Pages of Testimony, etc.) available on this website: https://yvng.yadvashem.org/

A list of all books available from JewishGen Press along with prices is available at: https://www.jewishgen.org/Yizkor/ybip.html

Translator's Introduction

Scouring archives and databases searching for historical resources to confirm my mother's testimony about her Holocaust experiences in Kovno, Lithuania, I was thrilled when I came across this book by Joseph Gar, published in Germany in 1948. I gleefully downloaded the entire book from the electronic archive of the Yiddish Book Center, in Amherst, Massachusetts. (Also available in the YIVO archive).

This book was written in the years just after the war and was based on interviews with Kovno survivors after their liberation. Most of these survivors were housed in the numerous Displaced Persons (DP) camps set up after the war mostly in the American Zone. Most Kovno Jews were in DP camps in southern Germany, with large numbers in the Landsberg DP camp, 100 km west of Munich. My aunt, Rivka (Sidrer) Baran, a survivor from Kovno, told me that her father, my paternal grandfather, Feival Sidrer, knew Joseph Gar. We assume that he possibly knew him from the Ghetto or from the DP camp, and perhaps even gave testimony to Gar for this historic account.

This is a photo of Joseph Gar in the uniform of the Lithuanian military, 1919. He was one of the volunteers, both Jewish and non-Jewish, who joined the military to fight for the Independence of Lithuania. My own maternal grandfather, Jacob Santockis, was also such a *Savanoris*, as related in my book, A Holocaust Memoir of Love and Resilience: Mama's Survival from Lithuania to the USA.**

My mother told us that the *Savanoriai* were highly recognized and honored in Lithuanian society. In fact, the President of Lithuania recognized them each year at the Independence Day parades and honored them with a medal and other benefits. However, Gar writes about the 70 *Savanoriai* who were to be shot at the Seventh Fort in July 1941. They were collected and taken away from the massacre site – but were later murdered. Nevertheless, my grandfather was lucky. He was not taken to be murdered, perhaps because he showed the shooter the medal that was in his pocket; this shooter sent him to the Gestapo jail instead. Wanting to retrieve this medal for our family, I purchased one from an antique dealer in Kaunas during my "roots" trip in 2017. I will never know if it was my grandfather's actual medal, but it does not matter. But, now I wonder if perhaps my Santockis grandfather knew Gar from their military service.

Image of the Savanoris Medal. Photo courtesy of Ettie Zilber

Joseph Gar was born in 1905 in Kovno to David Leib Gar and Esther Fainberg Gar. His Lithuanian name was Josifas Garas. He lost his wife (nee Shapiro) and baby daughter Gitele (b. 1940) during those years of horror. Gar was a writer and editor of various works before and after the war. Right after liberation he returned to Kovno and helped establish a children's home for those children who were saved by Christians. He eventually came to Israel but left in the early 1950s, immigrating to the USA where he worked as a research associate for YIVO, documenting the history of ghettos and concentration camps. In 1966, he edited a "Bibliography of Articles on the Catastrophe and Heroism in Yiddish Periodicals," a joint project with YIVO and Yad Vashem. He also narrated various stories about the Holocaust. Joseph Gar died in 1989 in the USA.

As I perused Gar's 400-page tome, I groaned as I realized the job ahead of me. I realized that I would have to reactivate my Yiddish language brain cells which had been lying dormant for too many years. My Yiddish neurological language center was formed at my birth, in the Displaced Persons Camp in Landsberg, Germany after the end of World War II.

While many children born to Eastern European immigrants or refugees might have acquired varying levels of spoken Yiddish, my mother was adamant that I become literate in reading and writing and in the beauty of the literature and culture. So, for seven years I attended *Yiddishe Schule* in Brooklyn and Manhattan. Sponsored by the *Arbeter Ring* (today, the Worker's Circle), I studied the classic works of Sholem Aleichem, Mendel Menachem Sforim, and others, and participated in numerous cultural events – all in Yiddish. It is hard to imagine that I did this all after regular school hours.

With the deadline looming for the publication of my book, I bit the bullet and dove into Gar's Table of Contents to find the chapters and topics that related to events that Mama mentioned in her testimony. While I trusted Mama's memory, I wanted to ensure that there were other sources that corroborated her memory of those horrific years - and Gar's opus was one of them.

Slowly, I began the painstaking process of translating those paragraphs and chapters with the aid of one electronic and two hard copy dictionaries. I was worried that the task was beyond my capabilities despite my years in *Yiddishe Schule*. However, I was pleasantly surprised that my literacy skills were alive and that I could still access those dormant cells, even after all the years of learning additional languages.

I was grateful to Mr. Gar for his efforts at collecting information from survivors right after the war and documenting their horrific experiences before many went silent. As I read the relevant chapters pertaining to my mother's account, I learned that Mama was very accurate in her memories. But I learned much, much more in the process.

After publishing my book, I closed Mr. Gar's book until the pandemic forced me to reopen it. I realized that I needed a Covid project during our isolation. Thus, I decided that I would translate the entire book – as a gift to the world, or, more realistically, to whoever might be interested. Thus, I embarked on the mission to complete the translation of every page. I was convinced that it was good for my brain cells - and my sanity.

Fast forward to January 2022 when I was encouraged by JewishGen's Yizkor Project to publish the translated book. Suddenly, my work moved from a "brain exercise" to a more serious goal – to offer Joseph Gar's work to a wider audience.

I was most impressed by Gar's details in this book, which were clearly based on interviews with Litvak survivors from Kovno and his own experiences. Many of the Litvak survivors were housed in the Landsberg DP Camp. This camp was famous for its size and the myriad of institutions which offered social, cultural, memorial, religious, educational, and sports initiatives. All the DP camps saw innumerable marriages, and the largest baby boom in the world. I was one of those baby-boomers.

Not only is this book a chronology and description of events, but it also details the inner thoughts, behaviors, and emotions of the Jews at every stage of their mental, physical, and spiritual suffering. It describes every horrific or heroic event, the daily struggle for survival, the fear, the desperation, the ghetto conflicts, and all the Jewish institutions that were established and functioning during the 3 years of the existence of the Kovno Ghetto. But even more, Gar succeeded in transporting the reader to the Ghetto to feel the angst, the fear, the anger, the exhaustion, and the injustices. He describes multi-faceted human behaviors under the most unconscionable and unimaginable conditions. Gar certainly did not shy away from exposing and criticizing the ugly underbelly of human behavior which shows itself when people are under existential threat. He causes the reader to contemplate: "what would I have done under those conditions?" Historian Peter Hayes* believes that such questions cannot be answered by those now living in "liberal and law-observing societies." Of course, no one knows how they would behave under these unimaginable life-threatening circumstances, where right is wrong and wrong is right...and certainly, no one should judge.

There are other testimonies and publications about the horrors that befell the Jews of Kovno. But, as my university professor said, "research is the continuous addition of another brick that creates a complete wall." I am pleased to know that my translation of this book will serve as an additional brick for English speakers to access details about the Holocaust in Kovno, Lithuania.

This translation was completed without any financial remuneration. After this labor of love, and after learning more than I ever would want to know about the day to day organizational, physiological, psychological, social, and emotional challenges of the Jews in the Kovno Ghetto and beyond, I am left with only one question: "Why was I the first one to translate this work to English - after 74 years?" While JewishGen did post an online translation of Gar's chapter headings, I am honored that I was able to share all of Gar's words and make them available to the English-speaking world.

Thank you for your interest in this tragic period of history.

Dr. Ettie Zilber, translator/editor

Phoenix, Arizona, 2023

*Hayes, Peter. (2017). Why? Explaining the Holocaust. W.W. Norton & Co., N.Y.
**Zilber, Ettie. (2019). A Holocaust Memoir of Love & Resilience. http://getbook.at/Zilber
****** ******************

Group portrait of soldiers in the Lithuanian Army.

Photograph | Photograph Number: 21954

Group portrait of soldiers in the Lithuanian Army.
Pictured on the right is Jacob Gar, the donor's uncle.

Date	Circa 1920
Locale	Lithuania
Photo Designation	LIFE BEFORE THE HOLOCAUST -- Lithuania -- Military
Photo Credit	United States Holocaust Memorial Museum, courtesy of Libbey Sansanowicz

Dedication & Acknowledgements

Translating an historical book that deals with a tragic and very personal family history is not just an academic exercise – it is an emotional one. Some of my mother's and father's families survived, but most did not. Their stories appear on each page of Gar's magnum opus. Thus, for me, this project was truly a labor of love – and deep pain.

Every word on every page of Gar's book brought me closer to visualizing the daily challenges and horrors of their lives between 1940-1950. And, on each page, I found myself wishing my parents were alive so I could ask them about this or that event. Or perhaps to ask forgiveness for not understanding their trauma earlier. Sadly, I could not.

Thus, I dedicate this labor of love to my Kovno family who miraculously survived the Shoah: my mother, Lottie (Zlata Santocki) Sidrer, my father Louis (Liova) Sidrer, my surviving aunts, Nechama (Santocki) Shneorson, and Rivka (Sidrer) Baran, my surviving grandparents, Chaja (Kamionski) and Feival Sidrer, and to those who were brutally killed: my maternal grandparents, Eta (Zivov) and Yakov Santocki, and their two daughters: Ida and Genya Santocki. I pray that they are all resting in peace – together again.

I would like to acknowledge my wonderful aunt, Reva (Sidrer) Baran. She is my father's younger sister. She survived life and labor in the Kovno Ghetto, the Kinder Action, the train transport, Stutthof Concentration and Labor Camps, the Death March, liberation, post-war reunification, and immigration to the newly established State of Israel.

Her numerous anecdotes about the family's war experiences helped me write the family memoir.[3] And her help was invaluable for this translation, as well. Whenever I had a question about life in the Ghetto, or the experiences of liberation and reunification, I would call her. When I was stumped for a word or a concept (these were often in Russian), I would check the time zone difference between Arizona and Israel and plan my call for help. She immediately gave me the answers I needed- with no hesitation. Her memory and her mind are still so sharp at 92 – it is impressive. She even recalls some of the song lyrics which appear in the last chapter of Gar's book. We are blessed to still have her with us. She is an inspiration.

And, I am so grateful to my loving husband, Yakov (Jake) Zilber, born and raised in Israel, who was always willing and able to help me translate some colloquial or Biblical Hebrew phrases with which I was not familiar.

I would also like to thank JewishGen for their tireless work in helping historians, genealogists, and researchers gain access to Yizkor books and data bases which bring us all closer to our ancestry and heritage. It was their offer to publish this translation which motivated me to complete it.

A graysen dank aych alemen. (thanks to you all)

Ettie (Sidrer, Santocki, Kamionski, Klempner, Kawoyko, Chodosh, Disner) Zilber

1. Zilber, Ettie. (2019). A Holocaust Memoir of Love & Resilience. http://getbook.at/Zilber Return
2. Hayes, Peter. (2017). Why? Explaining the Holocaust. W.W. Norton & Co., N.Y. Return
3. A Holocaust Memoir of Love and Resilience: Mama's Survival from Lithuania to America http://getbook.at/Zilber. Return

Photo Credits

Front Cover Drawing:
Road to the 9th Fort by Feival Sidrer, 1948
The drawing on the front cover of this book depicts the second day of the "Big Action" in the Kovno Ghetto, which took place on October 28 and 29, 1941. In the drawing you see a view of the Ghetto and the road leading up a hill. On this road, the tiny human figures represent almost 10,000 Jewish men, women, and children. These selected Jews were marched from the Kovno Ghetto to the 9th Fort, where they were shot and buried in mass pits – many who fell dead - and others, not quite. (See Gar, Chapter XIII). This date is recorded in infamy, and it became the official date of mourning and commemoration for the surviving Jews of Lithuania.

This scene is etched in the memory of all the surviving prisoners of the Kovno Ghetto; it was drawn in 1948 from memory by the translator's *Zeide* (grandfather), Feival SIDRER (1900-1979).
Choosing *Zeide's* drawing for the cover of this Yizkor Memorial Book is a great honor and a tribute to the SIDRER and SANTOCKI families - those who survived and those who did not. Photo credits: Sidrer-Baran family.

Background Photograph: *Old Beit Hamidrash* [prayer study house] in Kovno. Page 9.

Back Cover Photographs:
Hundreds of photos were taken clandestinely, and at great risk, by Zvi Kadushin/George Kadish (1910-1997), before, during and after the Kovno Ghetto years 1941-1944. After his survival, he returned to the liquidated ghetto to unearth and recover the numerous negatives he previously and carefully buried. His photography was an act of resistance. It is the greatest collection and documentation of three years of daily ghetto life, showing the world evidence of the daily trials of the Jews in the Kovno Ghetto. These are 4 of his large collection of photos.

Top left: *Portrait of two young boys wearing Jewish badges in the Kovno ghetto, taken shortly before their round-up in the March 1944 "Children's Action."* United States Holocaust Memorial Museum Photo Archives #06546. Courtesy of George Kaddish. Copyright of United States Holocaust Memorial Museum.

Top Right: *A pair of shoes left behind after a deportation action in the Kovno ghetto.* United States Holocaust Memorial Museum Photo Archives #81082. Courtesy of George Kaddish. Copyright of United States Holocaust Memorial Museum.

Bottom Left: *View of Krisciukaicio Street in the Kovno ghetto.* United States Holocaust Memorial Museum Photo Archives #81143. Courtesy of George Kaddish. Copyright of United States Holocaust Memorial Museum.

Bottom Right: *Ruins of the Kovno ghetto.* United States Holocaust Memorial Museum Photo Archives #81133. Courtesy of George Kaddish. Copyright of United States Holocaust Memorial Museum.

Geopolitical Information

Kaunas, Lithuania is located at 54°54' N 23°54' E and 58 miles WNW of Vilnius

	Town	District	Province	Country
Before WWI (c. 1900):	Kovno	Kovno	Kovno	Russian Empire
Between the wars (c. 1930):	Kaunas	Kaunas		Lithuania
After WWII (c. 1950):	Kaunas			Soviet Union
Today (c. 2000):	Kaunas			Lithuania

Alternate Names for the Town:

Kaunas [Lith], Kovno [Rus], Kovne [Yid], Kovna [Heb], Kowno [Pol], Kauen [Ger]

Nearby Jewish Communities:

- Aleksotas 1 miles S
- Vilijampolė 1 miles NNW
- Aukštoji Panemunė 4 miles SE
- Garliava 6 miles SSW
- Zapyškis 9 miles W
- Veiveriai 12 miles SW
- Rumšiškes 12 miles ESE
- Gyviai 13 miles SW
- Pakuonis 14 miles SSE
- Babtai 14 miles NNW
- Darsuniškis 14 miles SE
- Vandžiogala 15 miles N
- Kruonis 16 miles SE
- Vilkija 16 miles NW
- Gudeliai 17 miles SW
- Kazlų Rūda 18 miles WSW
- Prienai 19 miles S
- Jonava 20 miles NE
- Višakio Rūda 20 miles WSW
- Birštonas 20 miles SSE
- Ąžuolų Būda 21 miles SW
- Kaišiadorys 22 miles E
- Žiežmariai 23 miles ESE
- Kriūkai 23 miles WNW
- Seredžius 23 miles WNW
- Žeimiai 23 miles NNE
- Jieznas 23 miles SSE
- Čekiškė 24 miles NW
- Nemajūnai 24 miles SSE
- Josvainiai 24 miles N
- Balbieriškis 25 miles S
- Stakliškės 27 miles SE
- Kėdainiai 27 miles N
- Veliuona 28 miles WNW
- Antanava 28 miles WSW
- Punia 28 miles SSE
- Žasliai 28 miles E
- Griškabūdis 29 miles W
- Šėta 30 miles NNE
- Pilviškiai 30 miles WSW
- Čiobiškis 30 miles E

Jewish Population: 25,448 (in 1897), 40,000 (1914)

Map of Lithuania showing the location of **Kaunas**

Table of Contents

Preface	Reuven Rubinstein	3
Preface	Dr. Phillip Friedman	4
Forward	Yosef Gar	5
Photos from Pre-War Kovno		8

I. Remarks about the Situation of Lithuanian Jewry during the Years 1918-1940 — 10
- Some characteristics of the political, socio-economic, and cultural situation of the Lithuanian Jews in the period between the two World Wars. - Outbreak of WWII - Important events in the country until the entrance of the Red Army into Lithuania.

II. One year of Soviet Rule in Lithuania (June 1940-June 1941) — 15
- Radical changes in the life of the Jewish population in Lithuania, with the establishment of the Soviet regime in the country. -Hasty deportation of politically non-loyal elements right before the outbreak of the war between Germany and Russia. -Increase of the anti-Soviet and anti-Semitic feelings among the Lithuanians.

III. Outbreak of the German-Soviet War and the Panicked Evacuation — 18
- Armed fights between the Lithuanian "5th Column" against the retreating Red Army. - Partial evacuation of Jews to the far regions of the Soviet Union. -First Jewish victims of the war.

IV. First Mass-Actions Against the Jewish Population in Kovno — 19
- The situation in Kovno on the eve of the German occupation. -Anti-Jewish incitement on the Lithuanian radio. -Attacks against Jews in Kovno. - The horrible pogrom in Slobodka. - Bestial murders in the garages

V. Horrible Killing at the Seventh Fort — 24
- Murderous crimes by the Lithuanian Partisans against the 10,000-12,000 Jews caught and gathered in one place. -Shaming, raping, and shooting Jewish women. -Murder of about 8,000 Jews.

VI. The establishment of the Ghetto in Slabodka — 26
- The Creation of a Jewish Committee. -The Jewish population of Kovno and surrounding towns forced to relocate to the newly founded ghetto. - A flood of anti-Jewish orders. -The first Action of the Jewish Committee moving the population into the Ghetto.

VII. Jewish Victims Before Locking the Ghetto — 31
- The Action on the "infamous Thursday." - Death of over one thousand Jewish men. - Shooting of Jews while they were buying food products.

VIII.	**Action of the Intellectuals Right After the Lock up of the Ghetto**	33
	- Locking up of the Ghetto. - Order from the authorities to deliver 500 Jews for "academic" work in town. - Registering several hundred Jews for work. - Capturing Jews in the Ghetto. - Tragic fate of the 534 captured young Jews.	
IX.	**The Robbery of Jewish Belongings**	35
	- Systematic house-searching in the Ghetto with the purpose of robbing Jewish property. - Terror and victims during the house searches. - "Voluntary" delivery of money and all other valuables.	
X.	**Test Action**	37
	- Distribution of 5,000 "certificates". - Mass-Action in the Small Ghetto, whose process was stopped for unknown reasons after the first "selection."	
XI.	**The first "organized" mass Action in the Ghetto**	39
	- Provocation concerning the "attempted murder" of the Commander of the Ghetto Guard by a Jew. - The closing of an entire ghetto neighborhood and the first mass Action in the Ghetto.	
XII.	**Action and Liquidation of the Small ghetto**	40
	Unexpected Aktzia in the Little-Ghetto. - The course of the Aktzia. - Burning alive of the sick and the medical personnel in the Jewish Hospital. - Liquidation of the Little-Ghetto and transfer of the surviving Jews to the other part of the ghetto.	
XIII.	**The Big Action**	44
	- Disturbing rumors before the Big Action. - The order to the population to assemble in Democracy Square, without giving the reason for the assembly. - Increasing panic in the Ghetto. - The gathering of over 26 thousand Jews in Democracy Square. -The course of the selection, from morning to evening. - The selected Jews were taken to the 9th Fort. - Agitation in the Ghetto. - The horrible fate of over 10 thousand Jews.	
XIV.	**The situation in the Ghetto during the first few months after the Big Action (November 1941-January 1942)**	53
	- Depressed atmosphere among the ghetto Jews. - "Reassuring" announcements from the Ghetto Command and the Gestapo. Assembly of foreign Jews at the 9th Fort for their murder. - Hunger, cold and hard labor. - Good news from the Soviet front. - "The Fur-Action" - Guarding of the Ghetto by a N.S.K.K. unit.	
XV.	**The First Relocation Action to Riga**	58
	- On the eve of the relocation Action. - Early recruiting of people for the relocation. - The failure of the Jewish authorities in recruiting. - Means taken by the rulers to perform the recruiting. - End of the relocation Action. -The fate of the relocated Jews.	

XVI.	**Life in the Ghetto in the Period Between the Two Relocation Actions to Riga (February-October 1942)**	63
	- "Action" of books and holy books. - Partial stabilization of the situation in the Ghetto. - The problem of using the Jewish labor-force. - Large Ghetto Workshops. - Signs of intensification of social life. - The struggle between Kaspi-Serebrowitz and Liptzer about the management of ghetto life. - Remarks about Liptzer's role in the life of the Ghetto. - Problems of nutrition in the Ghetto. - Smuggling of food produce. - A few words about ghetto livelihoods. - Decrees and more decrees: a. clearing up of ghetto neighborhoods, b. prohibition of pregnancy, c. closing of religious schools and schools for young children d. establishment of a "no-money" economy, e. prohibition to import food produce, f. recruitment for labor camps.	
XVII.	**The Second Relocation Action to Riga**	83
	- Measures taken by the Jewish Ghetto administration to recruit the required number of people to be sent to Riga. -Tense course of events at the end of the recruiting period.	
XVIII.	**A Hanging in the ghetto**	85
	- The doomed young Jewish man, Mek, who shot a German member of the Ghetto-Command. - Immediate Gestapo investigation. - Arrest of the Council Elder and his release. - The public hanging of Mek.	
XIX.	**"The Stalingrad Action"**	88
	- The measures taken by the Nazis to prevent Jewish satisfaction and joy over the German defeat at Stalingrad. - The course of the Action, which claimed 50 victims from the Ghetto.	
XX.	**Important Events in the Ghetto in the Spring and Summer of 1943**	90
	- Conflict between the S.A.[a] and S.S.[b] concerning the management of the Ghetto. - S.S. - the new ghetto "owners". - The first steps of dividing up the Ghetto into separate labor camps. - How they recruited for the first small labor camps in the provinces. - Founding a Jewish authority to select the people for the camps (the "Kazernirungs Commission").	
XXI.	**Preparations to Turn the Ghetto into a Series of Separate Labor Camps**	98
	- Conflict between the S.A. and S.S concerning the managing of the ghetto. - S.S. - the new "owners". - The first steps of changing the ghetto into separate labor-camps. - How the first small labor-camps were first recruited in the Province. - Founding a Jewish authority to select the people for the camps (the "recruiting committee").	
XXII.	**Relocation Action to Estonia**	103
	- Preparations for recruiting 3000 Jews for the labor camp in Ezsheretshai. [now: Ezerelis] - The mood in the Ghetto on the eve of the relocation. - The arrest of the Jewish "wood-brigade." - The first day of the Relocation Action. - The situation in the Ghetto when they began catching Jews. - The fate of the people who were taken out. - The day after the events of October 26th.	

XXIII.	**From the Relocation Action to Estonia until the eve of the Action on the children, the old and the sick (November 1943-March 1944)**	109
	– Movement in the Ghetto to give the children to Christians. – Establishment of the first Jewish labor-camp in Alexot. – Jewish "life" in the labor-camp. – Founding the second labor camp in Shantz. – Clearing of the old ghetto region. – Further recruiting for Jewish labor camps. – Legendary escape of the Jewish labor brigade which worked in the 9th Fort burning Jewish corpses. – The situation in the Ghetto during the first few months of 1944: a. good news from the front, b. favorable economic situation, c. new obligatory registration, d. less recruiting, e. joining the partisans. F. Jewish fight against informers, g. Intensive building, h. Sending German "Kapos" to the Ghetto, i. Rumors, denials, etc., – More persons involved in connection with the Partisan Movement. – Individual and collective contact with private Christians.	
XXIV.	**Children, Old and Sick People Action**	134
	– Calm mood in the Ghetto on the eve of the Action. – "Innocent" organization of the Jewish Police to gather and learn how to protect themselves from attacks from the air. – Unexpected deportation of Jews to the camp in the 9th Fort. – The Action in the Ghetto and in the labor camps. – The situation in the Ghetto after the Action	
XXV.	**Difficult Situation in the Ghetto between April – June 1944**	144
	– Liquidation of the Jewish Ghetto Police. – Founding the "Service Order". – Arrest of the Elders Council. – Final liquidation of the ghetto "autonomy." – New and more severe directives in the Ghetto regime: a. Increased guarding over the Jews, b. Systematic counting of the Jewish population c. Dressing the Jews in striped concentration camp uniforms d. Hasty measures to recruit the rest of the Jews in the Ghetto. – The arrest of the Partisan leader Chaim Yellin. – Gestapo attack on a Jewish Partisan group.	
XXVI.	**Deportation and Liquidation of the Ghetto**	152
	– Kovno becomes a front zone. – Tense situation in the Ghetto on the eve of the deportation. – The course of the first days of the deportation. – The Gestapo's murderous measures during the last days of the deportation. – Horrible destruction of the Ghetto. – Terrible end for 1,500 Jews who were hidden	
XXVII.	**Fate of the Deported Jews**	161
	-What happened to the deported Jews when they arrived in Germany? -The painful road of the men in the Dachau hell -The fate of the women taken to the East-Prussian labor camps	
XXVIII.	**After Liberation**	172
	-New problems and worries for the liberated men and women. -The life of the surviving Lithuanian Jews during the first years of the "remaining-remnants."	
XXIX.	**Cruel Blood Reckoning**	176
	Over 90% of the Kovno Jews, who lived in Hitler's hell perished for being Jews	

MONOGRAPH: Jewish Institutions in the Kovno Ghetto

Introductory Remarks   Joseph Gar   182

I. **The Elder's Council**   183
Establishment of the Jewish Committee in the first weeks of the occupation and its further development. - Some main elements about the activity of the Elders Council as the highest representatives of the ghetto settlement. - About the Jewish ghetto administration in general and the politics of the Elders Council, specifically. - Leading persons of the Elders Council.

II. **Jewish Ghetto Police**   196
- Founding of the Jewish Ghetto Police and its basic tasks. - The role of the police in the ghetto life. - The Ghetto Police and the "Service Order". - The separate units of the police. - The Police Orchestra.

III. **Labor Office**   204
The significance of labor in the life of the ghetto population. - Early forms of forced labor for the ghetto Jews. - Gradual formation of stable Jewish workplaces in town. - First concrete steps to regulate the problems of forced labor. The organizational structure and basic activity of the special labor offices sections. - Important periods in the history of the Jewish Labor Office.

IV. **Economics Office**   225
- Founding of the Economics Office -Appointments and activities of the Economics Office and its functions at organizing economic life.

V. **Provisions Office**   231
- Official provisions for the ghetto population. - Institutions of the Provisions Office.

VI. **Housing Office**   234
- Painful question about living space in the Ghetto. - Extermination Action "to clear out" needed apartments. - Larger clear out of the ghetto areas. - Activities of the Housing Office.

VII. **Health Office**   238
- Problems of the state of health in the early months of the ghetto's existence - Medical institutions in the Health Office and their significance in ghetto life.

VIII. **Social Welfare Office**   242
- Necessary resources for large portions of the ghetto population. - Establishment of the Social Welfare Office and its activities.

IX. **Statistics Office**   244
- Representation in the Statistics Office and Address Bureau. - Establishment of the "Estates Office". - Attempt at creating an illegal mail connection between Kovno and other ghettos. - Use of the materials of the Statistics Office.

X.	**School Office**	247
	- Educational issues in the early ghetto months. – Founding and character of the children's schools. - Liquidation of the schools and the School Office. - Activity of the Vocational School. – Attempts to alleviate the cultural needs of the ghetto population.	
XI.	**Ghetto Court**	251
	- Origins of the Jewish court entity in the Ghetto. - Activity of the Ghetto Court and its liquidation. - Police Court.	
XII.	**Ghetto Firefighters**	254
	- Firefighters Commando and its additional duties.	
XIII.	**Drawing and Painting Workshop**	255
	- Completion of various graphic works	
	Addendum	
	1. Zionist Activity in the Ghetto	256
	2. Samples of Ghetto Folklore	259
	Index of Names - Original Text	277
	Name Index - English Edition	282

The Destruction of Jewish Kovno
(Kaunas, Lithuania)

54°54' / 23°54'

Translation of: *Umkum fun der Yidisher Kovne*

Edited by: Joseph Gar

Published in Munich 1948

Acknowledgments

Project Coordinator and Translator:

Dr. Ettie Zilber

This is a translation from: *Umkum fun der Yidisher Kovne*
The Destruction of Jewish Kovno
Editor: Joseph Gar, Munich 1948 (424 pages, Y)

Note: The original book can be seen online or purchased at the Yiddish Book Center site:
Umkum fun der Yidisher Kovne

This material is made available by JewishGen, Inc. and the Yizkor Book Project for the purpose of fulfilling our mission of disseminating information about the Holocaust and destroyed Jewish communities. This material may not be copied, sold, or bartered without JewishGen, Inc.'s permission. Rights may be reserved by the copyright holder.

JewishGen, Inc. makes no representations regarding the accuracy of the translation. The reader may wish to refer to the original material for verification.
JewishGen is not responsible for inaccuracies or omissions in the original work and cannot rewrite or edit the text to correct inaccuracies and/or omissions.
Our mission is to produce a translation of the original work and we cannot verify the accuracy of statements or alter facts cited.

יוסף גאר

אומקום
פון דער

יידישער קאוונע

אריסגעגעבן דורכן פארבאנד פון ליטווישע יידן
אין דער אמעריקאנער זאנע אין דייטשלאנד, מינכען

1 9 4 8

PREFACE
Content-Notes

[page 7]

In fire and flame, in suffering and wincing-agony of death, a large, beautiful, strong, succulent Jewish world was destroyed. European Jewry was stamped out under the boots of the bloody Nazi-German uniformed beast.

Hundreds of Jewish communities, cities, and towns, filled with Jewish life and spiritual creation were destroyed, and annihilated under God's skies. Among them, also, Jewish Lithuania. Among them, also, Kovno.

This was a city which first began its national Jewish splendor after the first World War, in the years 1917-1941. From a small provincial city, it grew into a modern city, and became heir to the best traditions of the historically famous Lithuanian Jewry, with traditions from the nucleus of Jewishness, culture, learning, modern social-political movements, and people of Israel.

Kovno became the representative of the Lithuanian-Jewish people, who were renown throughout the entire Jewish world with its steadfast Jewish genuineness and with its creative national potential.

During the horrific three years between 1941-1944, during the vile killings by murderous German occupiers and their cruel Lithuanian collaborators, this same Jewish Kovno was entirely cut down. Kovno shared in the fate of the murdered Jewish people.

The story of this slow, fatal annihilation is depicted in Joseph Gar's book. This is the first book about the life and liquidation of the Kovno Ghetto. It was written by a person who experienced the dreadful transformation of the life in the Kovno Ghetto, through which he, himself, went walking on the thorny road of death and destruction.

As an academic, a writer, an editor, a person with a high sense of responsibility and feeling for systematic knowledge, and one of the most important remaining representatives of the Lithuanian-Jewish intellectuals, Joseph Gar endeavors to unroll the horrible story of the destruction of Kovno in this monograph.

He describes the tragic events objectively, precisely, and scholarly. He suppresses the vestiges of his personal shocking survival and how they were even possible.

Joseph Gar is therefore the most honest and most convincing witness and historian to the horrific finale of Lithuanian Jewry. Herein lie the historical words from his work, in which he invested enormous energy, labor, and great gusto of literary composition.

We, the remnants of Jewish Lithuania, and all Jews in general, accept this valuable book with deep appreciation.
1. The Association of Lithuanian Jews in the American Zone of Germany was honored to help our friend, Joseph Gar, publish this book and owe him a debt of gratitude.
2. This is a story of suffering, tears, destruction, and dreadful life events of one of the most beautiful communities of our martyred and blessed people and will be immortalized for generations through this book.

Reuven Rubinstein
Chairman of the Association of Lithuanian Jews in the American Zone in Germany
Munich, May 9, 1948

[Page 9]

In a speech at the conference of Jewish writers in the Land of Israel, our great poet, David Schmonovitz, offered these advisory, sad, and bitter words:

> "…we know very well, what happened to the Jews in all the lands that were occupied by the Nazis. To the terror and horror of all humanity, we also know how small and feeble the reaction was on the part of the residents of the occupied lands against the dreadful events that happened to their neighbors. We know even more. We know that the Polaks, the Ukranians, and the Lithuanians, with all their possibilities, helped the Germans in their extermination of the Jews."

In no other country of Europe did the criminal Nazi-propaganda find itself such fruitful terrain, nor did it find such huge numbers of enthusiastic helpers for its bloody work, as in this accursed border-realm between East and West. These lands, where nationalistic hate and chauvinistic intolerance raged for decades, and where the strengthening of the generations-long political and social tensions and conflicts, turned to the heads of Jews. It became designated by the Nazis to become a mass grave for millions of Jews from all over Europe. According to the horrific crimes against Jews, the role played by the inhabitants of this realm, the performance in which they engaged, was already illuminated in numerous works and articles. At least it was in this manner that the Lithuanians participated, because they played such a fatal role in the macabre performance, and their dark Jew-hatred motivated them to spill Jewish blood widely throughout the borders of their land and made them conduits of mass murder in foreign territories and countries.

[page 10]

To my knowledge, Yosef Gar's book is the first work which gives us multi-faceted and clearly established material about the role of the Lithuanians during that tragic period. True, Yosef Gar's work does not include all of Lithuania, and it isn't competing to give a picture of the Lithuanian politic and of the Lithuanian murder of Jews over the wider territory, "just because it is there."

However, various methods exist to get to the bottom of the known truth. The nature researcher who plans to test the taste of ocean water, does not have to research by including the entire amount of water existing in the ocean. He takes in drops and lays it down under a microscope. From the microcosm, as it were, he teaches the meaning of the macrocosm. Yosef Gar took it as his goal to analyze one city, the capital city of Lithuania. He analyzes it perfectly and thoroughly. He analyzes the battle and the struggle, the worries and the laments of the victims, the abyss of villainy, murder, and outrage of the persecuted; and what we receive from this picture is the role of the "Aryan" neighbors in the capital. We can imagine how it approached the macrocosm, everywhere, where the Lithuanians "collaborated" with the Germans in their "solution to the Jewish question."

And then, from a different standpoint, this story of Jewish Kovno presents more than just a simple local concern. Kovno, like Lodz in Poland, was the only Jewish settlement in the Eastern region which was spared utter extinction by the Germans until the end of the Summer of 1944. Jewish Lodz and Jewish Kovno endured the suffering of destruction and agony for a longer time and a slower speed than the other communities. Here, the stages of decline and battle for life were stretched out longer. Here, specific characteristic processes of the tragedy came rife with expression, more than anywhere else. Here, the historian, studying the years of destruction, gets a more profound view of the painful and horrific details of its development, which in other settlements developed at rapid fire speed.

Josef Gar endeavors to disclose to us, step by step, the tied-up knot of these complicated processes in his home city, Kovno.

To control the enormous number of problems and materials, and shape them carefully and clearly for the reader, he divided his work in two parts:

[page 11]

The first dynamic part describes the breath-taking events in the Ghetto in chronological order, the struggle with the enemy, the shivering between life and death, the worries, the cruelty of the murderers, the resistance, the destruction, the tragic numbers of those liberated too late.

The second part is a static one. It is more analytical and reflective. He gives a systematic overview of the social structure of the Ghetto. He analyzes the complicated phenomena of the ghetto structure -both social and psychological (especially the "pros" and "cons" of the Elders Council and Ghetto Police).

Thus, this author put together, in story-like examination, all aspects of Jewish life during that tragic time. At the end, he also included political life and Kovno Ghetto folklore.

We lay down this book with the feeling that the editor has given us much material to construct a general picture of Jewish life, its decline during the Nazi era, and a lot of matters to remember.

Josef Gar's work is not simply a thorough chronicle or collection of facts and events. It is a serious attempt to go deep into the problems of that time, and to analyze them systematically. Gar's work is an important contribution to the history of the destruction years without any judgment. His serious, knowledgeable approach is a model for many authors who work according to a recipe of "a super-fast timeframe." They twist and vulgarize the story of the destruction years, have little use for the study of Jewish history and little honor for the dear memory of our martyrs. In the ocean of written works, Gar's work is to be welcomed like a rare exception and as a good example of responsible, conscientious research work.

Dr. Philip Friedman
Munich, May 11, 1948

[page 12]

FORWARD

In the book *The Destruction of Jewish Kovno*, the author endeavors to exhibit a picture of the horrific destruction of Kovno - the largest Jewish community in Lithuania, the city, and the people of Israel.

Jewish Kovno had the misfortune of being captured in the early days of the German-Soviet war at the end of June 1941. During the horrifying Nazi years, it went through a path full of suffering. In the final accounting, the Nazis brought most of the Jewish communities in the occupied domains to complete annihilation.

As we know, every Jew who languished in that Nazi hell, strove to survive until liberation. They also had a deep desire to tell the world about the appalling Jewish existence under Hitler's rule. This was especially the dream of those people who had some relationship with the pen.

However, conducting such record keeping was not a simple thing, particularly on site in the Ghetto. Such expository texts and such work were life-threatening. Unfortunately for us, most of the writings, scribed during that period did not survive. Together with the killing of the writers, no trace remained of their writings. That is why most of the published descriptions about those years were written after liberation.

[Page 13]

This work was also created in the post-war period. After a lengthy period, this heavy work was finally finished, and the book will be brought to the Jewish reader. At this opportunity the author allows himself to make the following comments:

    a. The book includes two basic parts:

        i. A chronological description of what the Kovno ghetto settlement was exposed to during the occupation period, and

        ii. A Monograph about the Jewish institutions in the Ghetto. During this period, the first part mainly exposed the deeds of the Nazi-murderers and their various collaborators toward the vulnerable Jewish population; then, in the second part, the activities of the Jewish ghetto institutions and their impact on shaping the relationship to Jewish suffering and on the innermost ghetto life. A few additional notes are included at the end of the book.

    b. The first pair of introductory chapters, such as, "Observations on the State of Lithuanian Jewry in the years 1918-1940" and "One Year of Soviet Rule in Lithuania" were to pitch out the most important features of Jewish-Lithuanian life during the period between the two World Wars. It finally clarified what the stages of the earlier periods were preceding the catastrophe, which in the early occupation days took on such an exceptionally bloody course. The aim of the last chapters, "After Liberation" and "The Horrific Blood-toll," was to give a picture of the destruction. At the same time, it highlighted the main problems of the cluster of Jews who became survivors during those early years after the destruction.

    c. Completely remarkable details, known only to certain people who were close to the leadership of the Jewish administration, are available in this martyrs' history of the Kovno Ghetto. The Jewish community was especially interested in the negotiations of the offices of the Elders Council, the highest representatives of the Kovno Ghetto collective. During that period, there were various decrees, for instance, Actions, relocations, and other abuses. The author did not belong to the best-informed people in the Ghetto, so, unlike an employee of the Jewish administration, he didn't have an opportunity to be in-the-know about the ghetto events more than any other Jew. Secondly, he had a longer time frame to collect information from competent people, to present a more complete description. And, finally, he made sure of the existence of the details in the book.

[Page 14]

    d.   Aside from the descriptions of the prelude to the extermination-actions, this book brings forth a major overview of "normal" ghetto life – from one slaughter to another. The Kovno Ghetto existed longer than other ghettos in the East for certain reasons, which are partially described in the book. So, in a certain way, it was a typical ghetto from whose story we can learn a lot about the tormented situation of the Jews during the occupation years. True, the Kovno Ghetto did not demonstrate armed resistance against the Nazis, like for example, the ghettos of Warsaw, Bialystock, Vilna, etc., not because of lack of courage, perseverance, and security. Although the Kovno Ghetto seemed superficially passive, it dealt with internal daily battles of the Jews to surmount all the harsh blows of immediate ghetto realities like, slave labor, hunger, cold, overcrowding, dirt, and other evils, to eventually survive until Hitler's downfall. And, in addition, with the partisan movement in the Ghetto, the construction of the bunkers, and the like, it becomes clear that the Kovno Ghetto conducted a heroic struggle to avoid being squashed between the stones of the Nazi death mill.

    e.   Not only dry facts were presented in this book, but the events of life in the Ghetto are also more or less commented upon. Thus, it is to be expected that certain differences of opinion and critique about specific facts would arise, specifically from one or another surviving Jew from the Kovno Ghetto. This is only natural because there can be various opinions about such fresh and sensitive material. In addition, it seems that each person views life through the prism of his own eyes and world view. Also, some will be unhappy that the book mentions the names of ghetto Jews who were active in the Jewish administration and, in certain cases, includes short characteristics about the role of these specific people in ghetto life. However, this was done because the editor was deeply convinced that ignoring the personal details would, without a doubt, negatively impact the wholeness and authenticity of the description.

[Page 15]

While writing this book the editor was committed from the start to only one goal: to give an exact and objective picture of what happened. While working all by himself, especially after the fact, with such rich and complicated material, and almost without documents on hand, understandably, work imperfections snuck in. In any case, the imperfections were not created deliberately, but only unintentionally. Regarding where and how many errors were allowed, the author saw to blocking them out, or at least to keeping them to a minimum. Whenever this essay will be updated, the improvements, made by those who are knowledgeable, will be taken into consideration gratefully, and the errors will be corrected.

The editor knows very well that whatever is included in the book, especially the first part, is not more than a very weak echo of what really took place. It would be foolish to think that the pen of a decent human being, a scribe, would be able to reconstruct what took place in that other horrific time, during the indescribable Jewish catastrophe.

The unique intent of this work is a double one: to construct a type of tombstone to the destruction and the destroyed past of Jewish Kovno and, to bring together some raw material for our historians and artists, to get an idea about this bloody topic: "Edicts 1940-1945."
    Y.G. [Yosef Gar]

Postscript

[page 16]

Finally, this author would like to express his appreciation to the other institutions and persons, who allowed him the opportunity to release this book. Firstly, the following should be recognized: the Union of Lithuanian Jews in the American Zone in Germany, at the head, the Chairman, the Manager and leader of Lithuanian Jewry, editor Reuven Rubenstein; the Secretary-General of the Union, Engineer Avraham Shuster; Management Committee members, Engineer Faivush Goldshmidt; Y.D. Sheinzohn for his title page drawings, as well as all the other good friends who in this, or in other ways, had a hand in the publication of the book.

A great thanks to the Central Jewish Historical Commission in Munich, and a host of other individuals for the few dozen photos included in the book.
D.Z.

Photos from Pre-War Kovno

Leisvus Aleya, one of the main streets.

The Jewish Central Bank

Health Center of the "Oze" Society

Old Beit Hamidrash [prayer study house] in Kovno
(constructed in the middle of the 19th century)

CHAPTER I

Remarks about the Situation of Lithuanian Jewry during the Years 1918-1940

-Some characteristics of the political, socio-economic, and cultural situation of the Lithuanian Jews in the period between the two World Wars.-Outbreak of WWII-Important events in the country until the entrance of the Red Army into Lithuania

[Page 17]

A Jewish settlement in the land of Lithuania is six to seven hundred years old, located in the not-large agrarian territory near the shores of the Nieman and Vilya Rivers. The Jewish-Lithuanian collective survived various historical periods over the course of their generations-long existence- some worse, and others considered better. Over the long centuries, the Lithuanian Jew, the "Litvak," acquired a character trait of a specific Jewish folk-type and, after a while, became well known throughout the global Jewish family.

The contribution of Lithuanian Jewry to our cultural-societal diaspora was quite large in the new period of our old and much-celebrated folk story. As we know, achievements in creative Jewish thought always reverberated loudly and warmly in the life of the Lithuanian Jewish people, as for example in religious Judaism, learning, political Zionism, Jewish Socialism, world culture in Yiddish and Hebrew, etc.

However, they not only excelled in general Jewish cultural creations, but Lithuanian Jewry excelled significantly in accomplishments and earnings. It was also well known that with their mastery and experiences and with their initiatives and entrepreneurial spirit in the economic realm, the Jews of Lithuania impacted quite a large portion of the development and prosperity of the local social and economic life.

[Page 18]

Up to the first World War, Lithuanian Jews were mainly concentrated in the smaller provincial settlements and, thus, had daily personal contact with their Lithuanian neighbors, and educated most of the general local people. Notwithstanding, the livelihood of the small-town Jew was dependent on the Lithuanian peasant. And, the Lithuanian villager couldn't survive without Jewish dealers, shopkeepers, and artisans, who were the economic middlemen between the village and the city.

In those times there reigned a natural state of peace between Lithuanians and Jews, who coexisted well, notwithstanding occasional misunderstandings. At that time, the Jews in Lithuania didn't have any basis to complain about dangerous Jew hatred from the Lithuanian people. In addition, when Lithuania was under the Czarist yoke, significant layers of the democratic and progressive Lithuanian society and the literate Jewish circles found a common language and created a partnership campaign against Czarism, etc.

In 1918, with the rise of an independent Lithuanian kingdom at the end of the first World War, a worsening of relationships became noticeable.

Among other factors, the establishment of an independent Lithuanian national government was also the cause of a marked change in the socio-economic structure of the Lithuanian people. Suddenly, in this context, it became favorable and conducive for the young Lithuanian bourgeoisie and intelligentsia to suddenly envision new and greater development opportunities for themselves.

In their urgency for expansion and hegemony, these same Lithuanian urban elements became offended by the natural reaction of the Jewish middle-class, who had holdings and great experience in the realms of industry, business, hand crafts and the liberal professions, which restrained their economic achievements.

In an open and masked battle to get their hands on key positions in the economic life of Lithuania, the aggressive fighters of the Lithuanian economic classes used the full backing and various privileges from the government hierarchy. Understandably, these same socio-economic contrasts between the Lithuanians and the Jews became noticeable in the form of opposing relationships between Jews and non-Jews in Lithuanian public life.

[Page 19]

In parallel to the growth of an economic appetite on the part of the Lithuanian nationalist circles, came the further strengthening of the anti-Jewish atmosphere among the Lithuanian people. The widening and deepening antisemitism in Lithuania in the later years was also noticeably influenced by the rapid advance movement of National Socialism in neighboring Germany. The anti-Jewish attitude in neighboring Poland, and in other countries in Europe also became evident.

Right in the first half of the 1920s, the reactionary class of the Lithuanian church, which was then supporting the regime, destroyed the institutions of Jewish national autonomy, which the Lithuanian Jews had established with great effort. Therefore, the existence of the duly recognized community was short, extremely short. That's why the Jewish National Council and a special Ministry for Jewish issues was established. After all these difficult battles and achievements for Jewish autonomy, in the final accounting, Lithuanian Jewry was successful in holding control of only the specific domain of school education.

The totalitarian regime, under the leadership of the regime President Antonas Smetana, who led the country for over 13 years (from the 17th of December 1926 until the 15th of June 1940), truly did not permit any anti-Jewish abuses, due to the government's fear of outside countries upon whom small Lithuania became strongly dependent. But the process of expelling the Jews from their well-established positions in business, industry, handcrafts, and the independent professions, went on with a feverish speed.

Thousands of Jewish families who went through this same battle for a Jewish living, were left without economic support and were forced to eke out a tortured living by being dependent on material support from relatives outside the country.

For the Jewish youth growing up in those years, the sole practical prospect for setting up their lives was immigration to the Land of Israel, and on a much smaller scale, also to wander out to the lands of Central and South America, South Africa, etc.

[Page 20]

Particularly difficult was the Jewish economic situation in Lithuania at the end of the 1920s and the beginning of the 1930s, when the general economic crises in the world also left deep tracks on Lithuanian economic life.

An interesting chapter took place in the Jewish social and cultural life in Lithuania. True, the 160 thousand Lithuanian Jews (without Vilna and environs) was quantitatively not one of the large Jewish collectives in the world, but that's why they lived a truly national-Jewish folk-life.

The scourge of assimilation, which so disruptively impacted the life of many large Jewish settlements, was not a problem at all in Lithuanian Jewish life. This might be explained by the fact that the young Lithuanian culture did not have the ability to attack the Jewish cultural position, which stood on a much higher level than the Lithuanian, or that the Lithuanian Jews gained more effective national immunity to assimilation than the Jews in the other lands; or perhaps both factors together played a role. In any case, Lithuanian Jewry did not suffer from the assimilation affliction. Aside from that, the Lithuanian Jewish intelligentsia was quite popular and felt tightly connected to all the sorrow and joys of the entire Jewish people.

The following were all the expressions of the national intense and lush Jewish folk life in Lithuania in the period between the two World Wars: study groups and Yeshivas, among them the world-famous yeshivas of Slabodka, Telz, and Ponevesh; kindergartens, public schools, secondary schools, teachers' seminaries, as well as many education and educational institutions from the Yiddishist-progressives; Jewish and Hebrew libraries; three daily newspapers of varying streams, like "Yiddish Voice" (generally Zionist), "the Word" (Zionist-Socialist); various newsletters in Yiddish and Hebrew; acknowledged theaters as well as Yiddish and Hebrew studios; more sport-unions, like "Maccabi," Hapoel", "YAC" (Yiddish Athletic Club); a wide network of public bank branches, at the head of which was the Central Jewish Bank; economic organizations of Jewish industrialists, businessman, artisans, grocery store owners, people from the free professions, etc.; institutional charity and all kinds of charitable associations; legal, and also, illegal parties, starting from the extreme right, "Agudas Israel" and ending with the extreme left Jewish Communists; youth organizations of various shades of society, etc.

[Page 21]

Kovno stood at the center of Lithuanian-Jewish social life– the biggest Jewish community in the independent Lithuanian Republic. It was the city of world-famous Jewish personalities: the Rabbi Hagaon Itzhak-Elhanan Zitchl, Abraham Mapu, great sage, etc., and the great minds of Israel, who made the name of Jewish Lithuania famous throughout the world.

When Vilna was occupied by Poland, Kovno was fated to become the Lithuanian capital.[a] This same fact greatly influenced the growth and development of Kovno, which, over several years took on the face of an official city.

From a population of approximately 50-60 thousand souls at the end of the first World War, Kovno grew into a city of 130-140 thousand people on the eve of the Second World War. This same boisterous growth of the general Kovno population strongly lowered the percentage composition of the local Jewish population. While in the earlier years, the Jews in Kovno made up about half of the general number of people in the city, on the threshold of destruction, the Jews were not more than a third of the general population.

As we know, due to the conflict between Lithuania and Poland over Vilna, no diplomatic relations were established for over 18 years[b], and each of the countries was bordered off from the other as if with a Chinese wall. The lack of active contact with Polish Jewish neighbors stimulated the Jewish community in Lithuania to become self-sustaining, in a national sense. The Jewish intelligentsia of Lithuania had to carry all the socio-cultural needs of Lithuanian Jewry on its own shoulders. This forced them to become active in all realms of Jewish national creation.

[Page 22]

As mentioned, the tone of Lithuanian-Jewish life was set by Kovno. In Lithuania, there were famous Jewish communities in Shavl, Ponevezsh, Memel[c], etc., but the initiative for various Jewish social activities always came out of Kovno, where the most important Jewish central institutions were found.

There was a strong flow of Jewish youth coming from the provinces to Kovno. From dozens of smaller and larger Jewish villages there was a continuous draw for groups of Jewish boys and girls to come to study in the higher and middle learning institutions, in the yeshivas, etc. Many provincial Jewish youth would get organized in various handicraft trades in Kovno, or according to employment in enterprises in the commerce industry. This *wanderlust* stream was particularly strong from the village to the city and it continued during the Soviet period in Lithuania.

All of this left an indelible Jewish stamp on Kovno – the metropolis of Lithuanian Jewry. Not only were there such purely Jewish city sectors like, for example, Slobodka, Altshtot, etc., but also, at every corner of the city there pulsed an intensive, effervescent, and creative Jewish life, full of Jews and Yiddishkeit.

At the outbreak of the Second World War, which started on September 1, 1939, during the armed conflict between Lithuania's two neighbors, Germany and Poland, Lithuania proclaimed itself neutral.

Due to the boisterous collapse of the Polish regime in the first weeks of the war, Lithuania became flooded with a large tide of Polish refugees, among whom were also many Jews. The Lithuanian Jews, according to their capabilities, made efforts to support their unfortunate brothers from Poland and helped them find temporary lodging in Lithuania. A Jewish refugee committee was specifically established, among others, to take care of immigration for those war-refugees, who had the opportunity to get out of the country.

[Page 23]

Also, due to many factors related to the war at this time, a period of so-called war prosperity impacted the economic life of Lithuania. This also trickled down to the local Jewish population, but the outbreak of war strongly disturbed the Lithuanian Jews. However, from that same new world slaughter, and despite the favorable economic juncture for the Jews, only the Jews saw the obvious; sadly, nothing good would come out of it for Jews.

Later, because of their previous agreement with Nazi-Germany, the Soviet Union started to spread their sphere of influence into the Baltic lands. There they installed the Soviet war bases, etc., where many Soviet garrisons were quartered.

The installation of the Soviet war bases in Lithuania had a strong impact on daily life. You could touch this small buffer of the Baltic lands with your hand. In war time, even more than in peace time, it was not more than an object of diplomatic "cow-trading" between the major powers.

As was expected, this newly established situation in the country strongly shook up the foundations of the dictatorship. They clearly felt that due to the development of international political events, their further existence was in jeopardy. Ruling Lithuanian nationalistic circles were even prepared to forgive the Soviets for their "gift" to Lithuania. This gift, which had been captured by Poland, was the reinstatement of its capital, Vilna, within the borders of the Lithuanian kingdom. If only things would remain like they were before.

In fact, we must say that the Lithuanian opposition and progressive elements – except for the Communists, of course, were also not too strongly enthusiastic about the growing Soviet influence in Lithuania. In this way they hoped that now they would finally succeed in achieving their long-term dream to throw off the Smetana-regime. During this regime, all democratic elements in the country were already forgotten. They wanted, once and for all, to bring a democratic royal ordinance to Lithuania.

[Page 24]

The overwhelming majority of the Jewish population in Lithuania were sympathizers with the side of the democratic forces, and most Jews, together with the opposition bands in the country, waited with impatience for the fall of the Smetana clique.

The incorporation of Vilna and environs into the borders of the Lithuanian Republic, enlarged the Jewish collective in Lithuania by more than 100,000 souls. At that time, when the 160 thousand Lithuanian Jews made up 7% of the general population in the country, the quarter million Jews now became 10% of the general population. From the start, the Jews thought that because of their aspiration to Lithuanianize the newly acquired areas, the Lithuanian government circles would have to consider the Jewish factor, especially in Vilna itself, where 75 thousand Jews lived. They thought this would benefit the general situation for Lithuanian Jewry.

These Jewish expectations were not considered. Instead, the chauvinistic Lithuanian elements tried to play the Vilner Polaks against the Jews. That way, for example, right after the entry march of the Lithuanians into Vilna, anti-Jewish Actions took place. After they divided up Lithuanian police and antisemitic Polaks, Jewish hopes ran out into the river…

In the meantime, the Second World War continued in the following way. Hitler's Germany went from victory to victory. After smashing Poland in September 1939, we know that in Spring of 1940, Denmark,

Norway and, later on, Holland and Belgium were occupied, and a German general attack was started against France. On the 14th of June 1940, Paris fell.

Thus, on the 15th of June 1940, one day after the fall of the French capital, the Red Army marched into Lithuania. President Smetana, it seems, did not calculate well and barely managed to run away to Germany. The dictatorship fell apart like a house of cards. It became established as a "people's government", and, at the head, the well-known Lithuanian writer, Professor Kreve-Mizkevicius (who, by the way, remained in Lithuania during Nazi occupation after the outbreak of war between Germany and Russia, and was, perhaps under pressure by the occupiers, and was publicly applauded by the Soviet Union.) He

was appointed as a substitute for the President by the Lithuanian journalist Justus Paletzkis, who, in that last year, was known for his pro-Soviet speeches.

These surprising political occurrences, which presented a stormy turning point in the newest story of Lithuania, soon caused far reaching changes in the life of the Lithuanian-Jewish collective.

Original footnotes:

  a. Formally: The Temporary Capitol
  b. From 1920 until 1938
  c. From 1923 until 1939 the Memel region belonged to Lithuania

CHAPTER II

One year of Soviet Rule in Lithuania

(June 1940-June 1941)

-Radical changes in the life of the Jewish population in Lithuania, with the establishment of the Soviet regime in the country-Hasty deportation of politically non-loyal elements right before the outbreak of the war between Germany and Russia-Increase of the anti-Soviet and anti-Semitic feelings among the Lithuanians

[Page 26]

As we know, on the 23rd of July 1940, after a five-week internal political judgment process, the newly selected Lithuanian "People's Group" proclaimed Lithuania a Soviet Republic, and it later became incorporated as part of the Soviet Union.

Understandably, the introduction of the Soviet regime order into Lithuania brought on widespread changes in all areas of public and private life in the country. These changes also affected the Jewish population in Lithuania.

In the legal-political sense, the Jews of Lithuania, for the first time in the history of this country, received complete equal rights with all the other citizens of the country. Being a Jew suddenly stopped being a reason for all sorts of national-political discrimination and persecution, as was the case until that time.

The new Soviet regime opened their doors wide to the Jews, just like for non-Jews. This new and uncustomary situation allowed the Jews in Lithuania, once and for all, to raise their heads freely and not think of themselves as lower class citizens.

The reorganization from a former capitalistic regime-order to a new Socialist foundation was very necessary, according to the knowledge and the understanding of the Jewish working intellectuals. They threw themselves into the work force with dedication and contributed to the rebuilding process. Jews played a visible role, not just in the administrative and economic structure, but also, in various instances, in the dominant party.

[Page 27]

The Jewish citizenry now had equal rights. But it was mainly because Jews acquired responsible positions in the regime and party system, that the Lithuanian anti-Soviet elements took advantage of it for their illegal agitation against the newly installed Soviet regime in Lithuania. Privately, antisemitism was useful material for them, and the Lithuanian pro-Fascist circles attempted to extract from this as much capital as possible.

We must say that the Soviet regime knew how to restrain these Fascist anti-Semitic people, and thus, no anti-Jewish occurrences took place.

Most Jews in the country had happy feelings because of their complete political equality in Lithuania. However, the process of nationalization of the larger and well-resourced trade and industrial enterprises from the larger homes, was quickly accepted as the result of the newly installed Soviet regime in the country. This caused the lowering of social class for large portions of the Jewish population.

Understandably, the declassified Jewish population was very unhappy with the economic changes that the Soviet regime introduced in the country. Those previously well-to-do families who received the order from the regime to leave their homes in the city were strongly shaken up. They had to move out somewhere else to the smaller towns in the Kovno environs. These unhappy elements had no choice and had to make peace with the newly established situation. So, they searched to find a way to grasp the order of the new regime organization.

Except for the Jewish Communists and their periphery, the turbulent liquidation of the entire previously active social and cultural life made a very painful impression on the Jewish population. The crisis came so fast and was also so severe, that there simply was no opportunity to adapt themselves gradually to all the fundamental changes.

[Page 28]

At this opportunity we must add that right after the Soviets marched into Lithuania, many Jews, mainly from the earlier well-established strata, as well as activists from the liquidated societies, parties, and organizations, made desperate attempts to get themselves out of Lithuania at any price. They tried to travel to Eretz-Israel, to the Scandinavian countries, or toward Japan, from where they hoped to get to America and other places.

The immigration scare was enhanced by a large portion of Polish Jewish refugees, who for political reasons, had reason not to remain under the same roof with the Soviet regime.

Many of these people would camp out daily at the institutions of HIAS, "Palestine Office", and "Intourist" (Soviet tourist society for foreigners), to find any opportunity to go anywhere. With no less difficulty, this was also related to receiving a permit to get out of the country.

Arrests were carried out from among the Jewish (and, also non-Jewish) leaders from their prior social life. This increased the drive for emigration for even more people. On the other hand, the danger increased when entering the institutions of the regime to try to emigrate, as this could awaken suspicion of anti-Soviet intentions. For those whose queue numbers were quite high, they suffered many difficult days.

And the Second World War continued. After achieving a military victory over France, in June 1940, the appetite of Nazi Germany became even more brazen and aggressive. Hitlerism swallowed new kingdoms: Yugoslavia, and Greece (April 1941), the island of Crete (May 1941), and finally in June 1941 the most important focus of their aggressive plans arrived: war against the Soviet Union.

[Page 29]

The detailed preparations by Hitler's Germany for a war against the Soviet Union (which, of course, did not remain a secret from Soviet Russia) advanced the timeline of deporting the traitorous political elements from Lithuania.

In Lithuania, in mid-June 1941, about a week before Germany's conquest of the Soviet Union, a hasty deportation of politically "unfit" people took place.

Completely unexpected, the Soviet regime started to deport the high-ranking persons from the previous Lithuanian administration. These deportations into the deepest areas of Russia included the officer circles of the previous Lithuanian army, the active leaders of the defunct political organizations, together with the previous owners of the larger establishments which were nationalized, etc.

This step by the Soviet regime also included many Lithuanian Jews, who were deported together with non-Jews. But the Lithuanian anti-Semitic elements turned the entire thing around and presented it to the Lithuanian people as, "the work of the Jews".

The provocation against Jews was disseminated and militant antisemitism started in no time. From day to day, new waves of gluttonous poison against the "Jewish" NKVD elements who conducted these measures, flooded the furthest corners of the Lithuanian provinces.

As mentioned, the Lithuanian antisemitism created a mood which made the Jews responsible for the harsh measures of the Soviet regime. This generally tense atmosphere in the country, combined with the exceptionally inflamed hatred against the Jews, led up to the day and the moment Nazi Germany so proudly pounced on the Soviet Union, on the 22nd of June 1941.

CHAPTER III

Outbreak of the German-Soviet War and the Panicked Evacuation

-Armed fights between the Lithuanian "5th Column" against the retreating Red Army-Partial evacuation of Jews to the far regions of the Soviet Union-First Jewish victims of the war

[Page 30]

The unexpected ambush of Red Russia, which took place in the early hours of Sunday, the 22nd of June 1941, made an exceptionally strong impression on the Soviets as well as on the Jewish circles in Lithuania.

At the same time, when large portions of the Lithuanian population received notice about the outbreak of war, they reacted with enthusiasm and happiness. This was especially evident among the Nationalist and pro-Fascist elements, who were terribly enraged and frightened due to the deportations to Russia. These Lithuanian circles were now seeing the realization of their dream: a war between Germany and Russia. At that time, they believed, with complete faith, that it would bring on the unavoidable destruction of the Soviet Union, and the re-establishment of their Lithuanian national independence.

The Red Army at this time did not engage in any great battle for the tract of Lithuanian territory and retreated to their Russian territory. Whether this was due to strategic reasons, or for other reasons, this offered the German army an opportunity to move itself quickly into Lithuanian territory. During the first days of war, large areas of Lithuania were occupied by the fast-marching German army divisions.

[Page 31]

In parallel to the retreat of the Red Army, and the hasty evacuation out of Lithuania of the institutions of the regime, the pro-Lithuanian-Hitlerite elements started raging, and immediately began to organize themselves into "Lithuanian partisan camps."

A few days after the outbreak of war, in addition to these pro-German elements, there were also political and mainstream criminals from Lithuanian jails standing on the Lithuanian streets. The Russians had not yet managed to evacuate them from Lithuania. Since the jails remained without supervision, the prisoners freed themselves.

This Lithuanian "fifth column" which, without a doubt, had already established prior contact with Nazi-Germany and had accumulated a secret arms reserve, soon armed itself. With arms in their hands, they started a battle behind the retreating Red Army.

In parallel to the battle against the Soviet army divisions, these Lithuanian armed forces started their long-dreamed bloody terror against the unprotected and extremely anxious Jewish population in Lithuania.

At this time, no one even thought about the possibility that the Hitlerite murderers would completely annihilate the Jewish people. Nevertheless, large numbers of Jews hastily started to evacuate themselves into the deeper domains of Russia. The first to leave were former Jewish officers and higher employees from the Soviet institutions, who expected strong reprisals in the event of a German occupation.

Due to the surprising speed of the evacuation by the military state institutions, there was a great shortage of means of transportation for civilians. This was one of the reasons why very few groups of Lithuanian Jews managed to evacuate in time.

By the way, we must also add that in the beginning, the Soviet border guards did not allow entry into the domain of Russia proper to those refugees who came from the Baltic countries or environs, which became part of the Soviet Union from the outbreak of the Second World War. Because of this, many refugees had to return to their previous homes from where they ran away, but these places were already occupied by Germans. A few days later, the Soviet regime opened the borders, and all the refugees were allowed to enter freely into the country. Because of the original prohibition on crossing over the Soviet border, many Jewish refugees, including those from Lithuania, fell into the hands of the Nazis.

[Page 32]

Those Jews who were allowed into Russia were among the fortunate ones. They were successful in avoiding the horrific Jewish slaughter that was conducted by the bloodthirsty Hitlerites with predatory cold bloodedness.

Large groups of Jews who did not have any means of transport, went on foot carrying their children in their arms or transporting them in children's carriages, leaving behind all their possessions in their abandoned homes. Almost all of them were caught enroute by the Lithuanian partisan groups. Many Jews were killed on the spot, a large portion of them were arrested, and the others, after much torture in the "partisan-headquarters," were forced to retreat through the danger-filled road to their old residences, which were already occupied by the Germans.

Add to this everyone's horror about the war operations of that time, mainly the ceaseless German bombardment of the roads on which the retreating Soviet military divisions and other evacuees travelled. It was clear what the Jews lived through during those horrific days of war.

Actually, the two main directions of the evacuees were toward Vilna and Dvinsk. During the first week of war, these roads were full of dead Jewish bodies while the final occupation of the Lithuanian territory was taking place.

CHAPTER IV

First Mass-Actions Against the Jewish Population in Kovno

-The situation in Kovno on the eve of the German occupation-Anti-Jewish incitement on the Lithuanian radio-Attacks against Jews in Kovno-The horrible pogrom in Slobodka-Bestial murders in the garages

[Page 33]

Already in the first hours of the war, Kovno started feeling the impact of the outbreak of the German-Soviet war. In the early morning hours of Sunday, the 22nd of June 1941, the city was bombarded by a German air attack. All day Sunday, the German bombardment was repeated many times. From the bombardments, more and more fires broke out. That same afternoon, the Soviet regime institutions began evacuating.

As one can imagine, the panic among the Jews became great. People ran to friends to consider what to do. Every Jew suddenly felt that the ground was burning under their feet. The evacuation of the Soviet institutions strengthened the agitation of the Jews. It was clear to most of the Jews, that if the Russians are evacuating the city, the Jews should not remain either.

The shock and disorientation of the Jews became so great with the outbreak, that at the same time one noticed how the Kovno Jews ran to the provinces, hoping that perhaps the awaiting storm would pass much easier over there. And Jews from the smaller settlements near Kovno ran into the city trying to find safe protection, because in the little towns there were very few Jews.

[Page 34]

On Monday, the 23rd of June, there actually was no Soviet regime in Kovno any longer. Since the Germans had not yet occupied the city, the actual bosses of the city were the self-established Lithuanian anti-Soviet partisan groups.

That same day, the Lithuanian leaders of the nationalist circles made an announcement via Kovno radio to the Lithuanian people. They declared that the re-establishment of Lithuanian national independence had finally been formed with a national Lithuanian government, headed by Colonel Skirpa, the former Lithuanian envoy to Germany.

We must note that when the Germans occupied Kovno, they did not recognize the Lithuanian proclamation of independence, not even the establishment of the Lithuanian government. In addition, they didn't even allow any Lithuanian "ministers", who were in Berlin, to come to Lithuania. From the start, the Germans agreed to recognize only the existence of a Lithuanian military command, and of a Lithuanian magistrate. Later, as we know, the "Lithuanian Quisling," General Kobiliunas, formed a Lithuanian government with "General Ratgeber." They were no more than lackeys of the German occupation forces.

To curry favor with the Germans, the pro-Hitler Lithuanian elements then started their anti-Jewish murders. They hoped that through such acts, like Jew-murders, they could convince the Nazis that they could leave it to the Lithuanians and could trust them fully.

From minute to minute during those horrifying days, the Jewish situation in Kovno became even more deplorable. The provocative radio proclamation by the Lithuanian military commander, Colonel Bobelias, said that, because Jews are shooting at the arriving German military, for every German soldier killed, 100 Jews would be shot; the pogrom atmosphere against the Jews became highly charged.

According to a previously prepared plan, the Lithuanian partisans then started their first mass Action against the Jewish population in Kovno.

[Page 35]

Carried out by the "highest partisan staff" the armed Lithuanian partisans scattered around various areas of the city and started attacking Jews in their homes. During these attacks, the partisans shot quite a lot of Jews on the spot and arrested many others. The arrested Jews were transported to the "partisan headquarters" in the just recently established Lithuanian Security Police, and in the jails. As a collection point for the Jews that were held in the Old City, the place was exactly on the same site of the neighborhood Council House. From the selected collection points, most of the arrested Jews, mainly the men, were later sent over to the 7th Fort (one of the forts from the past fortifications of Kovno; the first large mass-annihilation site for Kovno Jews.)

At that time, horrific scenes were being played out while the blood-thirsty Lithuanian partisans conducted their murderous acts on the helpless Jewish population. Here and there cries of lamentation were heard from the mortally frightened Jewish men, women, children, and elderly, who were being wildly and murderously rushed and kicked-out of their houses. Jews who were attacked and who dared bargain with the partisans not to arrest them, would be murderously hit and cursed with the worst curse words.

Surviving Jewish witnesses relate the following street pictures, about those past painful days for the Kovno Jews.

Groups of Jews, who were captured in Slabodka, were demonstratively taken through Leisvus Aleya, the central street in Kovno. Among the transported Jews, many were seen dressed in *tallit* and *tfilin* [*religious prayer items*], reciting *Tehillim* [prayers] out loud. These murderous processions were accompanied by beatings from rifles and intimidating gunshots from the accompanying Lithuanian partisans.

Not far from the Slabodka Bridge, on Yaneve Street, the Lithuanian murderers captured a group of about 25 Jews who were forced to dance, do various "sport exercises" and loudly sing Jewish religious prayers and Soviet songs. The bandits invited the passers-by to make merry over the tortured Jews.

[Page 36]

When the outcasts became bored with the blood-play, they forced the Jews to stand on their knees and they shot them all from behind. Among those shot was also the former editor and colleague of the Kovno "Folksblat" newspaper, Dr. Shmuel Matz (known under the pseudonym, "Shmulik").

One young Jewish man managed to extricate himself from the execution and jump into the Vilya River, but he was shot while swimming in the river.

A photographic essay of this execution was later published in a German illustrated journal with a caption: "how the native-born Eastern people take revenge on their enemies…"

In parallel to the murders, robberies of belongings also took place in many Jewish houses.

At this opportunity, it should be asserted that during those fatal days, when the previously mentioned murders of the Kovno Jewish population took place in front of all the world to witness, not one Lithuanian voice was heard. To the disgrace of the Lithuanian people, no one would weigh-in and condemn the horrible mass-murder of the Jews by the Lithuanian Hitlerites. That same shameful and tragic fact made a very strong impression at the time on the beaten Jews, and their hopeless situation under the government of the Nazis and their Lithuanian partners was already made very clear.

On the night of Tuesday, the 24th of June, when the first German military divisions showed up in Kovno, the murders by the Lithuanians were very strongly advanced. Most of the Kovno Jewish population hadn't managed to evacuate at the right time, and they started shutting themselves up in their homes in tremendous fear, waiting to see what the next day would bring.

[Page 37]

The building watchmen [concierge] played a significant role during those dark days of attacks on the helpless Kovno Jews by the Lithuanian partisan camp. Most of them suddenly wanted to settle accounts and get rid of their Jewish neighbors and did everything so that the wild partisans could capture as many Jews from their courtyard as possible. In this way, they could get their hands on Jewish belongings. Only a few watchmen didn't allow themselves to benefit from the greed of grabbing Jewish possessions, and they helped protect their Jewish neighbors somewhat, by telling the oncoming partisans that these Jews had already been taken away, or that in their courtyard there were no Jews, etc. Such virtuous and good people were very few among the watchmen of the buildings.

In the earlier few days, one could see some passersby on the Kovno streets, but later they became "empty of Jews." That's how, for example, on Wednesday, the 25th of June, you could notice how the few Jews were running through the streets with great fear and nervousness, like animals who were being persecuted by their hunter. Many Jews knew very well what kind of deathly danger was lurking for them from the Lithuanian partisans if they appeared on the street. People put their lives in danger to go out on the street with one goal: to contact relatives or good friends who live on other streets, in order not to feel so lonely and isolated during those horrifying days and nights.

However, at the height of those first mass Actions against the Jews, came a horrific pogrom in Slabodka. This horrific mass slaughter took place during the night between Wednesday, the 25th and Thursday, the 26th of June 1941.

Under darkness of night, murderous bands broke down the doors of the Jewish homes on the small streets of Slabodka. Among them were many Lithuanian students in uniform and partisan guards with guns, revolvers, axes, and knives. With murder previously unheard of, they shot, stabbed, hacked heads, etc. This slaughterous pogrom went on the entire night.

Human body parts, torn to pieces, were found in many attacked houses, and in the courtyards around the houses, because a portion of the murderers also used "dum-dum" bullets. After the pogrom, for example, on Yorbuker Street, where the Kovno Zionist community leader, Mordechai Yatkonski, lived, the head of Yatkonski was found in one corner of the room, and the rest of the body parts – on the other end of the room. The body of his wife (a dentist) was found with her breasts cut off.

[Page 38]

A dreadfully mutilated body was found in the apartment of the Slabodka Rabbi Osofsky with the Rabbi lying on top of a bloody *Gemorah* [holy book], which he was studying at night when the murderers came to kill him.

There was even talk that in one of the shop windows in Slabodka, decapitated Jewish heads were put on display.

On Krisciukaicio Street, opposite the Slabodka post office building, a Jewish house was set on fire. A few Jewish families who were shot were burned in the flames.

These are only a few details of the horrors of the Slabodka pogrom, in which about a thousand Jews were annihilated in this bestial manner.

On Friday, the 27th of June, the dead were collected on garbage wagons and a portion of them were buried in the Old Slabodka Jewish cemetery, and the rest in a mass grave on the edge of the Vilnya River, near Slabodka.

The Slabodka pogrom, as it turns out, did not quench the bloodthirst of the Lithuanian murderers. Their animal-like greed for Jewish blood demanded even more new Jewish victims. During those horrible days for Jews in Lithuania, the Lithuanian pogromists allowed themselves to satisfy their sadistic tendencies on a mass scale, which they could never ever have dreamt of. Confirmation of this can be found in the following horrific facts:

On Friday, the 27th of June, about 60 Jews, who were captured together in the district of Vitoft Prospect and Gedimin Street, were transported to the courtyard of the "Lietukis" Garage on Vitoft Prospect and were tortured to death in an extraordinarily horrific manner.

Witnesses from the neighboring houses described some dozen Jews being murdered by the Lithuanian mass murderers by battering them with auto instruments, shovels, and axes. Hoses, used to wash cars, were shoved into the mouths of a portion of the victims, and as the water was turned on, the Jews' bodies burst.

[Page 39]

After this bloody execution in the courtyard of the garage, a shapeless bloody mass of hacked human limbs was torn to pieces and left lying about.

Similarly horrific events took place at the same time in another garage in the neighborhood of Vytauto Prospect. Also in this garage, the murderers tortured their victims so long until the Jews fell, powerless. Then, they poured cold water on those powerless prone Jews to revive them, and then tortured them again. This was repeated so long, until the unfortunate Jews became totally tortured.

On the same day, in another part of the city, a group of captured Jews were forced to pull a Soviet tank out of the Nieman River with ropes. The tank had fallen into the water at the time of the battle near the river bridges. Because there was no way the Jews could accomplish such a heavy job, they were murderously battered by the Lithuanian partisans, who kept on screaming that the Jews "are too lazy to work…"

Unfortunately, the horrible Slabodka pogrom, the bloody Actions in the garages, etc., were nothing more than an introduction to the later inconceivable murders of the defenseless and desperate Jewish population, both in Kovno and in the provinces. In this mass slaughter there were representatives of all strata of Lithuanian people, like peasants, workers, intelligentsia, clerks, etc. They actively participated with genuine predatory, cold-bloodedness, and sadistic pleasure bathed in oceans of Jewish blood.

So, this is how tragically hopeless the Jewish situation appeared already in the first days of the Hitlerite occupation of Lithuania.

CHAPTER V

Horrible Killing at the Seventh Fort

-Murderous crimes by the Lithuanian Partisans against the 10,000-12,000 Jews caught and gathered in one place-Shaming, raping, and shooting Jewish women-Murder of about 8,000 Jews

[Page 40]

At the time of the mass arrest of the Kovno Jewish residents, the Lithuanian partisans (LAF) enjoyed capturing some 10-12 thousand Jews. As previously mentioned, the arrested Jews were from various collected towns, and were transferred to the 7th Fort, which is located near the Kovno suburb of "the Green Hill." [Zaliakalnys]

Only a few Jews managed to get themselves out of this hell, through bribery and some other kind of arrangements. All the others, among whom were mainly men and fewer women and children, remained arrested at the Fort. The women and the children were imprisoned in the casements of the Fort, and the men were held under the open skies.

During the lead up to the mass executions, the terror at the Fort was cruel. For the smallest "sin" they would be shot on the spot, without warning by the Lithuanian partisans who were guarding the arrested Jews.

[Page 41]

The men were being held in the terrible heat, under the burning rays of the sun during those many endless days. They were lying immobile and were not allowed to speak a word among themselves. If any one of the men lifted their head, or if they would move to get more comfortable, the partisans on patrol at that spot immediately would start shooting with their machine guns. There was no mention of food during the first days. The arrested were languishing for a drop of water. Some found an opportunity to drink from a nearby stream, but the partisans would shoot them on their way back, saying that it was for trying to run away.

To make the week more brutal and sadistic for the Jewish prisoners, they would systematically become drunk. Many soldiers would almost always be in a drunken state.

A separately horrible account was the situation for the young women. At nightfall, the drunken Lithuanian partisans started grabbing women from the casements and dragging out young Jewish women and girls to rape and then shoot them. The panic among the women reached the skies. Many of the victimized women lost their minds from the shock. These gruesome scenes took place over a few nights. Dozens of Jewish girls and young women were raped and shot during these night orgies by the wild Lithuanian scoundrels.

To make themselves undesirable to the partisan eye, the prettier and younger women and girls would smear their faces with mud, etc. However, this did not deter the beast-like sadists from their criminal deeds, and the toll of Jewish girls who were raped even increased. There were even cases among the raped girls and tortured women where young girls were raped together with their mothers.

The then Lithuanian Kovno commander, Colonel Bobelis, came to visit the 7th Fort and give the necessary directives to the guards himself.

One day he ordered a selection of those Jewish men who served as volunteers in the Lithuanian army. About 70 young Jewish men who served as volunteers in the Lithuanian military, were selected out from among the other men and imprisoned in a separate casement. These Jews were forced to sing and dance for the drunken guards, who at various times were overseeing them. Later, they were transferred to the Central Kovno Prison and, after some time, were murdered. Only a few of them were saved by various means, and from the jail were then able to get out to their families.

[Page 42]

Witnesses to the horrible murders at the 7th Fort gave testimony to this irrefutable scream-to-the-heavens fact: at the same time the captured prisoners were held at the Fort, there was a basketball game taking place in Kovno, between a German military team and a Lithuanian team. The Lithuanians were great experts in this sport and for a time were the basketball champions of Europe, so they had a victory match. As a "prize" every one of the victorious Lithuanian team members got the right to shoot a dozen Jews at the 7th Fort. A Lithuanian officer, Kirkila was there and because of his strong bestial bloodthirstiness, he himself shot hundreds of Jews. Tortured by his conscience, he committed suicide a few days later.

Afterwards, in the beginning of July 1941, as soon as the Soviet prisoners of war prepared the mass graves, the arrested Jewish men, totaling 7-8 thousand persons, were shot by machine guns.

Before the murder of the men, the Jewish women and children were transferred from the 7th Fort to the 9th Fort which is 4-5 km from the Kovno suburb of Slabodka. After a short time, they let most of the women and children go home, where a flood of plunder and persecutions awaited them.

And, once again, it should be stressed here, that during the enormous bloodbath at the 7th Fort, the slaughter was not only carried out by the Lithuanians, but together with the Gestapo, they were also the organizers of the mass murders. This specific appalling fact took place not only in Kovno, but also on a much larger scale in many places in the Lithuanian provinces where the Lithuanian Hitlerites murdered the resident Jews without any decree from the Gestapo. For generations to come, this will remain a mark of shame in the history of the Lithuanian people, whose sons and daughters carried out such horrific and shameful violations.

[Page 43]

The Jews around the world, and especially the Lithuanian Jews, will forever have etched in their memory these shameful and horrific killings on the part of the Lithuanians, who during this critical moment in our story of martyrdom, had a hand in spilling the blood of our innocent martyrs.

CHAPTER VI

The Establishment of the Ghetto in Slabodka

-The first Action of the Jewish Committee moving the population into the Ghetto-The creation of a Jewish Committee-The Jewish population of Kovno and surrounding towns forced to relocate to the newly founded ghetto-A flood of anti-Jewish orders

[Page 44]

A few weeks after the outbreak of the war, when the war operations were moved further behind the borders of Lithuania, the occupation powers started to "stabilize" the situation in the country in general, and in Kovno, in particular.

In the beginning of July 1941, the Kovno Gestapo started by calling on a few Jewish leaders, who were notified that the Lithuanians can never live together with the Jews in the city because "all the Jews are Communists." Thus, from the 15th of August of this year, a ghetto will be established for Jews in Kovno. The suburb of Slabodka was planned as the district for the Ghetto. The previously mentioned Jews were ordered to set up a Jewish Committee* in the Ghetto, which would deal with the Jewish abuses in the city.

At this opportunity the Gestapo "assured" the Jewish leaders that no further Actions against Jews would take place.

On the 10th of July an order was made public, according to which all those of Jewish heritage in the city of Kovno and in the surrounding towns must leave their homes by the 15th of August 1941. They must relocate to the town of Viliampole (Slabodka), where a ghetto will be established for Jews.

[Page 45]

In the middle of July, there came a short "quiet" pause after the first wave of unspeakable mass-murders against Jews in Kovno passed. At that time many Jews snuck into the city by various means and with great personal danger. These were the Jews who were caught enroute from their evacuation by the fast-advancing march of the German army division. These were people, who, for various reasons enroute, didn't fall into the hands of the Lithuanian partisans, or escaped from them after a variety of tortures and persecutions.

At that time in Kovno, there was a population of approximately 30,000 people. They were comprised of Jews who didn't manage to evacuate, and the few women and children who were arrested in the first days of the war and then released.

In truth, there were no more systematic attacks by the Lithuanian partisans on Jewish homes, as had taken place until this time, but walking on the street, especially for Jewish men, still entailed great danger. In those days, Jews were not only afraid of being arrested, but also of being caught at work by the Germans or the Lithuanian partisans, because at work they would murderously beat and jeer at them. Therefore, Jews hid themselves away with fearful heart palpitations, and waited with unease for the development of future events.

On the 17th of July 1941, in Kovno, a civil regime was finally established, that is, in the city a German City-Commissariat was established, which started organizing all issues of the civil population. The S.A.

Brigade Leader, Kramer, who was the former Mayor of Dachau was installed as the City Commissar, and as later shown, was a big Jew-hater.

The Lithuanian, Kaminskas, the former High officer from the Kovno Magistrate and for a short time, was Mayor of Vilna during the time of Smetana, was instated as the Councilor of Jewish Affairs in the City Commissariat. Later, the young Nazi from the German border town Eidkugen, S.A. Major Jordan was instated as the speaker of Jewish affairs in the City Commissariat. He was a Jew murderer on a mass scale, who on his own accord was responsible for thousands of Jewish victims.

[Page 46]

At this time, the authorities of the City Commissariat managed to publish the first anti-Jewish orders. As usual, there was a law for Jews to wear a yellow Magen David star on their chest, and a few days later a new order to wear a second Magen David star on the back. There was now a law that Jews were forbidden to walk on the sidewalks, like all other people, but they must walk on the edges of the street, near the gutters of the sidewalk. There were more laws forbidding Jews to show up in frequented areas, or use common means of transportation (like autos, horse-drawn carriages, etc.), have telephones, radios, have Christian employees, go to the market to shop for food, etc.

A special law also forbade Jews from selling or even entrusting their earthly possessions, whatever they were, to Christians, including furniture and homewares. As it later turned out, the purpose of this last rule was so that Jews and all their possessions would be transferred to the Ghetto for the Germans to rob them of everything.

These anti-Jewish laws were publicized in the name of the German City Commissar, or from the Lithuanian military commandant. Violations of these laws would receive death penalties.

After the bloody Actions against the Jewish population during the first few weeks of the Nazi reign, when thousands of Jews were killed, this wave of anti-Jewish laws bore bi-weekly witness to the situation for Jews in the world.

The tragic experiences up to this point, and the unsettling worry about the near future caused daily increase in depression and anxiety in the Jewish population. The Jewish faces mirrored their woes, problems, and sorrows.

In the first weeks of the occupation the Jews were completely broken down. Later, the Jews became partially hardened to the endless bloody events, and they became less sensitive to the various Nazi orders.

[Page 47]

Immediately from the beginning, the established Jewish Committee had a lot of work thrown upon them. On this Committee were assembled, among others, Dr. Grigori Wolf, Dr. Elhanan Elkes, Dr. Yefim Rabinowitz, Advocate Leib Garfunkel, Advocate Yakov Goldberg, Rabbi Shmukler, Rabbi Snieg, etc.

Although the "power" of the Jewish Committee, as one can imagine, was very minimal, the defenseless Jewish population, who were without rights, laid siege to the Committee on various issues, searching for help and advice, on a daily basis.

To model productive work, the Jewish Committee established various commissions, which were dedicated to issues, legal help, housing, work distribution, abuses in the Ghetto, etc.

At the start, the Committee had much to do with those Jews who returned from the city after an unsuccessful attempt at evacuation. They found that their apartments along with their possessions which were left after running away from Kovno were taken over by Christians. They had to find housing for these Jews, or shelter somewhere, and then retrieve at least a portion of their possessions. To regulate the housing situation for Jews within the Jewish Committee, a Lithuanian officer from the Housing Office of the magistrate was delegated to them. Getting back their possessions was dependent mainly on the Housing Administration, an institution which remained active since the Soviet days when the big houses were nationalized.

But, as mentioned, the prime task of the Jewish Committee was to organize and put order into the relocations into the Ghetto.

There was much to negotiate with the Kovno Lithuanian magistrate in establishing the ghetto domain. The Lithuanian tone setters of the magistrate were disposed to designating a somewhat smaller area for the Ghetto, in order not to, God forbid, "upset" the Christian population in Slabodka. The Jewish representatives, therefore, had to fight with the magistrate to add another street to the ghetto area, with a few dozen wooden huts.

[Page 48]

Under the supervision of the Lithuanian magistrate official, the Jews themselves had to fence in the ghetto quarter with a high fence of barbed wire.

As was foreseen at the start, Jews were also living in homes on both sides of Yorbuker Street, but the main street had to be kept open for non-Jewish traffic. So, they considered building an underground tunnel near Yorbuker street (not far from the Slabodka bridge) which was supposed to be designated for Jewish traffic. But, in the middle of construction of the tunnel it became clear that Jews would not be allowed to live on Yorbuker Street, so the work of digging the tunnel was cancelled.

Also, from the start, the ghetto domain included a part of Paneriu street, which had the uneven numbers, and in addition a few nearby little streets, for example, Naoialo, Lampedzshiu, parts of Dvara, Gashtauta, etc. This portion of the ghetto was called "the Small Ghetto."

Thus, because Paneriu Street was one of the central streets of Slabodka and led to important streets in the city, this specific street was also designated for non-Jewish traffic. That is, Jews lived in the houses on both sides of the street so the main street was separated from the houses by tall fences of barbed wire so that you could travel from the Small Ghetto to other parts of the Ghetto. It continued to Paneriu street (near the cross street with Dvara street) and a special wooden hanging bridge was constructed by Jews. (a viaduct).

To create space for the Jews in the previously foreseen ghetto concept, the local non-Jewish population had to leave their homes and relocate to the former Jewish homes in the city, or in the part of Slabodka where no Jews were allowed to be.

For a few weeks, long lines of hundreds traveled, packed up, loaded up with baggage and thousands on foot with packages on their backs stretched out on the streets of the city to Slabodka, and from Slabodka to the city. The first were Jews, the others - Christians. By comparison, it looked like a "people-wandering"-

a wandering, forced by the Gestapo, which had premeditated their horrific plans regarding the fate of the Ghetto.

Note: Specifics about the establishment of the Jewish Committee, see "Eltestenrat" in the Monograph "Jewish Institutions in the Kovno Ghetto."

Map of Kovno and the environs, in 1922

At the 7th Fort. Thousands of captured Jewish men,
who were murdered in the beginning of July 1941.
(The Kovno Jew, S. Burshtein got this photo from a German in Munich)

[Page 49]

Knowing that the order to transfer the Jews to the Ghetto will have to be fulfilled punctually by a specific time, a rush began among the Jews to find a house in the Ghetto. Those who could financially afford it, would offer a larger sum of money to Christian Slabodka house owners who had to leave their homes, and they would take over their homes. At this opportunity, there was plenty of deceit and more than a few tricks played on the part of dishonest Christians.

Meanwhile, among the Jews in the Jewish Housing Office, which regulated the housing issues in the ghetto area, there was a rumor that there were dishonest negotiations among corrupt Jewish officers, who wanted to create a source of "easy earnings" from the Jewish misfortune.

A large portion of the Jewish population, who were without means, and who were not able to acquire housing, simply attempted to transfer their belongings to the Ghetto and put them somewhere with a friend, in storage, in an attic, etc. There were rolled up packages with Jewish possessions near many houses in the Ghetto. Included were disassembled furniture, and various home items, which Jews brought with them to the Ghetto but did not have any personal corner to lay them all out.

The Destruction of Jewish Kovno

From one day to the next, new groups of Jews left their apartments in the city and resettled in the Ghetto. By the first week of August 1941, the largest portion of the Kovno Jewish population was already settled in the Ghetto. At that moment they could not yet foresee what kind of incredibly tragic fate awaited the ghetto Jews very soon.

CHAPTER VII

Jewish Victims Before Locking the Ghetto

-The Action on the "infamous Thursday"-Death of over one thousand Jewish men-Shooting of Jews while they were buying food products

[Page 50]

At the beginning of August 1941, several Jews were still living in the city. They were the ones who had not yet managed to relocate to the Ghetto, or those who didn't yet have an apartment in the Ghetto to which to relocate. In addition, many Jews, who were already sitting in the Ghetto had left a portion of their things in the city. Because of a shortage of means of transportation, these items could only be transferred piecemeal from the city to the Ghetto. Therefore, there was much traffic between the Ghetto and the city. On the streets of the city, many Jews were moving around.

This was on Thursday morning, the 7th of August 1941, when the full tempo of the transfer into the Ghetto took place, and many Jews were travelling from the city to the Ghetto, and back again.

Unexpectedly for the Jews, who were busy with the relocation into the Ghetto, the Lithuanian partisans started arresting Jewish men who were found in the homes and on the streets of the city. None of those who were caught had any idea why they were arrested, or where they were being taken.

At first, the Jews thought that they were catching them to take them to work, something which in those days would often happen. But the Lithuanian partisans ceaselessly hunted Jewish men, regardless of their age or physical health status, and they violently packed them into special cattle trucks which they had in their authority for this purpose. It turned out that the Jewish men were transported to the Kovno Central Jail station (the so-called, yellow jail).

[Page 51]

Within a few hours, the Lithuanian murderers managed to capture around 1200 Jewish men and bring them all to the jail.

As soon as they found out about the hunt for Jewish men, most men in the city and in the Ghetto started to hide themselves. Then, close family members of the captured men started searching for ways to free them from jail.

After tremendous efforts on the part of the relatives of the arrested men, they released about 150 old and weak men, but the rest remained in jail.

In the beginning, the Jews didn't manage to ascertain anything about the fate of these more than 1000 Jewish arrested men. Later, it became clear that a few days after their arrest, all were taken out of the jail and shot. Where they killed them remained unknown to the Jews.

In the history of the Kovno Ghetto, this round up was called: "the infamous Thursday Action."

Already from the first days of the Hitler occupation, Jews started feeling the shortage of food from one day to the next, in addition to all the other evils and calamities. There was no reserve of food among any of the Jews, and the little bit of food they did have from before was almost finished.

In truth, in the first month of the occupation, Jews received food ration cards, just like non-Jews, but because of the anti-Jewish abuses and arrests, many Jews were afraid to even go out in the street to pick up the food products with the ration cards. The terrorization by the Lithuanian partisans made it impossible for many Jews to step close to the food shops. For all these reasons, the question of nourishment was especially acute for the Jews.

[Page 52]

Forced by hunger, Jews took the risk and sneaked out on the streets behind the city to buy something from the peasants, who brought their products to the city. The Ghetto was not yet locked up at this time, so it was mainly the Jews who were already settled in the Ghetto who had to do this, because they didn't have anything to eat.

The occupation regime decided to end this Jewish "violation" in genuine Nazi manner.

In the beginning of August 1941, it was still possible to go in and out freely from the Ghetto Gate. Early one morning, when the relocations in the Ghetto were not yet completed, the Gestapo suddenly ambushed those Jews who went out on the streets behind Slabodka to buy some food from peasants who were driving by.

A few dozen Jews, who were on the streets, managed to hide, but 26 Jews fell into the hands of the Gestapo during this ambush.

Those who were caught by the Gestapo were taken away to the 9th Fort. There, they were forced to dig a pit for themselves, dance around their own grave, sing Soviet songs and then, they were all shot.

After shooting the captured Jews, the Gestapo murderers brought a few dozen Jews, who worked at the Ghetto Gate, to the site of the execution, and forced them to fill the pit with the murdered Jews.

Before returning these Jews to the Ghetto, the Gestapo told them that they should tell the ghetto Jews what kind of an end awaits any Jew who risks going out on the roads to buy food from the peasants travelling by.

And on the same day of the execution of the 26 Jews, the event was published in a special Gestapo announcement.

So, after this tragic murder, there is certainly no need to explain that the Jews stopped going out on the roads to buy food. Thus, the question of nourishment took on a catastrophic character for the Jews, very quickly.[a]

Original footnote:

    a.   More details about the issue – in the later chapters.

CHAPTER VIII

Action of the Intellectuals Immediately After the Lock up of the Ghetto

-Locking up of the Ghetto-Order from the authorities to deliver 500 Jews for "academic" work in town-Registering several hundred Jews for work- Capturing Jews in the Ghetto-Tragic fate of the 534 captured young Jews

[Page 53]

On August 15, 1941, the Ghetto was finally locked up. It is difficult to report details of how many Jews relocated from the city to the Ghetto. It is suggested that about 28 to 29 thousand Jewish people relocated into the Ghetto. Immediately after the Ghetto was closed, the guards took over authority of the Ghetto from the special German police division, and they had at their disposal many Lithuanian partisans.

After a succession of transformations from the earlier Jewish Committee, the Jewish Elder's Council[a] was established, headed by Dr. Elchanan Elkes. Their job was to fulfill the orders of the regime for the Ghetto and to carry out internal issues of ghetto life.

These first became recognized by the regime as the representation of the Ghetto settlement, and then as the Elder's Council. In addition to these Jewish representatives, a wide array of ghetto institutions was established, as follows: Jewish Ghetto Police, Jewish Work Office, Jewish Housing Office, Jewish Welfare Office, etc. According to the intention of the Elder's Council, all these ghetto institutions had to help establish some order in the internal life of the Ghetto.

[Page 54]

Only one day after the lock-up of the Ghetto[b], on Shabbat, the 16th of August, based on an order by the regime, Jews had to vacate a few streets where they had just gotten organized with such great difficulties like, for example, Raudondvariu, Degetoku, etc. The aggravation in the Ghetto became greater now that they had to transfer over to another ghetto area.

The Jewish population hadn't even managed to recover from the horrible punch of that infamous tragic Thursday, the 7th of August, when more than 1000 Jewish victims were caught. The murderous Hitlerites claimed hundreds of new Jewish victims to calm their insatiable thirst for Jewish blood. This time, the Gestapo call for Jewish blood was masked in a respectful manner:

Thursday, the 14th of August 1941, the then Councilman for Jewish Affairs in the city, the Lithuanian Commissar, Kaminskas, gave the Jewish Elders Council an order to assemble 500 Jews by Monday, the 18th of August. They were ostensibly needed to put order in a few archives in the city. Kaminskas stressed that for this specific job they needed mainly intellectuals.

The Jewish Work Office of the Elders Council sent out announcements, unsuspecting that this was part of a vile and a provocative trick by the brown-shirted executioners and their Lithuanian accomplices to kill a huge portion of the Kovno Jewish intellectuals. These went mainly to the Jews from the liberal arts, like for example lawyers, doctors, engineers, teachers, librarians, students, etc. They were told that they should report to the Ghetto Gate at a specific time, to go to work in the city.

[Page 55]

Also, the contemptible Kaminskas "assured" the Elders Council that nothing bad would happen to the Jews and that during the work time they would receive food three times per day, etc. After the announcement from the Jewish Work Office, not more than two hundred men responded by the specified time, among whom were, as mentioned, many of Kovno's intellectuals.

On Monday, the 18th of August, a large guard of Lithuanian partisans arrived, under the leadership of the Gestapo murderer Rauca, who later became tragically infamous as the biggest hangman of the Ghetto. He arrived at the Ghetto Gate to transport the Jewish men to "work." These Jews, who came voluntarily to the assembly point by the Ghetto Gate, were immediately surrounded by a large and strong partisan guard.

Because they were still short a few hundred men to fill this order, the Gestapo hangman, Rauca, ordered the partisans to go into the Ghetto and capture the missing number of Jews that were needed.

The Lithuanian partisans, with great murderousness, spread out across the streets of the Ghetto and, in a brutal way, chased and captured a larger group of Jews.

Together with those who came of their own accord, 534 Jews were assembled at the place near the Ghetto Gate under stronger guard, and they were transported from the Ghetto into the city, from where they never returned.

At first the Ghetto Jews didn't yet know that this was a masked Action, and the family members of those who were transported would run daily to the Ghetto Gate to wait for their own people who were supposed to come back from work.

The Jewish pleas to learn something about the fate of the captured victims were to no avail. Despite clear "assurances" from the various Nazi-big shots who oversaw the Ghetto that the 534 transported Jews were alive and working, it was quickly discovered, that on the same day that they were transported out of the Ghetto, they were shot at the 4th Fort, which is located near the Kovno suburb of Panemun.

[Page 56]

Once again, the Ghetto found itself in a difficult situation because of the murderous Gestapo, who, as noted, had greatly helped the Lithuanian Hitlerites.

Sometime after this Action, the former Ghetto Commander, S.A. Major Jordan, one of the most horrid hangmen of the Kovno Ghetto, told the Elders Council that the 534 Jews were shot as punishment for sabotaging their work because they wet and spoiled a wagon of sugar, which belonged to the Wehrmacht. Of course, this was not true.

Anyway, for the Gestapo, this was a "reason" to kill over 500 Jews, which included a huge number of the Kovno Jewish intellectuals.

Original footnotes:

    a.   Officially named: Altestenrat of the Jewish Ghetto, Local Community, Viliampole. The name "Eltestenrat" was adopted by the Kovno Ghetto Jews. This word was maintained and not Yiddishized.

    b.   About the activities and the roles of the Jewish ghetto institutions, see Monograph: "Jewish Institutions in the Kovno Ghetto."

CHAPTER IX

The Robbery of Jewish Belongings

-Systematic house-searching in the Ghetto with the purpose of robbing Jewish property-Terror and victims during the house searches- "Voluntary" delivery of money and all other valuables

[Page 57]

A few days later, after the entire Kovno Jewish population was finally locked up behind a tall fence of barbed wire and strongly guarded by a special ghetto guard, searches took place, day in and day out, in Jewish homes to confiscate money and other valuable items from the Jews. This took place over the course of two weeks, starting from the 19th of August and ending on the 4th of September 1941.

German police divisions would go from house to house under the supervision of the Chief of Police, Torenbaum. They conducted thorough searches and would take money, gold and silver items, better clothes, underwear, shoes, electrical machinery, medical and other instruments, nicer furniture and any other objects and items that they liked from the Jewish homes.

In the beginning, the ghetto Jews were determined to hide their better and valuable items from the German robbers. To this end, each one considered hiding his money and better objects somewhere so the Germans could not find them. Money, gold, silver, and other valuable items would be buried in the earth or hidden in such places which were not conspicuous to an outsider's eye. So that they would not seem unwelcoming and empty-handed to their "guests," the Jews would deliberately prepare a small amount of money and whatever else of their better things, so the Germans would not become suspicious that they were hiding something from them.

[Page 58]

Then, after the Jewish homes had already been searched one time, the Germans started to go through every Jewish house once again. Their goal was to disorient the ghetto Jews, so they couldn't prepare in time for another house search and hide their better objects. To do this, the German police would engage in various tricks. For example, after a day or two they would conduct the searches systematically, going from street to street, and suddenly they would attack one ghetto quarter and then another, etc.

The attackers had trucks with them, and a special work-command would immediately transport the robbed items to the city. The previous Jewish prayer houses in the old city were used as storage depots for the robbed Jewish items and furniture.

In an effort to scare the ghetto population so they would not dare hide any valuables and would give everything up during the searches, a few days after the start of the house searches, the Nazis brought a bloody terror to bear. Day in and day out, during the time of the searches, and without the slightest reason, the police would shoot Jews, mainly men. Dozens of Jews were shot in this manner. The shock and terror of the house searches was so great, that every time, when it was known that the attackers were already here in the Ghetto, the ghetto Jews would become genuinely confused. Jews at that time weren't as afraid of the Germans taking away valuable items, as they were afraid of, God forbid, becoming a human victim.

Equally horrible for the men was to be found in their home during the house searches, because the Germans would beat the men mercilessly and as was said, they might also be shot. The men would take pains to immediately disappear from those quarters, while the house searches were taking place.

Therefore, during the searches, only women and children were found in the houses. Searching the women, allegedly for plugging up gold, diamonds, etc. the women would be undressed completely naked, and they would be searched by the German police.

This terror by the Nazi robbers created such a panic and deathly fear among the ghetto Jews, that many Jews wanted to get rid of their property, just to save their lives.

[Page 59]

Thorough searches took place for more than two weeks, during which time a large portion of the Jews' belongings was robbed. Most of the ghetto Jews had huge difficulties hiding portions of their possessions from the Nazis during the searches.

After all the house searches, the Nazis decided to thoroughly squeeze the remainder of the possessions out of the Jews, which they succeeded in hiding during the life-threatening searches. To this aim, the then-Ghetto Commandant, Jordan ordered the Jewish Elders Council to order the Jews to deliver everything they had hidden themselves during the time of the house searches. To persuade the Jews that this time they should really give up everything they owned "voluntarily," the Ghetto Commandant gave notice that by violating this rule, not only would the guilty ones be shot, but their neighbors would be shot, as well.

Based on the decree by the Ghetto Commandant in the beginning of September, the Elder's Council notified the Ghetto population that by Thursday, the 4th of September 1941, all Jews must "voluntarily" give up items of greater or lesser value. This included: money (leaving out not more than 100 rubles for an entire family, which at that time was equal to 10 Reich-Mark), foreign currency, securities, gold items, including wedding rings, silver-workmanship, rugs, furs, textile material, electric and medical machines, collections, etc. This decree was accompanied by the pressure that not only the person by whom the items would be found would be shot, but those living nearby would also be shot.

Since the ghetto Jews already knew very well that the Nazi murderers would carry out these threats, there was no other choice but to comply with the decree. In addition, because of the warning that they would shoot neighboring people, the more honorable and responsible Jews complied with these demands by the regime exactly. They did not want innocent people to suffer due to their withholding items.

[Page 60]

During the first of the house searches, it was observed that the Jews had an attitude of hiding everything they could from the robbers. But this time, a hysteria developed to give everything up to the Nazis, so that there would be no excuse for new victims. Therefore, Jews started to unearth, or pull out of other hiding places all the valuables which they had hidden and prepared to deliver them to the regime. Every responsible Jew did this himself and convinced their friends that they should also do it.

Only the antisocial and amoral elements in the Ghetto were determined not to carry out this decree and thus, eventually put the people around them in danger. Most of the Ghetto Jews decided that their own lives and the lives of their neighbors had higher value than the valuable items, and, in this way, they showed higher social and moral consciousness.

From morning until evening, almost the entire Jewish population brought items consisting of generations of collected Jewish toil to the collection points with their own hands. Gold and silver cups, candlesticks, utensils, etc., were "voluntarily" given up, together with other valuable items, to the jurisdiction of the killers of the Jewish people. These items passed from generation to generation over dozens of years and were silent witnesses to a particular Jewish lifestyle in Eastern Europe.

During the next few days, exactly thirty thousand Kovno Ghetto Jews remained robbed and impoverished. Assessors estimated that the Jewish deliveries were worth tens of millions of Reichsmark.

Despite bathing themselves in the robbed Jewish belongings, in order to make sure that the Jews had given everything up this time, the Nazis then made an entire series of test cases in the Ghetto, to ascertain whether any of the Jews had, God forbid, not given up what they had to. It turns out that after they were finally convinced that the Jews really were left "naked and barefoot," no more house searches took place in the Ghetto. Such was the extent of the Nazi robbers' appetites.

CHAPTER X

Test Action

-Distribution of 5,000 "certificates"-Mass-Action in the Small Ghetto, whose process was stopped for unknown reasons after the first "selection."

[Page 61]

The Ghetto fell under the authority of the City Commissar. On the 15th of September 1941 the City Commissar gave 5000 certificates to the Elder's Council, through the Lithuanian official Kaminskas. They were to be distributed among Jewish craftsman and their family members. These printed certificates were drawn up by the then-Ghetto Commandant, Jordan. Thus, the certificates were called "Jordan-certificates."

In the Ghetto, it wasn't known at the start why these certificates were even distributed. There was a fundamental belief that those Jews who received the "Jordan certificates" would eventually be treated better than any Jew who didn't possess them. Various Jews in the Ghetto were therefore keen to acquire these "life-certificates," as the ghetto Jews later called the "Jordan-certificates."

When the Jews found out about the distribution of certificates, thousands and thousands camped out at the building of the Elders Council and its institutions on Varniu Street 49, wanting to acquire a "Jordan certificate." Understandably, the Elders Council couldn't fill everyone's request. Aside from that, there was a rumor among the ghetto Jews, that those who oversaw the distribution of the certificates were involved in various irregular activities. Therefore, there was a fierce struggle around the issue of the certificates. In addition to acquiring them through the Elders Council, Jews acquired a few "Jordan-certificates" directly from the German workshops where they worked.

[Page 62]

At this moment, it is important to note that these certificates did indeed play a big role during some future Actions. At the time of the Big Action, which took place on the 28th of October 1941, the Nazis didn't pay attention to any certificates, not even to the "Jordan-certificates." But, until then, the Jordan certificate really was, in a sense, a life-certificate, because it saved people during the selections which took place related to the extermination Actions.

On the night of Monday, the 15th of September, the Ghetto Commander, Jordan, came and confiscated the cash box from the Elders Council. Jordan did not reveal the reason for his act, so there was reason to be quite anxious about the upcoming plans of the regime regarding the Ghetto.

The later ghetto events demonstrated that this specific Jewish suspicion wasn't without cause.

At around 7-8 pm on Wednesday, the 17th of September 1941, a strengthened guard was set up around the Small Ghetto, where approximately 3000 Jews lived. Traffic between the Small Ghetto and the rest of the Ghetto was immediately closed off.

At the same time, German police troops came into the Small Ghetto, together with Lithuanian partisans, and they started chasing the Jews out of their homes. The Jews who were chased out were taken to a place which was in the Small Ghetto. When all the Jews were brought together on this site, they started a selection. Those who had a "Jordan-certificate" were sent to the "good side," all the others, to the "bad side."

During the time the Jews in the Small Ghetto were being chased to the site of the selection, the rest of the Ghetto went into an extraordinary panic. Jews thought that afterwards, when they finished with the Small Ghetto, they would get to the other ghetto quarters. So, they ran from one ghetto corner to another, understandably, not knowing where would be better.

[Page 63]

From far away, the Jews in the other sectors of the Ghetto started following everything that was taking place in the Small Ghetto. From minute to minute the tension grew. No one in the "luckier" side of the Ghetto knew yet what was really going on there. Some thought that the selected ones would be taken to be shot; others expressed suspicion that they must be taking them out of the Kovno Ghetto to Lublin, where there were communal dormitories for Jews, etc.

After the selection ended, those who were selected for the "bad side" were loaded onto trucks and transported in the direction of the 9th Fort. It became clear that an Action had taken place.

Suddenly, for unknown reasons, the Action was stopped. Those in charge of the selection started leaving the site, and the guards started chasing the Jews back home. From the 9th Fort they started bringing back those Jews who had been taken away.

It remained uncertain for the ghetto Jews if this time it was a real Action that was stopped for some reason, or this was a type of "war of nerves" against the ghetto Jews. Or perhaps it was just a type of "general test" for future mass Actions.

At that time there was also a rumor that the actual goal of this "test-Action" was to make a movie which would show that the extermination Actions against Jews were conducted by local residents, i.e.,

Lithuanians, and not by the Germans. To that end the Nazis mainly placed Lithuanian partisans on the selection work and then filmed the course of the sorting. This version remained only a supposition.

As it turned out, according to later unsubstantiated notices, this was all about a plan by the regime to leave behind only the 5000 holders of "Jordan-certificates" in the Ghetto and all the other ghetto Jews would be killed. At the last moment the occupation forces cancelled this plan. There were no successful findings and no authentic notifications about this event.

These events were called: "the Test Action" in the history of the Kovno Ghetto.

CHAPTER XI

The first "organized" mass Action in the Ghetto

-Provocation concerning the "attempted murder" of the Commander of the Ghetto Guard by a Jew-The closing of an entire ghetto neighborhood and the first mass Action in the Ghetto

[Page 64]

The first, "organized" mass Action in the Ghetto took place nine days after the "Test Action" on the 26th of September 1941.

Until then, the extermination of the Jewish population took place more randomly, without a "system." In this Action, the Ghetto entered a stage of organized mass Actions. This mass slaughter took place over one month's time, that is, from the 26th of September until the 28th of October 1941, resulting in the loss of approximately 13,000 Ghetto victims. The case of this Action took on a separate place in the martyr story of the Kovno Ghetto.

The "reason" for this Action, in which over 1000 Jews were killed, was the following:

A day or two before this mass Action, the Ghetto Guards informed the Elders Council that Jews shot at the then-Chief of the Ghetto Guard, Kozlovski, from a barn which was located on Krisciukaicio Street, near the Ghetto Gate.

The Elders Council was required to give up the guilty one to the Ghetto Guard for the "attempted assassination." If not, there would be unspeakable sanctions for the Ghetto population.

The entire story about the "attempted assassination" against the Chief of the Ghetto Guard was not more than a typical Gestapo provocation, which was intended to create a "reason" to carry out an Action in the Ghetto. All explanations and responses from the Jews from the beginning were doomed to be unsuccessful.

[Page 65]

There was no need to wait long to learn the true intention of the Nazis for the Ghetto.

On Friday, the 26th of September, around 3 o'clock in the afternoon, a few German police divisions and Lithuanian partisans marched into the Ghetto, and they encircled the entire quarter where the "attempted assassination" supposedly took place (capturing the streets: Vilianer, Mesininku, parts of Linkever, Ayrenoler, Krisciukaicio, etc.)

Thereafter, the entire Jewish population from that encircled sector was wildly and murderously kicked out of their houses and were collected in a neighboring place, and the selection began. Whoever could show that he worked somewhere in the city, was selected to one side. All the others were sent to the other side, among them many old and weak people, women without men on hand and with small children.

At that time, not all the Jews realized that the selection "to the right" or "to the left" meant a selection of life and of death. Many ghetto Jews still couldn't imagine that the Nazis were capable of such cold-blooded mass murders.

On that afternoon, over 1000 men, women and children were selected for death and were immediately transported in the direction of the 9th Fort. Those selected "for life" were allowed to return to their homes one or two days later, after the houses were thoroughly searched to discover "the hidden Jewish arms."

[Page 66]

At that time, no exact information about what happened to those transported Jews was available. Various rumors circulated. So, for example, a few days after the selection one version that was disseminated said that the transported Jews are located, supposedly, in Romayn, a village settlement near Kovno, where they are employed in field work. They even talked about a letter that was received from transported Jews to their friends in the Ghetto, from which it was believed that the Romayn story was true.

Even though many ghetto Jews talked about the letter, no one actually saw the letter with their own eyes. Then, as time passed, they realized that these rumors came from the Gestapo, which intentionally spread them, with the aim of disorienting and fooling the public opinion of the ghetto Jews.

From day to day, things became clearer, and that all the rumors about Romayn, etc. had no basis, and that the transported Jews were killed at the 9th Fort. Thus, the mood in the Ghetto became even more uneasy. It was obvious that everything that happened in the Ghetto until then was nothing more than a prelude. Unfortunately, the main point was that this unimaginably painful prospect would soon come true.

CHAPTER XII

Action and Liquidation of the Small ghetto

-Unexpected Action in the Small Ghetto-The course of the Action-Burning alive of the sick and the medical personnel in the Jewish Hospital-Liquidation of the Small Ghetto and transfer of the surviving Jews to the remaining part of the Ghetto

[Page 67]

As was mentioned at the start in the chapter "Establishment of the Slabodka Ghetto," the Ghetto area already included the portion of Paneriu Street which had the uneven numbers, and in addition some neighboring little streets. This same ghetto area was called "The Small Ghetto," and it was connected to the other part of the Ghetto through a special wooden hanging bridge.

The three thousand Jews living in the Small Ghetto had no idea of the tragic fate that very soon awaited them. A few Jewish institutions were set up in the Small Ghetto, for example hospitals for surgery and infectious diseases, a children's home, where the children from the previous orphans' home in Kovno were collected, a senior residence, etc.

At the end of September, the Christians who lived near the Small Ghetto started saying that soon the Jews will have to leave this area. Most Jews thought that the Christians were saying this probably because the previous Lithuanian owners of the houses in the Small Ghetto applied to the regime with a request. They asked that the Jews be removed from this area because their gardens and their businesses were located there.

As usual, the Jews listened to such rumors seriously, but at that time there was no ghetto Jew who could imagine that the Small Ghetto was on the eve of a catastrophe.

[Page 68]

On Sabbath eve, Friday night, the 3 of October and on Sabbath, the 4th of October 1941, the almost incessant shooting by the Lithuanian partisans who were guarding the fence around the Small Ghetto, became very suspicious to the ghetto Jews. True, the guardhouses of the Ghetto Guards would have shooting sprees at night, often for hours on end, which would make the ghetto Jews very nervous. But this time, the nighttime shooting spree was so heavy, that among the ghetto Jews, this was cause for great anxiety, especially for the Jews of the Small Ghetto.

It took place on Sabbath, at 7 a.m., when the Jewish night shift and the work brigade returned from the Airfield, and those who worked in the city went out to work. Suddenly the Small Ghetto was encircled with a stronger guard, armed with machine guns. On the bridge leading to the Small Ghetto, a special guard was stationed with machine guns, and the traffic between the Small Ghetto and the other sections of the Ghetto was blocked. Even the usual residents of the Small Ghetto, who were just returning from their night work at the Airfield, were forbidden to pass through the bridge to get to their homes.

Before this time, groups of German police, together with Lithuanian partisans, entered every house, kicked the Jewish population out onto the street, and lined them up in rows.

Not telling the Jews a single word about where and why they were forced out, they did not allow them to take anything with them. They were even told to take off their better clothes, coats, and leave them in the house.

When all the Jews of the Small Ghetto were kicked out of their homes, they started forcing them to a place, near the Small Ghetto, where they conducted a selection. The evening of the selection, the City Commissar, Brigadier General Kramer, notified the German police that during the selection they should only accept valid work certificates recognized as "Jordan certificates." After this decree, the selection began.

[Page 69]

Those lucky ones who possessed a "Jordan-certificate" were sent to the good side together with their families; all the others were collected for annihilation.

Before the selection was conducted, the Nazis set fire to the Jewish hospital for chronic infectious illness and over 60 sick people together with the medical personnel were burned alive in the flames.

At this opportunity it is worth mentioning, that at the start the Nazis captured a dozen Jews who were commanded to dig a pit near the hospital. As it turns out, they planned to shoot the sick and then bury them before burning the hospital. During the digging of the pit, a German police officer came to the Jews and told them to stop the work. Then the Hitlerites locked the doors and windows of the hospital and set it on fire together with the sick, who, as mentioned, were burned alive.

Long tongues of flames, encased in thick plumes of smoke, started shooting to the sky and announced to the ghetto Jews that in this moment more than 50 very sick Jews, together with their doctors and nurses, who did the hardest ghetto service of working to get them healthy, struggled in a formidable death.

This unprecedented barbaric act by the murderous Hitlerites made an extraordinary impression on the ghetto Jews, especially the Jews of the Small Ghetto, who were at that moment undergoing the selection.

The patients from the Jewish hospital for surgery and other illnesses, as well as the Jews from the old age home were packed into the trucks and all were transported to the 9th Fort. The work of loading the sick and elderly onto the trucks was done by those other Jews who dug the pits near the hospital.

As a reward for their "capable work" the Nazis later had them transferred to the other section of the Ghetto. Only two older Jews, who were kept back from the group to help set fire to the hospital, were killed by the murderers together with the sick.

In total, about 1500 Jews were selected, among them 200 orphans from the children's home in the Ghetto together with their educators and caretakers. After the selections ended, they started taking the selected to their death in the direction of the 9th Fort.

[Page 70]

Since the ghetto Jews were very aware of what kind of fate awaited them at the 9th Fort, the selected started to pull themselves out of the lines. The Germans and Lithuanians who were guarding them, started to beat them murderously with rifles and with preloaded guns. It played out in horrific and shocking scenes.

When those selected and destined for death were chased away a bit further from the selection place, the hangman, Kramer, who conducted the Action, addressed the Jews who were selected to "live," with the following words:

"Since the Jews in the Small Ghetto engaged in illegal activities through the Ghetto Fence, etc., from this day forth, the Small Ghetto will be liquidated. If the others standing in this square will be reasonable, they will be relocated to the remaining part of the Ghetto. If not, your route will be there!" And he demonstrated with his hand the direction to the 9th Fort.

A deathly silence was heard in the square where the Nazi boss held his speech. Those Jews who were still alive were standing stone-like, seized by a deathly fear, and through their sad looks, accompanied their brothers and sisters who were being taken to their death.

After the explanation by the City Commissar, Kramer, the Lithuanian partisans started chasing the "lucky" Jews in the direction of the little bridge, which went from the Small Ghetto to the other part of the

Ghetto. It was understood that there was no talk of going back into their houses to take something. The few surviving Jews, at that moment, had one and only desire: to leave the Small Ghetto as quickly as possible, where it smelled of death and extermination.

By climbing on the narrow and silent steps of the little bridge, the partisans once again started beating the Jews murderously, for going across the little bridge too slowly. Aside from the deadly beatings, they also threatened to send the Jews to the 9th Fort. While going across the little bridge, there arose a terrible congestion and panic. People crawled one on top of the other, trying to get themselves out of the Small Ghetto as fast as possible.

[Page 71]

Right after getting across the little bridge, the approximately 500 surviving Jews were able to catch their breath and recuperate from the horrific nightmare that they just lived through. As they were standing and walking, these people started to disperse among friends, to find a tiny corner to lay their heads. Those who didn't have anyone to go to, remained standing helplessly on the street, and waited until someone would take pity on them and invite them in.

A few days after the Action and liquidation of the Small Ghetto, the Jewish homes were completely robbed by the Gestapo, and in them remained only broken furniture and other worthless items. The Gestapo allowed the Jews from the liquidated Small Ghetto only one hour to go across to their previous residences to find something to take back to the other part of the Ghetto. Also, this "privilege" was only for those who could show a "Jordan-certificate."

One evening, Gestapo people came into the Ghetto. For one hour, they allowed hundreds of Jews into the Small Ghetto who had belongings there. Like a mighty stream, these Jews were waiting for hours to get over the hanging bridge. In a big rush, the Jews started carrying onto themselves bedding, old clothes, etc., and other things, which had no value for the Nazis.

For the people of the Small Ghetto, who were left "naked and barefoot" after the Action, any rag or any decent item had great value, and they therefore wanted to grab as many of their "treasures" during that one hour allotted to them. They hurried and rushed as if they were going to get the greatest treasures.

In this way, immediately at the beginning of the existence of the Ghetto, in true Gestapo fashion, the entire Small Ghetto was liquidated.

CHAPTER XIII

The Big Action

-Disturbing rumors before the Big Action-The order to the population to assemble in Democracy Square, without giving the reason for the assembly-Increasing panic in the Ghetto-The gathering of over 26 thousand Jews in Democracy Square-The course of the selection, from morning to evening-The selected Jews were taken to the 9th Fort-Agitation in the Ghetto-The horrible fate of over 10 thousand Jews

[Page 72]

Twenty-four days later, on Tuesday the 28th of October 1941, after the Action and liquidation of the Small Ghetto, an Action took place which acquired the appalling title: "The Big Action," because of the number of victims. Over 10,000 Jews were swallowed up!

Already at a certain time before this Action, rumors were circulating in the Ghetto that according to the comments of Christians in the city, large pits were being prepared by Soviet prisoners of war at the 9th Fort. There was serious reason to be suspicious that these pits were being prepared for the ghetto Jews. It caused huge confusion day after day, as these unsettling rumors became even more persistent, and the panic among the ghetto Jews strongly increased.

At midday, Sunday, the 26th of October, the then-Supervisor of Jewish Affairs to the Gestapo, Rauca, appeared in the Ghetto. He was already known in the Ghetto from the Action of the Intellectuals. He had a longer talk with some of the members of the Elder's Council, and finally gave the following "innocent" notice:

[Page 73]

Rauca declared, "The regime has decided to separate workers from non-workers in the Ghetto. To this aim, the non-working Jews will be divided separately, and they will be resettled in an area of the former Small Ghetto. The working Jews, the majority of whom are working at the Airport, and others who are working in essential war positions, must receive more and better food for them to do more work. Therefore, on Tuesday, the 28th of October, no one from the Ghetto will go out to work in the city, and an undisclosed division of the entire ghetto population will take place. The Elders Council must announce to the Ghetto population about the Tuesday gathering at the collection place." Thus, Rauca, the cold-blooded Gestapo hangman, ended his talk.

Based on the tragic words of the Gestapo notification, there was reason for anxiety about the real purpose of the notification to call together the entire ghetto population at Democracy Square.

Therefore, from the Elders Council there arose the question of whether they should or shouldn't publicize the notice about this decree from the regime to appear at the assembly place. After passionate deliberation, a few members of the Elders Council, headed by Dr. Elkes, went to Rabbi Shapira, on Sunday late in the evening, to hear his opinion about this question. Rabbi Shapira, who at this time was ill, asked for a bit of time to think about a response. First thing on Monday morning, Rabbi Shapira responded to the Elders Council, that they should indeed publicize the notice to the ghetto population.

The strain in the Ghetto was growing greater and reached a high point when on the morning of Monday the 27th of October, the Elders Council published a notification, which said that according to the decree from the regime organization, on Tuesday the 28th of October, at 6 am, the entire ghetto population, young and old, men and women and children, healthy and even sick must assemble at Democracy Square – the large space in the domain of the Ghetto. It stated in the notice that whoever was found at home would be shot by the German Police who will inspect the houses. Therefore, the houses must remain open. Not one word was mentioned by the Elders Council in their notice about the actual motive for this assembly.

[Page 74]

Right after becoming aware of this notice from the Elders Council, the Ghetto gave the impression of a sinking ship in a time of a great storm at sea…

The warning that they would shoot those who would be found in the homes, shut out the possibility of not coming to the assembly point. It must also be noted that at that time the thought of hiding themselves to avoid the order to assemble at the selection site, never entered the minds of the ghetto Jews.

From the latter half of Monday, and the evening between Monday to Tuesday there was great anxiety and restlessness. People ran from one to another to interpret the unreported aim of tomorrow's assembly at Democracy Square. One wanted to find a solution from the others to the painful question: what will really happen tomorrow?

As always, there was no shortage of restless rumors this time. There was no doubt that the Gestapo themselves spread the rumor that nothing bad would happen. They said it was only a matter of an innocent walk-through of the entire ghetto population, so that the regime representatives would have an opportunity to see with their own eyes the human resources of the Ghetto. They said that the regime organization would make a public announcement to the ghetto population, and that would be all, etc. But the 28th of October 1941 would become the blackest day in the history of the Kovno Ghetto community; a day that the greatest ghetto pessimists could never dare to foresee. It would be a day that would eliminate 40% of the population of the Ghetto.

Having experience with earlier selections, it was worthwhile to have the best work documents, from which it could be seen that one works, and one is a "useful Jew." Thus, on the next day, some ghetto Jews tried to acquire as many work-certificates as possible, to justify the pretense of being a living slave.

[Page 75]

The thousand Jewish aerodrome workers then paid greater attention to the work-bands[a] that were distributed among the German front construction people from the airfield.

Those aerodrome workers who had not picked up their work cards from the Jewish Work Office, quickly ran there to get them, hoping that this could have great importance for them. During the next day, the commotion in the Work Office was so great, that the uneasy mobs beat each other up to acquire the work card and demolished part of the Work Office.

The Elders Council, on their part, prepared the Ghetto population to group themselves at the square according to their various work details in this manner: Aerodrome, workshop work brigades, ghetto institutions, etc. And some workstations had a separate copy on which the workstation would be visible.

The other half day of the 27th of October ended, and the night passed between the 27th and 28th of October. Almost all the Jews spent that night in great anxiety due to the restless anticipation for the upcoming day.

The shooting stars were twinkling in the darkness of this late Autumn early morning, which had not yet become light. For the first time at the start of a winter, the earth was covered with a thin blanket layer of snow. It was frozen over and quite cold.

When the clock struck 6 a.m., suddenly Jews came out to Democracy Square from all the ghetto houses. Parents were carrying their little children in their arms or pushed them in carriages. The elderly and the weak people were held under their arms by their family members. The very sick people were taken on stretchers to the square. No one wanted to remain in the house and be exposed to the danger of being shot during the inspection of the houses. And, as was demanded by decree of the regime, the doors of all the Jewish homes remained open, free for inspection by the German police.

[Page 76]

As morning came, the entire ghetto population assembled in Democracy Square. In total there were over 26 thousand souls, every one of them desiring to be as close as possible to friends or acquaintances.

One and two hours passed, and nothing happened. Earlier, approximately 1,500 Jews from the Aerodrome arrived on the square. These were the ones who went out to work on the previous morning. On that day, that is, Monday the 27th of October, they were kept working at the Aerodrome and were held at work also for the night shift, because no workers were allowed out of the Ghetto for the night shift.

These Jews returned from the Aerodrome to the Ghetto. Not finding anyone in their homes, they ran around across the square to search for their family members among the masses of people. They were dead tired and exhausted from working in the Aerodrome for two shifts in a row, and they were covered in mud and lime from their work. (As the day progressed, it later turned out that their appearance stood out, and had a fatal impact on most of them during the selection.)

At 9 a.m., battalions of German police and large groups of strongly armed Lithuanian partisans started approaching the square, under the command of the Chief of Police, Torenboim. It became obvious that their unknown fate would soon begin.

As Rauca, the Gestapo murderer, arrived together with the Jew killer, Ghetto Commandant, Jordan, the huge square became deathly quiet, like during an extraordinarily tense moment. All the Jews on the square intuitively felt that something extraordinary will happen soon, something fatal…

Before anything else, a decree was delivered for everyone to stand 10 persons in a row and group themselves in columns of 100 people, keeping all families together. The family members of the Elders Council stood at the front, and behind them the Ghetto Police, together with their family members, the column of various Ghetto institutions, and then the Jewish workers, city brigades, the workers, etc.

[Page 77]

Before this, police and partisans were sent to conduct searches in the ghetto houses, to check if all the ghetto Jews appeared at the square. Those very sick ones who were left back in the houses and who could in no way be brought to the assembly place, were collected by the police and Lithuanian partisans, put on trucks, and were transported directly to the 9th Fort. At this opportunity, it is worth adding that a few

Lithuanian partisans, who could not overcome the evil instinct to steal, started robbing whatever there was from the Jewish homes. They were immediately sent in a convoy to the city by the Germans.

Finally, the murderers took to their bloody work.

After Rauca let the columns of the Elders Council and the Jewish Ghetto Police pass through, he started to select the columns of Jewish ghetto institutions, separating the elderly and weak people to the right side and the younger and stronger people to the left.

After ending the selection of the columns of the Jewish ghetto administration, the selection took on a more intense tempo. Standing with his face to the people assembled in the square, all the Jews had to file past him by rows, and he, Rauca, with a little stick in his hand, directed the people to go to the right or to the left.

Right from the beginning it became obvious that during the selection, Rauca was selecting mainly according to the physical appearance of the people, according to their clothing, cleanliness, family status, etc. The younger, stronger, and cleaner people, as well as, smaller families, which had few unskilled people were sent to the better side. The older and weaker people, families without skilled male workers, and others who looked unclean and were poorly dressed, were sent to the other side.

Absolutely uninterested in whether a particular Jew worked or didn't work, Rauca, didn't pay any attention at all to the work certificates, which some Jews had prepared to show him. There were many cases when long time craftsmen would file by Rauca and tell him that they are skilled workers who have already been working a long time in their trades. He would respond to them with a cynical smile: "very good! Just such artisans will be very needed here," gesturing with his hand in direction of the Small Ghetto.

[Page 78]

However, when he would get a notice from one of his servants at the square, that on the right, that is, the bad side, there were too few victims, then he would send to the right a larger number of Jews, without any criteria, just to even out his "count."

As lunchtime arrived, Rauca didn't stop his "holy" work. He continued with the same dedication as before, eating his bread and butter with great appetite, sending Jews to their death with his evil little stick.

At the beginning, Jordan did not select the people. He interested himself mainly with the general pace of the selection. Later, he became jealous of his "colleague" Rauca, and he actively started participating in the selection work personally.

Horrible and hideous scenes would play out during the selection, in cases when the Nazi murderer would tear an old father or mother apart from their children, or for no reason, according to their appearance, tear apart one or more family members and send them to the bad side.

A pitiful cry from separated family members was heard across the huge square. Each one was dominated by boundless despair and loss. Jews had the feeling that everyone was lost anyway. For one portion of the people, however, life was prolonged for the time being.

Before going through the selection, most of the younger people were terribly nervous, wanting as quickly as possible to know the verdict of their fate. However, it must be said, that the older Jews displayed greater calm and security. In all the rows, you could see and hear how older Jews unceasingly recited chapters of prayers with a tragic melody, as the corpses lay in the earth…

The horrific day stretched out like an eternity. Everything that happened on that square, looked wild, and incomprehensible, as in an evil nightmare. Unfortunately, it was not a wicked dream, but an existential tragic reality.

[Page 79]

Since the ones selected for the bad side would be transported to areas of the former Small Ghetto, at the square the Jews realized, or tried to convince themselves, that two ghettos would be established: a "better" ghetto, for the young and healthy people and a "worse" ghetto for which older and weaker people would be chosen.

And the sorting continued at full tempo. Unceasingly, groups of Jews would be sent to the bad side, and from there, to the Small Ghetto. Those family members who were ripped apart and would try to run over from the bad side to the better side, would be murderously beaten by the strong guards. According to the horrific attitude toward them by the guards, it was clear to see that what awaited the people would be very bad.

At this opportunity it should be mentioned that the Jewish Ghetto Police, who had to carry out various orders and job functions, had an early opportunity to move around in the square. During that horrible day, through various schemes, they helped many Jews to at least avoid the selection, or to sneak the chosen across to the good side, or, on a much smaller scale, right after the selection, grab them from the bad to the good side. That day, dozens and dozens of Jews survived a tragic death thanks to them.

The selection continued until the evening twilight. Many weak and sick people, who could not stand the lineup for an entire day on the field, died on the spot. Thus, after the selection, dozens of dead and a huge number of the sick and dying, remained lying on the assembly site. Those who were still alive were collected in trucks and were sent to the Fort to be exterminated in the morning hours.

Finally, at the end of the selection by the Gestapo murderers, it became known that for the bad side, over 10,000 victims were selected. When the last group of Jews selected for the bad side was transported to the Small Ghetto, those Jews who were chosen for the good side and had remained guarded for the entire day, were then allowed to return to their homes.

[Page 80]

In the evening darkness, the "lucky" Jews left their selection place and went home. But there was a colossal difference between the morning trip to the square and the return from the square in the evening: there was almost no family which returned with the same number of people they left with in the morning. In addition, hundreds and hundreds of entire families were sent away to the bad side.

Those returning home looked as if they were coming from a huge funeral, a funeral of over 10,000 people. Those who returned to their homes were dead tired, frozen, and hungry and could not revive themselves, because everyone was tortured by the question of the future fate of the chosen Jews in the Small Ghetto. Again, the night was a sleepless one.

The Jews transported to the Small Ghetto were ordered to take over the semi- destroyed residences where Jews had lived until the Action and liquidation of the Small Ghetto.

Not having any idea what kind of tragic end awaited them over the next day, the victims spread out around the Small Ghetto, to find a place where they could lay their tired heads. As it turned out, the majority believed that this would be their resting place for a longer time, so many of them wanted to take over a better apartment, etc.

During the night, the Chairman of the Elders Council, Dr. Elhanan Elkes, labored with the regime leaders to get permission to take 100 Jews out of the Small Ghetto. When he arrived at the Small Ghetto and started searching for the relevant people, the other Jews caused a terrible commotion around Dr. Elkes, and a Lithuanian partisan wounded Dr. Elkes in the head with his gun. In an unknown condition, Dr. Elkes was brought back to the Ghetto and nothing came out of this situation.

Map of the Slabodka Ghetto
(Compiled and drawn by the Engineer Yakov Peretzman)

Behind the barbed wire fence

The hanging bridge between the Small Ghetto and the rest of the Ghetto

[Page 81]

At first, during the morning hours of Wednesday, the 29th of October 1941, a commotion began in the Small Ghetto. The Lithuanian partisans woke everyone up and they were commanded to get themselves ready for the march. At the start, none of the victims knew where they were going to march.

When the Jews in the Small Ghetto were lined up on the street in rows and started to march, they saw that they are being taken from the Small Ghetto in the direction of the 9th Fort.

The murderous attitude toward the Jews by the stronger and larger guard, which was made up mainly of Lithuanian partisans, removed the possibility to even think about what was happening to the unlucky Jews.

The Ghetto became alarmed by the awful news that the Jews from the Small Ghetto were being taken to the 9th Fort. Everyone got up on their feet and hurried to the streets, from where they could see how they were taking the Jews to their slaughter. Unfortunately, all hopes and illusions about the fate of the selected Jews immediately became completely upended. The horrific howls and cries on both sides of the barbed wire reached the heavens. They were the horrific cries of a people who were being annihilated without any rhyme or reason.

The death column of over 10,000 Kovno Jews spread out for kilometers. This was their last march to one of the most horrible Nazi mass annihilation sites in Lithuania- the 9th Fort. Just weeks before Soviet prisoners of war were forced to prepare huge mass graves for the Jews.

Murderous Gestapo people, together with Lithuanian mass murderers, intoxicated with the poison of alcohol and driven by their animal instincts, were already there with automatic and dum-dum guns, ready to welcome the thousands of Jewish men, women, and children with a flood of fresh lead…

[Page 82]

After many days and nights, the late Autumn wind carried the echo of the incessant banging of machine guns to the Ghetto from the 9th Fort. This echo of the shooting announced to the ghetto Jews who were still alive, that at this moment hundreds of shot and half-alive naked Jewish bodies are piling up in layers in the mass graves. They squeezed their little children to their hearts, in this way, trying to protect them from the hail from the machine guns, sending hundreds of Jewish mothers falling into the pits together with their little chicks. With the last Shema Israel [Hear, Oh Israel prayer] of these holy victims and through their death howls, their bloody curse will remain forever– a curse which will hang on the heads of the horrible Nazi mass-murderers and their Lithuanian helpers…

Original footnote:

a. The work armbands would be worn on the left sleeve of the outer garment.

CHAPTER XIV

The situation in the Ghetto during the first few months after the Big Action
(November 1941-January 1942)

-Depressed atmosphere among the ghetto Jews- "Reassuring" announcements from the Ghetto Command and the Gestapo.-Assembly of foreign Jews at the 9th Fort for their murder-Hunger, cold and hard labor- Good news from the Soviet front-The "Fur Action"-Guarding of the Ghetto by a NSKK unit

[Page 83]

After the Big Action, 16,000 souls remained in total in the Ghetto, and the atmosphere was extraordinarily dejected.

At that time, the Jews were quite desperate, not just because of the huge victim count after the Big Action, but predominantly because of a general conviction, that, sooner or later, the same fate would also await the current Jewish survivors, just like their brothers and sisters who were killed. No one in the Ghetto could therefore see any sense in further suffering, as the chances of survival to liberation, at least for a small portion of the Jews, looked completely unrealistic.

The Big Action completely confounded the generally accepted belief that, as long as they needed Jews as a free labor force for various slave works, then the Nazis would allow them to remain alive for a longer time. But after the Big Action, when hundreds of the best Jewish artisans, thousands of young, healthy, and talented male and female workers, were taken to the 9th Fort to be killed, how could anyone believe that they would allow the Jews to remain alive? Would they have wiped them out for work?!

[Page 84]

It turned out that this opinion was correct. While the Jews lived in the Nazi hell, they had to work, and, like the more optimistic ghetto Jews figured out, it meant that while the Jews worked, they would allow them to live…

That's why the Jews in the Ghetto started relating to going to work with skepticism. That's when the ghetto Jews started to formulate the psychology of "there is nothing else to say; in any case our fate is sealed," etc.

When this desperate atmosphere reached the Nazi ghetto-administrators, the then-Ghetto Commandant, Jordan, came to the Elders Council and gave an "assurance" in the name of the regime administration, that "the Big Action was the "last" Action for the Kovno Ghetto," and that, "all Jews should be calm about their future fate," etc. etc.

And beyond that, Jordan requested that the Jews should punctually and conscienciously fulfill their work duties.

As "comfort" from the Nazis for the 10,000 Jewish victims and, in parallel, as a "stimulus" to motivate the Jews to want to work, Jordan gave the Elders Council a check for 10,000 Marks and ordered them to pay the Jewish aerodrome workers half a Mark per day. And, by the way, he "authorized" that the remaining belongings of those Jews who were taken away during the Big Action, be distributed among the poor unfortunate aerodrome workers.

A few days later, after Jordan's announcement, the chief-murderer of the Big Action, Rauca, came to the Elders Council and in the same spirit as Jordan, he also gave a "calming" speech about the future fate of the Ghetto.

Understandably, none of the ghetto Jews was convinced by these announcements from the Nazi murderers, Jordan and Rauca, and the Jews remained in the same desperate mood as before.

As additional proof of why they should not believe all these "promises" from the ghetto bosses, was the tragic fact that for over a month, that is, from the middle of November to the middle of December 1941, they were bringing larger groups of foreign Jews (Germans, Austrians, Czechs, etc.) to be exterminated.

[Page 85]

Thousands of foreign Jews were killed at that time at the 9th Fort. The foreign Jews were brought by train to Kovno, from where they would transport them on foot alongside the Ghetto to the 9th Fort. Most of the time it was done at night, so as not to draw the attention of the surrounding population.

From the various letters found[a] in the robbed belongings of the murdered Jews from foreign countries, they could discern the places from where they were brought. They were assured by the local regime that they were being relocated to "Estonia" for work, and they were allowed to bring with them a larger amount of their better items, a large amount of food, etc.

It turns out that the foreign Jews couldn't imagine the real motive for their "relocation" and believed that they were going to work somewhere in the occupied Soviet regions.

Some Jewish youths were captured in 1943 and sent to work at the 9th Fort. Their job was to excavate the bodies of the murdered Jews from the pits and burn them to erase the evidence of Hitler's horrors.[b] Many foreign Jews were found in the mass graves, dressed in their clothes. This happened because a portion of the foreign Jews refused to undress naked for the execution, as per the "regulations" at the 9th Fort.

Thus, the ghetto Jews felt extraordinarily pessimistic about the development of the events in the Ghetto. The questions of how to live and somehow how to survive from day to day became the greatest calamity in the Ghetto.

[Page 86]

More than half a year passed since the beginning of the Nazi occupation, and at that time the Jews had already experienced so many problems and so much pain, that they couldn't even mention other complaints. And they remained without any material means of existence.

As was mentioned in a preceding chapter, most of the Jews did not possess any food reserves when they entered the Ghetto, and the little food that anyone brought had already been finished long ago. Through their work in the city, Jews would smuggle food products into the Ghetto, which they would buy illegally from the Christians with whom they worked. At that time there were very few who could do it because most Jews worked at the Aerodrome and the Jews there would almost never come into contact with Christians, with whom they could exchange their last shirt or clothes for some sustenance.[c]

Exchanging their possessions for food products with the Christians who walked near the Ghetto Fence, later became connected with a death sentence, because the guards at the Ghetto Fence would shoot without warning at any Jew trying to get close to the fence.

The official allocation for the Jews by the regime was inconsequential (less than a third of the food distribution for a non-Jew!) Bread was a treasured find, which could rarely even partially satisfy any ghetto Jew, even if he could get it. Frozen, rotten potatoes and even potato peels were also a huge thing for the ghetto Jews.

Therefore, in hundreds of ghetto houses hunger, in the literal meaning of the word, became a real and constant companion, and day after day, it seized even more and more Jewish families.

Later, in the winter of 1941-42, the famous huge frost set in, and a terrible cold added to the hunger. The Jews didn't have any warm clothing to wear, and they would have to work in the cold open fields of the Aerodrome from early morning until the evening.

[Page 87]

Aside from this, thousands of Jews would also have to march approximately 10-12 kilometers every day, going from the Ghetto to work and back. So that winter, hands and feet were frozen, and Jews became handicapped.

There was not even a piece of wood to warm up the oven after coming home. Therefore, Jews started tearing down wooden fences around the unoccupied houses of the Ghetto, tearing them into splinters. Whoever had the opportunity, would carry a piece of wood on himself for 5-6 kilometers from their workplace, until they got back into the Ghetto. However, it was common for Jews to arrive at the Ghetto Gate and have their heavy piece of wood confiscated by a guard.

A large portion of the German bosses maintained a cruel attitude toward the aerodrome workers. They would beat them brutally for the smallest "sin" and, for many Jews, destroyed their strength and ruined their health.

This is the way the Jews were plagued in Hitler's hell, and very often they envied their murdered brothers and sisters, who were spared so much inhumane suffering and persecution.

The suffering and gloomy ghetto Jew had only one comfort that gave great hope and raised his spirits: the strategic situation on the German-Soviet front during the winter of 1941-42.

During the period leading up to the Big Action, and for a certain time thereafter, it looked to almost everyone in the Ghetto, like the Nazis and their collaborators, might, heaven forbid, give up their predatory war goals and then there would no longer be the minimal illusion about the fate of the Jews who were still alive. The Soviet attacks and their victories over the Nazi armies gave a little spark of hope and spirit for better times.

As the winter progressed, the difficulties for the German military became more apparent. This brought great satisfaction for the ghetto Jews for all the persecution and attacks they suffered from the Germans.

[Page 88]

While the Jews themselves suffered terribly from the extraordinarily cold winter, it was everyone's desire that the winter should be harsher, and it should last longer…

At the end of December 1941, in the early morning, the Ghetto experienced a huge shock "for a change." A totally unexpected order was publicized from the Elders Council. According to an order from the regime, the Jews must give up their available furs within the hour, including even simple furs which Jews wear to work.

Just like at the beginning, it was predicted by this decree that if the Jews had to give up their furs, they could not go to work in the city that day, and everyone would have to assemble on the tragically infamous Democracy Square, where on the 28th of October 1941 the selection of the Big Action took place. So, the Jews interpreted the situation of giving up the furs as a special assembly by the Gestapo, to go through a selection connected to an Action, once again.

As a result, the Ghetto became very anxious and almost all the Jews decided that under no circumstance would they go to the Democracy Square. Jews considered it better to be shot in the Ghetto, in your own home, rather than go to the Square and from there to the 9th Fort.

When the Gestapo figured out the atmosphere of the ghetto Jews, they backed off the original plan for the Jews to assemble at Democracy Square. They agreed that the Jews should give up their furs at specially designated collection points instead.

The ghetto Jews were already happy, that instead of an Action against the Jews, it ended up only as an Action of Jewish furs. So, they brought their better furs, as well as their own simple torn work furs to the collection point. It would have been very dangerous to attempt to hide them from the big house searches this time in the Ghetto, in the Autumn of 1941.

[Page 89]

As it turns out, the hard winter of 1941-42 went deep into the bones of the Hitlerites, so that they didn't even feel ashamed to confiscate the Jews' worn out and torn work furs and send them to their frozen army divisions on the Soviet front. Nevertheless, the Ghetto had a day of deathly fear and a difficult experience because of the fear of an Action, which luckily did not take place.

During this "Fur-Action," the figure of a young Jewish man, Benno Liptzer, boldly swam to the surface of ghetto life. He was the Brigadier of the Jewish work brigade in the Kovno Gestapo.

Because of his association with a line of leading Gestapo people, Liptzer quickly started to play a powerful role in ghetto life. Liptzer and the Kovno Ghetto – this is a theme, which begs separate attention in the story of the Kovno Ghetto settlement and deserves broader scrutiny at another opportunity.

In the middle of January 1942, a division of the Kovno G.S. K.K.[d] took over the guarding of the Ghetto.

Until that time, the guarding of the Ghetto lay in the hands of a division of the German Police, which had at its disposal a larger group of Lithuanian partisans. Both the command of the Ghetto Guard, as well as the guard posts near the Ghetto Fence had their quarters in the neighborhoods of the Ghetto. They would only enter the Ghetto itself when they would have to take care of service issues.

When the G.S.K.K. people took over the guarding of the Ghetto, the command of the Ghetto Guard organized itself inside the Ghetto. This alone meant a change for the worse, because until then, they would see those of the Ghetto Guard infrequently, and now there were many of them in all corners of the Ghetto.

[Page 90]

Aside from that, from the beginning, they immediately introduced terrible terror near the Ghetto Fence. From the first days of their takeover of the Ghetto Guard station, they shot a few Jews who attempted to approach the fence to exchange something for food-products with a Christian passer-by.

Also, they immediately assessed the need to install stronger control near the Ghetto Fence over the Jews who were coming back from their work in the city. This took away the little food which the Jews had illegally procured through their work. This meant a terrible verdict of hunger for the Ghetto.

Already on the first day, they set the example that they were serious about their new powerful control near the Ghetto Fence. Thus, they shot a Jew, by the name of Gempel, who wanted to escape out of their control.

They also didn't forget to "order" the issue of how the ghetto Jews must greet the German Ghetto Guard (even from far away, when seeing a German, a man would have to take off his hat, and women walking by would nod with their head.)

Seeing the outcome for the Jews regarding the G.S.K.K., the Lithuanian partisans became jealous that their German "colleagues" were not being greeted "properly." Thus, a murderous Lithuanian partisan passing by on one of the streets of the Ghetto, shot the Jewish doctor Gerber, without any warning. All these things together threw the Ghetto into a horrible fear of eventual abuses from the new Ghetto Guard.

One day later, however, people from the strong G.S.K.K., became more permissive and after a while they became lax on their original terrorization of the Ghetto population. This was the result of receiving fat Jewish "gifts." Nevertheless, their takeover of the guarding of the Ghetto, as we have seen, cost the ghetto Jews a long list of victims and a huge amount of alarm.

Original footnotes:

    a.   The letters were found by Kovno Ghetto Jews who were workers for the Kovno Gestapo and there they organized the belongings of the murdered Jews.
    b.   See "Legendary Escape of the Work Brigade, which worked at the 9th Fort, burning the excavated corpses."
    c.   More details about this issue in later chapters.
    d.   "National-Socialist Kraftfar-Corpus" – a Nazi military formation which had to do with motorized transport routes.

CHAPTER XV

The First Relocation Action to Riga

-On the eve of the relocation Action-Early recruiting of people for the relocation-The failure of the Jewish authorities in recruiting- Means taken by the rulers to perform the recruiting- End of the relocation Action- The fate of the relocated Jews

[Page 91]

It was suddenly in the second half of January 1942, when the Ghetto had not yet managed to catch its breath from the horrible experiences of the Actions and other afflictions that took place, that rumors started circulating that they needed 500 Jews from the Ghetto to go to Riga.

We must say that at first, few paid enough attention to all these rumors. Later, these same rumors became much stronger, until it became entirely clear that it really had to do with an order from the regime unit to the Elders Council. By the end of January, it was completely certain that during the upcoming days the Ghetto would have to cope with a difficult and painful experience.

According to the regime, the official reason was that Jews are being sent to Riga to work. However, based on the tragic experience of the multiple mass Actions, the Jews didn't believe the regime's official version and considered it an Action, under the overcoat of traveling to work in Riga. Therefore, the atmosphere in the Ghetto became more tense day by day.

At this opportunity, it must be added that at that time, the institutions of the Elders Council, especially the Jewish Ghetto Police and the Jewish Labor Office, managed to set up specific organizational formats and began leading "normal" activities. The Jewish ghetto administration already managed to conduct an exact registration of the remaining Ghetto population after all the extermination Actions, and had information about each ghetto Jew, their residence, workplace, family status, age, etc.

[Page 92]

The regime unit ordered the Elders Council to organize the recruitment of the needed number of people. Thus, during the compilation of the list of persons chosen for Riga, the Elders Council decided to look for candidates according to the following guidelines: in first place they took into consideration skilled men or women who are not supporting families, as well as heads of households who don't have any small children.

The unrest in the Ghetto became greater during the first days of the month of February, when it finally became clear that in the upcoming days, they would have to recruit people for Riga.

Because the ghetto population didn't know exactly on which day this would take place, they were afraid that any day, upon their return from work, a portion of them would be caught at the Ghetto Gate to go to Riga. So, many people, mainly the younger and independent ones, stopped going to work in the city and sought to hide themselves until the Riga issue passed.

We must add, however, that at this time in the Ghetto they had not yet constructed any special hiding places, "*malinas*," as they were later called. The hiding places were then mostly primitive, for example, somewhere in a cellar, in an attic, in a stable, or in an uninhabited building, etc.

Those Jewish workers who worked in the city and managed to establish better relations with whichever German in the workplace, could arrange with the German to allow them to remain overnight somewhere in the workplace in order not to have to go to the Ghetto and be exposed to the danger of being captured for Riga.

Finally, the 6th of February 1942 arrived – the day when the Jewish ghetto administration had to collect the pre-selected persons for Riga. Considering that certain Jews would put up resistance against the unarmed Jewish Ghetto Police when they came to take them to Riga, the Jewish Police arrived in the evening to collect them, accompanied by German guards from the Ghetto Guard.

[Page 93]

By nightfall, no movement was seen on the Ghetto streets. Furthermore, like every day, this evening the little ghetto houses were sunk in darkness. Jews who didn't even have any underlying suspicion of being included on the lists for Riga, were also sitting at home anxiously awaiting the inevitable events.

At around 9 o'clock in the evening, a bigger group of guarded N.S.K.K. people came into the Ghetto and they, together with the Jewish Ghetto Police, started going into the houses to collect the pre-selected persons.

But right from the start, it turned out that many of the identified persons were not in the houses, because they were in hiding. Those people, who were found at home – especially single girls and women, older men, etc., were taken into the building of a former small synagogue (on Velioner Street), which was set up as a collection point for the collected Jews.

The hysterical screams and cries were carried through the streets of the Ghetto, disseminating the terrible horror throughout that dark freezing night.

Those who strongly opposed and didn't want to go with the police, were aggressively dragged to the collection point.

For hours during that tragic night the orgy continued in the Ghetto. It was heartbreaking and horrible. Even after the police collected everyone according to the special lists, they didn't manage to get more than about 200 persons, the majority of whom were women, elderly, and weak people.

Among the captured ghetto Jews there were many people of little means, so the Elders Council saw to it that they got some underwear, warm clothing, a little food, and a few dozen German Marks before departure. The unlucky Jews didn't even consider taking that little bit of help from the Elders Council and they didn't stop complaining about their tragic and bitter fate.

[Page 94]

In the dimly lit synagogue building, the people selected for Riga were collected and held. These unlucky ones were seated on the floor and with uneasy heart palpitations, they awaited their fate with uncertainty. The outstretched shadows on the abandoned walls of the synagogue made the entire tragedy even more horrific. It was a true picture of another Hitler-style forced Action over the Jews, who were, thusfar, still allowed to live.

Around 3-4 o'clock at night, they brought together the entire group of Jews under a strong convoy of the Ghetto Guard and took them off to the train station.

When they arrived at the train, the bosses of the Ghetto, the City Commissar Kramer and his "Jew-representative," Jordan, were already waiting for them. They saw that first, instead of 500 Jews, as were ordered, there were not more than 180, and secondly, most of the collected Jews were women and older weak men. So, they decided to send the entire transport back to the Ghetto and, without Jewish assistance, they would collect the people for Riga from the Ghetto by themselves.

In the morning, it was unexpected for the Ghetto population to see the people who were transported to Riga being brought back to the Ghetto. Jews understood that today and tomorrow would be a dark time in the Ghetto, because it was more than certain that the recruitment would be conducted by the Germans themselves.

Those persons, who were brought back from the train station were allowed to enter the Ghetto freely. They immediately ran to hide themselves before anyone else, so that they shouldn't be able to find them a second time to take them to Riga.

In the morning the Jews who worked in the city did go out to work, as usual. Figuring out that something would happen in the Ghetto this day, this time there were many more people than before who went to work in the city, not wanting to remain in the Ghetto.

At around 11 o'clock in the morning, the Ghetto commandant, Jordan, appeared at the Elders Council and made a real scene there, accompanied by various rumblings, because the Elders Council showed themselves to be unskilled in organizing the recruitment. Thus, he delivered the following order:

[Page 95]

The entire adult population, which does not go out to the city to work and remains in the Ghetto, excluding the workers from the Ghetto workshops and the colleagues from all the Jewish Ghetto workshops, must appear at 12 o'clock noon at Democracy Square, where he alone would recruit the Jews for Riga.

The connection that Democracy Square conjured up because of the selections during the Actions, didn't bode well among the ghetto population.

Many ghetto Jews decided not to go to Democracy Square, and they hid themselves wherever they could, just not to be in the house when they came to check houses for whoever remained. At the assembly place about 1000 men were collected, among them almost all colleagues from the Jewish ghetto administration, workers from the ghetto laundry, etc.

Jordan appeared at the site at around 1 o'clock, accompanied by a larger group of German guards, and he started the recruitment. Many employees from the Jewish ghetto system were found among the people who were selected for Riga, as well as older and weaker people who appeared on the Square, being certain that they would not be taken to Riga. During the selection, even Jordan failed to attain the full count of the required 500 persons.

The ones selected for Riga were immediately taken and chased out of the place to the train, accompanied by a strong guard. Those who were not able to keep up with the march to the train were murderously beaten by the accompanying guards. This all reminded the ghetto Jews of the tragic scenes during the infamous Actions that took place. It also strengthened their suspicions that the people are not being taken for work in Riga but are being taken somewhere to be exterminated. Therefore, the panic grew minute by minute.

Thereafter, as they transported the pre-selected party of Jews out of the Ghetto, inside the Ghetto, groups of German police spread out and started going through the houses to capture Jews.

Before that, those Jews who were away working in the city started to return to the Ghetto. Because the German police caught too few people in the houses, because of those who managed to find themselves a hiding place, the needed count of 500 Jews was not yet complete. It became clear that these remaining missing Jews would be taken from among those returning from work through the Ghetto Gate. And that was what happened.

[Page 96]

Of those Jews who returned from the city, some were taken at the Ghetto Gate and selected for Riga. This same selection was conducted by the Germans together with representatives from the Jewish ghetto administration. The panic and confusion of the Jews who were returning from work was great. Not to underestimate the shock for their family members, who didn't know the fate of those returning from work. In a few hours, the removal of the Jews took place directly from the Ghetto Gate and they were transported in columns to the train to Riga.

Between 7 to 8 o'clock in the evening the storm in the Ghetto slowly quieted down. The families of those who were caught for Riga were terribly upset because of the misfortune which befell them.

Certain high Jewish ghetto officials, travelling with the Jews to the train, had the opportunity to free a few captured persons during the morning selection by Jordan. But then many people whose close family members were taken, started running to these Jewish ghetto functionaries, to get them to return their relatives from the train. This, however, did not help, and the transport with the exact number of 500 Kovno Ghetto Jews left for Riga.

The relocation Action to Riga was mainly conducted by the German themselves, and the last tally absolutely did not account for whether the hidden persons did or did not leave behind families in the Ghetto. Thus, this caused many families to be torn apart.

Many families then remained without a breadwinner when the husband or grown son was sent away to Riga. That is why the material situation of these families became pitiful. The little material help from the Jewish ghetto institutions was trivial according to the minimum requirements for existence. So, this relocation Action left behind long term after-effects on ghetto life.

[Page 97]

A short time later, a few messages arrived in the Ghetto from those Jews who were sent out, saying that they really found work in Riga. These regards impacted and calmed the Ghetto, because the suspicion that the people were taken somewhere for extermination finally fell apart.

Finally, it must be added that in the Spring of 1944, on the segment of the northern front, the Soviet offensive forced the Germans to "clear up" in Estonia and Latvia. Thus, from Latvia a specific number Kovno Ghetto Jews, who were dragged to Riga during the two relocation Actions in 1942, were brought to Ponevesh. In Ponevesh at that time a Jewish work camp was established to build the Aerodrome there.

Due to the approach of operations on the front in July 1944, the Jews from Ponevesh were deported to Germany together with other Jews from the rest of the Jewish labor camps officially belonging to the "Kovno Concentration Camp." There, they shared the fate of all the Jews who were taken into the German camps.

CHAPTER XVI

Life in the Ghetto in the Period Between the Two Relocation Actions to Riga

(February-October 1942)

- "Action" of books and holy books- The problem of using the Jewish labor-force-Partial stabilization of the situation in the Ghetto- Large Ghetto Workshops. - Signs of intensification of social life-The struggle between Kaspi-Serebrowitz and Liptzer about the management of ghetto life.- Remarks about Liptzer's role in the life of the Ghetto-Problems of nutrition in the Ghetto-Smuggling of food produce- A few words about ghetto livelihood- Decrees and more decrees: a. clearing up of ghetto neighborhoods, b. prohibition of pregnancy, c. closing of religious schools and schools for young children d. establishment of a "no-money" economy, e. prohibition to import food products, f. recruitment for labor camps.

[Page 98]

After all the Actions and decrees which had the underlying goal of physically annihilating the Jews, there came to the Ghetto an Action of books, holy books, and other published items.

It turns out that our murderers' intention was not just to kill, to defeat, and to annihilate us Jews, but at the same time also to decimate our cultural creations, our spiritual treasures, so that there would remain no trace or remnant of us.

According to a decree from the regime organization, all ghetto Jews had to hand over to the regime all religious books, secular books, and other published items in whichever language, by the 18th of February 1942. As was always the Nazi style, this order was accompanied with much pressure for not obeying the decree punctually.

[Page 99]

When the Jews entered the Ghetto, almost everyone brought with them many of their books and holy books along with their possessions and household items. They thought that the book and the scroll would be the only spiritual nourishment for the brain behind the barbed wire. And that was really the way it was.

The decree announcing the relinquishing of all available books and holy books was not accepted with a light heart by the ghetto residents. For the ghetto Jew, the book was, for a while, the only means of removing from one's head the leaden thoughts of what was happening in the world. Many were served by the Public Ghetto Library, which existed in secret near the Synagogue Office[a] of the Elders Council.

Whoever had the possibility and character, took some of the books which were especially dear to him, and hid them. Others decided that it was better to burn the books rather than give them up to the hands of the Nazis.

At this opportunity it is necessary to add that during the Book Action some youths who belonged to the Zionist youth organization "Abetz"[b] succeeded in smuggling out a few thousand more important works, especially in Hebrew, from one of the collection points set up to deliver the books. A high functionary of the Jewish Ghetto Police, I. Grinberg[c] helped them. Later, the above-mentioned youth group established an illegal library of these books, which mainly served Zionist youth. Aside from that, other social groups hid huge numbers of books which had special interest for them.

Finally, tens of thousands of books and holy scriptures were requisitioned by the regime. Among the books that were given up were many valuable and rare works in various languages.

[Page 100]

As was known, the Third Reich employed the "Reich's operational staff person, Rozenburg" to "order" the looting of Jewish libraries, archives, museums, and other spiritual treasures. These had affiliates in all locations where there were larger Jewish communities before the occupation. In Kovno, there was also a division of Rozenberg's "operational staff" which, among other things, was involved in confiscating the books in the Ghetto. During the sorting of the collected books, these ghetto Jews were also employed: Lemchen (liberated in Dachau), Kizel (died in the liquidation of the Ghetto), Gutman (shot in 1942 for smuggling food), etc.

The more valuable creations, mainly of a Judaic character, together with the most important works from the confiscated Jewish libraries, archives, and other Jewish documents and materials from this Nazi "scientific" institution were sent away somewhere in Germany. All the other stolen books and holy books were given over to a paper factory to make them into paper.

Discounting the few saved books and holy books, the Ghetto remained almost "book-free" after this "Action" and for the common ghetto Jew, a book became a dear treasure.

After the first accursed Action to Riga, the situation in the Ghetto became more stable. This change for the better was first characterized by no further mass Actions, during the period between the accursed Action to Riga, that is, from the beginning of February to the end of October 1942.

The truth is that during this time, dozens of Jews were killed by the Gestapo in individual ways. There were those who fell into their hands at various moments, usually by going out of the workplace to trade with the Christians for food products, or by other attempts to meet familiar Christians. However, as mentioned, these were individual cases.

In a certain sense "lenient" relations between the occupation forces and the Ghetto had, at this moment, caused an estimated rise in an economic sense, and a period of "prosperity" began in the Ghetto. This increase in economic well-being took place mainly due to the changes in transforming the work activities of the Ghetto.

[Page 101]

In the first days after the establishment of the Ghetto, when there were exactly 30,000 Jews in the Ghetto, the issue of properly organizing Jewish work duty was not known. The Jewish Labor Office, whose task was to satisfy the demands of the regime for Jewish labor, would carry out their functions with the help of the Jewish Ghetto Police, who would from time to time bring together, more correctly said, would capture the necessary number of Jewish workers.

Later, due to the implementation of the mass murders, the Jewish ghetto population became smaller by almost half. Yet, the demands from the regime for Jewish workers increased. So, after some time, the Jewish Ghetto administration introduced a work-duty schedule for the Ghetto. The work duty consisted of men between the ages of 14 to 60 and women, from 15 to 45, and later, to 55 years[d].

Until that time, that is, starting from Autumn 1941 until the start of Spring 1942, most Jewish workers were utilized for work at the Kovno Aerodrome. The remaining Jews worked in various military workshops in the city.

At the start, mainly Soviet war prisoners were employed in the building of the Aerodrome. But already by the 21st of September 1941, for the first time, the Ghetto needed to provide 500 workers for work at the Aerodrome.

At this opportunity it is worth mentioning that on Erev Rosh Hashana 1941, when aerodrome soldiers came into the Ghetto at night to take Jews for the night shift, the Nazi murderers captured Jews at work and shot about 10 Jews near the Ghetto Gate for no reason.

From day to day the demand for Jewish aerodrome workers increased, since the largest portion of Soviet prisoners of war died due to the inhumane living conditions, and those remaining were transported elsewhere for work.

[Page 102]

The night before the Big Action, the number of Jewish workers at the Aerodrome each day was approximately 4000 persons. At the Aerodrome, the work continued around the clock each day, in various work shifts.

Work at the Aerodrome was exceptionally difficult and punitive hard labor in dampness and cold, in open fields over a long workday (alongside prior Jewish hunger, abuse, and lack of minimum clothing and shoes). For the ghetto Jew, work at the Aerodrome meant a life of hunger. It was because Jews who worked there never encountered Christians with whom they could possibly exchange the remnants of their belongings for food products. Thus, for the ghetto Jew, working at the Aerodrome meant not having any possibility of staying close to the family, slaving hard, total exhaustion, and having to accept the hunger rations which the regime would deign to throw to the ghetto residents.

Going out to work at the Aerodrome was one of the harshest punishments for various violations between Jew and Jew, according to the "legal code" of the Jewish ghetto administration. But even the regime institutions would typically send a Jew to work at the Aerodrome as a hardship punishment, for violating a "rule" of the occupation regime.

To compensate the Aerodrome worker for his especially difficult fate, the Elders Council, on their part, introduced various bonuses for the punctual aerodrome worker, i.e., for those who worked the entire 6-7 days a week. The weekly supplement of food would consist of 2 kilograms of bread, a few kilograms of potatoes, a few hundred grams of flour, etc.

In addition, the aerodrome workers at that time had a "privilege." During the time when the Jews from the other work units would have to go through the Ghetto Gate where there was an inspection to confiscate illegal commerce in food products, the aerodrome workers could go through the Ghetto Gate without risk.

Truth be told, the inspection of the aerodrome workers wasn't strong, because they would come back from their work with empty hands, and the inspection for smuggled food would be for naught.

[Page 103]

These "bonuses" and "privileges" affected the aerodrome workers very little, as their goal was: the faster they could finish with the aerodrome, the faster they could get a different work detail. The "Aerodromer," which means a worker at the Aerodrome, was therefore a derogatory name and meant that they found themselves at the lowest level of the social ladder of the Ghetto. And even folk songs were created lamenting the bitter fate of the Aerodromers[e]

The situation of the other ghetto Jews was not much better, as they worked in various smaller work brigades in the city. Here, in the city, the Jews encountered Christian workers with whom they worked. At these opportunities, they would exchange items for food products with the Christians, which they would bring back and smuggle into the Ghetto.

True, at the Ghetto Gate there was an inspection by the Ghetto Guards, to confiscate the products that the Jews would bring into the Ghetto illegally. Jews would take a risk by bribing the guards at the gate, so that while going through the Ghetto Gate they would conduct a superficial check or give back some confiscated products to the owner. An important role was played by these functionaries at the Ghetto Gate.[f]

At this opportunity it must be added that, over time, the Jews learned tricks to hide smaller amounts of products. Thus, many Jews would succeed in getting through the checkpoint in peace. At the time there were the following types of masquerades, for example: in a long, narrow sack they would fill up flour or grain and tie it around the body like a compress (this was really called: "making a compress"). Or, for example, in the leaden eating utensils, which were taken to work with them, there would be a double cover and in between the covers there was a space to put a piece of butter, bacon, cheese, meat, etc. These individual inventions would very often become true curiosities.

Aside from that, the price difference for foodstuffs between the Ghetto and the city was great. Thus, it was still worthwhile, as it was called, to "burn" at the checkpoint from time to time. "Burn" meant letting them confiscate a portion of the products. The loss of the products which were confiscated was covered by selling the products that got through.

[Page 104]

Thus, for the ghetto Jews, working in the city brigade was considered a privilege to make a living, to be able to afford to eat better, and to always have a few extra Marks.

The previously mentioned social contrasts between the aerodrome workers and the city brigade workers were visible, so that even by their external physical appearance and self-esteem, you could differentiate between Aerodromers and a worker in the city brigade.

At the time, the Aerodromers usually appeared torn and disheveled like a genuine pauper. They would look unfortunate, gloomy, and anxious, by comparison to the workers in the city brigade, who were better dressed and, for the most part, made a satisfied and cheerful impression.

At the start of Winter 1941-42, the occupation regime in Lithuania started mobilizing Lithuanians – "in a good way" – for various border construction works and, also, for work in Germany.

Through various open and masked terror strategies, the occupation forces succeeded in collecting thousands of Lithuanians as "volunteers," and send them to the Nazi "Reich service work." In many city factories and other workplaces there developed a phenomenon with a considerably exclusive composition of various factory specialists and assistants.

The pace of the war, especially those exhausted by the German winter battles, forced the German hinterland to work with full steam to be able to cover the needs of the poor fate of the Eastern front.

At that time, the Kovno City Commissar found himself slowly forced to use the Jewish craftsman forces, which were, until then, not proportionally used for their specialties, and who were mostly working out at the Aerodrome like common laborers. The reserve of the under-utilized Jewish craftsmen had to be urgently utilized in the city factories and work sites.

[Page 105]

For the Ghetto, this phenomenon had a double meaning: first, for the Jews, it strengthened their hope to remain alive; they need the Jews, right? And second, it aligned strongly with the economic needs of the Ghetto: by working in the city, Jews would be able to buy food products – one of the most important issues for the ghetto Jew, if he didn't get killed…

With the arrival of Spring 1942, the Kovno City Commissariat, the boss of the Ghetto, started allowing various military and civil workplaces to employ Jewish craftsmen and assistants more often. This shrank the Jewish work contingent at the Aerodrome, and because of this, the number of Jews working in the city places increased.

For those Jews who were removed from work at the Aerodrome and transferred to work in a city brigade, it meant a real transition from darkness to light. That meant that their economic situation strongly improved, and the question of sustenance became easier, as opposed to working at the Aerodrome.

In March 1942, an affiliate of the German Labor Office in Kovno was established in the Ghetto. The first step of the newly established German Labor Office was to introduce a general registration in the Ghetto. Many Jews, who were not even artisans, registered themselves as skilled laborers, with the belief that the chances of an artisan would eventually be better than an unqualified worker.

According to this registration, it turned out that there was a large reserve of under-utilized artisans in the Ghetto, and this made it possible for the German Labor Office to be generous and give employment possibilities to Jewish artisans in city workplaces.

[Page 106]

All the people from the German Labor Office in the Ghetto were designated to S.A. Captain Herman. He was not too big a Jew enemy. Aside from that, he would go on a spree with the frequent and fat Jewish "gifts." (When the Ghetto was taken over by the S.S. in Autumn 1943, and converted into a concentration camp, this S.A. man, Herman, had to leave his warm bench in the Ghetto. However, he had the sense to extract a written document from Dr. Elkes, that the Ghetto didn't have any grievances against him. Thanks to this letter, after the Nazi capitulation, he saved himself from various unpleasant punishments in the American Zone in Germany, in connection with Nazification.)

Through the Elders Council, the newly established German Labor Office in the Ghetto appointed Dr. Itzhak Rabinovitz,[g] a well-known Kovno resident, and, by the way, a close relative of the famous, righteous Kovno Rabbi Itzhak-Elhanan, R.I.P.

Due to all these planned factors, the number of newly established Jewish work-brigades in the city increased. This meant that from week to week the economic status of new families was improving. Then the Ghetto slowly started to recover materially. Fewer ghetto Jews had no source of sustenance. This process of economic improvement took place in the Ghetto during the entire Summer of 1942.

In parallel to the growth of the Jewish work-brigade in the city, the noisy construction of ghetto workshops began. This took the place of the Jewish work at the Aerodrome.

The manner of development of the large Ghetto Workshops belonged to one of the most interesting and studied chapters in the history of the Kovno Ghetto settlement, and it would be worthwhile writing about it in a larger monographic work. At this juncture, it is worth telling only the most important details about these workshops.

The idea of establishing special workshops in the Ghetto, where Jews would work on various orders of merchandise for the German Wehrmacht, was started at the end of 1941, when the Ghetto started to slowly recover after the Big Action in the Ghetto. The plan to establish these workshops came from the Jewish side, and it was accepted by the German ghetto bosses.

[Page 107]

The Jewish calculations were as follows: first, most ghetto Jews suffered terribly by the inhuman service of forced labor at the Aerodrome. The reader can get an impression about this slave labor in the previous chapter. Jews wanted to create easier work conditions in the Ghetto itself, which would be appropriate mainly for women, weaker men, youth, etc.

Secondly, by then, Jews had in mind that the existence of the ghetto workshops could, with time, raise the degree of the Jewish "usefulness" in the eyes of the occupation powers – a factor which, admittedly, was justified in huge measure.

From the perspective of the German ghetto governors, they were interested in the establishment of the Ghetto Workshops for the following reasons:

With the looting of Jewish belongings, which took place in Autumn of 1941, the boss of the Ghetto, the City Commissariat, aside from money, gold, and other valuables, also brought in large amounts of clothes, furs, footwear, etc. In addition, the City Commissariat would also get his "portion" of the items, shoes, etc., which were collected from the murdered Kovno and foreign Jews. The City Commissariat would store these items in various warehouses in the city, mainly in the buildings of the City Council House, in former prayer houses, etc.

A Jewish work commando, called "the Jordan-Brigade" named after the big Jew murderer, Ghetto Commandant Jordan, worked on the organization and sorting of these items. The best Jewish artisans in this brigade of tailors, furriers, shoemakers, jewelers, watchmakers, etc. worked on private orders for these officials of the City Commissariat and their families.

For various reasons, the Germans from the City Commissariat advised relocating these Jewish workshops into the Ghetto itself. In addition, they knew very well that they would gain great capital from the Jewish ghetto workshops. And this was how it really was; over time these workshops became an inexhaustible source of robbery, bribery, and other combinations.

[Page 108]

So, why at that time did Jewish and German interests in establishing these Large Ghetto Workshops coincide?

After long preparations by the Jews, various large spaces at Krisciukaicio Street 107 were remodeled. Here there was once a Lithuanian vocational school and in the Ghetto times, it was the biggest refuge for ghetto Jews without shelter. On the 18th of January 1942 the large Ghetto Workshops were finally opened.

In the beginning, only a few small workshops were established for tailors, and shoemakers, and then the Jewish workshops from the previously mentioned "Jordan-Brigade" were also brought over.

The Large Ghetto Workshops grew very quickly to a wide branched combination of various workshops, like, for example, tailor shops, shoemaker, knitting, hat and furrier shops, laundry, locksmith, carpentry, basketry shop, brush shop, and many other types of workshops. From the beginning a few hundred Jews, and later, three to four thousand Jews worked in two shifts: daytime and nighttime.

The work in the Ghetto Workshops was quite comfortable, like the work in the city, but here in the Ghetto Workshops where the Jews were assigned, no one, neither Germans nor non-Jewish supervisors, sat on your head.

In addition, while working in the Ghetto Workshops they would not have to deal with the long trip to work in the city and back, day in and day out. Many city workplaces were located 4-5 kilometers from the Ghetto, if not further. Walking there and back was approximately 10 kilometers to travel daily across the city bridge in the rain, in the heat and in the cold, etc.

Working in the Ghetto Workshops lessened the exhaustive procedure and extremely high tension of going through the Ghetto Gate in the morning on the way to work, and at night through the checkpoint for incoming foodstuffs. These were indeed the benefits of the Ghetto Workshops.

[Page 109]

The disadvantages were obvious in that the workers in the Ghetto Workshops didn't have any opportunity to procure foodstuffs for cheaper prices than what was available in the city. Therefore, in the Ghetto Workshops the only ones who could afford to work there were those of more means in the Ghetto. And that was the way it was from the beginning.

In addition to the genuine artisans, the Ghetto Workshops would take in such ghetto Jews who, because of their age or health status, were not assigned to a job in the city. Many older and weaker men and women and many grown youths worked there.

It was not so easy at that time for someone from a city workplace to get into the Ghetto Workshop. The Jewish Labor Office, which always filled shortages of those interested in going to work in the hard and distant workplaces, especially at the Aerodrome, would control transfers from the city to the Ghetto Workshops very strictly.

The Ghetto Workshops played a great role in the life of the Ghetto. They were a significant factor in the structure of the Jewish work responsibility. At the end of 1943, quartering took place in the Ghetto. That meant, the separation of the Ghetto into separate Jewish work camps. In Spring of 1944, after the Action of the children, elderly and infirm, the role of the Ghetto Workshops grew even more for a variety of reasons. At that time the Ghetto Workshops were an important factor in sustaining the existence of the Ghetto community.

In 1943, the youth started the movement to get out to the partisans in the forest. With arms in their hands, they could go to fight against the Nazi enemy. So, in the Ghetto Workshops they would secretly steal German military uniforms and other items that were necessary for those going out into the forest.

In order to maintain control over the activities of the workshops, the City Commissar had his officials there. A few of them were big monsters and the Jews would suffer greatly from them.

[Page 110]

In Autumn of 1943, when the Ghetto was transferred to the authority of the S.S.[h] the workshops stood on the edge of a crisis, because the new Camp Commander, Goecke, was set against the existence of the workshops from the beginning. Thereafter, when he "tasted the taste" of the workshops, he, too, became an advocate for their existence and designated his substitute, S. S. Captain Ring, as the supervisor of the Large Ghetto Workshops.

From the beginning of the establishment of the Large Ghetto Workshops, G. Gemelitzki was involved. He was an old timer from the Economics Office of the Elders Council. But later, right after their establishment, the Elders Council set up Jewish management of the workshops, headed by M. Segalson.[i] Aside from him, the workshop activities were managed by the previously mentioned Gemelitzki, B. Friedman, Ch. Kagan (all the persons mentioned were liberated in Dachau), H. Brick (saved himself in a ghetto bunker during the liquidation of the Ghetto), Y. Shwartz, Agr. Kelzon (both died in Dachau), etc.

Some specific people from the management of the Large Ghetto Workshops were as good as useless and set the tone for the other ghetto institutions, which were not free from favoritism, bribery, corruption, and other amoral and asocial impairments.[j] These workshops, as previously mentioned, played a very important role in ghetto life.

The Ghetto Pottery Shop, which until the Nazi occupation belonged to the Slabodka Jewish residents, the Michles brothers, was also formally attached to the Large Workshops. The potters' shop was located on Aldonos Street number 9.

[Page 111]

They started to work in the potter shop during the Summer of 1942, when the Large Ghetto Workshops were flourishing, and they opened a complete line of new divisions. Thereafter, the Ghetto mental institution, which from the beginning was quartered in the spaces of the potter shop, was transferred to another location, so the potter shop renewed its work.

Together with the former owners of the potter shop, about 30 Jews in total were employed. In the potter shop they would manufacture various clay utensils, like bowls, pots, etc. The manufactured utensils would be exchanged among the residents of the Ghetto and later, in the Jewish camps which belonged to the

Ghetto. In addition, the potter's shop would manufacture drinking jugs, etc. ordered by the Nazi ghetto rulers.

The prior owners supervised the work of the potter shop, as did a German ceramic artisan, George Hauer (by the way, he was not a bad German and later, for unknown reasons, he ended his life by committing suicide).

The potter shop existed until the liquidation of the Ghetto in July 1944. During the ghetto deportations, in a well-hidden bunker in the potter shop, a dozen Jews were successfully hidden and, a few weeks later, were saved after the liberation of Kovno by the Red Army.

In addition to the Large Ghetto Workshops, Small Ghetto Workshops also existed in the Ghetto. As noted, if the Large Ghetto Workshops were working for the needs of the German military institutions, the goal of the Small Ghetto Workshops was to serve the residents of the Ghetto and of the Jewish work camps which belonged to the Ghetto.[k]

The situation in the Ghetto became relatively more peaceful and the state of the ghetto residents improved. Various ghetto institutions were stabilized under the authority of the Elders Council. The Ghetto started showing signs of an anticipated social life.

[Page 112]

The socially active people from the former parties and administrations, especially from among the Jewish youth, started to take on leadership in the Ghetto. They organized secret social activities in homes with their ideological supporters.

A separate activity started to exhibit itself in the various Zionist groupings, on the one hand and the left leaning elements on the other.

In the case of Zionism, whose ideology was to solve the ongoing Jewish diaspora problem, the ghetto Jew didn't need clarification what diaspora means! As well as with the Soviet Bund, the big and powerful kingdom, which carried on its shoulders the heaviest burden of destroying the murderous Hitlerism, the biggest blood-enemy of the ghetto Jew! On both sides, the social consciousness of groups of ghetto youth was strongly awakened.

The strategies of a few of the above-mentioned social groups were on the periphery and maintained the mood, through covert organizational activity, kept up by a sympathetic cheerful spirit, and a guardedness regarding the events in ghetto life.

The left-leaning elements in the Ghetto not only managed to organize their supporters, but at the same time they tried to set up contact with left-oriented elements in the city.

Little by little, specific contacts between the various social groups in the Ghetto started to get set up, with the aim of establishing coordinated activities on the part of all the socially active leaders. Later, from this same collaborative work of the disparate streams, the united movement of ghetto youth grew with the aim of escaping to the partisans in the forest, to stand up as fighters against the Nazis.[l]

Later, when the building of "*malinas*" in the Ghetto became actualized, that is, bunkers to hide oneself in the time of roundups and captures, these organized groups were the first active builders of *malinas*.

A warning not to come close to the Ghetto Fence

Benno Liptzer, one of the most important Jewish authority figures in the Ghetto

Left: Dr. von Renteln, General-Commissar of Lithuania, Hans Kramer, Kovno City Commissar

Right: Lithuanian troops were sent over the borders of Lithuania to carry out "special" assignments, Kaunas Newspaper, number 27, November 11, 1941

[Page 113]

Aside from this illegal organizational work among the youth, a semi- legal cultural activity was started at that time in the Ghetto (of course, in very borderline measure), which was organized by the School Office of the Elders Council.

They opened a few public schools for the children of school age at that time. A vocational school with a few departments to learn a trade was opened for the older children. From time to time, they would also organize semi-legal lessons, recitations, and cultural presentations, which would bring in a huge audience.[m]

Frequently, on Saturday and Sunday, a Jewish orchestra was organized in the Ghetto.[n] The orchestra gave concerts in one of the buildings of the once famous Slabodka Yeshiva, to which, aside from Jews, representatives from the City Commissariat and ghetto command also "deigned" to come.

For just a moment, there was the impression that a thin film was slowly covering up the open wounds of the ghetto population. But only for a second could the ghetto Jew forget his historically tragic fate. The Nazi regime in and around the Ghetto ensured that the Jews should feel their place is in the world wherever they turned.

In the Kovno Gestapo circles, for a specific time (from the beginning of the occupation until approximately Summer of 1942) a visible role was played by the Lithuanian Jewish young man Caspi-Serebrovitch. Already from the time of the Smetona control in Lithuania, this young man had a dark past behind him and during the Soviet regime in 1940-41, he was placed in jail together with many others who were arrested. He was liberated by the Germans when they entered Kovno.

[Page 114]

Due to his connection with the Gestapo, Caspi-Serebrovitch received the right to live in the city, ignoring the fact that he was a Jew. By the way, he was the only single Kovno Jew who enjoyed such an outstanding "privilege" from the Gestapo. In the Gestapo, Caspi was active as an official for Polish or other issues and in addition, was empowered by the Gestapo to supervise the Ghetto. Furthermore, he really showed an active interest in Jewish life in the Ghetto and would come to the Elders Council very often for guidance about the Jewish Ghetto Police.

Due to their fear of his position with the Gestapo, the Elders Council agreed to all his wishes and opinions about various issues of ghetto life, especially in determining the higher functionaries of the Jewish ghetto hierarchy.

At this opportunity it would be interesting to add that Caspi stood close to the Revisionist movement in Lithuania before the war. He tried convincing his Gestapo bosses that the old-time Revisionist stream of Achimeir's "Against the Tide," was an anti-English argument, and it sympathized with Hitler and his state. In this manner he wanted to establish more "security" and supervision in the Gestapo's eyes. By coincidence, a package of letters sent from the Kovno Ghetto to Vilna fell into the hands of the Gestapo.[o] As the researcher of this issue, Caspi wanted to protect his Revisionist friends who sent the letter to Yosef Glazman in Vilna, when their letters also fell into the hands of the Gestapo.

Caspi-Serebrovitch's influence on the Elders Council revealed the jealousy from another Jewish young man, Benno Liptzer, who, as already mentioned, was the Brigadier of the Jewish work brigade in the Kovno

Gestapo. He also had special connections with high Gestapo people. Liptzer also tried his influence on the Elders Council.

The camp competition between the previously mentioned Jewish young man and Liptzer continued for a few months until the beginning of Summer 1942. Liptzer at last, using an opportune situation against Serebrovitch, achieved his goal. For specific reasons, Caspi-Serebrovitch fell out of favor with his Gestapo bosses, and they killed him and his family on the way from a mock assignment to Vilna. Liptzer then became empowered by the Gestapo to oversee the activities of the Elders Council and their institutions.

[Page 115]

Before the war, Liptzer was a salesman for the Kovno radio company. He was a person in his 40's, almost without education, and only with a strongly developed ambition for power. In the Ghetto he always loved to allow people to feel his power status and would speak with the tone of a high "lord." Thanks to his close connections with specific Gestapo big shots, he became the uncrowned Jewish "dictator" of the Kovno Ghetto population.

In truth, we must also add that dozens of Jews who, for various reasons fell into the Gestapo's hands, were saved from certain death due to Liptzer's familiarity with the then representative of Jewish issues in the Gestapo, the hideous Jewish murderer Shtitz,[p] who he would "grease" with great amounts of bribes.

There were also cases, however, when Liptzer would allow himself to save the life of one arrested Jew instead of another one. This was because very often the Gestapo was only interested that a Jew be killed - and it was not important which one.

In any case, Liptzer's influence in the Gestapo circles very strongly impressed the ghetto Jew, legally or protectively, especially the brow-beaten "folk" person from the Ghetto. There were dozens of stories and legends about how Liptzer saved Jews from death at the very last minute before being transported to the 9th Fort to be shot. These stories circulated among the ghetto folk and his high esteem and popularity in the Ghetto grew very strongly.

Indeed, with his demagogic appearances in favor of the simple folk, he very quickly gained their sympathy. He would take on complaints and requests from the Jews about past injustices by the Ghetto institutions and would give appropriate orders to the indicated institutions, which would carry out his decisions punctually, just like an order from the regime.

[Page 116]

Going to complain to Liptzer was a threat not only for a lowly official from a ghetto institution, but also for the leading functionaries from the Jewish ghetto administration.

In November 1943, when the Ghetto was converted into a concentration camp and S.S. Captain Goecke, was designated as Camp Commander, Liptzer's star started to decline. His esteem sank even more, when his work brigade stopped going to work in the city at the Gestapo because in the Ghetto itself, workshops were organized especially for the Gestapo workers. His contact with the Gestapo was thus made more difficult and his influence in the Ghetto became greatly reduced.

Liptzer played a very suspicious role during the time of the arrest of the Ghetto Police, which took place at the end of March 1944, and at the same time during the Action of the children, elderly, and infirm.[q]

After the liquidation of the Elders Council in Spring of 1944, Liptzer, became Chief of the "Service workers."[r] These Service Workers had to replace the liquidated Jewish Ghetto Police, and his star started to lose its shine again. His newly acquired influence held on until the deportation and liquidation of the Ghetto.

At the time of the liquidation of the Ghetto, Liptzer hid himself in one of the ghetto-*malinas*. His hideout was uncovered by the Gestapo, and they forced the people to climb out. Prior to that, Liptzer managed to take poison, but it didn't take effect. Liptzer wanted to go with the deported Jews, but the Camp Commander, Goecke, searched for him for a few days, while he hid out in the *malina*. The Gestapo had their eye on him because he knew too many "secrets of the court." They didn't allow him to go with the deported Jews. The next morning, Liptzer was shot and, as witnesses recounted, was thrown into the flames of the burning Jewish hospital while still alive, where he was burned together with other murdered ghetto Jews.[s]

[Page 117]

Chaim Matematik, a co-worker from his brigade was also shot, together with Liptzer. This young man would hear secret foreign radio news in the Gestapo, which he would relay to the Ghetto.

Although Liptzer's connections in the Gestapo remained unclear, it is almost sure that he played a very suspicious role regarding the Ghetto. It was particularly clear to see his provocative double role at the arrest of the Jewish Ghetto Police. It was also almost certain that he "contributed" to the liquidation of the Elders Council.

The fact that he was in contact with the sophisticated Gestapo Jew murderer, Kittel, the tragically infamous liquidator of the Vilna and Kovno Ghettos, is evidence that in the last critical period of the Ghetto, Liptzer, maybe against his will, brought many problems into the Ghetto.

As noted, Liptzer played a colossal role in the peculiar service of life in the Ghetto and, he and his name are tightly bound with the most important events in the Kovno Ghetto community.

As was mentioned many times, one of the most important existential questions of the Ghetto was the problem of nourishment. The largest portion of food products which the Ghetto needed was brought in by the workers of the city brigades.

The fear of hunger prodded the Ghetto Jews to take risky steps to procure food. As usual, they removed the yellow patches and "posed as non-Jews." They would circulate among the Christians at the workplace, from whom they would be able to buy something.

More than a few Jews at this time fell into the hands of the Lithuanian police, who would immediately extradite the "guilty" directly to the Gestapo. For such "sins" the Gestapo would send them to the 9th Fort.

Furthermore, in cases where a Jew was caught in the city, the former horrific Gestapo murderer Shtitz, the one in charge of Jewish issues, would immediately shoot not only the perpetrator, but his entire family at the same time. In this manner, dozens of Jews, together with their families, paid with their lives for attempting to acquire a piece of bread and something with the bread, for themselves and for their children.

[Page 118]

For those ghetto Jews who were taken to work somewhere in the provinces for a day or two, it was a great stroke of luck. By the way, this was the best opportunity to acquire food for cheaper prices, and with less risk of capture by the Gestapo. In such cases, those traveling to the countryside would be greatly envied. Many ghetto Jews wished to have this right to be able to travel to the countryside at least once. In the Ghetto it was called "to make a good package," which meant, to be able to buy food products for lower prices.

In the Summer of 1942, they also started taking Jewish women and youth to work in the gardens and fields in the big homes around Kovno. For the Ghetto, this was again a double opportunity: first, the opportunity to steal vegetables, grain, and second, to buy various food products from the peasants nearby.

During the time of the existence of the agricultural work brigades, the Ghetto had enough vegetables to satisfy their appetite.

When the German military or agricultural organizations would take Jewish women to pick potatoes, vegetables, etc., or they would require Jewish workers to load grain, and other food products, in these cases the Jews, with or without the approval of their supervisors, would also steal some potatoes, vegetables, grains, etc., for themselves.

If a Jew was caught in such a "violation" he would be beaten murderously, and very often would be given over to the Gestapo. It was worthwhile to "organize" something, as it was called in the Ghetto and in the concentration camp. They would bring full backpacks into the Ghetto and there was enormous happiness.

The smuggling of food products through the Ghetto Gate also played a specific role in nourishment. In the Ghetto there were special gate managers who had connections with the city merchants, who would set them up with various food products in greater amounts. Of course, in such a business there were also specific guards spread out around the Ghetto Gate, which without their agreement, this kind of smuggling would not be possible.

[Page 119]

The gate managers would sell the food products to illegal food stores in the Ghetto for resale. The competition between the gate managers themselves actually regulated the prices of the food products on the "ghetto market."

Very often, it would happen that upon bringing larger amounts of food products into the Ghetto, the difference between the prices of these products in the city and in the Ghetto were so minimal, it was simply not worthwhile purchasing such products in the city.

Therefore, it would be better for Jews, to buy such products inside the Ghetto, even paying a bit more for it. In this way they would minimize the danger of harm when the inspection at the Ghetto Gate would eventually confiscate some of the purchased food products from the city.

For a while, the Jewish Ghetto Police even attempted to establish regulated prices for the food products in the ghetto shops, so that they would not tear the ghetto residents apart.

The gate managers were the best situated Jews in the Ghetto. The majority were bold and cunning youth, and they would be stuffed with thousands of Marks.

The truth is that more than a few of them paid with their lives when they fell into the hands of the Gestapo in cases when there was a failure. The biggest earners among the gate managers would not stop the other gate managers from earning a living, which played a very important role in feeding the Ghetto.

There were various ways for the ghetto Jews to make a living. A large portion of workers made a living from the better city brigades. A smaller number of workers made a living from the good workplaces at the Aerodrome. Details of the best ways to make a living: First, on the way to work they would bring products with them to the workplace, various clothes, shoes, underwear, etc., to sell for money or exchange for food or things which were still found in the Jewish network. Second, on the way back from work they would bring food products into the Ghetto, a portion of which they would use for themselves, and the rest they would sell to other Jews for prices which would obviously make a profit.

[Page 120]

In this way the workers who were in the better jobs would, on a given day, have double earnings: once in the city upon selling the items, and a second time in the Ghetto, by selling the food products.

In the Ghetto there were also special middlemen, who dealt with supplying various items to the workers from the workplaces to sell in the city. They would buy these items from various ghetto Jews, who could not go into the city to work themselves. There were also middlemen in the Ghetto who sold the food products which were brought into the Ghetto. Both types of middlemen also had a way of making a living.

We must not forget about the issue of clothing and that the clothes of the Jews deported from the Actions were usually transferred to their relatives, or to their neighbors, and often even to unfamiliar people. A portion of these clothes would also be transferred to the network of social offices, to distribute to ghetto Jews who were without means.[1] At that time, there were sixteen thousand Jews in the Ghetto, who, in fact, earned money from the clothes which belonged to the nearly thirty thousand Jews who entered the Ghetto in August 1941.

The truth is that the better Jewish clothes were robbed during the big house searches, which took place in Fall of 1941. But even the simple clothes had a value in the city. The Christian population in the city and especially in the villages eagerly purchased even the used Jewish clothes. Because first of all, new things were then very difficult to get, and secondly, the Jews would give away their very good clothes for small amounts of food products.

The craftsmen, for example, a tailor, a shoemaker, etc. at that time, when they were free from their work duty, would make private orders in their homes, either for the ghetto Jews or for selling in the city. In this way these craftsmen earned well.

There were also Jews who took advantage of the dearth of items, such as women's kerchiefs, shirts, hats, etc., among the Christian population in the villages.

[Page 121]

Thus, in the Ghetto, an "industry" was developed which would produce these items. In this Ghetto production more people were pulled in. Some of them would occupy themselves by going around the Ghetto homes buying up used sheets, pillowcases, linen, etc. and others would occupy themselves with decorating these fabrics, by painting ornaments on the various kerchiefs, so it should look as if it was manufactured in a factory, etc.

In the Ghetto, Jews would also produce baked goods, poppy cakes, and sweets to sell in the city. Dozens of Jewish families made their wretched ghetto living, from such "illegal" businesses. In addition, in this way they could spite their bloody enemies with whatever it took, to survive all the horrors, in order to see the defeat of the Nazis.

During the intermediary time between both abusive Actions to Riga, the Nazis didn't forget to "favor" the Ghetto with an entire new list of decrees and 'little' decrees, which had a serious impact on the life of the Ghetto. We will note only the most important ones.

The Ghetto population was often hit with decrees to clear out Ghetto quarters. Because living space for the ghetto Jews was minimal, even after the reduction of the Large Ghetto, one can understand how great the crowdedness in the Ghetto would become with another decree to reduce specific ghetto areas.

During extremely freezing temperatures, like the freezing weather of those days in the middle of January 1942, suddenly the ghetto Commandant, Jordan gave the Elders Council an order to reduce quite a huge ghetto quarter. Within a time-period of just a few hours, this Vienazshinski area of the Ghetto had to be vacated. Jordan's "motive" was - on this same day 5,000 Jews from Vienna would come to live in the houses in the cleared-out areas.

The Ghetto area was cleared up in the required time, but no Viennese Jews came to the Kovno Ghetto. At first, we thought the whole story about the Viennese Jews was just an "excuse" to reduce the Ghetto area, or Viennese Jews actually came, but instead of bringing them into the Ghetto, they took them to the 9th Fort. It turned out that a group of Viennese Jews were, indeed, brought to the Riga Ghetto. It was originally planned to bring them to the Kovno Ghetto, but at the last moment they transported them to Riga.

[Page 122]

Later, this specific area in the Ghetto was reinstated and in the beginning of October 1942 it was once again taken out of the Ghetto domain - this time for good.

A second ghetto quarter clear-out took place in May 1942, when Paneriu Street was cleared out. Also, the remainder of the Jewish houses which were located on the side with the odd numbers, and all the Jewish houses from the neighboring little streets were all cleared out.

On the 7th of May 1942 the regime announced an order to the ghetto population, which forbade any Jewish woman to be pregnant. For breaking this specific rule, the death penalty was expected for the pregnant woman and for the child.

The dreadful experiences due to the Actions, the daily decrees, and, in addition, also malnutrition caused atrophy and worsening of life for the ghetto population. For example, young men became impotent and young women lost their menses.

At the end of 1941, the wave of mass murders quieted down and in Spring and Summer of 1942 the economic situation in the Ghetto was somewhat better than before. Thus, the horrible life of the ghetto population returned in stages to its more- or- less normal character.

Many women became pregnant, but they each explained it with the same reasons. Since they did not have their menstruation, they themselves didn't know they were pregnant in the early months. In this regard, menstruation was a dependable source in the earlier ghetto times.

Regarding the rule about forbidding pregnancies in the Ghetto, the Jewish Health Office sent nurses and midwives around to the Jewish houses. They demanded that young women who didn't menstruate come to the Ghetto clinic for an examination, to know if this specific symptom was not connected to pregnancy.

[Page 123]

If it was determined that these women were certainly pregnant, they had to have an abortion. Among the pregnant women who were in their later months, they tried to cause early births. These women would not show themselves on the street, so that they would not be noticed by the Germans, and the births would take place in their homes and not in the hospital.

The new-born children would in such a case be registered in the Statistics Office of the Ghetto with a date from before the rule, so that they would be "legal."

Therefore, performing abortions in the Ghetto was not only lawfully allowed, but, even more - it became obligatory.

The Nazi bosses in the Ghetto wouldn't rest knowing that in prayer houses in the Ghetto, Jews were conducting religious prayers to the Jewish God. Also, they couldn't understand why Jewish children, who would sooner or later be killed, should study in the children's schools.

To regulate these issues in the Ghetto, a law was announced on the 26th of August 1942 from the powers, to lock all the prayer houses and prohibit Jews from holding religious prayer in public. In truth, the Jews continued to pray in the homes in Minyans, as always, but the power organs were not supposed to know. At the same time, the children's schools were locked up.[u]

A ghetto Jew must not have any money, was a rule the entire time since the Nazis robbed the Jews of all their possessions.

The Elders Council oversaw an entire list of institutions, which would take various fees from the population, such as in the food stores, where the Ghetto population gave out the official food rationing, in the Ghetto Gardens, pharmacy, hospital, Small Ghetto workshops, etc. They had to pay the price officially determined by the Workshop Office of the Elders Council.

[Page 124]

From these payments, the Elders Council would have quite a large income, which they would utilize at their own discretion.

In the month of August 1942, the previous ghetto boss, Von Kepen appeared at the Elders Council quite unexpectedly. He confiscated the treasury box of the Elders Council which contained the sum of 30 thousand Marks. Other than that, it was strongly forbidden for the Jewish ghetto administration to take any payment money.

From then on, in the Ghetto a "non-monied" economy was introduced. That is, all the needs of the ghetto Jew, like nursing, medicine, clothing, etc. had to be satisfied without any reward. However, illegal payments for all these things remained as it was before.

To end the illegal smuggling of food products in the Ghetto, the Gestapo announced that starting from the 26th of August 1942 it would be completely forbidden to bring rationed food products (and almost all food products were then rationed) into the Ghetto.

Since these orders were announced 4-5 days earlier, Jews wanted to take advantage of the time to prepare a small reserve of food products, so that they should not have to be dependent on the official hunger rations in the future.

Just during these days, hundreds of men and women who were working in the Ghetto Workshops, or in the ghetto institutions, or those who were freed from work due to their age or health condition, would come to the Ghetto Gate in the morning to go along into the city with a work brigade and buy some food products there.

In those days around six to seven thousand Jews would line up by the Ghetto Gate, together with the permanent city workers and, with all their strength, would fight to get into a better city brigade, where they could have more favorable conditions to procure food products. The noise and the hurly-burly near the Ghetto Gate were like at a gigantic holiday market.

The prohibition against bringing in food products to the Ghetto held for a short time. But, from day to day the actual harshness of the prohibition became weakened and quickly the Jews continued to bring in vital sustenance, illegally, just like before.

[Page 125]

One time, in the Summer of 1942, the Ghetto had to give up a specific number of Jews to the work camp in Palemon (a railroad station near Kovno), where various foreign workers were dragged in and worked at hard labor.

The recruitment for the Palemon work camp was conducted by the Jewish institutions, and it took place with all the well-known sad accompanying phenomena like coercion, crying, wails, and helplessness coming from those who were assigned to travel out there.

One of the transports to Palemon left on the first day of Rosh Hashana 1942, giving the Ghetto a true "holiday."

At the end of the Summer, rumors were circulating around the Ghetto that the regime was going to demand people for work in Riga for a second time. Finally, it became clear that there was such an order. The Ghetto suddenly forgot the day-to-day worries and started "living" with this standing decree, and there was nothing to stop it.

Original footnotes:

    a. See "School Office" in the Monograph "Jewish institutions in Kovno Ghetto."
    b. See "Zionist activities in the Ghetto"
    c. See "People who were involved with the partisan movement in the Ghetto"

d. Details about the question of forced labor -see Chapter "Work Office" in the Monograph "Jewish Institutions in the Kovno Ghetto."
e. See "Samples of Folklore in Kovno Ghetto"
f. See "Labor Office" in the Monograph: "Jewish Institutions in the Kovno Ghetto."
g. For particulars about him, see "Work Office" in Monograph, "Jewish Institutions in Kovno Ghetto."
h. See, Chapter-Cut off: "Fight between S.A. and S.S. for leadership in the Ghetto" and "S.S. – the new ghetto bosses."
i. By the way, he played a big role in ghetto life, when the Ghetto was under the authority of S.S. Captain Goecke.
j. For more about these specific issues – see the Monograph: "Jewish Institutions in Kovno Ghetto"
k. About the Small Ghetto workshops: see "Workshop Office" in Monograph "Jewish Institutions in the Kovno ghetto."
l. Details about this issue – in the later chapters.
m. See "Shul Office"
n. See "Police orchestra" in Monograph: "Jewish Institutions in the Kovno Ghetto"
o. See "Failure of the illegal letter connection between Kovno and other Ghettos" in Monograph: "Jewish Institutions in Kovno Ghetto".
p. In the Summer of 1943, Jewish partisans conducted an attack against Stitz near Vilna, from which he died a few days later
q. See Action of the Children, Elders and Infirm
r. See Capital-segment "Establishment of the Service-workers
s. See "Deportation and Liquidation of the Ghetto."
t. See "Social Office" in the Monograph "Jewish institutions in the Kovno Ghetto"
u. See "School Office" in the Monograph: "Jewish Institutions in the Kovno Ghetto."

CHAPTER XVII

The Second Relocation Action to Riga

-Measures taken by the Jewish Ghetto administration to recruit the required number of people to be sent to Riga-Tense course of events at the end of the recruiting period

[Page 126]

By end of October 1942, when it became clear that for the second time the Ghetto must give up 300-400 Jews to work in Riga, the situation in the Ghetto once again became tense.

Of course, at the start, the atmosphere for the second relocation Action wasn't as desperate as it was during the first relocation Action in the beginning of February 1942. The most important difference was that this time no one doubted that this was truly about traveling to work and not, God forbid, about an extermination Action.

The regards sent from those who were transported to Riga eight months prior, were not too bad. At that time, in Riga, the Jews also worked in varied forced labor and lived in conditions similar to the Kovno Jews.

Here, no one wanted to lose their established position acquired during the time of the "achievements." They didn't want to start from the beginning, building a new life somewhere in new, unfamiliar conditions.

The situation for those Jews was different. In the first relocation Action they were transported with close family members, full of people like a husband, a wife, children, elders, etc. So, right at the start they were prepared to go to Riga, even voluntarily, to be together with one's own.

The Elders Council was given the task of recruiting people for Riga by the regime. Understandably, they tried to take advantage of this atmosphere and got volunteers by even promising material support to go to Riga.

The total number of volunteers for the pre-registration, however, was not large. Therefore, also this time, it was more than certain that they would have to recruit people in a coercive manner.

Once again, a panic and a nervousness arose from those ghetto Jews, who they themselves bet that they would eventually fall onto the list of persons who would be forced to go to Riga. This panicked atmosphere negatively affected the position of those who volunteered, as well.

So, day by day, the total number of volunteers going to Riga actually diminished. The original registrants who voluntarily registered to go to Riga, renounced their readiness to travel in large numbers.

These same people who renounced their registration, were still being considered by the Jewish ghetto administration as the most suitable candidates for the relocation to Riga - whether they wanted to go, or not.

A few days before the people were to be sent off to Riga, when the Jewish Ghetto Police began detaining the designated people, the atmosphere in the Ghetto became highly charged. People started taking the only possible measure: to hide themselves from the Ghetto Police.

Many also stopped going to work in the city, so they wouldn't be stopped at the Ghetto Gate on their return from work. Once again, the air in the Ghetto became filled with horror and pain.

At that time, the Ghetto Police continued detaining the designated people. As was the case when the recruits were transported, this time many detained people who also had connections with whomever from the higher Jewish ghetto administration, tried through their close connections to get themselves freed. In place of those who were allowed to go free, they had to detain other persons. The feeling of torture and shock increased even more.

A day before the departure of the transport, they still didn't have the needed count. The rest were captured for Riga near the Ghetto Gate from those returning from work. This time the Jewish authorities carried it out themselves.

In order not to raise the suspicions of those who were stopped at the Ghetto Gate, the Jewish Ghetto Police carried out an unexpected search of those returning from the city. This search was about whether their yellow patches were attached according to the regulations of the regime.

Those people whose patches were not in order, that is, those who they wanted to detain, were taken into the Ghetto Jail which was located near the Ghetto Gate.

This "fabrication" by the Ghetto Police was figured out very quickly. However, those who were detained were already in the Ghetto Jail under guard and had no choice but to make peace with their fate to be relocated to Riga.

The Jews were deathly afraid of the Gestapo murderer, Shtitz, because of the great number of Jewish victims he killed. This same person, in charge of Jewish affairs in the Gestapo, could at any moment, without the slightest reason, deport Jews to the 9th Fort and shoot them there by his own hand. At the Ghetto Gate, this proved to be the most awful strain for the ghetto folk during the time the transport was sent to the train.

On the neighboring street around the Ghetto Gate many friends and acquaintances came to accompany those Jews who were to be sent off. But, with the arrival of the hangman, Shtitz, this meeting place immediately emptied of people. Each one was afraid to find himself in the proximity of the Nazi murderer whose name alone would conjure up horrific associations of bloody executions of Jews at the 9th Fort.

Even those Jews who were sent by transport, had to control their strained feelings with all their friends and acquaintances while leaving the Ghetto for the last time. They did not make a sound as they marched by the bloodthirsty Jew-murderer, Shtitz.

Going through the Ghetto gate and seeing Shtitz in the distance about a hundred meters away, they could have cried out their fate undisturbed – the bitter fate of the ghetto Jews, who were condemned until their destruction to suffer in the horrible Nazi hell…

CHAPTER XVIII

A Hanging in the Ghetto

-The doomed young Jewish man, Mek, who shot a German member of the Ghetto Command-Immediate Gestapo investigation-Arrest of the Council Elder and his release-The public hanging of Mek

[Page 130]

After the second relocation Action to Riga, a few, so-called, quiet weeks transpired without any shake-ups in the Ghetto. A critical moment for the Ghetto took place in the middle of November 1942. This specific, unexpected crisis took place in the following way:

It was Sunday night, the 16th of November 1942. A Jewish young man by the name of Mek, a man in his 30's, a former owner of a watch and jewelry shop in Kovno, together with two other friends, decided to pose as non-Jews and sneak out through the Ghetto Fence at a specific time to "arrange" something in the city. One of the three youngsters managed to get through the Ghetto Fence successfully, and Mek went after him. But he got caught up on the barbed wire of the fence, and because of that he was noticed by one of the guards who ran to arrest him. The third young man, who was supposed to go through the fence after Mek, understandably didn't go, and immediately disappeared into the Ghetto.

By coincidence, a high functionary of the Ghetto Guard was in the vicinity - a Viennese German named Fleishmann. When Fleishmann ran up to Mek to arrest him, Mek grabbed a revolver out of his pocket and started to shoot. He didn't hit anyone, but he was immediately arrested.

Notification of this specific surprising event spread through the ghetto population with lightning speed. It created unexpected confusion, because this was the first instance where a ghetto Jew dared to raise arms against a German, especially against such a high German ghetto official. It stood to reason that this would levy a huge toll of victims on the entire Ghetto. Not to mention the mere fact that there was a Jewish attack on a German, they were afraid that this incident would serve as a pretext by the regime to accuse the entire Ghetto of having personal arms.

[Page 131]

At this moment, Jews reminded themselves that in Autumn of 1941, there was no more than provocative confusion about a so-called shooting of Kozlovski, the former chief of the Ghetto Guard, by a Jew. Thereafter, the first mass Action in the Ghetto took place, which cost the ghetto population over 1000 victims. What awaited them today in the Ghetto when an attack against a German by a Jew really did take place?! That's how the Jews explained and imagined horrific scenes. Therefore, it was with great nervousness and strain that the Jews awaited the sanctions for the Ghetto from the occupation regime.

In an hour or two after this event, the representative of the Gestapo, together with the chief of the German Protection Police arrived in the Ghetto and started an investigation of the issue. The strain in the Ghetto became even greater when it became known that because of the first investigation, all the members of the Elders Council were arrested, except for Chairman, Dr. Elkes, who was at that time sick in bed.

From the investigation, the Jewish Ghetto Police was ordered to immediately arrest 20 Jewish hostages, until Mek's friend, who got through the Ghetto Gate and disappeared, was found. Since it was crucial to wait, because the hostages could become victims if they weren't successful in finding Mek's friend, the Ghetto Police detained hostages from among men and women from the mental institution and those hopelessly sick, etc. This was done so that no healthy persons or heads of family should suffer in case there would be bloodletting.

[Page 132]

Right after the first investigation, the members of the Elders Council were transported to the Gestapo. The Jews perceived the arrest of the members of the Elders Council as a bad sign, and it strongly increased the unrest in the Ghetto, because of the anticipation about the next day, when the mood of the regime would become clearer in resolving this issue.

At this time the Jews used everything in their power to "soften" the hearts of those Nazi-rulers, on whom the course of the investigation was dependent. The fact that in the shooting, Mek did not target the German, Fleishmann, and that he only shot in the air, played a certain role in the investigation, which was the real gift that benefitted the Ghetto.

Finally, through many efforts, they succeeded in placing the entire issue on such a plane, that Mek was not a public emissary of the Ghetto and that his act was committed on his own initiative. He wanted to run away from the Ghetto for fear of an extermination Action. Aside from everything, it turns out, the Kovno Gestapo this time didn't have a great desire to make a big deal of this issue and the next morning freed the members of the Elders Council from arrest and sent them back to the Ghetto.

Despite everything, the Gestapo had already decided to hang Mek in the Ghetto. True, when the judgement of the Gestapo became known, the Ghetto breathed easier, because they had expected sanctions on a mass scale. Nevertheless, they ordered the execution of Mek by hanging. This pained everyone strongly because this was the first case of hanging of a Jew in the Kovno Ghetto.

Tuesday, the 18th of November, was the day when it was decided to carry out Mek's execution. The Jews themselves had to prepare the gallows, which was stationed in an open plaza opposite the Elders Council building. While Mek was in the Gestapo, he was already murderously battered up until the hanging. However, he held himself valiantly, very tranquil and his first question before going to the hanging was about the fate of his mother and sister, with whom he lived in the Ghetto.

[Page 133]

The representatives of the Jewish Ghetto Police, who had to prepare the hanging, and be present at the execution, calmed him, saying that all is in the best order. The truth was that the Gestapo had already sent his mother and sister to the 9th Fort where they were shot, even before they hanged Mek.

The then-representative for Jewish affairs in the City Commissariat, the S.A. man, Miller, didn't idle in running into the neighboring Jewish houses, in order to force the available Jews to be present at the execution. All Mek's possessions[a] were transferred into the private custody of the Gestapo murderers, who dealt with the situation.

Mek's body hung on the gallows for a long period of time. It is not difficult to understand the feelings of the Jews that day. A cold late Autumn wind blew Mek's small and stretched out body back and forth on the gallows. The noose on Mek's neck, even more than any other day, didn't allow the Jews to forget their tragic hopeless fate.

After it became clear that the Mek issue was finally over, the hostages were freed. After a while, the Ghetto quieted down, but not for long, because a new period of permanent unrest started for the Ghetto with the arrival of the year 1943. This was a period when important changes took place in ghetto life, which had a decisive impact on the future fate of the ghetto Jews.

Original footnote:

    a. By the way, according to the Gestapo division, as it turned out, Mek had items of great value in his residence, as he didn't deliver his valuables during the time of the robbery of Jewish possessions in the year 1941.

CHAPTER XIX

"The Stalingrad Action"

-The measures taken by the Nazis to prevent Jewish satisfaction and joy over the German defeat at Stalingrad-The course of the Action which claimed 50 victims from the Ghetto

[Page 134]

In January 1943, the situation became more critical for the encircled German forces near Stalingrad. It was sensed by everyone that here, near Stalingrad, the downfall of the German Army on the Eastern Front would begin. Thus, the mood in the Ghetto became more cheerful day by day. Jews clearly saw that their long-dreamed hope to be freed from Hitler's hell, slowly started becoming a reality.

As they got closer to the end of January, even the German military High Command couldn't hide its reports from the front. With the indomitable German catastrophe near Stalingrad, the faces of the ghetto Jews started shining and expressed happiness and revenge. Finally, the historic Battle of Stalingrad ended with a roaring win for the Soviet Union, and with a shake-up defeat for the Nazi-Germans.

When the Third Reich proclaimed a day of national mourning pertaining to the defeat near Stalingrad, it was a real, long-awaited holiday for the ghetto Jews. Not only in the Ghetto, but even in the city at work among the Christians, Jews shared their feelings of happiness and held their heads higher.

On the other hand, however, it was to be expected that the Nazi murderers would mar the happiness of the Jews. Unfortunately, the Jews didn't have to wait long for such a step to take place by the Gestapo. They soon made them forget about the German defeat and move on with their own problems.

[Page 135]

On the 3rd of February 1943, a few days after the final German defeat near Stalingrad, a few dozen Jews were arrested in the city by the Lithuanian police, according to a decree from the Gestapo. Until then, Jews would very often go out in the neighborhood near their workplace to illegally buy some food products. Most of the time they would get through successfully. But on this day in the city, any Jew who tried to walk even a short distance from their workplace, was arrested.

Truthfully, Jews themselves took great care not to fall into the hands of the Gestapo. They knew in advance that the murderers were infuriated because of the German defeat, and now more than ever, would not let the Jewish victims out of their grip under any circumstance. So, on this day in the city a few dozen Jews were arrested for buying a loaf of bread, a few potatoes, a newspaper, etc.

In addition to the Jews arrested in the city, the murderer Ratnikas, the Chief of the Lithuanian Police of the Ghetto Guard, also arrested a certain number of Jews inside the Ghetto. These were mainly the bosses of the secret food stores. His "pretext" was fighting against black marketeering in the Ghetto.

Those arrested in the city were taken to the Gestapo, and those arrested from the Ghetto – to the Ghetto Jail. The Gestapo also ordered the Jewish Ghetto Police to detain all the family members of the arrested, both from the city, as well as from the Ghetto.

Knowing what kind of tragic fate awaits their family members, most of those Jews arrested in the city, would not divulge that they had family members in the Ghetto during the Gestapo investigation. In this way many family members of those arrested men were saved from a certain death. In total, close to 50 Jews were detained, both from the city as well as from the Ghetto, among them men, women, and a few dozen children.

On the morning of February 4th, 1943, while transporting the arrested from the Ghetto Jail to the Ghetto Guard, gruesome scenes played out. Finally, the arrested were seated on sleds in which they were transported to the Ghetto Guard, where Gestapo people were waiting for them.

[Page 136]

The convoy of sleds, on which were seated those convicted to die, looked like a funeral of living dead. They knew all too well what awaited them in a few hours at the 9th Fort. Exhausted physically and spiritually from the horrible experiences, they prepared themselves mentally for the upcoming execution, and looked at the Ghetto with resigned looks - for the last time in their lives.

At this time, the tragic and infamous truck of the Gestapo was seen as it passed by the Ghetto in the direction of the 9th Fort, in which sat the Jews arrested in the city. Twenty minutes later the same truck came back from the Fort and drove to the Ghetto Guard to collect the rest of the Jewish victims.

The Gestapo executioner, Stitch, who conducted the execution, came to the Ghetto Guard to oversee the transport of the Jews convicted to death. His presence near the Ghetto population raised the possibility of getting closer to the Ghetto Guard and for the last time, getting a look at the few dozen Jews who would, in an hour or two, be killed. Among the victims was also the well-known Kovno Russian Jewish journalist Boris Oretshkin, and his wife. They were arrested just the day before by order of the Gestapo because their child, who was hidden in the city by Christian people, was discovered there by the Gestapo.

[Page 137]

It was a cloudy winter morning, when the Ghetto paid with the lives of exactly 50 Jews. The blood bath was organized by the Gestapo to eliminate any happiness about their defeat. The Hitlerites only partially accomplished their goal. The mood in the Ghetto was really very low due to the murdered victims, but this atmosphere of grief couldn't completely erase the Jews' elevated feelings of happiness and revenge.

In the history of the Kovno Ghetto, this Action comes under the name "The Stalingrad Action."

CHAPTER XX

Important Events in the Ghetto in the Spring and Summer of 1943

-The project of relocating some 4-5 thousand Jews from the Vilna region to the Kovno Ghetto-Also bringing some 800 Jews who worked in the Zhezhmer area to the Kovno Ghetto-The Gestapo accusation that the Ghetto Jews were sending "signals" to Soviet aircraft-Vague rumors about the Warsaw Ghetto uprising-Attempts by the first Jews in the Ghetto to join the partisans in the forest

[Page 138]

With the arrival of Spring 1943, the signs became clearer, from one week to the next, that the Ghetto was heading for an indomitable crisis. The reason for this upcoming crisis, first lay in the situation of the war operations on the Eastern Front. It was becoming clearer that the Red Army was overpowering and forcing the Germans to retreat from the occupied Soviet areas. Because of this, the Nazis became even more irritated than when they were certain of their victory. This nervousness of the Hitlerites in this regard, was felt in their relations with the clusters of still-existing ghettos.

For some specific reasons, the Kovno Ghetto colony had a longer, comparatively peaceful break, when no significant events took place. At that time, the Kovno Ghetto Jews started to strongly feel changes for the worse. Moreover, the Jews in the Ghetto actually felt that the problems were "closer, rather than, further." But the degree of uncertainty about when, and mainly how the ball of thread will unwind itself, kept them from enjoying the worsening of the German campaign on the fronts. This situation forced the ghetto Jews to keep their eyes open for everything happening around them.

In the beginning of March 1943, the occupation regime from the Vilna region decided to liquidate the remaining smaller ghetto colonies in Oshmene, Smargon, Olshan, Kreve, Varnian, Michalishok, Svir, etc. In these points around Vilna there still were approximately 5,000 Jews. These steps by the regime were based on its plan to slowly clean out the few surviving Jews from the Eastern areas. What was the connection between the Jews from these smaller ghettos around Vilna? We must say that they were viewed with an evil eye by the regime, because these ghetto colonies were close to the partisan nests in the forests between Vilna and Minsk. An apparent movement to leave the Ghetto to go to the Partisans, was already noticeable.

As we know, at the end of 1941, the area above White Russia was transferred to the general region of Lithuania. By that time, the extermination of the Jews in the provinces had already ended, and in White Russia they just started the systematic extermination Actions on a wide scale. The remnants of the Ghettos remained in existence thanks to the accident by which they became incorporated within the borders of Lithuania.

At first, the Kovno City Commissar and boss over the Ghetto agreed to allow the Jews of the Vilna region to be brought into the Kovno Ghetto. The Vilna Ghetto, at that time, was already standing on the eve of liquidation, so there was no discussion about transporting the Jews from the Vilna Ghetto.

The Elder's Council of the Kovno Ghetto, on their part, had already anticipated a plan of how to bring these Jews into the Ghetto, and set them up with a roof over their heads. But, at the last minute, the Kovno Gestapo did not allow these Jews to be brought into the Kovno Ghetto, even if it could take responsibility for them, because "they are all partisans…"

[Page 140]

The issue ended fatally for these Jews. In the beginning of April 1943, the local regime organization reported to the Jews that they are transporting them over to the Kovno Ghetto. At first the Jews believed it and let themselves be transported. Enroute, they saw that their train was really being brought to the Ponar station. A horrible panic broke out among the Jews, and they started tearing up the closed wagons in which they were being transported, trying to run away. The accompanying guards immediately opened fire on the Jews with machine guns. Many Jews put up resistance against the murderers and killed a few of them. As a result of this fight, a few dozen Jews succeeded in disappearing, but all the others were shot in Ponar.

The horrible fact that the Jews from the Vilna area were killed, completely frustrated the illusion for the majority of Kovno Ghetto Jews, that the time of mass-murders was already over and there would be no more such killings of Jews. On the contrary, it was obvious to see that the infuriated evil Hitlerite animal had not completely given up its original program of total eradication of the Jews who found themselves in their grasp. And if Jews had reason to be pessimistic, unfortunately, it was quickly confirmed.

Between us, a bigger group of Jews from the aforementioned ghetto colonies from the Vilna neighborhood were employed in the construction of the Vilna-Kovno highway. In May 1942 approximately 600 skilled men and women from the Ghettos in Oshmene, Smargon, Olshan, Keve, etc. were brought to Zheshmer[a] during the construction of the highway. These Jews worked at "O.T.," i.e. Organization Todt."[b] A second group of Jews worked on the same highway not far from Yavieh, near Vilna.

In Zheshmer, the Jews were quartered in a former Beit Midrash [house of study], and in a movie house. In these same buildings, in unsanitary conditions, were held Soviet prisoners of war before the arrival of the Jews. Therefore, right after the Jews' arrival, an epidemic broke out from which many people died, among them also the Jewish leader of the camp, Reuven Segalovich, from Olshan.

[Page 141]

The Jews lived together fairly well with the people from the "O.T." So, for example, each week a car would travel from Zheshmer to bring food products for the Jewish camp from their homes near Vilna. Together with food, relatives of the Jewish workers would also join and stay to work in Zheshemer.

On the eve of Spring, 1943, when they were about to liquidate the Ghettos around Vilna, there were another 700 Jews, among them many small children, who were brought to Zheshemer. In the Zheshmer camp in total, there were about 11-12 hundred Jewish souls.

In the summer of 1943, the work of constructing the highway ended. About 300 Jews from "O.T." were brought to another workplace. It was unknown at first what they would do with the remaining Jews. However, the danger was understood- they would be killed because they were "unnecessary" Jews.

The Kovno Elders Council, which was previously in contact with the Jews in Zheshmer, started to use their connections with Herman, from the German Work Office in the Ghetto. They wanted him to arrange permits through the City Commissar for these Jews to be transferred to the Kovno Ghetto. The City Commissar had to officially state that they were needed as a work force for important workplaces.

Finally, the regime divisions agreed that the skilled Jewish workers be allowed into the Ghetto. The person from the German Work Office was not trustworthy to choose the suitable people, therefore, a few higher Jewish Ghetto officials went together with him. With the people from the German Work Office, they were successful in silently transporting into the Ghetto not only the skilled workers, but all the Jews from the Zheshmer camp. About 800 Jewish men, women and children were brought into the Kovno Ghetto in June 1943, and, in this way, they saved them from certain death.

[Page 142]

In the beginning, the "Zheshmer Jews," as they were called, were very warmly received in the Kovno Ghetto. According to their various means, they were willing to help them with whatever was possible. Unfortunately, we must establish that later the Jewish Ghetto Administration was not always objective toward these Jews. Looking at them as "inferior" Jews, they would, for example, plug them into all the slots when they needed people for difficult work positions outside the Kovno Ghetto.

The largest portion of these Jews were taken to Estonia during the Relocation Action, which took place on the 26th of October 1943.

In the Spring of 1943, the Soviet air war visited Kovno from time to time, and bombed the city a few times. Needless to say, the Jews got great enjoyment from the bombing and saw this as the start of their salvation.

The Kovno Gestapo circles were not unfamiliar with the attitude of the Jews to the Soviet bombardment. To keep the Ghetto in a permanent irritated mood, the Gestapo blamed the Ghetto for signaling to the Soviet airmen during the time of the air attack.

In addition, at that time, the entire issue became more intense due to the following events:

Among the German labor positions, where ghetto Jews were then working, there was also a Jewish work brigade near a large munitions camp, which was located at the 5th Fort, near the Kovno suburb, Panemun.

To get arms for the youth who were preparing themselves to go out of the Ghetto into the woods to the partisans, the leftist circles in the Ghetto sent a few of their members to this very brigade. They would find suitable opportunities at work to steal arms parts and afterwards smuggle them into the Ghetto when they returned from work.

[Page 143]

One day in March 1943, at the Ghetto Gate, the checkpoint where all Jews were checked before going in or out of the Ghetto, one young Jewish man, by the name of R. Berman, was detained from the aforementioned brigade, as he was smuggling a small rocket part into the Ghetto. The young man was arrested, of course, and was immediately taken to the Gestapo.

Because of Liptzer, who had high connections in the Kovno Gestapo, and who, by the way, also wanted to maintain good relations with the leftists in the Ghetto, he did everything he could to free Berman.

After a few weeks, Berman was actually freed, but the Gestapo already had another "argument" to strengthen its provocative charge - that the Ghetto was "signaling" to the Soviet fliers.

This issue, which went on for a few weeks, caused the Ghetto plenty of anxiety, because there was a suspicion that the Gestapo was looking for a "reason" to conduct an Action. The situation in the Ghetto became particularly strenuous just during the week of Passover. It gave the impression that the Gestapo was doing everything purposely to put augmented strain on the Ghetto during Passover time so that the Jews should have a disturbed "holiday."

Finally, the Elders Council succeeded in washing the Ghetto clean of this Gestapo provocation after long arguments and answers.

Although the Ghetto was strongly isolated from the outside world, news arrived about the uprising and liquidation of the Warsaw Ghetto. Additional details about the uprising were not known in the Ghetto. They only knew that at the liquidation of the Warsaw Ghetto, the Jews set up an armed uprising and the Germans had to bring in special tanks, artillery, and even airplanes against the Jews.

[Page 144]

To get credible news about the issue, the Elders Council tried to connect with contacts in the Vilna Ghetto, which was geographically located closer to the Warsaw Ghetto and were able to get more news than in the Kovno Ghetto. They also tried to reach Christians in the city. Individually they were only successful in reaching a Christian who had travelled through Warsaw just during the days of the revolt and heard the cannon fire of the fighters and saw how the Ghetto was burning in flames.

The more settled ghetto Jews took the news about the uprising in the Warsaw Ghetto with a strong tense feeling. However, the news about the revolt made a strong impression on the active youth and stimulated them to quickly search for resources and strategies to stand up among other fighters against the Hitlerites. Just then, certain social circles took on greater importance in the life of the Ghetto and called for groups of youths to get organized and go out of the Ghetto into the forest to hook up with the Partisans. After a while, from the fright in the Ghetto, an entire movement started to take on an unexpected role in ghetto life.

The news about the revolt and liquidation of the Warsaw Ghetto strongly shook up the Ghetto population and forced every ghetto Jew to think even more about their future fate.

As is known, the strategic situation on the German-Soviet Front later in the Summer of 1943 became even more catastrophic for the Germans. Despite all that, the Soviet victories strongly contributed to the growth of greater partisan forces behind the enemy lines, which undid German contacts both in people, and in war materials.

At that time, in the Kovno region there was no partisan activity for two fundamental reasons: firstly, Kovno was very far from the front lines, and secondly, the Lithuanians, almost as a rule, were hostile to the partisan movement. The closest partisan nest in the forests around Vilna were approximately 50 kilometers distance from the Ghetto.

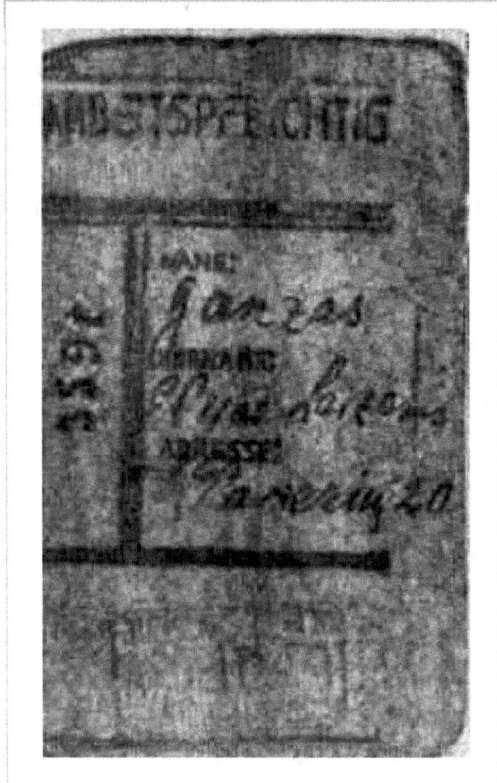

Jews at slave labor under the Nazi government
Top left: A work duty card from the Kovno Ghetto

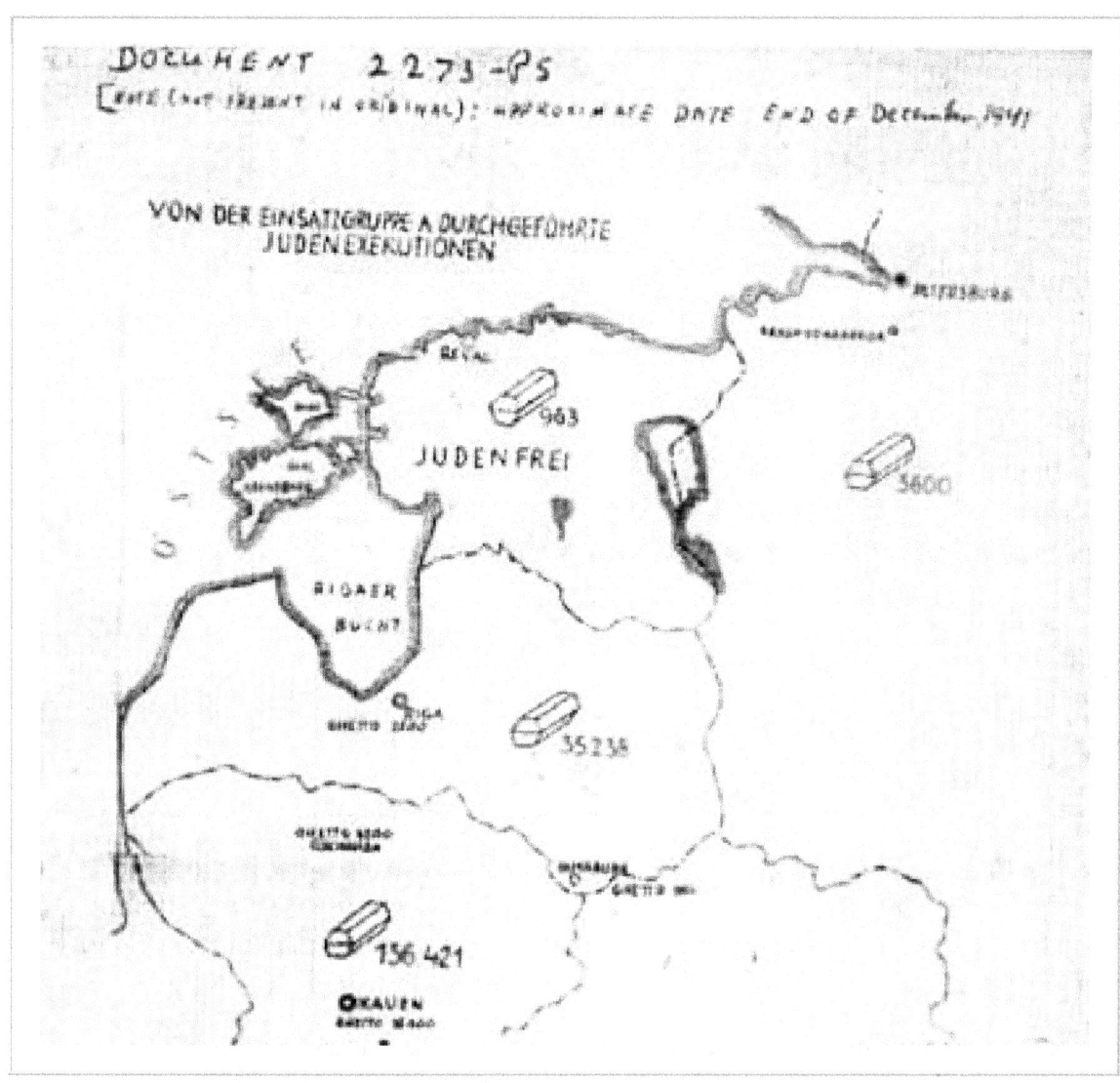

Map of the massacres of Jews, conducted by the Gestapo and its accomplices, at the end of December 1941 in Lithuania (excluding Vilna and region) as 136,421 Jews were already murdered. The only ghetto settlements that remained were in Kovno (16,000 people) and Shavl (4,500).

The 9th Fort, where the majority of the Kovno Jews were killed

[Page 145]

Therefore, there was no objective possibility that larger groups of Jews from the Kovno Ghetto would be able to link themselves to the partisan movement. However, the drive of the ghetto youth to get out to the Partisans was growing, in parallel to the Soviet victories and to the German defeats.

At that time, the first concrete steps were actually taken so that groups of youths could get out to the Partisans in the forest.

The initiative to organize the partisan movement came from the leadership of the left-leaning elements in the Ghetto, at the head of which was a Kovno young Jewish writer, Haim Yellin.[c]

Not only in the Ghetto, but even in the city of Kovno itself, the underground leftist movement at that time was very weak. But that movement started to revive itself and displayed signs of greater activity.

The contact between the left-leaning elements in the city and the Ghetto didn't take long to set up. Therefore, the various groups of youth, who were ready to leave for the partisans in the forest had to do it without informed help or instructions from outside the Ghetto.

A few dozen youth decided to go out of the Ghetto in various groups, and set out for the forests around Vilna, to find partisans. But the situation was such that it wasn't possible in any way to protect the route from these "spies," and it wasn't known where one could find the partisans. But these youth were determined not to remain in the Ghetto, and they got themselves out in various ways – by smuggling themselves out through the Ghetto Fence, or by running away from the workplace in the city – abandoned out on the road.

The result of this first attempt to escape to the partisans was very tragic. Almost all those who left the Ghetto were arrested on the way by the Lithuanian Police, who delivered the Jews to the Gestapo.

[Page 146]

Not knowing the fate of the first group, a few other groups of people went out and fell into the hands of the Gestapo. When it first became known that this is not the right way, no more people from the Ghetto were allowed to go this route in this manner. They started searching for safer ways and means to get through to the partisans.

But not only the left-leaning elements had the urge to go out to the forest. Also, many young people from the other social groups were ready to put themselves in line for armed resistance against the Nazis. Thereafter, a more developed idea arose in the Ghetto - to create a secret committee of representatives of the various social streams, like the Communists, Zionists, etc. Thus, the partisan topic could be planned on a broader plane, according to safer possibilities than before.

At this opportunity, it is important to add that at the beginning of Spring 1943, a certain Christian woman from Poland, Irena, had a secret meeting in the Kovno Ghetto. Irena, a middle-aged woman, who as a student, got close to Jewish life, and had a great interest in Zionism, especially for "Hashomer Hatzair- [the Young guard]". During the Nazi years she was mainly devoted to establishing contact with the Jewish Ghetto settlement in Poland.

She came to Kovno from the Vilna Ghetto. The Vilna PPA (United Partisan Organization) had her assigned to reach the Kovno Ghetto and do what she could to connect the Ghetto defense to the partisan movement. Through her, they learned that the Ghettos in Warsaw and Bialystock were getting arms and preparing themselves to have a revolt against the Nazi murderers. The Vilna Ghetto was going the same way.

She was in the Kovno Ghetto for a few days and managed to hold secret consultations with "Matzok"[d] and with a few leading people from the social groups. She strongly promoted the idea that the only way is for the youth to tear itself out of the Ghetto and get out to the forest to the partisans.

Her visit indeed contributed to the fact that the partisan movement in the Ghetto soon took on actual and realistic expression.[e]

Original footnotes:

a. A small town on the road between Vilna and Kovno
b. As we know, Todt was a famous German engineer who, when he was Minister of Armaments in the Third Reich, conducted large military construction works.
c. For more about him – see "Arrest of the Jewish Partisan leader Haim Yellin."
d. See "Zionist activity in the Ghetto."
e. More about this in the later chapters

CHAPTER XXI

Preparations to Turn the Ghetto into a Series of Separate Labor Camps

-Conflict between the S.A.[a] and S.S.[b] concerning the management of the Ghetto- S.S. - the new ghetto "owners"- The first steps of dividing up the Ghetto into separate labor camp.- How they recruited for the first small labor camps in the provinces- Founding a Jewish authority to select the people for the camps (the "Kazernirungs Commission")

[Page 148]

In the Summer of 1943, the Ghetto went through a very strained atmosphere. They received tragic messages from the Ghettos in Vilna and Riga, where the occupying regime energetically conducted the liquidation of the Ghettos. They transported most of those Jews to specially established labor camps. This news robbed the Kovno Ghetto Jews of the bit of, so-called, tranquility which they had until then.

Over the past months, the Jews in the Kovno Ghetto lived in conditions that were relatively more favorable than the Jews in Vilna and Riga. After a while, those Ghettos took the remaining surviving Jews out and transferred them to labor camps. Since almost all the Kovno Jews still lived in the Ghetto, their situation was privileged by comparison to their brothers in Vilna and Riga. But this short tranquil pause ended for the ghetto Jews in Kovno, and the sky above the Kovno Ghetto was slowly starting to be covered with thick clouds.

[Page 149]

Changes for the worse began for the Ghetto with a conflict between the old bosses of the Ghetto, the representatives of the German civil management, headed by the Kovno City Commissar, S.A. Brigade Fuhrer, Hans Kramer, on one side, and on the other side, the representatives of the S.S., the new pretenders over the opinion makers of the Ghetto settlement.

The German strategic situation on the Eastern Front changed after the catastrophic defeat near Stalingrad. Thus, the possibility of a future retreat from the occupied Soviet areas, among other reasons, forced the "Jewish desk" in the Nazi party to prepare proper preconditions for the liquidation of the remaining surviving Jews in the few Ghettos of "Estonia." For this purpose, the Ghettos first had to be quickly converted into labor and concentration camps for all those Jews still alive to date.

The Nazi experts on the Jewish question knew very well that transporting the Ghettos to separate labor camps, with extremely strict regimes, would give them easier entry to conduct their plan designed to exterminate the remaining Jews in the occupied eastern areas. In the high Nazi spheres, it turns out, they believed that the extreme S.S. men were more suitable to conduct this operation, than the "moderate" S. A. people.

The old bosses of the Ghetto, the S.A. people, gained great material advantage from the Ghetto. Therefore, for this S.A. clique, losing power over the Ghetto meant losing a source of bribery, theft, and various other schemes, which they had in quantity, thanks to the Ghetto. Because of this, they did not want to give up their positions so easily. In addition to the many tangible reasons, it also gave them the possibility of sitting in the quiet hinterland and not have to go to the Front. Therefore, a miserable struggle developed, which reached as high as the Central Party sphere in Berlin, over the question of management of the Ghetto. After a long stubborn fight, the S.S. finally came out victorious, and the Kovno S.A. people had to take leave of their warm benches.

Truth be told, during this dramatic struggle between the two blood brothers from the brown-executioner-family, the Jews were interested in having the former ones remain, as this had already translated into Jewish blood. They preferred falling under the tail of the S.A. people, rather than the evil and strict S.S. men, from whom new and heavy decrees were awaited. Unfortunately, it didn't turn out the way the Jews wanted.

In the beginning of September 1943, a tall S.S. functionary, S.S. Major, Wilhem Goecke, appeared in the Ghetto and hastily took over the administration of the Ghetto from the City Commissariat. With his appearance in the Ghetto, the new ghetto boss created great confusion among the Jews. In a sense, the Jews felt that with his arrival in the Kovno Ghetto the "seven good years" were over and the Ghetto was stepping into a difficult period.

In the Ghetto they received news that Goecke was the executioner of Jews at a large massacre and the "high echelons" gave him a proxy to act according to his own vision. Thus, the Jews interpreted his arrival in the Kovno Ghetto as a sign that the Ghetto is on the eve of liquidation.

Additionally, at the start of September of this year, the liquidation of the Vilna Ghetto took place. The largest portion of Jews were taken to Estonia for forced labor in the local camps. The older, weaker, adults and children were exterminated in Ponar, and the remaining few thousand Jews were resettled in a few labor camps near Vilna. The atmosphere in the Kovno Ghetto clearly became tense.

From his external physiognomy, Goecke immediately commanded fear in the ghetto Jews. He was a real tall Prussian-type, with wide shoulders, always in military style, a stretched-out body, a sad head, and a pair of deep penetrating eyes. Moreover, he started taking the management of the Ghetto into his own hands.

[Page 151]

Seeing a refined Jew-killer with a large amount of "singular-Nazi intelligence," it turns out that Goecke decided that this time he would achieve his goals regarding the Ghetto "through the gentle path," which meant that before all else, he would establish a certain trust between himself and the Jews. He started on this path by enlarging the food distribution for the Ghetto. The former ghetto boss, the City Commissar, would simply steal the meager food-allotments for himself, despite its being designated for the Jews. He might also throw in a hundred grams of bread a day per person for the Jewish population, and from time to time some rotten potatoes. But, Goecke ordered not only the established food distribution for the Jews, but he also cozied up to the Jews, so to speak, not to offend. And he even designated additional distributions of food products for the hard-working population.

Aside from the enlargement of the official distributions, he also didn't bother the Jews when they brought food products into the Ghetto, which they would buy illegally in the city during their work time. Superficially, at the start he gave the impression that the new bosses of the Ghetto are not worse than the old ones, but, on the contrary, in certain details, for example, individual distributions, they were even better than the others. But very quickly Goecke started to betray himself through his new steps regarding the Ghetto.

He quickly started moving ahead to prepare the conditions to transform the Ghetto into a concentration camp. During the relocation of the largest portion of ghetto Jews to special Jewish labor camps, Goecke started his plan. He first renovated a large military building near the Kovno Aerodrome. This building was formerly a camp for Soviet prisoners of war. He ordered the Jewish Work Office to conduct the renovation of this building, as soon as possible. Although the ghetto Jews supposed that the newly renovated camp would be for them, there was no confirmation about this from the Ghetto Commandant.

[Page 152]

Secondly, before his arrival, the situation in the Ghetto was that over 5000 Jews worked together with Christian workers in about 200 city workplaces spread-out over-all corners of the city. This was excluding the Aerodrome where about 500 Jews worked. According to Goecke's plan, quick steps were taken to liquidate the distribution of Jewish workplaces and at the same time establish 5-6 large workplaces for Jews in the Kovno suburbs. During the establishment of the work positions and labor camps for Jews, Goecke hoped to achieve the following goals:

a. the Ghetto with its compact load of about 16,000 souls would be divided up over a few labor camps, each one separated from the other.
b. Jews being taken out of jobs where they worked together with non- Jews, removed the opportunity for the Jews to meet Christians – a factor which took on terrible significance for the Jews.
c. having the labor camp near the work site itself, avoids having to transport the Jews from the Ghetto to the city to work and return, and…
d. …this is the main thing! At the appropriate moment, when the time came to liquidate the remaining Jews, it would be much easier to achieve, because the Jews would find themselves in small, isolated work camps under a strong regime, rather than a larger number of Jews concentrated in a ghetto, where Jews had comparatively much more freedom of movement than in a labor camp.

According to Goecke's order, from day to day they closed more and more labor brigades in the city. The Jewish workers from the liquidated brigade would automatically be transported to the workplace especially established for Jews near the military commissary organizations[c] in the Kovno suburb of Shantz.

In addition to everything, these phenomena had a negative economic impact on the ghetto Jews. While working in a smaller workplace together with Christians, Jews had opportunities to exchange their last bit of clothes for food products. By forcing the Jews to work only in an environment of Jews, with no contact with non-Jews, it took away their opportunity to subsist. Therefore, the economic situation in the Ghetto started to sink very rapidly, and the largest portion of Jews started living worse than before.

[Page 153]

In the time approaching the summer of 1943, before the Ghetto was transferred to the authority of S.S. Major, Goecke, the ghetto population was recruited to three Jewish work camps in the Lithuanian provinces: 1) in Keidan – near the construction of that Aerodrome, with about 500 Jews, 2) In Palemun – in brick and peat-work, with about 300 Jews, and 3) in Kashedar – in peat and forest work, with about 300 Jews.

The recruitment for these labor camps was conducted by the authority of the Elders Council in the following way: every time it was necessary to recruit a specific number of Jews for the designated labor camp, lists of suitable candidates were put together for the camp. The following criteria were formally used during the assembly of these lists: first, single young men and women; second, families without little children, and third, it was commanded that only physically healthy and skilled people be considered to send to the camp.

The Jewish ghetto leaders weren't too meticulous about following the previously mentioned, straightforward guidelines. In ghetto life there was no shortage of connections and immoral phenomena, like corruption, influence, etc. So, we must truthfully say that, in fact, the lists were mainly made up of those who were standing on a lower rung of the social ladder in the Ghetto. These helpless and unprotected folk were the same obligated resource for the forced relocation to the labor camps.

To make people available for a possible earlier establishment of the labor camp, the lists would always be marked with a much larger number of people than was necessary for the camp.

[Page 154]

Practically, the recruitment for the labor camp would take place like this: a few days before the deadline to send the Jews off to the camp, the noted persons would be detained, unexpectedly, mainly at night by the Jewish Ghetto Police. They would be held in the Ghetto Jail, until being transported to the camp. During these days and nights, the Ghetto would experience huge strain and upset. Those not yet detained dreaded that they would be detained, and the already detained would, through their friends and acquaintances who were free, apply various lobbying attempts to free themselves.

During recruitment time, many young and skilled single persons who were then the most suitable candidates for the labor camp, took pains to hide themselves somewhere in a hideout, so as not be found in their homes when they came to look for them. They would manage to do this until the transport to the labor camp would already leave and it was clear that the danger of being sent away to a camp was finally over - this time.

Just before the departure of the human transport to the camp, higher officials from the Elders Councils together with a Jewish medical commission, would come into the Ghetto Jail and finally decide who must go to the camp. In these closing hours, the area in and around the Ghetto Jail would buzz like a beehive. Those who would even have the slightest chance not to go, would try to use it during these same last minutes.

The climax of these painful and tragic ghetto events would heighten in that moment when they would begin transporting the people from the Ghetto Jail to the camp. A special convoy of Germans, Lithuanian partisans or Ukrainian Vlasovites [Soviet deserters] would come to pick up the Jews. Friends and acquaintances of the Jews selected to go to the camp came together around the two Ghetto Jails, where they held the collected people, and with wailing, like at a funeral, they escorted their dear ones. Horrible scenes would play out at the departure of the people. Cries, screams, hysterical episodes from women, etc., all mixed together and created a shivering picture of Jewish "life" in the Ghetto.

After the departure of the Jews for the labor camp, for a certain time there was a feeling of mourning in the Ghetto because of the departure of the people. But the arrival of more evil decrees and problems pushed aside the prior happenings. The Ghetto would "live" with the new evils and afflictions. And it continued like this without an end.

[Page 155]

When Goecke took over the leadership of the Ghetto, it became clear to the entire ghetto population that his aim would be to transfer the entire Ghetto to the labor camps in stages. So, to regulate such a painful process to ghetto life, the top representative from the ghetto collective, the Elders Council, established a Kazernirungs Commission[d] which dealt with all the issues about transferring Jews from the Ghetto to the labor camps. Those active In the Kazernirungs Commission were Police Chief Moshe Levin, Dr. Valsonok, Engineer Ratger, David Ratner[e] N. Markovski (liberated in Dachau), P. Margolis.[f]

The Kazernirungs Commission quickly got into its work. An entire "staff" of workers was set up under its authority. The work of the Commission took place through the day and night. First, the Kazernirungs Commission drew up a plan how to divide the entire ghetto population. Depending on family condition, workplace, work skills, age, profession, etc., special categories were established to orient them to which work camp this or that Jew would eventually be quartered.

Aside from the people selected by the Elders Council, the Kazernirungs Commission also dealt with the representatives of the illegal social groupings in the Ghetto, like from the Communist, Revisionist, and Zionist streams. The task of the members of the Kazernirungs Commission was to defend the interests of their people regarding the quartering.

Since that time, the importance of the socially active elements continued growing, mainly because of their activity regarding the departure from the Ghetto to the partisans in the forest. The Kazernirungs Commission strongly considered their wishes and desires.

[page 156]

Aside from the ghetto Jews who had some loyalty to the social streams, at the first quarterings they were protective of those partisans who had good relations with the leading functionaries of the Jewish ghetto organization. Therefore, during the recruitment for the labor camps, the above-mentioned regular Jews, who built most of the buildings for most of the ghetto population, became exposed to the discretion of the Kazernirungs Commission.

True, the ghetto Jew formally could complain to the Elders Council against the decisions of the Kazernirungs Commission. Truth be told, such complaints would rarely ever be taken into consideration. The Jew who was designated for a labor camp had to fulfill the orders of the Kazernirungs Commission, willingly or unwillingly.

The first real assignment of the Kazernirungs Commission, under orders from Goecke, was the quick preparation of a list of 3000 ghetto Jews, to establish a Jewish labor camp for peat and forest labor in Ezheretshai.[g]

Original footnotes:

- a. S. A. Shturmabteilung = Assault Division
- b. S.S. Schutzstaffel = Protection Squads
- c. H.V.M. -Heeresverpflegungsmagazin=Army catering magazine, and H.B.A.-Heeresbekleidungsamt= Army Clothing Office.
- d. In the Kovno Ghetto, the transfer of Jews from the Ghetto to special Jewish work camps was called "Kazernirn" from the German word "Kazerneh"-Kazarmeh, which means quartering the Jews in Kazarmes or barracks at the labor places. The authority which had to do with these issues, was called: "Kazernirungs Commission".
- e. About all of these see "Persons who were involved with the Partisan-movement."
- f. See "Labor Office"
- g. A village settlement near the town Sapitshishok, about 40 km from Kovno.

CHAPTER XXII

Relocation Action to Estonia

- Preparations for recruiting 3000 Jews for the labor camp in Ezsheretshai. [now: Ezerelis]- The mood in the Ghetto on the eve of the relocation- The arrest of the Jewish "wood-brigade."- The first day of the Relocation Action- The situation in the Ghetto when they began catching Jews- The fate of the people who were taken out- The day after the events of October 26th

[Page 157]

As we saw in the previous chapter, the Ghetto Commander, Goecke, ordered the Elders Council to prepare a list of 3000 Jews for a new labor camp in Ezsheretshai, near Kovno. The Kazernirungs Commission, together with the Elders Council, worked at "full speed," to finish the list of suitable candidates for Ezsheretshai as fast as possible. That was in the middle of October 1943.

The Elders Council trusted Goecke's explanations that the 3000 ghetto Jews were really needed for Ezsheretshai. The Elders Council then made all the preparations for the Jewish labor camp to be set up on a proper basis. For that purpose, in Ezsheretshai, they planned to prepare associates from the various ghetto institutions of, for example, the Labor Office, Social Office, etc., just like in the Ghetto. This would establish a Jewish structure which would serve the camp population.

The recruitment of people for Ezsheretshai was not a secret for the ghetto Jews. Unlike the prior recruitment for labor camps, when they viewed it as a misfortune, now many Jews did not take it as tragically. Some Jews in the Ghetto knew that, first, they would sooner or later fall into a labor camp anyway, and second, the camp in Ezsheretshai was not worse than the other labor camps.

Both the efforts of the Elders Council to set up a bit of order, as well as the "assurance" of Goecke to establish living conditions at the peat forest work in Ezsheretshai that were not any worse than in the Ghetto itself, significantly neutralized the fear of becoming destined for the new labor camp.

True, some ghetto Jews wanted to remain in the Ghetto, rather than go to Ezsheretshai. But, as mentioned, it was not considered a great tragedy.

Regarding the Ezsheretshai issue, it didn't even enter their mind to disregard such a tragic demand.

The atmosphere in the Ghetto became quite strained like always before such happenings. It was as if the ghetto Jews intuitively felt that a great danger was approaching them, when it became clear that in the coming days, they had to prepare themselves for the recruitment to the new camp.

To finally convince themselves of the truth of the explanation from the Ghetto Commandant, that the Jews will be relocated to Ezsheretshai and not anywhere else, Dr. Elkes once again spoke to Goecke. Goecke conveyed "assurance" that it is only about going to the Ezsheretshai camp.

Finally, Goecke communicated to Dr. Elkes, that the departure of the people to the new camp would take place on the 26th of October.

On the afternoon of Tuesday, the 25th of October, as they were loading wood not far from the train line, Jewish workers from the "wood-brigade" who worked in Alexot[a] noticed that there were many wagons with barbed-wire windows standing at the station. When the Jews tried to find out for whom these wagons were waiting, they received an elusive answer.

[Page 159]

Although the Jews from the wood brigade never suspected anything evil, a few hours before finishing work and going back to the Ghetto they saw Gestapo men come and order them to end their work and climb into the trucks which they brought with them. From the beginning the Jews thought that it was about an inspection by the Gestapo of the illegally purchased food products. But there was no inspection. The Jews couldn't figure out what was happening here. They saw that the Gestapo people were taking them in the direction of the 9th Fort, from where no one returns. Thus, as they drove by the Ghetto, the people cried and screamed to the ghetto Jews that they are taking them to the Fort. Even in the Ghetto, no one knew what happened to the people from the "wood-brigade."

During the night between the 25th to the 26th of October, after a stop at the Fort, the petrified Jews were all returned to the Ghetto in the morning, where, as we would later see, the collection of the people had already taken place.

Thereafter, it became clear that the Gestapo took the workers from the "wood brigade" to the Fort, because they feared that the Jews who noticed the prepared wagons, would tell what they saw upon their return to the Ghetto. In this way, however, the ghetto Jews would not have any suspicion that the wagons were possibly prepared and designated for them.

The Gestapo preparations for the next day didn't remain totally secret in the Ghetto. The Jewish brigade workers from the labor brigade, H.K.P.[b] as well as those from the "Power Office", Kauen[c] came back from work Tuesday evening and brought the confidential news that through the aforementioned German service positions, the Gestapo ordered a larger number of trucks for the next morning. This gave them serious cause to be suspicious that on the next morning, a day of only painful and difficult experiences would begin for the Ghetto.

[Page 160]

A few Jews had already prepared a hiding place to disappear until the rage would pass, but almost the entire population helplessly allowed themselves to be carried along with the flow of their fate. During the night, many ghetto Jews prepared a backpack for every adult family member with the most necessary items, in preparation for any eventuality.

Once again it was a night of sadly famous sleeplessness in the Ghetto, when no one was sure if he would still be in the Ghetto the following night, or if he would be dragged somewhere to be killed. In the early morning, the familiar strengthening of the guard around the Ghetto Fence was clearer proof that nothing good would happen in the Ghetto.

In the early morning of Wednesday, the 26th of October, all the ghetto Jews were already awake and prepared for a difficult experience-filled day. Very early a published order from the Elders Council announced to the ghetto population that the Elders Council received an order from the regime to collect 3000 Jews for work in Ezhereshtai. In the decree, it was unknown that there were lists of Jews chosen to go to the new camp- already prepared. The Elders Council called on the ghetto population to carry out the instructions exactly. The Ghetto Police would be coming into the homes to take the relevant people designated to go to Ezhereshtai. At the end, the Elders Council said some comforting words to those Jews who came out to go to the camp, wishing them luck in their new "home."

They didn't allow the Jewish city workers out to work that day. In the early morning hours, groups of Jews were already congregated near the houses and, with great nervousness, awaited the upcoming events.

At around 7-8 am, a strong guard force of German police, Gestapo, and civilian dressed Lithuanians from the Lithuanian Security Police, started to enter. The Jewish Ghetto Police with the prepared lists of persons designated for Ezhereshtai, went around through the ghetto homes collecting and escorting the designated persons.

[Page 161]

Many people who were expected to be on the lists were at first found at home because of the following reasons: first, no one knew if he was or wasn't on the list; second, the preparedness for escape by the majority of the ghetto Jews was paralyzed, as they believed what was previously said - that they were really going to Ezhereshtai, a place near Kovno. And third, at that time, the total number of hiding places in the Ghetto was very low and Jews simply did not have a place to hide.

When entering a house to take people away to the camp, they would allow them to pack up only the most necessary items, which they would transport to the assembly point near the Ghetto Gate, on Varniu Street.

By lunch time, many ghetto Jews started doubting whether the assembled persons were really going to Ezsheretshai. There was the assumption that from the Ghetto the transports were not going to the Nieman port where they should have gone in the case of travel to Ezsheretshai, but rather the people were being transported to the Aerodrome.

From hour to hour the atmosphere in the Ghetto took on a more panicked character and each one tried to hide wherever possible, to avoid falling in among those collected according to the prepared lists. Therefore, the process was slowed down.

The Kazernirungs Commission received news from the Jewish Ghetto Police that they were almost at the end of the prepared lists but were still missing many people, because many were hiding. So, with great speed, they started creating new lists, not keeping within any guidelines, so long as they fulfilled the demand of the regime to recruit the needed number of Jews. But even these quickly-put-together lists did not help much because the people became more difficult from hour to hour.

The Gestapo, which conducted the Action, still waited for such an opportunity to carry out their piece of "work."

[Page 162]

At around 2-3 o'clock in the morning, the Gestapo, together with staff of the Ghetto Commandant, Goecke, saw that about 1000 were missing. At that time, they let a large gang of sworn-in Vlasovites [Russian turncoats] into the Ghetto, who were hiding somewhere in the neighborhoods of the Ghetto since the morning. They were given a command to encircle the large block houses, where hundreds of Jews lived and, without selecting, chased all the Jews out to the street.

With the wild murderous enjoyment of pogromists, the Vlasovites tore into the Jewish homes and let loose with their loaded rifles, guns, and hooligan curse-words. They threw themselves on men, women, and children, healthy and sick, young, and old, without exception, and chased them to the assembly point by the Ghetto Gate. There they were packed into trucks which would transport them from the Ghetto.

After chasing the Jews out of the large block of houses, the houses in the neighboring streets were attacked, and from there they also started chasing the Jews to the trucks. The bacchanalia of these wild murderers lasted a few hours. By that time, a horrible panic and pogrom atmosphere ruled the Ghetto. People started hiding themselves wherever they could. They ran like crazy from one corner to another. The screams and wailing were heard from those who were being dragged by the Vlasovites. These murderers also looted the Jewish houses which they attacked.

In this way, approximately 500 men were caught by the Vlasovites in a few hours.

As night fell and the needed total of Jewish victims was collected, the Gestapo camps and Police, together with their "colleagues," the Lithuanians and Vlasovites, slowly started leaving the Ghetto. On the streets of the Ghetto, it took a long time to see any human being. The ghetto Jews waited in deathly fear for what would come next.

[Page 163]

When it became clear that the Action was over, the hidden Jews slowly started to climb out of their holes. The Ghetto looked like a scene after a horrible pogrom. In many houses whole families were missing and a few individual persons were transported out of the Ghetto. In total, there were 2700[d] Jews taken that day.

As was later explained, they brought the Jews from the Ghetto to the Kovno Aerodrome. The S.S. and Gestapo were already waiting for them, and at the head, the infamous leader from the Big Action, Captain, Rauca.

The following "arrangement" ruled at the Aerodrome: as soon as a truck with Jews arrived, the Nazi murderers would encircle the transported Jews and conduct a selection. The children were immediately taken away from their parents; anyone daring to say anything or resist would be beaten murderously. The older and weaker men and women were divided separately.

The younger and healthier men and women were loaded in the nearby cattle wagons, 100 persons in a wagon. The loaded wagons were immediately encircled. The little wagon windows were lined with barbed wire. The crushing and screaming in the packed wagons were tremendous. People were squashed like herring in a barrel. There was no talk about eating or drinking. The Jews even had to unload their human needs in the same wagon.

The entire look of the Aerodrome was reminiscent of the horrible familiar pictures of the extermination Action. The laments and screams of the painfully-torn-apart family members were heartbreaking. It rained down on Jewish heads from all sides by the murderous beatings from the thieving S.S. and Gestapo people.

According to information clarified later, they took the children, older and weaker men and women and transported them to Auschwitz, where they were gassed and burned. The number of victims who were exterminated could not be determined.

[Page 164]

The division between the male and female skilled workers only started late in the evening. The Jews in the wagons saw that they were being transported somewhere. However, they didn't know where they were being taken.

Going over the railroad bridge, where there was a work position for ghetto Jews,[e] the people from the wagons threw out little notes on which they wrote to the Jews in the Ghetto, that they are being taken in an unfamiliar direction. Such notes were also thrown out near Keidan, where there was a Jewish labor camp. While they went through Shavl, the Shavl ghetto Jews who worked not far from the train comforted the Kovno Jews that they are being taken not for extermination but for work in Riga.

It was heard that a few days later the division arrived in Estonia and the Jews were settled in the work camp around Vayvara (near Narva) and around Klooga, where they had already found Jews, dragged out from the Vilna and other ghettos.

The largest portion of the Jews dragged out from Estonia died from the hard punitive labor and from the inhuman living conditions.

In July 1944, when that Soviet summer offensive took place, the Nazis quickly started evacuating the eastern labor camps. After many rounds, about 4000 Jews from the camps around Vayvara were evacuated to the concentration camps in Germany. Because of the fast advance of the Soviet troops, the Hitlerites had not yet managed to evacuate the remaining Jews from the camps around Klooga. In the beginning of August 1944 these Jews were shot and laid out, ready to be burned on the pyres. The murderers hadn't yet managed to burn the victims because the Russian forces reached the site and found the shot Jews there, all prepared for burning on the pyres.

[Page 165]

A few dozen Jews did manage to get out of that mass slaughter and hide out in the Estonian forests. The largest number of them however, died as they fell into the hands of the Nazis, or died of hunger or disease. A few persons managed to overcome all these horrible experiences and were liberated exactly two months later.

Those evacuated toward Germany also shared the same fate as all the other Jews trailing into German concentration camps where survival to liberation was the exception.

As night passed after such a nightmarish day, the next morning the Jews themselves did not go to work in the city. Near the collection point by the Ghetto Gate from where they caught the Jews to send them in the trucks, there was a mountain of bags of Jewish clothes. At first the Jews wanted to take their clothes with them but seeing that they are not being taken to Ezsheretshai, as was discussed, rather to some unfamiliar place, maybe even to be killed, no one even thought of taking clothes with them. Later, these remaining clothes were taken by the Social Office.

The first thing in the morning, each one ran to reach their friends and acquaintances who were transported out the previous day. Those remaining in the Ghetto cried for those transported out and some of the ghetto Jews awaited their own difficult unclear future, with dread. Now everyone was sure that after the liquidation of the Vilna ghetto, the turn to liquidate the Kovno Ghetto would also come. They had the conviction that the future existence of the Ghetto is only a question of a few weeks, or maybe a few days. They only wanted to have a break, if only for a few quiet days, to catch their breath.

The same day, that is, Thursday, the 27th of October, Goecke ordered the Elders Council to clear out the large housing blocks on Varnius street and the little housing blocks on Mildos Street within a few days. The Nazi murderers didn't allow the remaining ghetto Jews to even grieve. Hundreds of families were forced to leave their homes and search for new accommodations somewhere, entirely unexpectedly.

[Page 166]

The picture in and around the large housing blocks looked horrible after the previous Relocation Action. Feathers from torn bedding mixed with broken furniture, household items, and the like were strewn about. Everything together gave witness to the pogrom by the Vlasovites. In addition, everyone was still forced to do the urgent reduction of the district. Jews from these ghetto districts carried necessities on themselves, like housewares and quartered themselves in other areas of the Ghetto. All looked like mourners who had been condemned; tomorrow, or the next day, their turn would come. And the painful gnawing question that didn't stop for even one minute - what next?

In a few days after the Relocation Action to Estonia, Goecke, in a conversation with Dr. Elkes informed him that starting from the 1st of November 1943, the Kovno Ghetto would be converted into a concentration camp[f]. What kind of a fuzzy meaning would this conversion of the Ghetto into a concentration camp have for the ghetto Jews? At that moment, it was not yet entirely clear. In any case it was reason to expect that this meant a change for the worse – not for the better… and, unfortunately, that is exactly what it was.

Learning this, the atmosphere for the ghetto Jews changed. There was no purpose to go to work, because anyway the Ghetto will finally be liquidated. So, Goecke "succeeded" in getting the Jews to calm themselves after the previous events and convince each one that they should go to work punctually, like before. And, if not, he would apply stronger sanctions on the ghetto population.

As a result of the tragic events of the Relocation Action to Estonia, the ghetto Jews came to the following important conclusions:

First, whoever had the smallest chance to leave the Ghetto to go to the partisans in the forest, or to familiar Christians in the city, or in a village, should not wait even one day longer. Now is the last moment to do it; if not, it would be too late.

Second, whoever does not have the opportunity to leave the Ghetto, should quickly start building a "*malina*," that is, a well masked hideout, where they could hide themselves during such horrible days as those of the 26th of October. Their experience showed that those who were hidden in a hideout somewhere during the Relocation Action, remained peacefully in the Ghetto. That is why, from that moment, a feverish construction of "*malinas*" began– a movement in which many ghetto Jews were caught up.

Original footnotes:

- a. A Kovno suburb near the Aerodrome.
- b. H.K.P. Heereskraftfahrpark
- c. The Nazis changed the name Kovno to Kauen.
- d. On the day of the relocation-action they estimated that over 3000 persons were transported. The error was clarified by counting the people at the selection at the Aerodrome.
- e. A division of the German company "Demog."
- f. Formally called: K.L. Kauen.

CHAPTER XXIII

From the Relocation Action to Estonia until the eve of the Action on the Children, the Old, and the Sick

(November 1943-March 1944)

- Movement in the Ghetto to give the children to Christians- Establishment of the first Jewish labor-camp in Alexot- Jewish "life" in the labor-camp.- Founding the second labor camp in Shantz- Clearing of the old ghetto region.- Further recruiting for Jewish labor camps- Legendary escape of the Jewish labor brigade which worked in the 9th Fort burning Jewish corpses- The situation in the Ghetto during the first few months of 1944: a. good news from the front, b. favorable economic situation, c. new obligatory registration, d. less recruiting, e. joining the partisans. f. Jewish fight against informers, g. Intensive building, h. Sending German "Kapos" to the Ghetto, i. Rumors, denials, etc.- More persons involved in connection with the Partisan Movement-Individual and collective contact with private Christians

[Page 168]

The ghetto Jews hadn't yet managed to calm down from the huge blow of the relocation Action when nearly 3000 Jews were transported to Estonia. It was ten days later, when a notice was distributed in the Ghetto that on the 5th of November 1943, an Action on children, elders and the sick took place in the Shavl Ghetto. This action cost the Shavl Ghetto over 800 victims, mainly children up to 12 years old, older people over 55 and, in addition, the sick and disabled. When this became known in the Kovno Ghetto, the Jews became terribly upset, because it was expected that whatever happened in the Shavl Ghetto must, sooner or later, also happen in the Kovno Ghetto.

[Page 169]

Many older and disabled people, who, according to their age or illness, were no longer able to do work duty and who happened to be without a work card, tried to acquire a workplace mainly in the Ghetto Workshops, where the work conditions were not as desirable as in the city workplaces.

It was difficult to figure out what to do with the children. Since they believed that the children who learned a trade in the ghetto trade school were in less danger than children who were at home, the parents started sending their children to the trade school.

Regarding the elderly and sick, there was no way they could help themselves, and they had to wait for the horrible day when the evil Hitlerite animal would come to devour them. The worry about the fate of the little children didn't leave them in peace. So, they started looking for opportunities to transfer children to the city or a village and give them up to Christian families. However, this was an extraordinarily difficult undertaking which ran into countless difficulties.

Before anything else, they had to find such a Christian family which would be prepared to take a Jewish child and, by doing so, risk the lives of all their family members, in case they were discovered by the Gestapo.

Secondly, they had to possess a large sum of money to compensate the Christian family for taking and sustaining the child. Those parents who had no resources managed to create the necessary resources to arrange for the child to stay with the Christians.

Even more important than financial means, was the basic question: where do you find a suitable place to give up the child? And this question was not so simple either.

Too many abuses and tricks took place by individual crooked Christians. These Christians would take money and items from the Jews and right afterward they would try to get out of taking in the child, or a short time later they would send him back to the parents in the Ghetto, saying that the Gestapo was following them, and they could not keep the children any longer in their home. There were cases when children went from the Ghetto to the city and returned three or four times until they found a shelter. There was no shortage of cases of blackmail, pranks, and other pressure ploys from dishonest Christians, for whom the tragedy of the Jewish child was a good opportunity to make "easy business…"

[Page 170]

There were not many Christians who were inspired mainly by humanitarian motives, and who dared take in a Jewish child. A humane understanding of saving Jewish children did show itself in certain persons from the Kovno Catholic clergy, like for example, the very endearing priest Paukshtis, the Jesuit priest Aloiz, the nun, Ana Brokaitite, and others. Some of them did it for purely humanitarian reasons; others did it for missionary motives: converting the Jewish children and raising them like Christians. Whichever, it was, thanks to the Catholic clergy, many children from the Ghetto were saved.

Aside from this, it was also no small problem to carry the children out of the Ghetto and place them with the Christian families. Specifically, most Jews coped in the following ways:

For a good reward, certain guards of the Ghetto Guard, during their gate duty would allow the child through the Ghetto Gate. Not far from the gate, one of the Christians would already be waiting, and would immediately take the child and transport him to his own home. However, the majority would be forced to place the children with Christians in the city.

With the help of various arrangements many children would be carried out through the Ghetto Gate. For example, after putting them to sleep with a narcotic, the small child would be covered up inside a bag or a backpack, and while going to work, they would carry them into the city. Or, for example, a strongly built man would tie up the sleepy child within his coat and, in this way, carry the child through the Ghetto Gate unnoticed.

[page 171]

Jewish carts from the ghetto institutions and from the ghetto workshops were often used to transport many children out of the Ghetto. These carts would travel into the city for various services, like bringing fertilizer to the Ghetto, taking away, or bringing, material for the Ghetto Workshops, etc.

In such cases, the guards at the Ghetto Gate were well rewarded by the parents of the children. When the regime in the Ghetto became much stricter, and Jewish carts started being accompanied by German guards, the Jews managed to get along with the guards, and they would close their eyes to what was being transported on the carts…

As mentioned, the children would be put to sleep with a type of narcotic just before being carried through the Ghetto Gate. This was so that the smaller children would not start crying during the transport out of the Ghetto and endanger themselves and their parents.

There was no shortage of cases when children would wake up just on the evening of the transport out of the Ghetto. Then they would have to turn back home and, in a day or two, try to put the child to sleep again. The danger was also great when the child would wake up on the other side of the gate too early, that means, before they arrived at the site.

In general, it was easier for Christians to take in girls, rather than boys. Since boys were circumcised, it was much harder to bring them to the city.

Another problem was also that the child had to know some Lithuanian to be understood in the new environment.

Then, there were Christians who would only be willing to take younger children. Others would only want to take older ones.

To deliver a child to the city, one had to manage all these issues, and only then come to the main issue: carrying the child out of the Ghetto.

At this opportunity we must note that the young Jewish man, Yankel Verbovsky[a], who worked at the Ghetto Gate, personally helped transport children out of the Ghetto.

[Page 172]

Despite all the enormous difficulties, a large movement was initiated in the Ghetto to get the children set up in the city, as fast as possible. Those parents who had contacts with Christian acquaintances in the city or in villages and managed to acquire the necessary resources to carry out this very difficult operation, weren't deterred, and did it as fast as possible. The prospect of being caught by the Gestapo for setting the child up in the city and paying for it with the life of the entire family, didn't scare any of these parents. The ghetto Jews would do anything, just to save their children.

In this way, dozens of children were saved from the Ghetto, but hundreds of children had to remain in the Ghetto because their parents were not successful in finding a suitable place for them in the city.

A separate chapter was also taking place in this silent, but deep tragedy of the Jewish child who did get set up in the city with Christians. Not knowing the language to make themselves understood with the new people, the longing for their parents, the transition period of acclimating themselves in their new "home," etc., is a theme which awaits future examination.

This movement to hand over the children to Christians in the city or the villages continued until, and after, the Children's Action, which took place in the Ghetto at the end of March 1944.

In the beginning of November 1943, as mentioned, the Ghetto was converted into a concentration camp. At the end of November, it became clear that later, at the Kovno Aerodrome (in the same building the Jews had constructed) they would establish a labor camp for 1500 ghetto Jews, called "Alexot Labor Camp."

Right afterwards, they found out that they would have to finish the wooden barracks especially for Jews at an additional labor camp for about 1500 Jews in the Kovno suburb of Shantz. A third camp was planned for Petrashun, about 7 kilometers from Kovno, where about 700 Jews who worked for a German military service for Auto-Renovation ("H.K.P."), were quartered. In addition, they had to enlarge the already available labor camps in Keidan, Palemon, Kashedar, etc. for the Kazernirungs Quartering Commission. Large tasks were set up and they started to speed up the tempo of work.

[Page 173]

According to the orders of the Camp Commander, Goecke, they had to transport about four to five thousand Jews from the Kovno Ghetto to the labor camp as soon as possible.

Inside the Ghetto about seven to eight thousand Jews remained temporarily: 1) those working in various ghetto workshops; 2) the few, still functioning, Jewish work brigades in the city, and 3) the network of Jewish institutions serving the population of the Ghetto and the surrounding Jewish labor camps.

In the plan to accommodate the total ghetto population, it was foreseen how to quarter the remaining Jews inside the Ghetto. However, this was left for the same finale as with the quartering. In the first place, they had to establish the labor camp at the Aerodrome. The camp was set to be established on the 30th of November 1943.

Finally, the Kazernirungs Commission finished making the list of the people for the Alexot camp. Since it already became clear that every ghetto Jew would have to get through a period of being quartered in a work camp, and that avoiding such a thing would not be possible anyway, so now they didn't have to take the earlier measure of applying force to recruit people. Orders were sent a week earlier that the persons listed for the camp had to be prepared to be quartered.

Immediately from the start, most of the ghetto Jews who received such orders made peace with the thought of becoming quartered because they knew that this is an "illness" that some ghetto Jews would have to get through… and if so, what good would it do to remain in the Ghetto a few more weeks? This is pretty much what the average ghetto Jew thought.

[Page 174]

This psychological preparation to become quartered contributed to these Jewish "suppositions" along with the following:

First, those who were now being quartered, supposedly knew that this is their last place. They now believed that they would either be freed by some miracle, or, at a critical moment, they would be killed.

Second, those who remained in the Ghetto could only expect various surprises. Many ghetto Jews speculated to themselves, as follows: since they needed more people for labor, and since there were still many Jews in the Kovno Ghetto, they would "logically" take them not from a work camp but from among the not-yet quartered ghetto collective. So why be dragged somewhere to the unknown, under who knows what conditions there would be, and where all the family members would be. So, it was "worthwhile" for them to be quartered in the vicinity of Kovno together with the entire family.

In addition, many ghetto Jews voluntarily allowed themselves to be quartered for the following serious reason:

As mentioned, at the beginning of November the Action on children, elderly and sick had already taken place in the Shavl Ghetto. Since the Action in the Shavl Ghetto happened in the Ghetto itself, the Kovno Ghetto Jews figured that the children, elderly, and sick would be "safer" in the work camp than in the Ghetto. Not a single ghetto Jew had any doubt that sooner or later such an Action would also take place in the Kovno Ghetto.

After putting aside, the last doubts about quartering, it was also the order from the Camp Commander, that right after the quartering at the Alexot Camp, the old ghetto area would be cleared out. So, this also contributed to the decision. That meant that in the original sector, where about 6,000 people lived, mainly Jews would become candidates for the work camp. Knowing in advance how many difficulties there would still be to find accommodation in the remaining ghetto area, where there would be no more than one and a half cubic meters of living space per person, most of the Jews who decided on quartering in Alexot absolutely didn't try to negotiate about remaining in the Ghetto. So, everyone was more than sure that when the day came for the quartering in Alexot, there would be, without a doubt, no shortage of Jews for the camp.

[Page 175]

A few days earlier, the Jews who were assigned to the work camp, packed up their few soft rags, leaving behind furniture and housewares, etc. in the houses. They were prepared to get through the new, and, as everyone hoped, last stage on the sorrowful road in Hitler's hell.

On the morning of the 30th of November 1943, the designated people started gathering at the Ghetto Gate to go to the Alexot work camp. The hundreds of men, women and children were convened in family groups and with packs on their backs they waited for the order to leave the Ghetto and get on the road. The psychosis of being quartered made the masses of convened people impatient, so when ordered to go through the Ghetto Gate, they started to push through the gate as if they were being freed from the Ghetto.

But when the German convoy of soldiers came, standing with rifles stretched out in columns to guard the marching Jews, their hearts sank. Friends and acquaintances came to accompany those marching to the camp. The goodbyes took place in a very tense atmosphere: they cried bitterly, kissed each other warmly, and in this way wished them well wherever they should be. At that moment, it was very difficult to distinguish who was smarter: those who were going to be quartered, or those who remained in the Ghetto.

After the transport got to the work camp, those Jews who were working on this relocation returned home at night. They were immediately heard describing the terrible welcome received by those who were relocated. These people were chased into large barracks where hard wooden grooves of three levels were prepared. The families were immediately torn apart, because the men were separated from the women, and the children were divided up: the older boys had to be with the father, the younger children with the mother.

[Page 176]

The guarding of the camp was very tight, and the impression was that it was not much larger than in the Ghetto. The items that were brought were immediately taken away to a separate storehouse, giving each one only the basic necessities in their hand: a portion of bedding, a pair of underwear, a towel, etc. Getting more items was only allowed once in two weeks. They would not be able to live off the official allotments, so Jews had to exchange their last items with Christians to get some food products. Losing the ability to freely use their own items was a hard blow.

The next morning, those who went out to work were not only the men and women who worked in the Ghetto, but even those who were free from work because of age or illness. In the camp there only remained those bed-ridden sick ones and elderly. Children up to approximately 10 years old were supervised the entire day by the few healthier older men and women. There is no need to describe what kind of supervision that was.

After a cold and wet winter evening of work on the open field of the Aerodrome, the Jews came back from work in the evening frozen and soaked. Returning from work, they no longer had a warm or peaceful family corner, like in the Ghetto. They only had huge barracks with taped-up grooves, one on top of the other, and one near the other. Understandably, in the din of about one thousand five hundred men, there was no way to get any rest. During their time in the Ghetto, each one still had the possibility of preparing food for himself according to his material possibilities, but in the camp, they had to be satisfied with a portion of soup from the common cauldron. And above everyone was the camp leader, the S.S. man, Miya, a real murderous soul with a history of service in other concentration camps.

Because of the murderous camp leader in Alexot, the work camp was transformed into a dreadful hell. For the smallest "sin" he would murderously beat them with his long whip, especially on the face. And he would always find a "reason" to beat and whip, at every step.

A group of Jewish partisans from the Kovno Ghetto in the Rudnitzki forests
(Vilna area)

Rabbi Ben-Eliezer, commander of the partisan camp "Kortshagin"

Heroic partisan Haim Berman (16 years old)

After carrying out an important partisan mission. All his friends were killed, so he blew himself up with a hand grenade, and in this way, he killed more S.S. people.

Murdered camp inmates from the Estonian concentration camp, Klooga. Because of the Soviet offensive, the Nazi murderers didn't manage to burn the dead on the pyres.

[Page 177]

According to the expected camp regime, they would conduct roll calls[b] twice a day on the campgrounds, during which he would unceasingly wave his whip to the right and to the left - for not standing as they should, for saying a word during line up, etc.

In the camp, men were not allowed to see their own wives. Even if they met on the stairs or in a corridor, they wouldn't dare stop to say a few words. For violations of this order, the camp leader would use his whip.

If he would catch someone going to work carrying another shirt or something else to exchange for food, he would not only confiscate it from the Jew for this resistance but in addition, he would beat him heavily. He also liked to supervise the Jews returning from work, and if he would find purchased food products, the whip would fly like hail again. It was like this, day in, day out.

These tortured Jews had no way back and they were therefore forced to suffer and to shut up. If someone "won" by being seriously ill and would have to be sent to the Ghetto hospital for a specific time, he would consider it rare luck, even for a short time, to get out of this hellish nightmare of "Labor Camp Alexot," under the supervision of the S.S. sadist, Miya. The people who would come from the camp to the Ghetto would look, with envy, at the ghetto Jews who had the good fortune to find themselves in the circle of their family, sleeping in their own bed and not having the cruel camp leader around at every step.

After such inhumane and insufferable experiences in the Alexot camp, the desire to be quartered fell strongly, and recruiting for future work camps became more difficult than before.

[Page 178]

After the establishment of the work camp in Alexot, recruiting for the Shantz labor camp began, where Jews themselves built the wooden barracks for the camp. In Shantz there was an S.S. man by the name of Bentzko who was expected to become camp leader, but fortunately, he was not a murderer like his "colleague" Miya in Alexot. In a certain way, this eased the recruiting for the Shantz camp. Aside from that, the Ghetto at that time still lived in fear of the anticipated Children's and Elders' Action, and many Jews accepted any difficulty of camp life with love, believing that in this way, maybe they would be able to save their children or elders.

Finally, on the 22nd of December 1943 the reduction of the old ghetto area was also decided. It was certain that to delay the reduction any further wouldn't be possible. Once again, many Jews allowed themselves to be quartered, because the prospect of finding a small corner in the remaining ghetto area where they could lay their head, was very slim.

On the 19th of December 1943, a few days before the reduction of the old ghetto area, exactly 1000 Jews became quartered in the Shantz camp. About 500 remaining Jews were quartered a bit later.

In the Shantz work camp, they managed to set up a much easier regime than in Alexot. The camp leader, Bentzko allowed himself a fling and because of that he didn't bother the Jews too much in their inner camp life. Therefore, for the ghetto Jew, to be quartered in Alexot or in Shantz, was not the same.

At this opportunity it is interesting to add that in the beginning of July 1944, a few days before the deportation from the Kovno Ghetto and the surrounding work camps to the German concentration camps, Bentzko ran away from the camp together with a Jewish woman with whom he developed a strong relationship. In the beginning of August 1944, after the liberation of Kovno by the Red army, he appeared in Kovno accompanied by his Jewish lover, and let's say, he hoped to be well liked by the Bolsheviks, due to his better treatment of the Jews in the Shantz work camp. But before his arrival at Shantz, during the Soviet regime, his sins in the camps for Soviet war prisoners were established, and according to the judgment of the war tribunal, he was shot.

[Page 179]

On the 22nd of December 1943, thousands of Jews from the old ghetto area, from the abovementioned first sector, were forced to leave their homes and live in the remaining portion of the Ghetto.

The reduction of the ghetto area had a painful impact. Starting from the early morning hours until the hour when they were permitted to stay in the cleared-out quarter, thousands of Jews carried bags, "furniture", and other housewares on their backs. Understandably, there was no talk about transportation.

One could see, for example, how one Jew carried something on his shoulders; a second Jew had whatever packed in a washtub or in a little basin wrapped with a rope, he carried it like that on the ground; a third carried something of his "riches" on a broken little wagon or a sled on the sandy little streets of the ghetto;

a fourth, not being able to carry his little table or closet any more, gave up and abandoned it. The entire day was noisy like at a fair on the small and twisting little streets of the Ghetto. The noise was like during a big fire. Each one, however, was predisposed to saving his things and bringing them over to his new furrow.

After the reduction of the old ghetto area, that area of the Ghetto became much smaller. In just a few hundred little wooden houses and in a few larger housing blocks seven to eight thousand Jews had to squeeze together. Because of the large crowding in many houses, they were forced to set up two levels of beds and remove furniture and less necessary items from the homes to fit in more beds.

That's why these Jews hung on to remain in the Ghetto as long as possible, and at any cost. They just did not want to be quartered in a labor camp where the living conditions were worse than in the Ghetto, even in these worsened conditions.

At the same time, while the recruiting was taking place for the large labor camps in Alexot and in Shantz, small camps in the province, like for example in Keidan, Koshedar, Palemon, were also enlarged. Later, new smaller labor camps were established in Raudondvaris, Bobet, Kazlove-Rude, and at other points near Kovno.

[Page 180]

After the Action of the children, elderly and sick, the largest portion of Jews from the labor camps in Alexot and in Keidan were transferred to Ponevezsh, where at that time a Jewish labor camp was established near the building of that Aerodrome. As mentioned in a previous chapter, Jews were brought to the Ponevezsh labor camp from Latvia. Among them, a specific number were Kovno Ghetto Jews, who were dragged to Riga on all fours during the two relocation Actions, which took place in February and October 1942.

As we will later see, at the end of June 1944, just before the deportation and liquidation of the Ghetto, the majority of the Jewish work brigades which worked in the city, hastily became quartered, but, by that time, the work brigade didn't live in the Ghetto. These brigades were quartered in the Alexot or Shantz camps.

The camp leader, Goecke, also planned to quickly quarter the Jewish work brigades which were working in the Slabodka factories, to the labor camp in Petrashon and, in addition, also to quarter them in the Kovno suburb of Slabodka. However, he didn't succeed in carrying out these quarterings, because on the 8th of July, the deportations and liquidations began in the Ghetto.

In the year 1943, a distinctive breakthrough on the eastern front took place in favor of Soviet Russia, and the Germans were forced to retreat in stages after their catastrophic defeat in Stalingrad. Among other things, the issue of removing the evidence of their past horrific acts in the occupied territories as fast as possible, became very real for the Nazis.

At the 9th Fort[c] the Hitlerites set up the largest mass murder site in Lithuania, where tens of thousands of dead were lying in the mass graves. In addition to Kovno Jews and foreign Jews, Soviet prisoners of war, and non-Jewish victims of the bloodthirsty Nazi regime were also murdered. However, the majority of the murdered were Jews.

[Page 181]

At the end of the Summer, 1943, they started digging out the dead bodies from the mass graves at the 9th Fort and burning them on pyres. A brigade of 64 men were employed for this work. Aside from the few dozen Soviet Jewish prisoners of war, who were already working a long time at the Fort burying the people after the executions, almost all the other brigade workers were Jews from the Kovno Ghetto.

The majority of the Kovno Jews who got themselves out of the Ghetto enroute to the forest to join the partisans in the Summer of 1943 were youth. On the way, they fell into the hands of the Lithuanian Police, who delivered them to the Gestapo. The Gestapo murderers kept a few dozen Jews at the 9th Fort, preparing the ongoing burning of the murdered. A certain number of Jews were recruited from the Ghetto itself from those work brigades near the Gestapo, which Camp Commander Goecke, liquidated at that time as part of the quarterings from the Ghetto.

According to the Gestapo plan, this pressing work had to be finished by Spring, 1944 at the latest. Therefore a "policy" was decided that the brigade had to burn about four to five hundred dead every day. The people from the brigade were divided into separate work groups, and each work group had to fulfill a specific task, like, for example, pulling the dead out of the graves, preparing the pyres, laying out the dead on the pyres, burning them, etc.

Not to mention the heinous work of digging up and burning the dead. These people knew very well that when they finished the work, the Gestapo would definitely kill them all so as not to leave any living witness who could tell the world what they saw and heard at the 9th Fort.

The more energetic people of the brigade therefore got the idea to search for a way to escape from the Fort. It is certainly unnecessary to mention that the Gestapo guarded the 9th Fort "appropriately."

[Page 182]

Among the prisoners of war was a former Soviet officer, who was an engineer by profession. He had already worked at the Fort for a while and was on the work brigade longer than others. He was oriented to the environment of the casement where they were held. With the collaboration of a few prisoners of war and a few youngsters from the Ghetto, he actively started exploring the possibility of escaping from the Fort.

After long observations and explorations about how possible this really was in the framework of the harsh regime at the Fort, this small group of people succeeded in learning that in the vicinity of their chamber there was a tunnel through which they could break through to the exit of the Fort. It was possible to get to this tunnel through an iron door which was near their chamber but was bolted from the inside of the tunnel.

Among the people of the brigade there was also a Jewish doctor, Dr. Portnoy, who for whatever sin was brought to the Fort, where he performed the duties of a doctor for the brigade.

One young Kovno man in the brigade, Pine Krakinovski,[d] was a locksmith and belonged to the leadership group. For a while, he simulated a disease so that the Jewish doctor would free him from going to work and let him remain in the chamber. With the help of a self-made drill made from a little pocket-knife which they found in the clothes of the dead, he stealthily succeeded in drilling a hole in the door, which led into the unknown tunnel.

When this important work was finished the leaders decided to make the last preparations to escape from the Fort. Because it was just before Christmas, 1943, it was decided to conduct the escape on the night of the 24th of December, when the guards of the Fort would certainly be inattentive and not as alert, due to the festival.

[Page 183]

At this opportunity we must add that the Gestapo gave the brigade men plenty of food and, from time to time, distributed cigarettes, and schnapps. The Gestapo did it for two reasons: first, so the people should be physically able to endure and complete the expected work, and second, to paralyze them from any urge to escape the Fort. After finishing the work, the Gestapo already planned to kill them on the same pyre where they burned the bodies.

The leaders of the brigade would take pains to show the Gestapo supervisors that they were good workers, and they did everything so that between the brigade and the Nazi guards they had, as they say, good relations. And, from time to time, before going to sleep, the brigade men would organize "parties" with songs and dance, in which guards from the guard post of the Fort also joined.

Regarding the weekend, on Christmas Eve they ended work earlier than other days and the brigade also received schnapps, cigarettes, etc. as gifts for the "holiday."

At night the leaders of the escape reported to all the others in the brigade that they prepared a possibility to escape from the Fort and that it would happen that night.

We can imagine the surprise of the people who for the first time found out about the whole plan…they were given the details when and how this would happen and immediately told that they should maintain strong discipline and punctuality and follow the instructions of the leader. There was no compassion for any objection as it would spoil and disturb the general escape plan for all of them.

On Christmas Eve a party took place in the brigade's chamber with songs, dances, etc. and a portion of the guards came to the "ball." The men from the brigade already arranged for the schnapps that they received to be drunk by the guards…

[Page 184]

After the party, the guards left and the gang went up to their bunks, as if, to sleep. When the light was turned off, all laid down on their beds, dressed, and held their breath, waiting for further orders. All felt that their fate would quickly be decided. Life – or death?

A long time passed, and it became very quiet around their casemate. The leaders of the escape gave the order for groups to come out of the chamber quietly, holding their shoes in their hands, and closed the door that led to the tunnel.

With great care, all managed to get out to the door, slowly and without noise through this drilled-out hole in the unlocked door. The hall was lit up with portions of light which allowed them to get through the tunnel to the exit. After a longer search they came to the exit which was located just in front of a high walled fence encircling the entire Fort building.

The guards were in the vicinity that separated the exit from the tunnel up to the entry to the fence around the Fort. So that the dark silhouettes of the escapees would go unnoticed on the snow, a pair of men held a stretched bedsheet like a linen screen, and the men came out in groups until they got to the fence, hiding under the linen.

With the help of the rope ladders, which were pre-arranged and made from hand towels, all the people got to the fence safely. All managed to climb over the fence and they found themselves in the fields outside the Fort.

Then everyone dispersed in small groups or individually, and quickly managed to get out of the area of the Fort. A portion went to the Ghetto in the middle of the night, which was about 5-6 kilometers distance. They snuck inside the Ghetto itself, or into the cleared-out area of the old ghetto, from where they later somehow got themselves into the ghetto domain. The other men went in the direction of the forests around Kovno.

One can imagine the teeth-grinding at the Kovno Gestapo when they learned about the escape from the Fort. Sadly, the Gestapo had a disrupted Christmas. Wanting to avoid a devastating scandal from the higher Nazi spheres in Berlin for allowing such a terrible event, the Gestapo quickly organized a chase after the escapees. Many escapees were killed while being pursued or fell into in the hands of the Gestapo – still alive.

[Page 185]

A few dozen men, mainly those who managed to sneak into and hide out in the Ghetto, later got out to the partisans with arms in their hands, to take revenge against the Nazis. A portion of them got through the partisan period safely and eventually survived to liberation.

All those who were captured by the Gestapo were immediately shot. To recruit a new work brigade, the Gestapo collected Jews from the Ghetto and also from the labor camps, according to the instructions from the German Labor Office in the Ghetto. At that time, they told the ghetto population, the creation of a list of people for this same brigade took place with the "collaboration" of some higher Jewish ghetto functionaries who had influence over the activities of the German Labor Office in the Ghetto. The newly organized brigade had to finish the work that had been started in burning the excavated dead bodies. These men were now kept under very strong guard, and after the end of the work – they were killed.

The ghetto Jews, understandably, took strong pleasure in the heroic story of the escape from the Fort. The fear was that the Ghetto would have repercussions but, luckily, it turned out to be unfounded. The Ghetto did not suffer because of this event.

The first few months of 1944 went by in a relatively calm atmosphere in the Ghetto. The Camp Commander, Goecke, during the New Year, went away for a few weeks leave. During the time of his leave, all assumed that no serious events would probably take place. And so, it was.

During this period, life in the Ghetto was characterized by the following happenings, which had varied importance:

[Page 186]

The worsening military situation for Nazi Germany and their collaborators on all the fronts, had a strong soothing effect on the ghetto population and strengthened the hope for better times. These included, the unheard-of retreat of the German forces from most of the occupied territories of Russia, and from Italy where the western allies had noticeable victories, the systematic bombardments of the German industry-centers, ports, large cities, etc. It then became very clear that if the Hitlerites got caught up for an additional day, it would be one day closer to their ruthless defeat. The main question was only: who among the ghetto Jews would survive to the moment of liberation?

General and political news at that time about the situation on the fronts, would reach the Ghetto from various sources: from the Lithuanian and German newspapers, which were purchased illegally at work in the city and afterwards smuggled into the Ghetto, and from those Jews who worked as radio mechanics and found appropriate opportunities at work to listen to foreign radio. Aside from that, for a certain time, the leftist elements in the Ghetto had a home-made radio unit and disseminated the news mainly from Moscow radio.

The most important news from various sources went from person to person and would be disseminated among the ghetto population with the speed of a blitz. Understandably, due to the topics, the interest in political and military events was great among the ghetto Jews. A few Jews in the Ghetto knew very well that their personal fate was, in great measure, dependent on the outcome of the wider world events.

The economic situation in the Ghetto was not bad at that time. Aside from the official disbursements, which were much better than when the City Commissar ruled the Ghetto, the Camp Commander, Goecke, practically didn't disturb the Jews from bringing in food products which they would buy at work in the city.

True, some ghetto Jews lived according to what their material circumstances allowed. No one suffered from hunger at that time in the Ghetto.

At this opportunity it is necessary to note that more than a few people from the "ghetto aristocracy", that means higher functionaries from the Jewish ghetto units and those "connected" to the German regime leaders, would from time to time even have parties in their home where our people would get drunk all night and allow themselves to go on a spree of other earthly pleasures.

[Page 187]

This conduct from a specific portion of "big-shots"[e] stood as an offensive blow to life for most of the ghetto population, who carried the yoke of ghetto exile with great suffering.

In general, there was the impression that Goecke deliberately allowed the living standard to rise in the Ghetto to this level, to paralyze their preparedness to leave for the forest or for the city. These political ploys by Goecke, we must admit, were successful. Many ghetto Jews who had specific difficulties and who could create the opportunity to get out of the Ghetto, allowed themselves to maintain the "good" life in the Ghetto, and thought less about going out into the city.

In the balance we must therefore admit that regarding the economic situation, the ghetto population didn't have any reason for strong complaint.

At the end of January 1944, Goecke ordered a registration to be conducted of the entire population in the Ghetto and in the labor camp, including children, non-working elders, sick, etc. Formally, this registration was related to the setting up of a specific file of the entire Jewish population which belonged to "Concentration Camp Kauen". So, for the ghetto Jews, the Action that took place in the Shavl Ghetto on children, sick and elderly, was fresh in their memory and there was a suspicion that such an Action could soon await the Kovno Ghetto. Thus, the fear of registering their younger children was understandable. Also, the older people were afraid to add their real age at the registration.

The families which had little children or elders and sick members, worried terribly about this issue of registration.

During the first two months of 1944 a large quartering meeting took place in the Shantz work camp, and, in addition, smaller quartering meetings took place in the other work camps. The smaller quartering meetings dealt with a few topics: first, in general, it was necessary to enlarge the number of people in the camps. Second, a few people were liberated from the labor camps because of sickness or good connections with the relevant local Jewish ghetto rulers, and they now had to send new people in their place.

[Page 188]

Quartering a person in a labor camp, especially in the Alexot Camp, was a special tragedy for a ghetto Jew. By the way, it was also one of the punishments for violations of the rules of the ghetto policies.

The motivation to break out of the labor camp was very big. Whoever had the smallest chance of freeing himself from the camp, would do so. The contrast between living standards in the Ghetto and in the labor camp was so glaring that a ghetto Jew couldn't be indifferent to the question about remaining in the Ghetto or being sent out to a labor camp.

At this specific time, an intensive movement spread among the ghetto youth - to get out to the forest to join the partisans. At that time in the Ghetto, an illegal organization was established which was involved in recruiting and transferring people to the partisan camps. The secret Partisan Committee was made up of representatives from the former social groupings in the Ghetto. Members of Elders Council and respected people from the Jewish Ghetto Police also belonged. This fact was very significant for the development of the partisan movement in the Ghetto.

At the beginning, the initiators of the partisan movement had to be careful not only because of the non-Jewish factors outside the Ghetto. They also had to be careful, partly because the Jewish administration, just at the last moment, had been phased down, and this was very significant. Moreover, this coordination of the various social groupings in the Ghetto, including the highest divisions of the Jewish ghetto administration, the Elders Council, and the people from Jewish Ghetto Police, suddenly opened entirely new and relatively wider perspectives for growth of this Jewish resistance movement against the Nazis.

[Page 189]

While this specific movement widened its base inside the Ghetto, steps were taken by the leftist elements to set up tighter contact and collaboration between this organization in the Ghetto, and the leftist circle in the city. This was done with the calculation that everything that is related to this specific work should move along as always.

The collection of money in the Ghetto was carried out mainly from the well-situated brigade people. This would cover the expenses of purchasing arms for the departees going to the forest and getting trucks to send people over as close as possible to the partisan nests. This entire movement engaged large groups of young people and it was impressive that neither the Gestapo, nor the Camp Commander, Goecke, were informed about what was taking place in the Ghetto.

Meanwhile they managed to take advantage of the favorable circumstances, and in this sense, it was lively.

Since this all took place with the knowledge and support of the Jewish ghetto institutions, everything in the Ghetto stood at the disposition of this movement. The Jewish functionaries at the Ghetto Gate played tricks and twisted the head of the German guard, so when a Jewish group from the Ghetto would go out to the partisans with arms in their pockets, the guards would say - here goes a brigade to work in the city.

Or, similarly, as mentioned, when they would smuggle items like German military clothes, boots, and other necessary clothes out to the partisans from the Large Ghetto Workshops where Jews worked in various jobs for the German Werhmacht, it was done with the knowledge of the Jewish leaders from the Workshops.

To make it easier to get out of the Ghetto, they also managed to take advantage of the fact that at that time there was a bigger work brigade[f] which set up an underground telephone and telegraph cable between Kovno and Mariampole. Since, at the beginning, the Jewish workers would travel daily from the Ghetto to their work and back, many of the youth who were prepared to leave for the partisans would join them on the Kovno-Mariampole highway on their way to work, and from there, the youth would disappear. Later, this same brigade became quartered in Mariampole, where it remained until that time when the work was finished.

[Page 190]

Because of all these things, that period could be counted as the "golden era" in the story of the partisan movement in the Kovno Ghetto.

The activities of these movements became more difficult when the mass murderer, Kittel, arrived at the Kovno Gestapo. This tragically famous liquidator of the Vilna and other ghettos was the Gestapo "specialist" for Jewish issues. He took active interest in ghetto life. Finally, the smashing blow for the partisan movement came from the Gestapo through the Children's Action and the arrest of the Jewish Ghetto Police at the end of March 1944.

It is necessary to mention the names of the most important ghetto Jews who were personally active in the secret organization to recruit partisans and send them off into the forest:

A. From the leftist circles:

    1. <u>Chaim Yellin</u> – head leader of the Partisan Movement. The reader will find more details about his personality in the other chapters of the book.[g]
    2. <u>Dima Halpern</u>: a young man from the assimilated Jewish intelligentsia of Kovno. His father, by the way, an apostate, was a lawyer in Kovno. Dimke, as they would lovingly call him, took an active leadership role in the resistance movement. A good person, very accommodating in the real meaning of the word, sympathized with all social streams in the Ghetto. He managed to survive the Dachau Concentration Camp and after liberation, he returned to Lithuania.
    3. <u>Engineer, Shimon Ratner</u> – at first, he was a colleague of the Jewish Work Office. In stages he became close to the left. Later, he became one of the leading people of the Secret Committee. In mid-April 1944 he was shot by the Gestapo when a Jewish partisan group was attacked not far from the Ghetto.[h]

[Page 191]

    4. <u>Yerachmiel Berman</u> – during the Soviet period in Lithuania he was active as an artist in the Jewish theater. He did a lot to purchase arms for the partisans. As previously mentioned, in March 1943, he was arrested while bringing a rocket into the Ghetto. Thanks to Liptzer's intervention he was freed. He was in the previously described Jewish partisan group, which was attacked by the Gestapo. After surviving the shooting, he reached the partisans. After liberation he left Lithuania with the stream from the Bricha.

    5. <u>Menashe Sapoznikov</u> – he was a painter by profession. Was active in the criminal division of the Jewish Ghetto Police. Was a very bold and energetic young man who did a lot for the left, and also for the partisans. Was killed in the previously mentioned attack of the Jewish partisans.

    6. <u>Dr. Rudolf Valsonok</u> – a well-known journalist. Was a very educated and skilled person. In the Ghetto, at first, he was in the Aerodrome division in the Jewish Labor Office. Later, he became a part of the Statistics Office. One of the most important members of the "Kazernirungs Commission" who had to decide on the people for the labor camps. Personally, he had many sins on his conscience. In the Ghetto, he held close to the left. Like a former officer of the Polish army, helped by the military issues of the partisan organization, he was taken to Dachau Concentration Camp. After liberation he started the publication of a Jewish newspaper[i] with a Latin alphabet, in the Landsberg D.P. camp. He was a sick man and after an operation he died in Munich on the 31st of December 1945.

    7. <u>Moshe Sherman</u> – a young man who was active in the leftist circles for a long time. Left the Ghetto for the partisans. After liberation, he returned to Kovno and did a lot for the Jewish Children's Home.

    8. <u>David Ratner</u> – he was sent by the left to work in the Jewish Ghetto Police and in the "Kazernirungs Commission." Did a lot to send people into the forest. Later, he went out to the partisans himself. Was killed in the forests around Kazlove-Rudeh a few days before this vicinity was freed by the Red Army.

[Page 192]

B. from the Zionist stream:

    1. <u>Moshe Levin</u> – was chief of the Jewish Ghetto Police for a long time. Belonged to the Revisionists. Had many enemies in the Ghetto because he was a strong man and would often become too harsh. Raised large sums for the partisan movement and for building "hideouts." During the arrests of the Jewish Ghetto Police, at the end of March 1944[i], the Gestapo devil Kittel tortured him terribly and shot him right afterwards. During the interrogations at the Fort, he held out very boldly and admirably.

    2. <u>Hirsh Levin</u> – one of the leaders of the Revisionist movement in Lithuania. After the Soviets marched into Lithuania, he was arrested and sat in jail. When the Germans occupied Kovno, he, together with other arrestees were let out of jail, because the Bolsheviks didn't manage to evacuate the arrested. In the Ghetto he was a leading person in the Elders Council. He was one of the most active members on the secret Partisan Committee. After the arrest of the Ghetto Police and liquidation of the Elders Council he was hunted by Kittel. However, he managed to hide himself in the Ghetto and then in the city where he survived until the liberation. After liberation he helped found the Kovno Jewish Children's Home. According to a report by a young Jewish man, during the Big Action, Levin refused to ask the Gestapo murderer, Rauca, who was conducting the selection, to free the young man's deported parents. Levin did do this for other Jews. He was arrested by the Soviet Security Service and disappeared without a trace from Kovno. According to later notices, he might have been sent to a labor camp in the northern Soviet region.

3. <u>Itzhak Grinberg</u> – a higher functionary of the Jewish Ghetto Police. Was a leading member of the Zionist Youth Organization in the Ghetto "ABZ"[k], was a heroic young man who did a lot for partisan issues. Was a very honest person and fought the anti-social phenomena of ghetto life to the best of his ability. During the arrest of the Jewish Police, was shot at the 9th Fort.

[Page 193]

4. <u>M. Bramson</u> – was a teacher by profession. Previously an officer in the Lithuanian army and a leader in "Union of the Jewish Front Fighters in Lithuania." Took on a higher position among those of the Jewish Ghetto Police. Helped the Partisan Movement, especially in its period of organization. Was taken to Dachau. Being a passionate smoker, he would give away his last piece of bread to get something to smoke. He died of hunger just before liberation.

At this opportunity it is also necessary to mention some Jewish women who were active in the Partisan Movement.

1. <u>Olia Meizel</u> – was strongly devoted to partisan issues. Also was active in the left-wing circles. Left for the forest where she became sick and died.
2. <u>Aidl Pilovnik</u> – helped a lot by smuggling arms into the Ghetto for the partisans. Was in the forest and survived to liberation. Her brother,
3. <u>Tuvia Pilovnik</u> – a young man of 18 years was arrested on his way to the partisans and was sent to the 9th Fort to burn the unearthed dead bodies. After escaping from this brigade, he hid out in the Ghetto, from where he went into the woods. While carrying out a mission for the partisans, he was shot in Spring of 1944 near Kovno.
4. <u>Leah Senior</u> – worked a lot for the partisan organization. Was also in the forest and survived to liberation.

With the partisan issues, in addition to the listed people, there were a whole line of other men and women who were also involved, for example: Elchanan Kagan, Alte Borochovitz, etc., who in various ways helped the resistance movement against the Nazi murderers.

In addition to the organized Partisan Movement there were also individuals and smaller groups of Jews, in that period, who went out of the Ghetto to get things organized with Christian acquaintances in the city or in the villages, who prepared special hideouts for them.

These ghetto Jews who had a place to hide somewhere, managed to get there. In this case, the majority had to sneak themselves out through the Ghetto Gate or disappeared during their work in the city, and with great care, found Christian acquaintances, as soon as possible. In the dark of night, so no one should notice them, G-d forbid, these lucky Jews arrived at their place with the Christians, entered and quickly hid themselves in the prepared hiding places.

[Page 194]

The number of such Jews who left the Ghetto was not big. For various reasons, many of them fell into the hands of the Gestapo who killed them. Others didn't even manage to get to the Christian acquaintance and were arrested on the way.

The following tragic accident happened to a larger group of Kovno Jews who hid out in a bunker near Yorborek:[l]

About 100 Jews hid in that same bunker which was in a forest. In Summer, 1944, when the Red Army was about to liberate Lithuania, many large battles took place around Yorborek.

One day, the Jews noticed two Latvians around the bunker who told them that they were deserters from the German army, and they were looking for a place where they could hide. Since the Latvians promised the Jews from the bunker that they would be helpful with their military practice, the Jews agreed to allow them into their hiding place.

After spending a certain time together with the Jews, the Latvians declared that they wanted to go get arms for the people in the bunker. The Jews did not foresee anything bad, and they let them leave the bunker. On the way, the Latvians fell into the hands of the Germans who took them for spies and wanted to shoot them. Wanting to save their own lives, the Latvians promised to show the Germans where a bunker of Jews was located.

In a day or two after the departure of the Latvians, the bunker was suddenly attacked by a large group of Germans. The assaulted Jews maintained heroic resistance, but almost all were killed in the battle. Only a few Jews who, by coincidence, were away in the woods at the moment of the attack, were not in the bunker. They survived the destruction and later survived to liberation.

Among the Jews killed were also small children who, after great sacrifice, had been saved during the Children's Action in the Ghetto.

[Page 195]

At the same time, the Ghetto undertook an intensive movement to hand over the children to Christians. Anyone who had even a small possibility to do it, gave up the child to someone in the city or the village.

It was a fairly quiet period at that time in the Ghetto, so many Jews tried to talk themselves into the possibility that there would not be a Children's Action in the Kovno Ghetto, like in the Shavl Ghetto. Thus, quite a few parents who had difficulties keeping their child in the city, brought them back to the Ghetto. The largest portion of these returning children were caught during the Children's Action at the end of March 1944.

When the United Partisan Committee became a prominent factor in the Ghetto and its authority grew stronger over the ghetto Jews, the time came to begin an energetic fight against Jewish stooges and other scoundrels.

The first concrete case happened one night at the end of 1943. While they were looting, some underworld characters from the Ghetto shot three Jews.

The members of the Jewish Ghetto Police, together with the secret Partisan Committee, decided this time to punish the guilty ones themselves. They did not want the Gestapo to research the issue and start asking the question: from where did the murderers get arms? Such a question by the Gestapo would cost the Partisan Movement dearly.

Through various means, they succeeded in finding the guilty ones and they enticed them into the hands of the Partisan Committee. After determining their guilt, a death sentence was pronounced which was immediately carried out in secret.

At the same time as the fight against the looting, a campaign began against the operatives who served in the Gestapo and who violated the ghetto interests in various ways.

Catching a Jew in their hands, the Gestapo murderers would very often give them the following alternatives: either they would be shot together with their family at the Fort, or they could provide the Gestapo with information about the Ghetto - and they would be "freed."

[Page 196]

No one should, God forbid, judge those Jews who wanted to save their own lives for the price of informing on other Jews. We must, however, also not forget the psychological condition of those unlucky Jews who, by accident, fell into the Gestapo hands and were suddenly placed in such a difficult situation.

On a separate note, Kittel very much liked using Jewish stooges. This way he would have double the sadistic enjoyment: on one hand a Jew dies, and on the other it goes through a second Jew.

When the provocative activity by these Jewish stooges would take on a dangerous character, there was no other way to get rid of them except to clear him out of the way.

There was also a case when a certain Jewish young man, Mony Levin, conducted a robbery together with Lithuanian Police and squealed about a well-organized hideout which was in the cleared-out old ghetto area. There were no victims, but the bunker was discovered and robbed by the Lithuanian Police. This same Jewish scoundrel was also shot, according to a verdict from the Secret Committee.

Truth be told, it must be said that such "political murders" were very few in the Ghetto. In total it only reached a count of about a dozen.

After the elimination of an operative, Kittel did not wait for his agent according to the prearranged time, and immediately came into the Ghetto to look for him. Understanding that the Jews got rid of him he told the Jewish ghetto administration, with various threats, that they should give up those who kill people in the Ghetto. With great difficulty, the Elders Council or the Jewish Police succeeded in getting themselves out of Kittel's demands.

Such energetic actions by the Secret Committee served as a warning to both the Jewish stooges and the simple scoundrels, that they should be cautious about their criminal activities.

The total number of Jews who tore themselves out of the Ghetto was relatively very small. Therefore, they had to think about how to organize certain security measures inside the Ghetto. The only practical way was the construction of special hiding places, bunkers which the Ghetto called "*malinas*."

[Page 197]

Just after the relocation Action to Estonia, as previously mentioned, a movement began to build hiding places in the Ghetto where they could hide themselves in moments of trouble. Those who had a place to hide might survive the Action. Therefore, it was understood that they should expect Actions any day in the Ghetto, especially a Children's Action. So, many Jews got caught up in the movement to build hideouts.

The building of a *"malina"* was however, not a simple and easy thing and was full of all types of difficulties. For your information, there were various types of *malinas* in the Ghetto and it is worthwhile expanding on this.

The majority of real, specially built, *malinas* were built in this way:

Under the floors of the house, or in another building (stable, storehouse, etc.) in the vicinity of the apartment, a big pit was dug out, which, with the help of thick wood, and other facilities had to be strengthened so it shouldn't fall in. The entrance to the *malina* was one of the most important problems in the construction of the bunker. First, the entrance would have to be well-camouflaged, so that no outside people could easily notice it. Second, it would have to be organized, so that one could get into the bunker as quickly as possible. The *malinas* had various masked entrances and inventions were very creative. So, for example, the entrance to the *malina* could be through an oven, through a cabinet, through a cellar, etc. There were *malinas* in which the entrance was through a bathroom, through a well, and the like.

A second important problem in the building of a *malina* was to arrange for air and water. Air would flow with the help of pipes, which were pulled from the bunker to an unnoticeable exit around the building where the *malina* was located.

[Page 198]

In the larger *malinas* they would dig out a pit until they would find a layer of water inside the *malina*. Otherwise, they would have to prepare water in larger utensils, barrels, etc.

In the *malinas* they would also prepare food products for a longer time. So that the food shouldn't become rotten, they would have to prepare preserved and dried food products, like bread-zwieback, preserves, and smoked meat, and fish, etc.

The *malinas* would possess various interior facilities like, for example, where to sit, sleep, have the natural needs, and the like. To provide hidden light in the *malina*, they would string up the bunker with an electric current and bring in light. They would also use the electric current to cook.

The *malinas* would possess radios, to maintain contact with the outside world.

Building a *malina* would take a long time and would, by the way, cost a lot of money. Therefore, only those ghetto Jews who could afford it could build well-organized *malinas*.

The first and most important work in the building of a *malina* – the digging of the hole- mostly had to take place at night so that they could carry out the excavated earth without being disturbed and spread it out in the garden around the house.

In the Ghetto at that time, Jews didn't have to be so careful about building a *malina* because the Jewish Police and the Jewish ghetto institutions unofficially supported the building of the bunkers. The situation in the Ghetto changed after the Childrens' Action and the liquidation of the Jewish Ghetto Police. In its place, the Gestapo set up the "Service Order" where more than a few Gestapo agents were allowed in.

In building a *malina* they had to be very careful of the dozens of S.S. men from the Camp Commandant. They would have to be especially careful of the Camp Commandant, S.S. Sergeant Major Pilgram, a big hooligan, who would wander around every corner of the Ghetto, day, and night.

Specially built *malinas* would be built in the Ghetto with a few families together. This would happen for two reasons: first, during the entire work of digging the hole, etc., they would have to use mainly their own people, so that fewer outsiders would know the details of the *malina*. Second, it was a huge financial expense.

[Page 199]

In addition to the bunkers of private people there were also a certain number of "communal *malinas*" in the Ghetto, built by social groupings. Like for example, the leftists had their *malinas*, the Zionists- theirs, etc.

In those houses where it wasn't possible to build any *malina* underground, they would make other hideouts: for example, they would build a double wall of planks or of bricks and decorate it like all the other walls in the room. Through a hidden entrance they would go into the middle space between the natural and the built walls. In such a hiding place they would be able to hide in an emergency.

Ghetto Jews without resources, who could not afford to build a special *malina*, would seek any kind of hiding place in their houses, for example, in the attic, in the cellar, in a wood storehouse, etc., to have a place where they could hide until the rage had passed.

As we will see later in the days of the Action on Children, Elders and Sick, the Gestapo undertook a step to discover the *malinas*. This work was conducted by the Gestapo-murderer, Kittel, who already had a lot of "experience" at this job from liquidating the Vilna Ghetto, where there were also many bunkers. They were successful at uncovering many *malinas* and blowing them up.

Quite a few *malinas* remained undiscovered. In place of the destroyed bunkers Jews built other hiding places.

At the beginning of July 1944, when the deportation and liquidation of the Ghetto was ordered, and Jews were determined not to allow themselves, under any circumstances, to be deported, most of the Jews hid in *malinas*, and other hiding places.

The Gestapo, which conducted the deportations with the help of special bombing commandos and sniffing dogs, spread out over all the houses in the Ghetto to find the *malinas* and hiding places. Since every covered space was bombed with hand grenades, all the bunkers were discovered.

In the last days of the deportation, the Gestapo set fire to the Ghetto and all the houses and the yet-to be-discovered *malinas* were burned, along with many Jews who were hiding in them.

[Page 200]

From all the ghetto *malinas* only two remained undestroyed: one of these *malinas* was built very deep under a cellar in one of the tower housing blocks. When the block was blown up with dynamite, the explosion didn't reach the *malina*. In this *malina* a few dozen Jews were saved and lived to liberation. The second, a smaller *malina*, remained whole because it was not built under a house like most of the ghetto *malinas*, but in a garden. Also, this *malina* remained undiscovered and in it 15 people were saved. Not a trace remained of all the other *malinas* in the Ghetto.[m]

At that time a few dozen German Kapos were sent into the Ghetto. Who they were, and what kind of function they had in the Ghetto was at first unknown. Various rumors circulated about them.

After a while it was clarified that these German Kapos were former German criminals. A few of them were also political criminals. They came to the Kovno Ghetto from other concentration camps where they conducted various duties supervising and guarding camp prisoners.

Already from their external appearance it was noticed that they were "skilled" in their duties and, as it turns out, had a lot of experience in this area.

Jewish work brigades which worked in the city had Jewish brigade leaders (Brigadiers) appointed by the Labor Office. Now, Goecke ordered a German Kapo to oversee everything that happened in every larger brigade.

As we know, most of the Jews took advantage of their work in the city to engage in opportunities to purchase food products or stay in contact with Christian acquaintances. By sending the German Kapos into the Jewish work brigades the fear was understood that the Jews would no longer be able to do business on the brigade or meet with Christians. Right from the beginning, the Kapos started showing what they can do, and even started beating the Jews at work.

[Page 201]

However, the Jews, very quickly managed with these guys. They would stuff their mouths with bacon, eggs, and other necessary items. Since they were transitory youths, they understood that if they kept good relations with the Jews, they would have it better than if they would strictly follow "the law." Jews later started feeling as undisturbed as before the arrival of the Kapos in the brigade.

One of the German Kapos got along so well with the Jews that when the ghetto deportations took place, they ran away from the camp command and hid out until the arrival of the Russians.

When the Soviets freed Kovno, these "freed" German Kapos went out on the streets and felt like real kinsmen… however, they were later arrested by the regime, and they disappeared from the Kovno horizon.

The situation in the Ghetto during the first few months of 1944 was relatively calm for ghetto life and there were no extraordinary happenings. But from time to time there were quite a few rumors which caused much confusion among the ghetto population.

Most of the rumors described the fact that a larger group of Jews had to be transported out of the Ghetto. These rumors were mainly started by Christians in the city. How these Christians received this information was difficult to ascertain. In any case, the Ghetto was strongly unnerved because of these tense rumors.

Wanting to find an authentic clarification of all the tense talk, the ghetto Jews, who had access to various higher German ghetto functionaries, had a chat with them about this topic. We must say that these Germans would always deny that something bad was going to happen in the Ghetto. If they were, or were not, aware of this question, or if they were telling the truth or not, understandably, it was difficult to discern.

[Page 202]

There were a few times in the Ghetto when various German commissions and inspections would hold consultations about ghetto issues together with Camp Commander, Goecke. Also, at this moment, the Ghetto would become strongly unsettled and would look to ascertain what they said and what was decided during the consultation. If anyone got even a little piece of news, it would immediately be spread among all the ghetto Jews.

In the beginning of March 1943, weighty rumors started to circulate in the Ghetto that soon there would be transports of a few thousand Jews from the Ghetto to somewhere. They even said that this would take place around the 15th of March.

When the rumors started to spread from person to person, it caused Chairman Elkes of the Elders Council to visit the Camp Commander, Goecke, to find out something about this issue. It was March 14, 1944.

Goecke categorically denied these rumors. He shared that he believed such rumors had provocative intent and were coming from the Lithuanians. They were trying to create panic among the Jews so that the Jews should start running into the city and they, the Lithuanians, would meantime take the opportunity to pressure the Jews for money and other valuables.

To finally "calm" Dr. Elkes, he told him that if something were really supposed to happen in the Ghetto on March 15, he, the Camp Commander, should already have had notice on the 14th of March – meaning, only one day in advance.

In any case, Goecke's clarification gave the impression that in the run up to the coming days nothing bad would happen in the Ghetto.

Slowly the panic started to pass, and the Jews started to talk themselves into the idea that maybe Goecke was actually right; that nothing was going to happen in the Ghetto. Again, the Ghetto calmed down and ghetto life went back on its "normal" path.

But, this time, unfortunately, for only a very short time.

Original footnotes:

    a.   About the role of the Jewish functionaries at the Ghetto Gate, especially about Verbovski, see "Labor Office" in the Monograph: "Jewish Institutions in the Kovno Ghetto."
    b.   In the morning, immediately after wake-up, and in the evening, after work.
    c.   One of the forts from the former Kovno fortresses.
    d.   After liberation he gave this editor the descriptive details
    e.   The groups of the higher Jewish ghetto offices in the Ghetto were called "***Yales***." [big-shots] About the concept of "Yales" see "Observations about Folklore in the Kovno Ghetto."
    f.   This was called: "shiny cable".
    g.   Mainly in the chapter-segment: "Arrest of the Jewish partisan leader Chaim Yellin."
    h.   See "Gestapo attack on a Jewish partisan group"
    i.   "Landsberger Lager-Cajtung."
    j.   See "Unexpected Removal of the Jewish Police to the 9th Fort.
    k.   See "Zionist Activity in the Ghetto."
    l.   A little village on the Nieman River not far from the German border.
    m.   See "Deportation and Liquidation of the Ghetto"

CHAPTER XXIV

Children, Old and Sick People Action

-Calm mood in the Ghetto on the eve of the Action- "Innocent organization of the Jewish Police to gather and learn how to protect themselves from attacks from the air-Unexpected deportation of Jews to the camp in the 9th Fort-The Action in the Ghetto and in the labor camps-The situation in the Ghetto after the Action

[Page 203]

As was said, the last half of March 1944 went by in an atmosphere of relative quiet in the Ghetto. Something noteworthy at that time was the disquieting rumors about whether to get people out of the Ghetto. Absolutely no one imagined or suspected that this was the quiet before the big storm, which would soon take over the Ghetto settlement and the outlying camps and would take approximately 2000 victims.

In one row of ghetto houses, the religious Jews were baking matza, little by little, so that their Pesach shouldn't be disturbed. This was done in the strictest secrecy, so that, God forbid, the S.S. people from the Camp Commandant shouldn't notice.

The favorable news about the military situation on the fronts, the beautiful and sunny spring days which suddenly arrived, together with the Pesach atmosphere, threw brighter streaks of light on the mood of the downtrodden ghetto Jews.

[Page 204]

In truth, the painfully haunting dream about liberation and redemption during this pre-Pesach time did not seem to be realistic, like in the past or even earlier. While waiting for deliverance for the ghetto Jews, an uneasy feeling developed with the approach of the front lines. Logically, the liquidation of the Ghetto would have to come. But many ghetto Jews wanted to believe that no matter what would happen, perhaps they would be among the chosen ones who would in some indirect way survive the barely conceivable luck of redemption and liberation.

On the night of Sunday, the 26th of March 1944, the Camp Commander, Goecke, informed the chief of the Jewish Ghetto Police that tomorrow, Monday at 8 a.m., the full complement of the Jewish Police should assemble in the courtyard of the Camp Commander. There, they will receive instructions about protecting the Ghetto from air strikes. Never had there been any talk by the regime about air protection in the Ghetto. At that time, no one was suspicious of anything bad in this "innocent" information from Goecke, believing that Ghetto Jews are not privy to such genteel matters like protection against air attacks.

On their return, the ghetto optimists saw this specific announcement as a demonstration that these are "different times." That means that the ghetto Jews were no longer helpless in the time of an air attack, until now.

The Jewish Ghetto Police, which included in their ranks about 130 men, prepared themselves to line up in front of the Camp Commander, in full regalia, dressed up in military drill, like for a celebratory parade.

A sunny pre-spring-like day arrived on an early Monday morning, the 27th of March 1944.

As always, the Jewish workers who worked in the city and in the various ghetto workshops, went out to work. Only those who worked the night shift in the Large Ghetto Workshops, and the old people, sick ones, and children remained in the Jewish homes.

[Page 205]

Just after they let the Jews out to work, around 7:30 in the morning, a strengthening of guards was seen around the Ghetto Fence, a phenomenon which didn't bode well for the Ghetto. However, at that moment we didn't contemplate anything bad, and, anyway, very few Jews noticed that the guards around the Ghetto Fence were strengthened, so there was no commotion. Before that time, the Jewish Ghetto Police collected themselves in the courtyard of the Camp Commander.

Around 8 a.m., when the Jewish Police were already standing in military drill at the Camp Commander's courtyard, ready to hear the announcement about the air attack, Goecke stood before them and called the Jewish policemen who played in the Ghetto orchestra out of the columns and ordered them to enter into the Commandant building. All the other Jewish policemen received an order to sit on the ground, and to their great surprise were encircled by a strong guard. At this time Gestapo cars entered the Ghetto and a taxi started driving all over the ghetto streets, ceaselessly repeating the following phrase through a megaphone:

"Attention, Attention. Everyone must remain in the house. Anyone found outside their house will be shot."

While the Gestapo shouted the "good news" through a megaphone to the Ghetto residents, the Jewish policemen were forced to climb on all fours, to be caged in the trucks in which they were taken in the direction of the 9th Fort. A Jewish policeman, Levner, whose feet became cramped from fear and could not fulfill the order to get into the truck, was immediately shot on the spot.

Approaching the Fort, two Jewish officials from the Ghetto Police, Advocat, Zilberkweit and Levin, jumped out of the truck and started running. But they were immediately shot by the Gestapo accomplices.

At the Fort, they first took away everything that the Jewish policemen had, they tortured them murderously, and afterwards confined them in the casements of the Fort.

Later, the refined mass executioner, Kittel, approached them, and through all kinds of pressure and blackmail, tried to press information out of them about the existing bunkers in the Ghetto and about the activities of the youth who went out into the forest to the partisans.

[Page 206]

The first ones taken for interrogation, was the Chief of the Jewish Police, Moshe Levin, and his assistants Itzhak Grinberg and Yudel Zupovich. Afterwards, they were murderously tortured to get any information, (in which, by the way, the Gestapo investigators were not successful). They were shot and their bodies were burned on the pyres, as they previously burned the dead who were excavated.[a]

At the same time as the Jewish police were taken away to the 9th Fort, the Gestapo groups, together with the Ukrainians, tore through the Ghetto, and spread themselves out to all corners of the Ghetto.

It now became certain that this was an Action. But at the start, it was still not known what 'type' of Action it was.

Those who had specially built *malinas* or other kinds of hiding places, hid immediately. In any case, each person found wherever they could to hide and not be in view of the oncoming murderers.

After the first attack on the ghetto houses, they started dragging out children, the elderly and the sick. It then became clear that this time it was about that which caused such painful anxiety for such a long time; but right now, it was totally unexpected.

Just like the case of the Shavl Ghetto, the Kovno Nazis, it seems, had a decree to take away the children who were younger than 12, men and women who were older than 55 and, in addition, all the sick and invalids, regardless of their age.

Earlier on, many children had already arranged to get work cards wherever possible, indicating that they were 12 years old or older, but it helped little, because the Gestapo didn't pay much attention to these work cards. For them, the only measurement was the physical look of the child.

[Page 207]

A similar situation also happened with the elder people. For them, the age indicated on the work card was not as important as the general impression from their physical appearance.

Those bed-ridden sick people and invalids were taken away without any accounting of their age.

In the houses where they did not have any hiding places, or where they didn't manage to climb into them yet, they quickly hid the small children in many ways. For example, they hid children in the bedding, in the clothes, in furniture, in trenches in the yard, in the toilets, in the attics, in the cellars, etc. The mothers were motivated to think up all sorts of inventions for hiding the children, just to delay the danger of having their children torn away forever.

There were instances when the children were suffocated in the hiding places. To keep the smaller children from crying and screaming in the hiding places, and thus, being found by the murderers, they would put them to sleep with the help of narcotics. There were more than a few unfortunate accidents from overdoses.

When the Gestapo, together with their assistants, the Ukrainians, stormed through the Ghetto, they got to work with great haste. They dragged children, the elderly, and the sick from the houses, from all corners of the Ghetto, loaded them onto trucks with dark windows and transported them out of the Ghetto. The screams and the wailing reached to the skies.

Trying to muffle the lamentations and crying of the children and the mothers who were forced with their own hands to give up their own little infants to the trucks, the Gestapo, played loud recorded music in the circulating buses. The heartbreaking scenes could not be drowned out by any jazz music. The cries of tortured Jews, who in the middle of the day were set upon by the Nazi murderers, were heard all over the Nazi area of the Ghetto.

[Page 208]

Specially trained dogs tore wildly at the unfortunate Jewish mothers who didn't want to give up their children, biting them with their very long teeth, until the mothers fell from weakness, and let go of the children from their arms. Then the Gestapo murderers would throw the children into the trucks.

The stubborn mothers, who did not let go of their children, were shot on the spot, or they were thrown into the trucks together with their children.

Considering that a portion of the Jews were hiding in their bunkers, or wherever they could hide themselves, the child-murderers were prepared with sticks and iron bars. Every wall, every door, every attic, every cellar that they considered suspicious and where they might find hidden Jews, was broken into and thoroughly ransacked.

They would get to work in such a thorough manner that in the cases where they uncovered a *malina*, they would use grenades. It would not take too long until they would either uncover the *malina* and collect the victims, or they would convince them that there is no way to hide.

Every house was ransacked a few times. Often, they would use chalk, with previously arranged markings, to indicate to the new Hitler commanders what the previous Gestapo had found from their search.

In the houses where Ukrainians themselves would carry out the orders - without the Germans - they would first take an offered bribe from the Jews and either take away the victims, or they would go away and immediately send in their friends to do it.

Around the Big Ghetto Workshops, from early in the morning, a guard was stationed who did not allow anyone in or out during the entire day.

The death factory in Dachau Concentration Camp

Above: A mountain of bones of the dead camp prisoners;
Below: The crematoria

Tombstone of Dr. Elkes at the mass grave in the former Camp 1 site near Landsberg.
Michael Burstein renown Polish-Jewish script writer. Was in Kovno Ghetto and died in Dachau.
An earthen hut in one of the Dachau labor camps.
Mass graves of dead camp prisoners near Schwabhausen (near Munich) on the eve before liberation.

[Page 209]

The misfortune was foreseen in the Ghetto Workshops, where many older people worked and a quite a few children were located. With urgency, they started hiding many children, and a portion of older people in the numerous buildings in the furthest situated corners of the workshops. The chase for victims took on a dramatic race, because there were children and older people who were hidden under huge piles of German military clothes, shoes, bolsters, etc., things that Jews were working on. In specific hiding places dozens and dozens of children and older persons were lying hidden, and while holding their breath, waited for a long time, and wondered how it would all end.

During the first Action Day in the Ghetto Workshops, through these various strategies and with great danger, they succeeded in avoiding a greater toll of victims.

Even worse, children were cut off from those who were hidden in the workshops, where Jews worked exclusively for the Gestapo. The Gestapo collected the hidden children and with murderous fury, they demonstrated their genuine Nazi "gratitude" to these Jewish craftsmen, the parents of these children, who slaved day in and day out, at their jobs.

The wild hunt by the murderous Nazis continued for an entire day. About 1000 children, elderly and sick persons were caught during the first day of the Action.

At that moment it was unknown where they took the victims. Later, it was understood that the victims of the first Action Day were taken away to Auschwitz, where they were gassed and burned in those gas chambers and crematoria, like millions of other Jewish victims.

From the Ghetto, they would transport the victims in trucks to the train where a special troop transport was prepared for them. At that time, it was said that the Action of children, elderly and the sick took place at the same time in the Vilna Jewish labor camp, and the transport with the Vilna victims met up with the Kovno troop transport at the Kovno railroad station.

Before nightfall, around 6 pm, the Action was halted. The murderers left the Ghetto area. The Jewish work brigades started returning from the city, and the special guards were disbanded from the Ghetto Workshops.

[Page 210]

The people who returned from work in the city or who were freed from their work in the Ghetto Workshops, ran wildly to their homes to see who was missing. There was almost no house where someone wasn't missing and taken away in the Action. Appalling and fearful scenes played out in the houses; people were crying hysterically over the victims, pulling their hair out of their heads, and fainting on the floor.

There were no words to comfort each other. The pain was horrible, and everyone was utterly broken up.

While crying over the victims of the previous day at the same time, each one was also thinking: what will happen tomorrow? Will the Action really be ordered for tomorrow also?

Nothing more can be said about what the Ghetto went through that night.

The night passed, and the following day was a sunny morning, Tuesday the 28th of March 1944. No one in the Ghetto knew whether the Action was over or not. Thus, all who had a place, hid their children and elderly.

On this Tuesday, the Jewish workers who worked in the city, were let out to work as usual. In the morning, several children aged 10-12, as well as elderly people succeeded in smuggling themselves through the Ghetto Gate into the city, alongside the workers brigade. In this way they avoided the tragic fate of the second day of the Action.

At eight in the morning, the murderers came into the Ghetto again and the Action was renewed.

Right from the start, it was seen that the main goal of the second day of the Action was to uncover the ghetto *malinas*. Right from the morning hours the sound of the grenades were heard. Two-faced human animals together with bloodhounds energetically and thoroughly ransacked every place in which there was suspected to be a *malina*.

[Page 211]

On the first Action Day when they would uncover a bunker, mainly to take away the children, elderly and sick, the young and healthy ones would be murderously beaten up and left in the Ghetto. But the second Action Day was different. From every uncovered *malina* they took everyone away-- whoever they found and transported them out of the Ghetto.

On the second Action Day some of the Jewish Police who were transported to the 9th Fort during the first Action Day, were seen seated together with the Gestapo in some Gestapo taxis, showing the Gestapo where *malinas* were to be found.

As it was later discovered, the murderous Gestapo Kittel, applied such aggressive measures on the arrested Jewish Police, that some of them who had a lower moral level, couldn't hold out and agreed to tell the Gestapo all he knew about the *malinas*, and in addition, certain details about the partisan movement in the Ghetto. These specific informants among the Jewish Police now participated in uncovering the *malinas*.

As previously mentioned, a very covert role was played by Benno Liptzer who had a "connection" with the Gestapo circles, and specifically with Kittel. To everyone's surprise, he was transported with the arrested Jewish Police to the Fort during the Action. According to later information, his "arrest", as it turns out, related to helping Kittel break the morale of the arrested Jewish Police.

Because of this informant, several *malinas* were discovered. There were cases where their own family members were inside the *malinas* which they betrayed. It was difficult to know whether these same informants knew what was taking place back in the Ghetto while they were sitting at the Fort. In any case, after their liberation from the Fort, they were considered by the Ghetto Jews like Gestapo agents, and they would watch out for them.

[Page 212]

At this opportunity, it is worthwhile adding that a few of these Jewish Police informants, who succeeded in hiding themselves during the Ghetto liquidation, were liberated by the Russians. They were later tried and judged by the Soviet Judicial Courts, to 10-15 years hard labor. Others, who were taken away in the deportation to the Dachau camp together with all the Jews, died in the first few weeks, because the Jews themselves terrorized them with beatings and persecution.

Not looking at the specific cluster of informants, the Jewish Police didn't betray the Ghetto during their arrest. As it will be submitted in later broader descriptions, there were then 40 Jewish policemen. Among them, the chief himself, together with his two helpers and almost all the higher police functionaries were killed at the 9th Fort in a horrible way. They sacrificed their young lives for their people.

The terror on the second day of the Action was more horrific than the first day. The Hitlerites and the Ukrainians went wild. In an unmerciful mood toward those Jews discovered in the *malinas*, they were shooting left and right.

During the second Action Day approximately 300 victims were caught, mostly from the *malinas*. As was later clarified, the victims from the second Action Day were taken to the 9th Fort and there they were all shot and immediately burned on the pyres, where they continued burning the dead who were excavated.

Once again, the Ghetto went through a horrific day that cost the Jewish residents a few hundred victims.

Night fell. Completely unexpectedly, the weather started to change. It started to storm. It snowed heavily and it became the start of a real winter. The snowstorm started in the morning of Wednesday, the 29th of March. It was unknown whether the Action would continue for a third day. As it turned out, the wonderfully bad weather disturbed the Gestapo from continuing the Action.

Wanting to find out directly from Goecke, the Elder Council was told that the Action absolutely must continue for a third day, because according to the recent compiling of registration from the ghetto residents, there had to be many more children and older people than were found during the two Action Days. So, Goecke took on the responsibility "to bring order to the issue" himself - the Action was stopped.

[Page 213]

While the Action was taking place in the Ghetto, the Gestapo also conducted a similar Action in the Jewish labor camps, which were located around Kovno and in the provinces.

In the work camps where the Jews lived cramped in barracks under a continuously strong guard, it was easier for the murderers to achieve their predatory goal. Here there wasn't even the smallest possibility to hide the children or the elders, which was the case in the main ghetto.

In all these labor camps approximately 500 victims were captured and were taken in an unknown direction to their annihilation.

In total in this Action of children, elders and sick, the toll of Kovno Jews was approximately 1800 victims.

This was the most dreadful Action in the Kovno Ghetto. In the previous mass murders, the Ghetto lost 20,000 souls, when mainly entire families would die together, but this Action was even more hostile, because children were torn away from their parents.

During this Action, the smallest hopes and illusions became utterly upended even among the more optimistic ghetto Jews. All assumptions about the end of the big mass murders of the Jews were now burst, like a soap-bubble. It was certain that no Jew would be able to get out alive from the devil's hand, unless there would be some indirect miracle.

Together with the grief of the victims of this horrific Action of the 27th and 28th of March, on the 29th of March the most painful and urgent question now developed: what to do with the hidden children? They were sure that the Ghetto would be attacked suddenly, and the surviving children would have the same fate as the victims of the Action.

[Page 214]

The answer to the posed question was clear: they had to get the children out of the Ghetto as soon as possible and give them over to some Christian families, who were not so reliable, but it couldn't be worse than in the Ghetto.

On the morning just after the Action, they very energetically mobilized to get the children out of the Ghetto, as fast as possible.

Officially, it was said that there were no longer any children younger than 12 years old or people older than 55 years old left in the Ghetto. Thus, it was decided to hide the smaller children in the house until whatever happens, and the children, from 7 or 8 years old were sent to the Ghetto Vocational School. The older people quickly started to get themselves a place to work in the Big Ghetto Workshops, in the Ghetto Gardens, in the lighter workplaces in the neighborhoods of the Ghetto, etc.

So that everything would be in order, they would make the children's work cards older than 12 years, and for the elderly ones, not older than 55 years.

To make the older people look a bit younger, they started dying their grey hair a dark color, and men started cutting off their beards, etc.

They started dressing the younger children in clothing of older children, in shoes with higher heels, etc. to make the little children look older.

It was extraordinarily painful to see the involuntary "rejuvenation" of the old people and the "aging" of the children.

About the children, it is necessary to note something: 3-4 months after the Action, that means, in the middle of July 1944, because of the approaching front line, the Ghetto, together with the surrounding work camps, were deported toward Germany. They were sent to the sorrowfully-infamous transit extermination camp – Stutthof, near Danzig. There, a selection of the transported women from Kovno took place.

Those women, whose children were taken from them during the Action, came to Stutthof alone, without children, and from there they were dispersed and sent to forced labor in the camps of Prussia. Several of them succeeded in surviving until the liberation.

[Page 215]

All those women, whose children were saved during the Action and had their children with them in Stutthof, were sent to Auschwitz for extermination and none of them remained alive.[b]

This is the strangely tragic fate of the Jews under the extermination system of the Nazi murderers…

Original footnotes:

    a. Regarding the fate of the other Jewish Police – See "Extermination of the Jewish Ghetto Police" and "Establishment of the "Service-Orders."
    b. See "The Fate of the Deported Jews"

CHAPTER XXV

Difficult Situation in the Ghetto

between April - June 1944

Liquidation of the Jewish Ghetto Police. - Founding the "Service Order". - Arrest of the Elders Council. - Final liquidation of the ghetto "autonomy." - New and more severe directives in the Ghetto regime: a. Increased guarding over the Jews, b. Systematic counting of the Jewish population c. Dressing the Jews in striped concentration camp uniforms d. Hasty measures to recruit the rest of the Jews in the Ghetto. - The arrest of the Partisan leader Chaim Yellin. - Gestapo attack on a Jewish Partisan group.

[Page 216]

A few days after the Action on the children, sick and elderly, the fate of the arrested Jewish policemen, and the existence of the Jewish Ghetto Police in general, were all clarified.

As was mentioned earlier, a total of 130 members of the Jewish Police were arrested. Thereafter, the Police Chief, together with his two assistants, were shot at the Fort. It seems that Kittel, with knowledge from his confidant in the Ghetto, B. Liptzer, carried out the following decision: about 40 responsible functionaries from the Jewish Police will remain in the Fort "until further notice." All others (90 some-odd men) would be freed from the Fort and be brought back to the Ghetto.

Approximately 40 higher officers of the Jewish Police, mentioned above, were later shot at the Fort. Kittel had doubts about shooting them because he had earlier wanted to extract money from the Jews for, let's say, freeing them. He did manage to extract a huge sum of money from the interested family members, but he never freed any of them. After shooting the policemen, their clothing, shoes, and boots were brought from the Fort and distributed to the German Kapos in the Ghetto.

[Page 217]

Aside from this blood bath of the Jewish Ghetto Police, the Gestapo decided to liquidate the Jewish Ghetto Police, and in its place established a Jewish "Service Order."

The "Service Order" consisted of 50 people. It only included those from the prior Jewish Ghetto Police, for whom the Gestapo didn't have any contempt. Understandably, with the ascension of the "Service Order" they worked with those who informed about the *malinas* during the Children's Action, and other morally dubious people from the former Jewish Ghetto Police.

There was a very essential difference between the entire liquidated Jewish Police and the new Gestapo "Service Order." While the Jewish Ghetto Police was an institution that was founded under the authority of the Elders Council, the "Service Order" was nominated and stood at the disposition of the Camp Commander, and, also under the Gestapo.

Regardless of all the shady sides of the Jewish ghetto informants in general, and of the Jewish Ghetto Police in particular, the Jewish ghetto institutions, for the most part, advanced the general Jewish interests.

The "Service Order," however, from the beginning until the end was an institution which had consistently collaborated with the Nazis against the interests of the ghetto population.

The ghetto Jews started relating to the members of "Service Order" with great suspicion and distrust. In Jewish families where children who were hidden from the Nazis during the Action were still found, they made sure to hide them, not only from the S.S. men, but also from the Jews who served in the "Service Order." Jews were also afraid that someone from the "Service Order," God forbid, should know about the *malinas*, or any other hidden items they possessed.

Later, when harsh directives were introduced to prevent Jews from leaving the Ghetto, the "Service Order" inflicted much damage on the Jews. When they learned about it, they were, directly and indirectly, responsible for many Jewish victims.

[Page 218]

One of the higher leaders of the "Service Order" was a specific Jewish young man named T. Arenshtam. While he was a high police official at the Ghetto Gate, he fulfilled his duties exceptionally well, with a brutal relationship toward the ghetto population. As the head boss of the "Service Order" he would go wild. Thus, after the liberation of Kovno he was sentenced to 15 years hard labor in jail by the Soviet court authorities.

In parallel to the liquidation of the Jewish Ghetto Police, the turn also came to liquidate the Elders Council, and the entire Jewish ghetto "autonomy."

On the afternoon of 4th of April 1944, Kittel came to the Ghetto and arrested the Elders Council, including the Chairman, Dr. Elkes, a few additional people from the Housing Office, from the Social Office, and the printers of the Elders Council. All those arrested were immediately transported to the 9th Fort.

After all the tragic experiences related to the Action on the children, elderly and sick, after the happenings with the Ghetto Police, this arrest of the Elders Council, including leaders of the ghetto institutions, created an extraordinary panic among the ghetto Jews. The Jews saw a sign through these arrests, that the regime was hastily advancing the liquidation of the Ghetto. Specifically, the arrest of Dr. Elkes was a huge surprise for the ghetto Jews, because everyone knew that the Camp Commander, Goecke, counted on him for the most part. So, the Jews thought that if he, Goecke, allowed Dr. Elkes' arrest, this probably had a very bad meaning for the Ghetto. In the Ghetto, all hell broke loose, and the Jews were horribly restless.

As it later turned out, this arrest stood in conjunction with the desire of the Gestapo to investigate details related to the building of *malinas* in the Ghetto, etc. Kittel decided to bring the arrested men to the Fort as a greater death shock, so that they would reveal everything they knew about the issue. Kittel knew very well what the symbol of the 9th Fort meant to the ghetto Jews.

[Page 219]

On the next day after the investigation, all the arrested were brought back to the Ghetto, except Advocate L. Garfunkel, the Vice Chairman of the Elders Council, and Advocate, Y. Goldberg, a member of the Elders Council.

After energetic Jewish intervention through Goecke, Advocate Goldberg was also freed after a few days.

The Jewish Ghetto Police and the Finance Office, among others, were overseen by the Elders Council under the competence of Advocate Garfunkel. Advocate Garfunkel was held at the Fort for a week's time, where he was tortured terribly. He was barely alive and with great effort was brought back to the Ghetto. The Gestapo ordered him not to leave the house until his wounds would heal a bit, so that the ghetto Jews shouldn't see how badly he was battered at the Fort.

After this arrest, Goecke informed Dr. Elkes that the Elders Council was liquidated. Dr. Elkes was appointed as the "Elder Jew" of the ghetto settlement. But, no counselor or colleague of Dr. Elkes was appointed, and his "power" was very restricted.

Together with the liquidation of the Elders Council, a final resolution also took place about the other remaining Jewish ghetto institutions which were barely alive, like the Jewish Labor Office, the Workshop Office, etc.

We must say, however, that since the Ghetto was converted into a concentration camp, the ghetto "autonomy" in fact, ceased to exist, because the Camp Command itself took over the order of all the ghetto issues, which until then were organized by the Jewish ghetto institutions.

Jewish "issue workers" were active in a few sections of the command, for the officials of the Camp Command to orient themselves easily into the management of ghetto matters.

Although initially the Jewish ghetto institutions still existed, their capacity shrank from day to day until they were ultimately liquidated. The last functions of the liquidated Jewish ghetto institutions were then transferred to the Camp Command.[a]

[Page 220]

These last events in the life of the Ghetto had such an impact, that a few Jews started actively feeling that the earth in the Ghetto is burning under their feet.

Whoever had even the smallest possibility of contacting a Christian acquaintance in the city or in the village, to be hidden by him, didn't consider anything else, and was prepared to do it as fast as possible. Anyone who even had the slightest possibility of shelter outside the Ghetto, started leaving the Ghetto.

In order to stop the Jews from escaping from the Ghetto, a hailstorm of decrees and directives came down on them. Let's mention only a few of the most important ones:

First, the guard around the Ghetto Fence was strengthened so that a Jew who wanted to leave the Ghetto would not be able to sneak out so easily.

Truth be told, Jews were able to get around this decree. With the help of the Jewish functionaries at the Ghetto Gate, they managed to find those guards who would be willing to take bribes. The Ghetto found out which of the guards took bribes, so if someone had to leave the Ghetto, he would seek out the "good" guards. to allow passage through the gate.

Also, the number of guards who accompanied the Jewish work brigades into the city to their work was strongly increased. For example, in 1942, there was a time in the Ghetto when the Jewish work brigades would go to work in the city without German guards at all, only accompanied by Jewish Ghetto Policemen. Later, some work brigades had only a few guards. Now, they introduced a very harsh order: for every 5-6

Jews who went into the city to work, there would have to be one guard. A workplace which could not get the proper military employees for the needed number of guards, could not use a Jewish worker from the Ghetto.

[Page 221]

Both at work, as well as around the workplace, the guarding was very strong. To smuggle oneself out of the workplace became much more difficult.

But not everything could be totally supervised to avoid Jewish escapes. Those Jews who had somewhere to go would find various ways to disappear and get to their Christian acquaintances.

To draw in the Jewish brigade leaders in the battle against Jews escaping from work, they put personal responsibility on the brigade leaders for those cases when a Jew in their brigade would disappear. At the Ghetto Gate there would be strong control by the guards on the number of Jews, in case anyone, God forbid, was missing. In the morning, upon exiting the Ghetto Gate to work and at their return at night from work, they were counted.

When all these measures couldn't stop Jews from leaving the Ghetto, Goecke got help from his Jewish "consultant" who thought of new stronger orders.

Controlling the number of Jews in a labor camp was very simple: they would conduct a roll call two times a day, in the morning and at night.

In the battle against escape from the Ghetto, Goecke, from time to time, would call the entire ghetto population together in a place, to conduct a roll call.

Officially, after the Children's Action only skilled workers remained in the Ghetto. Each ghetto Jew had to have a work post in the Ghetto or in the city. As confirmation while they worked, they earned a work card, which would be given out by the German Labor Office in the Ghetto. As you can imagine, little children or elderly people hidden from the Action could not get a work card, because they were "illegal" in the Ghetto.

[Page 222]

The Gestapo was "talented" in taking care of these issues, as was seen by Kittel's actions. Once, when he was in the Ghetto, he held up an old woman who didn't have a work card and he immediately transported her away to the Fort and shot her.

Such a roll call of the entire ghetto population had to take place at an open place, and there would not be any way to manage the hidden children or elderly people. Nor was it possible to take them with them to the roll call because they did not have any work cards, nor would they be able to leave them in the house, in case the homes were searched, and the children found.

Finally, Goecke was successfully persuaded to agree that the Jewish "Service Order" carry out the count alone, while searching in the homes of the ghetto population.

Later, the following order was established: all residences in the Ghetto were numbered according to the row and a few houses were counted for a separate block. In each block the "Service Order" appointed a block manager.[b] Twice a day, in the morning before going out to work, and in the evening before going to sleep, each block manager would visit all residents from the block, to personally determine if any one of the residents was missing.

The "Service Order" had formulas prepared especially for the task, by which the block-managers, after the count, twice a day, would have to stand up in the center of the "Service Order" which had already, from their side, sent the report over to the Camp Commandant.

By introducing such strong and systematic control over the ghetto residents, they would be able to determine who was missing from the Ghetto on the same day.

Since all this was not by force, nor did it hold up the functioning of the Ghetto, the "Service Order" thought up new draconian measures:

[Page 223]

If the "Service Order" was suspicious of a few Jews who had an escape from the Ghetto in mind, they would be arrested and held in the Ghetto Jail, until the arrested would put up great amounts of ransom money and a personal guarantee from a random ghetto resident, that the arrested would not leave the Ghetto. Then he was let out of jail and held under police supervision. Also, it was not a radical remedy to block those who had prepared to leave the Ghetto.

Later, it was ordered that in the case of someone leaving the Ghetto, from whichever block, the nearest family members, or even anyone nearby in the same block, would be turned over to the Camp Command. This was to encourage Jews to spy on one another.

As mentioned, by setting up these stricter rules for the Ghetto, the tone-setters of the "Service Order" and other Jewish ghetto authorities played a great role. They did everything to charm Goecke, the almighty boss of the Ghetto.

To make it more and more impossible for Jews from the Ghetto, or from the labor camps, to run away to Christians, the Camp Commander, Goecke, decided to take the clothes away from the Jews and dress them in striped clothing, as was the "fashion" in all German concentration camps.

By ordering the Jews to wear concentration camp clothes, the Camp Commander wanted to achieve a few goals at the same time: first, a Jew dressed in striped concentration camp clothes, as well as yellow patches on the breast and on the back, would stand out in the non-Jewish population. If they wanted to run away, it would be a major disturbance for the Jew, because they would immediately be recognizable wherever they would be seen. Second, by taking away their clothes and dressing the Jews in concentration camp clothes, they would not have anything to exchange when they would eventually have the possibility to run away. By the way, it was also a new opportunity again to rob the Jews of the remnants of their baggage. Third, taking clothes away from the Jews removed the most important material item with which to entice the Christians to hide a Jew with them, since they wanted to receive something tangible from the Jews, like their clothes.

[Page 224]

We must say that this decree to wear concentration camp clothes and at the same time take away the former clothes, was taken very badly by the Jews; it was very painful.

At first, only the Jews from the labor camps had to put on concentration camp clothing. Entirely unexpectedly, S.S. men arrived one day at the Alexot Labor Camp, and took away almost all of the Jews' clothes and dressed them in the concentration camp clothes. A few days later this also took place in the Shantz Labor Camp.

As was mentioned earlier, the Shantz camp leader, Bentzko, had a fairly good relationship with the Jews. He actually told them beforehand, which day they would come into the camp to dress them in the concentration camp clothes. In this way the Jews had an earlier opportunity to hide their clothes either in the camp itself or take them out to hide somewhere in the workplace. Thus, in the Shantz camp they managed to take away fewer Jewish clothes.

While all the Jews in the labor camp were already "dressed up" in the concentration camp clothes, they were supposed to have their own clothes transported into the Ghetto. But they didn't manage to do it due to the Soviet offensive of June 1944. Thus, they quickly had to schedule the liquidation of the entire Ghetto.

Despite all these restrictions and decrees that were declared by the Camp Commander to strengthen the ghetto routine, they absolutely could not avoid the possibility of Jews running away from the Ghetto. Aside from that, Goecke knew very well that due to the general events on the fronts, the liquidation of the Ghetto would eventually come much earlier than was originally planned.

It was already previously stated that the occupation regime at that time considered it worthwhile to hold the Jews in labor camps, where it was possible to set up an even stronger regime than in the Ghetto.

[Page 225]

Therefore, they quickly started to liquidate the rest of the Jews from the work brigades in the city and divide them up among the existing camps in Alexot or in Shantz, depending on which workplace was closer. Again, some hundred ghetto families were quartered in the camps. Now came the turn to quarter about 700 Jews in labor camp Petroshun, where they only had to finish building the barracks. In addition, they had to quarter the Jewish work brigades which worked in Slabodka factories. The camp command decided to carry out these quarterings in the shortest possible time.

Once all the Jews who worked in the city were quartered, the turn would finally come to also quarter Jews who worked in the Ghetto itself. That meant, those from all the ghetto workshops and in the ghetto administration.

The Soviet offensive destroyed all the plans of the Camp Command, thus, Goecke was not fated to execute any concrete plan on how to quarter the Ghetto itself.

On the day of the liquidation of the Ghetto, in the beginning of July 1944, there were approximately 7-8 thousand Jews still in the Ghetto.

As mentioned, Chaim Yellin was the head leader of the ghetto movement to escape into the forest to the partisans. He was a young man from Kovno, who before the war stood close to the leftist circles, and also belonged to the Jewish progressive group of typesetters in Lithuania.

Chaim Yellin, a mid-height, thin young man of about 30 years old, demonstrated an outstanding heroism and boldness in this specific work.

To illustrate his habits and courage one can judge from the following facts: at the time many young Jewish people were killed when they fell into the hands of the Gestapo while searching alone along the way to find the partisans. Since in the Ghetto they were missing the needed connections to get to the partisans, he set out enroute searching for partisans, so that the ghetto youth would have someone to help them.

[Page 226]

After getting through a round trip of 400 kilometers, he finally got into the Rudnicki forests around Vilna, and there he made contact with the leader of those partisans.[c]

As a result, one of the most important questions was solved once and for all: they now had a real address for the partisans to receive the youth from the Ghetto. It is certainly unnecessary to say that such a "saunter" was deathly dangerous at that time.

Or, for example, such a fact: dressed in a uniform from, let's say, a train official, properly made up, he would often go around the Kovno streets with arms in his pockets, in order to organize the transport of people to the partisans.

In later days, he was actually outside the Ghetto more than inside. The major activities of the partisan movement in the Ghetto lay in his hands and he had great results.

After the Action on children, elderly and ill, as well as on other severe measures by the Gestapo on the Ghetto, Kittel decided to capture Chaim Yellin at any price.

One day at the start of April 1944, Chaim Yellin was going on an important mission on a side street in Kovno, when a suspicious looking Lithuanian passerby appeared. He was an agent of the Lithuanian Security Police who wanted to arrest him. Chaim Yellin in broad daylight took the revolver out of his pocket and shot him on the spot. He managed to disappear over a fence.

Because of the shooting, a noise arose, and a collection of passersby, and military men chased him and tried to catch him alive. Chaim Yellin however succeeded in evading his pursuers. Through courtyards and detours he got into the courtyard of an acquaintance where he wanted to hide.

[Page 227]

As he ran into the courtyard, a German officer wanted to arrest him because his external appearance showed that he was being pursued by someone. A Lithuanian policeman who was passing by came to help the officer. Chaim Yellin opened fire on them and in the chaos that arose, he disappeared and climbed into a cellar in the courtyard. It took a long while until he was discovered by the police in his hiding place. Not wishing to fall into the hands of the Gestapo alive, and not having any more bullets to commit suicide, he tried to cut his veins with his shaving blade. They brought him, wounded, to the Gestapo.

Kittel, for whom the arrest of Chaim Yellin was an unexpected surprise, did everything so that Chaim Yellin should recover as soon as possible, in order to interrogate him and get important details out of him about the partisan movement.

Various versions circulated around the Ghetto about the end of Yellin's arrest. According to the general widespread version, Chaim Yellin decided, as they say, to take Kittel to hell. He calculated that by going close to the partisan nest, maybe Kittel would fall into the partisan hands. So, he told him that he would take him to show where the partisans are located.

Kittel understandably hoped to achieve his own goal: to get to the hiding place of the partisans.

So, for a while, there took place, so to speak, a "cat and mouse game" between Kittel and Yellin. Kittel, however, it seems, didn't have a great desire to stick his nose too close into the partisan nest, and he did away with him.

Understandably, it is hard to know whether this version is true or not. In any case there is no doubt that Chaim Yellin was shot by the Gestapo.

Chaim Yellin's outstanding courage and detachment was truly a wonder. Specifically, those who knew him well from those days were surprised, because he was a quiet and modest person, who didn't look skilled for such heroic actions at all.

[Page 228]

In the story of the Kovno Ghetto settlement, Chaim Yellin will be remembered as a symbol of the outstanding heroism and courage of a young Jewish man who was resolute in an unequal battle against the blood thirsty Nazi murderers, who were armed from head to toe.

After all these happenings in the Ghetto, when Goecke decided to take all the ghetto Jews firmly into his hands, and specifically after Chaim Yellin's arrest, it became clear that the most important leaders of the partisan movement could not remain in the Ghetto because the Gestapo took measures to find and arrest them. These people therefore had to leave for the partisan nests as soon as possible.

As had always been arranged, a car was supposed to pick them up in the vicinity of the Ghetto and take them to pick them to a predetermined point from where they would be able to get to the forest.

On Shabbat, the 14th of April 1944, around 8 or 9 o'clock at night, a group of about 12 Jewish young men and women got into the car which was supposed to take them from Slabodka to their nearest point.

While travelling across the Slabodka bridge and driving on Janover Street, suddenly the driver started to drive slower. The Jews asked what happened, to which he responded something about a problem with the motor. The youngsters immediately started to suspect that something in this story is not right and with guns in their hands they were ready for any surprises. Suddenly the driver stopped the car and said that he must get out to look at the motor.

In that same minute when the car stopped, suddenly a hailstorm of bullets came from all sides into the car. It was later understood that the driver was a traitor, and he informed the Gestapo about the entire story of travelling to the partisans.

Gestapo and S.S. men, under the leadership of Kittel and Goecke, were hiding behind a house and waited for the car. They opened fire on the Jews with automatic weapons and machine guns.

[Page 229]

Without getting lost in the moment, the Jews first shot the driver and started responding with heavy shooting in all directions. Eight Jews were killed immediately on the spot. In the darkness the four remaining Jews, with guns in their hands, managed to tear themselves out of the encirclement and disappear.

These four heroic youngsters later got to the partisans in the woods. Two of them were killed in a battle against the Germans, but the other two succeeded in surviving until liberation.

The earlier attack on Chaim Yellin, and then the attack on the Jewish partisan group, combined with the newly strengthened regime introduced in the Ghetto, paralyzed the small but energetic resistance movement in the Ghetto.

Original footnotes:

    a.   About the activities of the Jewish ghetto institutions and about their role in ghetto life, see Monograph: "Jewish Institutions in the Kovno Ghetto."
    b.   There were more block managers in the larger blocks.
    c.   This was the Lithuanian-Jewish Communist activist, H. Zieman, who, as a Soviet parachutist, landed in the forests around Vilna in 1943 and, under the name "Yorgis," conducted partisan activities in that neighborhood.

CHAPTER XXVI

Deportation and Liquidation of the Ghetto

-Kovno becomes a front zone-Tense situation in the Ghetto on the eve of the deportation-The course of the first days of the deportation-The Gestapo's murderous measures during the last days of the deportation-Horrible destruction of the Ghetto-Terrible end for 1,500 Jews who were hidden

[Page 230]

On the 6th of June 1944, the long awaited second front in Eastern Europe was finally opened. The quick and safe landing of huge numbers of people and war materials of the exemplary military undertaking of the western allies would, without a doubt, sooner or later be crowned with great success, according to primary witness accounts.

The news of the invasion into northern Germany had an impact like a spark in a strongly cloudy dark night. Even for the biggest Ghetto pessimist it became clear that, thanks to this magnificent military campaign, the final defeat of Nazi Germany and its collaborating servants would be greatly sped up.

After the opening of the second front in the west, it was only a matter of time for the front to open on the east. The combined military forces would soon start war operations on the largest scale as soon as possible, in order to put an end to the most dreadful bloodbath in the world. On the 22 of June 1944, the large Soviet offensive began 16 days after the beginning of the invasion of Normandy, on the central Russian front sector near Vitebsk.

[Page 231]

During the first days of the offensive, the noisy tempo of the Soviet assault brought surprising success for the Soviet Union. At many sites, they broke through the German front legions, and the Red Army cut very deep into the German positions.

During the first days of July, Kovno fell into the front zone. This was completely unexpected for the Germans in Kovno and for the Lithuanian people. After the liberation of Minsk and the approach to Vilna in the beginning of July, they started evacuating the most important German military and civil institutions from Kovno. At the same time, the civilian people closer to the German border domain started evacuating.

After the hurried and unexpected evacuation of the Germans, almost all the Lithuanian people were caught in real shock and panic. The Lithuanians were afraid of the Soviets because they knew full well the kind of great sins they committed during the first Soviet occupation: the armed campaign against the retreating Red Army in June of 1941, the active participation in the massacre of the Jewish people, the open cooperation with the occupation, etc.

The forward movement of the Red Army on the segment front between Minsk and Vilna slowed down for about 1 or 2 days, so the evacuation from the city stopped. Bit by bit the various evacuated institutions started to return. But quite rapidly, the momentum of the Soviet offensive was reinforced, and it became clear that the Germans will not be able to hold their positions. Then the evacuation from the city started up again and this time continued definitively.

In these days, the agitation and the shock were unimaginable for the Germans and the Lithuanians in the city. The mood of the Ghetto Jews was in visible contrast. On the one hand, there was stirred-up happiness due to the realization of their multiyear dream to survive the disaster of the Nazis. But, on the other hand, there were deeply upsetting feelings as they awaited the decisive fateful days for the Ghetto.

These feelings and the mood were characterized by the old time Ghetto saying: "salvation is on the nose and the slaughter knife is on the neck."

[Page 232]

What will the Nazi murderers do with the Jews now? This was now the actual burning problem among the Ghetto folk, and it didn't allow even one minute's peace- neither during the day, nor at night.

Simple logic indicated that first, the Nazis absolutely would not leave the Jews in Kovno when everyone from the city was quickly evacuating. Secondly, it was certain that now, as the Red Army was getting closer to the gates of Kovno by the hour, the Nazis would not hesitate to burn down the Ghetto site, which, together with the labor camps around Kovno, amounted to 10,000 people.

Thus, there is only one possibility: deportation. But, how and to where?

This is how the early days of the month of July passed, with such tension and uncertainty about the future fate of the Ghetto.

The upheavals at the eastern front and the feverish evacuation from Kovno caused the following: the strong severity of the ghetto regime suddenly collapsed like a house of cards. The block managers stopped conducting their roll call, the Service Order became very lax in their harsh attitude toward to the Ghetto folk, etc. Every Ghetto Jew really felt that the dilemma was hanging in the air: either – or? That is, either salvation will arrive in the coming days, or the end will come to the seventy years…

On Wednesday, the 5th of July, nests of machine guns and a strengthened guard presence of Lithuanian S.S. men was set up around the Ghetto Gate. It was plain to see that guards were being prepared for various eventualities on the part of the Ghetto folk, who may attempt to tear through the fence to run away from the Ghetto.

At first, during these days of turmoil, Jews were still allowed to go out to work in the city. But, day after day, the number of runaway Jews increased, and the runaways left in masses. So, Goecke, the Camp Commander, prohibited the Jews from going to work in the city workplaces.

[Page 233]

It was still officially unclear what the Camp Commander was planning to do with the Ghetto Jews. In a conversation with the head Jew, Dr. Elkes, Goecke expressed his hope that the German army would surely manage to hold off the Russian onslaught and "everything would end peacefully."

Meanwhile, the panic in the Ghetto was growing by the hour. Similarly, Thursday the 6th of July, after noon, Goecke sent for Dr. Elkes and officially shared that the regime decided that the Ghetto would be transported to Germany. At this opportunity he told him the following:

The Ghetto would be evacuated to the outskirts of Danzig. All the Ghetto workshops would be transported there, and a work camp would be established for the Jews from the Kovno Ghetto. The evacuation will start on Shabbat in the morning, the 8th of July, and will be completed over a few days. But due to transport difficulties, it was not possible to procure the necessary train wagons, so the evacuation probably would go by water, with boats on the Nieman to the sea, and then by sea to Danzig. None of the Ghetto Jews should even think of escaping the evacuation, because there would be searches in the homes and any others caught in hiding, would be shot on the spot.

Thus, the Camp Commander's cards were opened. When the notice by the Camp Commander became known, the atmosphere in the Ghetto became highly charged. Groups of Jews started gathering around the houses to talk about the upcoming deportation.

The general dominant opinion was that the Jews would not allow themselves to be deported. Everyone was sure that after occupying Vilna, the occupation of Kovno would only be a question of a few days. In this respect the most important issue was – to gain time. Even in the most serious case, that is, if, God forbid, one was not fated to survive to liberation, it is better to die on the spot in the Ghetto, rather than be dragged somewhere else to be exterminated.

The Ghetto Jews connected Goecke's communication about deportation by boats, to the various reports from the foreign radio, which recently described how the Nazis started to destroy Jews by sending them out on a ship in the open sea and there sinking the ship together with the Jews.

[Page 234]

Therefore, it was understandable why Goecke's announcement about shipping the Jews by water, even strengthened the fear that they were transporting the Jews not for work in Danzig, but rather somewhere on the open sea to exterminate them. This even validated the objective that in no way should they allow themselves to be deported.

Therefore, the Ghetto Jews, with incredible speed, started preparing themselves to hide in the *malinas* the moment the deportations would begin. Other Ghetto Jews, who didn't have their own *malinas*, urgently started searching for opportunities to partner-up with people they knew to get into someone else's *malina*.

A few, who could afford a watch, a gold ring, a bigger sum of money, etc., started looking for a way to bribe a soldier at the Ghetto Gate, who would allow them the opportunity to get out of the Ghetto. At that opportunity, there were more than a few criminal stories about some delinquent soldiers who would take the Jews' valuables or money, and then not let him through the Ghetto Gate, or after letting them through the gate, they would shoot them down.

From Thursday night to Friday a larger group of Jews, who already got through the Ghetto Gate, were shot right near the Ghetto. Due to a denunciation by the soldier who allowed them through, or even without a denunciation, these Jews were killed by the S.S. sniper, Pilgram, who was lurking near the gate with a machine gun. Among those who were shot was also L. Yellin (the father of the Partisan leader, Chaim Yellin). In Kovno, he was well known by the nickname, "lover of knowledge," as a person from the large Jewish library and book camp.

Friday, the 7th of July, was the last "free" day in the Ghetto. Almost no one was allowed out to work in the city. And no one went to work inside the Ghetto either. All the Jews were occupied with only one sole thought- how can we avoid the deportation?

The authorized Jewish Ghetto rulers attempted to "serve the Ghetto" until the last minute. They were occupied with preparing lists of the first groups of Jews for deportation. But as was seen, this time their work was totally for naught.

To convince the ghetto Jews that they should "willingly" allow themselves to be deported, an order was announced – that with the first deportations, they would allow the older and weaker persons to travel together, something that was not altogether assured in the deportation of later groups, and maybe later they would have to walk. Many Jewish families, who had older or sick people, and who didn't have a place to hide, allowed themselves to be influenced by these rumors. But, as was said, most Jews, were determined not to go.

By nightfall, the number of Jews in the streets became smaller and smaller. The Camp Commander knew very well that the Jews had decided not to allow themselves to be deported. He knew that they were getting themselves ready for the moment when the Gestapo would come into the Ghetto and would start catching Jews for deportation. Each person, therefore, was immediately ready to climb into their furrow and wait there for further occurrences.

That night, a sudden air-raid signaled the arrival of the Soviet airplanes. The arrival of the Soviet Air Force, this time more than ever, set the Ghetto Jews in motion, most of whom were already lying in their hiding places. But that night, no bombing took place. Squeezed into their *malinas*, the Jews were ready not to give in to the bloody enemies and somehow carry on until liberation, which was, according to everyone's assessment, only a matter of days.

The night passed and the coming day was a hot summery Shabbat day on the 8th of July 1944 – the first day of the deportation. In the streets of the Ghetto, movement was almost completely dead. Here and there you could see a policeman from the "Service Order." With great anxiety, the Jews awaited what would come.

[Page 236]

When parties of Germans came into the Ghetto, they began to collect people. An entire Ghetto quarter (the small wooden block of houses on Mildas Street and the neighboring streets) was surrounded, and the Germans started their work: chasing them out of the houses and taking them to a place near the camp command post. During the first day of deportation the Germans satisfied themselves with a superficial search for the hidden Jews. They hadn't yet applied any sharp measures.

The newly caught Jews were transported to the Nieman port, where they were loaded onto boats and transported on the river in the direction of Tilzit, to the sea.

Starting on the Friday, they started collecting the Jews from the Small Workshops in the neighborhoods of Kovno, like Palemon, Kazlove-Rude, Roitn-Hof [Raudondvaris], etc. to attach them to the deportation of the Jews from the Ghetto. The Jews from the workshops in Kaydan and Ponevesh were taken to Shavl. And from there they were transported to Germany.

At this opportunity, it is worthwhile relating an interesting case that happened with the workshop in Kozlove-Rude, 40 km. from Kovno.

In the Kozlove-Rude Camp there were some four-five hundred Jews. By marching them on foot from Kozlove-Rude toward Kovno, they met up with a larger group of German soldiers, among whom were also a few Ukrainians. Since they saw that the Soviets were quite close, the Ukrainians, who, at the last moment, wanted to procure a little piece of the "next world," took it upon themselves to volunteer their services to a group of Jews. They offered to run away together with them to the Soviet partisans, who were located in the surrounding forests.

The leaders of the guard told all the soldiers that if anyone would notice any danger from a partisan ambush they should immediately shoot in the air and thereby signal all the soldiers and the Jews to lie down on the ground.

In the evening, the transport arrived in the forest. Wanting to make the rest of the soldiers lie down on the ground and thereby give the group of Jews, together with Ukrainians, an opportunity to run away into the forest, the Ukrainians suddenly shot up in the air. The German soldiers immediately laid down on the ground, and approximately one hundred Jews, together with the Ukrainian soldiers, ran into the forest and disappeared. As they recovered, the Germans started shooting at the runaways, but they didn't succeed in catching anyone. German soldiers were afraid to chase the runaways into the forest at night.

[Page 237]

The only Jews who ran away were those who were in the back rows and knew the plan with the Ukrainians. The remaining Jews were thus, very upset, as they saw that a portion of their friends escaped, and they remained. The largest portion of the runaways, however, were killed by the Germans and Lithuanians, who in another neighborhood persecuted the Soviet partisans.

The Jews who were brought from the labor camps into the Ghetto were allowed by the Camp Commander to freely disperse, because they didn't evade the deportation. Many of them, who had friends and knew of their *malinas,* also crawled inside. That is how the deportation days went by.

Sunday, the 9th of July, was very quiet in the Ghetto because Goecke couldn't procure boats for the deportation. To procure rail cars was even more difficult because the trains were specifically reserved for military transports.

A radical change in the search for the hidden Jews took place from Monday, the 10th of July, in the morning. From the early morning hours, it was plain to see that the Gestapo, which came into the Ghetto to find the hidden Jews, received strong instructions.

They deployed to all the corners of the Ghetto where they very energetically and thoroughly started searching for the *malinas* and other hiding places where Jews were hiding. In each place where they uncovered a hiding place, they started setting the grenades in motion. The Gestapo also brought with them German shepherds, which helped them in their work to uncover the Jews.

[Page 238]

By such drastic means the Gestapo succeeded in finding many Jews. Throwing a grenade into the area of a *malina*, the children in the hiding places started screaming and crying from fright, and thereby everyone was found out, even before being discovered by the Gestapo.

With great barbarity, the Gestapo would pull the hidden Jews out of their hiding places. The deathly shocked children would faint in a lamentable cry and, in great fear, clung on to their parents. With their heads down, like a prisoner of war after a lost battle, the Jews were chased to the assembly square under a tight convoy of Gestapo. There was no question about taking any clothing or food products with them.

The bangs of the grenades, the barking of the German shepherds, the swearing of the Gestapo, the screams of the children, etc., all mixed together in an orgy of tears and blood.

In this manner a greater number of hidden Jews was discovered on this Monday. They were transported to the port, from where they were to be shipped with boats, like the Saturday's transport. However, no boat succeeded in coming and they had to risk bringing the people back to the Ghetto, where they were held in a gated place near the Camp Commandant.

On the same day, they collected the Jews from the Aleksotas labor camp, and they were brought to the train, which took them directly to Germany.

Tuesday, the 11th of July, the search for the hidden Jews continued with the same ferocity as on Monday. During this Tuesday, there were hundreds of Jews who were pulled out of their holes and were taken to the assembly place near the Commandant.

Since Goecke could not procure any more boats and he didn't have any wagons available for the deportation, the Jews who were captured on the Monday and Tuesday, were held under the open sky until Wednesday morning, the 12th of July. Then all were shipped by train towards Germany.

[Page 239]

Wednesday, the 12th of July, was designated as the last day of the deportation. On this day they were supposed to deport the remaining Jews from the Ghetto, including locking up the Jewish officers near the Camp Commandant, and the workers from the various ghetto workshops, etc.

In many places in the Ghetto, more houses and other buildings went up in flames with tongues of fire from the grenades. This was the fate that awaited all the Ghetto houses including all the Jews, everything inside, and everything hidden underneath.

There were also cases when hidden Jews who discovered that the last transport had left, had to decide whether to die under the ruins of the bombed houses, or be shot in the act of being discovered. They themselves got out of their hiding place and willingly joined the deported Jews, who were seated on the pavement of Varniu Street.

Meanwhile, the search for the hidden Jews by the Gestapo and S.S. continued with boisterous tempo. Minute by minute, Jews were being discovered, exhausted, half naked, dejected, with infants in their hands. They were brought to the Jews who were seated on the ground, waiting for the order to march out of the Ghetto. Sick and weak people, who could not be deported because of their health situation, were ordered to be taken to the Ghetto Hospital. Later, they were burned to death when they bombed and burned all the houses in the Ghetto, as well as the hospital.

Wednesday morning, a large transport of Jews had already left by train, and that afternoon Goecke acquired more transport wagons for 3000 Jews.

Around 12 o'clock there was an order to line up in columns of 100 people and under a strong convoy of Gestapo carrying automatic rifles, the transport of over 2000 Jews started marching through side streets of the city to the train station in Alexot.

During the march out of the Ghetto, the sky almost symbolically, became covered with black clouds. It started thundering strongly and a downpour began.

[page 240]

On the way, many Jews were able to tear themselves away from the columns and run away. The automatic weapons from the accompanying Gestapo started banging all over. Quite a lot of Jews were shot on the spot; only a few succeeded in disappearing from the transport.

At the platform 40 transport wagons were waiting, the majority of which had small square windows and a special guard in each separate wagon. They were carefully guarded.

The Jews from the Shantz Labor Camp were brought to this train transport. As mentioned earlier, the camp leader, Bentzko Hart, ran away before the deportation, with his Jewish lover. In the meantime, before Goecke sent another camp leader, a few Jews ran away from the camp. A mass runaway didn't take place because the Jewish camp leaders foiled any mass size escapes, so that those Jews who couldn't run away and had to continue with the deportation, shouldn't suffer.

More than 3000 Jews were crammed together like herring in a barrel, in the transport wagons, when the train started to move out. It did not stop at any one of the stations enroute and the train transport hurried in the direction of Germany.

Enroute, a few dozen Jews succeeded in jumping out of the speeding train. Some of them died after jumping, because they fell into the hands of Germans or bad Lithuanians who killed them. Others were killed through the risky jump out of the high windows of the transport wagons. Only a few individuals succeeded in getting through all the mortal danger and waiting 3-4 more weeks for the Red Army to finally free them.

In one transport, which left in the morning, the accompanying soldiers noticed that Jews were jumping from the train. They stopped the train, and in each wagon, they designated hostages who were responsible for anyone running away from the transport. In fact, in other wagons they shot Jews, just to scare others from thinking of running away.

[Page 241]

Knowing how many Jews were supposed to be in the Ghetto and how many Jews had already been deported throughout that time, Goecke saw that many Jews were still lying hidden in the *malinas*, that is, in hideouts.

Just after the departure of the daytime transport, the Gestapo started to search for the remaining hidden Jews with great care. Through the application of all kinds of terror-strategies, the Gestapo succeeded in uncovering more Jews. The newly captured Jews were held near the workshops.

Thursday, the 13th of July, many houses were already in flames. Wanting to uncover even more hidden Jews, the Gestapo started applying various provocative measures. Thus, as a trick, the Gestapo took away the children from the discovered Jews and promised to give them back to the adults only when the adults would tell them where there are other hiding places, and where there are more hidden Jews. With the help of these vile provocations, the Gestapo wanted to demoralize the Jews and prod them into squealing, to make reaching their goal easier: the continuous uncovering of the hidden Jews.

Only a few Jews allowed themselves to be persuaded by the Gestapo to squeal about hideouts in exchange for "saving" their children.[a]

The killing and the violence by the Gestapo rose hour by hour. The deportation transport on Thursday didn't take any Jews who had been pulled out of the holes and dens, looking totally black, exhausted, and broken up. These people were left in the Ghetto, where they later shot them and threw them into the flames of the burning houses. In the end, the Gestapo was successful in collecting over 1000 Jews who were deported to Germany on Thursday.

[Page 242]

This was the last large deportation transport from the Ghetto.

After the departure of the last transport of Jews, the Gestapo saw that they could no longer find the remaining hidden Jews, because their hideouts were very well hidden, and they could not locate their traces. So, the Gestapo stepped up and carried out the last point of their plan to liquidate this ghetto: blowing up and setting fire to some ghetto houses and burning any Jews who were still not uncovered.

Friday, the 14th of July in the morning, together with the Kovno section of the Waffen S.S., a few dozen Jews from the work brigades who were working the whole time for the S.S., were deported. Thereafter, a special bombing commando came into the Ghetto, and with great vigor started their extermination work. Liquid burning material was spilled on every wooden house and then blown up and burned up. The few houses made of walled blocks were blown up with the help of dynamite.

In the various *malinas* there were still about 1500 Jews hiding. When the bombing or the fire reached the *malina* where Jews were lying hidden, they tried to save themselves from the burning hideouts (if they could still manage).

All around, the burning houses were patrolled by German soldiers who immediately shot any Jews who would want to save themselves from the fire, and then throw them back in the flames. There were many cases where the Germans also threw Jews into the fire while still alive.

Long tongues of fire wrapped in thick smoke clouds shot out to the sky from the torn up and torched Ghetto houses. The Ghetto continued to burn for several days, and under the burning houses hundreds of Jewish men, women and children were struggling with a cruel death. None of these martyrs succeeded in saving themselves from the frightful destruction in this hellish fire.

Saturday, the 15th of July at night, the Gestapo, together with their Lithuanian helpers at last left the area of the Ghetto after finalizing their murdering and leaving their destructive and gruesome tracks behind. Only a week before there existed a settlement of between 7 to 8 thousand Jewish souls.

[Page 243]

Kovno was liberated by the Red Army on the 1st of August 1944.[b] A few days later, little by little, the few miraculously surviving Jews started to return to the city. Everyone's first task was to run and see what the destruction of the Ghetto looked like.

The images that they saw on the site of the former Ghetto were horrific; in the Ghetto not one single house was left intact. All the wooden houses were completely burned. The large, massive walls of the brick block of houses were lying in ruins, like after an earthquake. Throughout entire areas of the Ghetto the monstrous skeletons of dead and burned Jews were seen. In full view of the blown up *malinas* heaps of Jewish dead were lying. According to the cramped-together, still incompletely burned bodies, one could recognize the worrisome struggle that these victims went through in the dying moments during their violent death.

Witnesses described the boundless murders by the Nazi mass murderers and called the world to take bloody revenge on the most horrific barbarians of all times – the brown Teutons of the 20th century.

Original footnotes:

    a. In any case, the children were sent away together with their mothers to Auschwitz to be killed a few days later.
    b. After occupying Vilna on the 13th of July, the Russians didn't go directly to Kovno as the Jews anticipated, but rather, they left Kovno out for earlier strategic reasons. As a result, the Nazis had much more time to do whatever they wanted with the Ghetto.

CHAPTER XXVII

Fate of the Deported Jews

*- What happened to the deported Jews when they arrived in Germany?-
The painful road of the men in the Dachau hell- The fate of the women
taken to the East-Prussian labor camps*

[Page 244]

Two transports of Jews which left Kovno by train on Wednesday, the 12th of July, arrived in the morning and afternoon at the Tigenhof train station, not far from the Stutthof Concentration Camp, on Thursday, the 13th of July 1944.

Just as they arrived in Tigenhof, the afternoon transport from both sections were divided: men separately, and women with children, again separately. A certain portion of older boys succeeded in remaining together with the men. All the younger children remained together with the women.

In Tigenhof, Dr. Elkes approached one of the S.S. men and asked why families were being torn apart. He then added that at the evacuation, the Kovno Ghetto Camp Commander, Goecke, promised that this would not happen. So, he received the answer to his question - a few fiery slaps from the S.S. man.

There was a tremendous commotion among the women because of the separation from the men, as they believed that this was about an extermination Action. A few Jewish doctors tried to commit suicide by injecting themselves with poison. Dr. Levin, a young Jewish female doctor died in Tigenhof from this injection.

[Page 245]

On the same day the column with the men was transported from Tigenhof. The men travelled without knowing where they were being taken. Most of the men were sure that they were being taken for extermination. In a few of the wagons the men gave public confessions and cried bitterly; each one said goodbye to the other.

The train, however, went further on its way until finally on Sunday it arrived at the station of Kaufering, 5 kilometers from the Bavarian town of Landsberg [60 kilometers from Munich]. This is the same Landsberg where, in 1924, Hitler, may his name be erased, sat in jail for his coup against the Weimar Republic, and composed his "work" – the gospel of the people and genocide – "Mein Kampf."

Around Landsberg there were labor camps which belonged to the Dachau Concentration Camp, and that is where they brought the men.

As soon as the men's transport left Tigenhof, they immediately took the women and the children who were with them and transported them to Stutthof, from where they sent them out either for work, or to the death factories.

A strong guard of S.S. men came to pick up the transport of women from the train station in Stutthof. At first the women thought that they are all being taken to be exterminated. Therefore, screams and a terrible panic broke out among them. They calmed down afterwards when they saw that they are being taken to the barracks of the concentration camp.

The Jews who were transported from the Alexot work camp were found in Stutthof. A few days later the deported Kovno Jews who were taken from the Ghetto arrived on the 8th of July, as well as the transport which left Kovno by train on Thursday, the 13th of July. Also, the men from that transport were sent away from Stutthof to the labor camps near Landsberg and the women with the children remained in Stutthof.

A week later a selection took place in Stutthof among the women. Those women who had children with them were sent, together with the children, to Auschwitz to be exterminated. All the other women, regardless of their age, remained in Stutthof.

[Page 246]

A few days after this selection came a second selection of the remaining women. The older and weaker ones were left in Stutthof where the largest portion of them were later killed in that crematoria.

The younger and skilled women were sent to the labor camps around Torun, Strasburg, Elbing, and other points in Prussia where, at that time, urgent fortification work was needed. A small number of Kovno women, together with other Jewish women, were sent to the Dachau labor camps, where the men were working, and a specific portion of skilled female workers remained working in Stutthof itself.

Thereafter, just as soon as they brought the men into the labor camps around Landsberg, the first thing done was to take away all their personal items. Those Jews who went through Stutthof and were already there in the time of their "redemption" were completely robbed.

They even took away the shoes and clothes they were wearing, and they dressed them in striped concentration camp clothes and in large wooden clogs.

Not wanting their money and valuables to fall into the hands of the S.S. men, a portion of the Jews threw their money and valuables into the filth of the toilets. When this information reached the camp administration, they chose a group of Jews during a roll call who, in everyone's absence, had to climb naked into the filth of the toilets and remove all the money and valuables which were thrown in there by hand.

Quite a few young ones from Tigenhof came together with their fathers to the labor camps around Landsberg. On Shabbat, the 22nd of July, a registration took place of all the youth. The 131 registered youth were sent off the next morning to Dachau and from there to Auschwitz. From the inhumane living conditions some youth died and almost 80 children were killed on the second day of Rosh Hashana, 1944, when thousands of Jews were sent to the gas chambers and crematoria of Auschwitz. Only a few strong youths managed to survive to liberation.

[Page 247]

On the way to Auschwitz, two youths succeeded in escaping by jumping from the moving train. One of them, Daniel Burshtein,[a] hid out with peasants and remained alive.

One week later, when the men were brought to the labor camp, they were divided into work columns on Monday the 24th of July. Thus began the actual concentration camp life with all its "famous" accompanying phenomena.

The Jews worked in various construction companies. Among others they worked at the tragically famous "Molel Construction Company," where thousands and thousands of Jews were tortured, day and night by the hard labor. At that time, they were building the "Me 262 Messerschmidt" and underground airplane factory, which was supposed to improve the campaign of the smashed German Air Force, as much as possible.

Just like in the Ghetto, here they also had various skilled people, but they did not receive more favorable work conditions than the non-qualified workers. Therefore, the largest percent of those who collapsed from work were the simple laborers who had to carry the heavy yoke of this unbearable back-breaking work on their shoulders.

For the unqualified workers there was also a big difference between those who worked day jobs and those who worked at night. Despite their difficult, straining work at night, the night workers couldn't even rest during the day because during the day most of them were chased out to various jobs in and around the camp.

Therefore, the first victims of the concentration camp hell were those coming mainly from the night workers. Over a few weeks, these people would literally fall off their feet and completely break down. The Jewish Kapos had much blame for the quick death of hundreds of night workers, as they didn't do anything to equitably distribute a little horrible soup to all their workers who were doing this hard labor work.

[Page 248]

The antagonism between Jews who came from other countries also played a certain role. For example, if the Kapo was a Lithuanian Jew, he would, usually protect Lithuanian Jews over Jews from Poland, Hungary, etc. If the Kapo was a Polish or a Hungarian Jew, it was the opposite.

There were some very morally corrupt elements among the Jewish Kapos. They didn't concern themselves about organizing the work so that the weaker people would be sent on available work that was a bit lighter. On the contrary, they would sooner send healthy and strong people on a lighter work assignment, so they could receive some material compensation. In this merciless camp reality, they could not expect any material compensation from a physically exhausted person who was completely helpless.

Up until Dachau, the Kovno Jews had gone through three years of ghetto life and were already used to life as Jewish slaves under Nazi sovereignty. Thus, they considered themselves better than the Hungarian, or Czech Jews, etc., who, until Dachau, had not yet gotten through the "school" of Hitler's ghettos and concentration camps. But here, the Kovno Jews also started collapsing very quickly from the unbearable concentration camp conditions.

We must mention their slave labor under the open sky in rain, in wind and in cold for 13-14 hours per day[b]. The majority worked 7 days a week, with a "rest" of not more than 6-7 hours a day. Each day they got through a long haul to go to work and return in the wooden clogs, which from the earliest days caused great wounds on the feet. The hunger-rations consisted of 300 grams of bread per day with watery soup without meat or fat, and which had not more than a few hundred calories daily, while doing physically straining work. The techniques were of long duration, with roll call twice a day: in the morning before going to work and in the evening after returning from work. The dirty earthen huts in which the people were kept were always crowded. And the worst plague of camp life – the lice, feasted on the people day and night, making horrible wounds on the body, causing thousands of people to leave this world.[c] The camp regime was extraordinarily strict, where, without any reason a Jew could be beaten murderously and terrorized. And, above all, the psychological depression of Jews in a Hitlerite camp due to the various moral humiliations doled out both by the German rulers, as well as by the loyal Jewish creative servants. Thus, it became clear why the life and soul of the Jews in the camps was destroyed so quickly.

[Page 249]

Right after the first months in the concentration camp, Jews started collapsing. The sick wards were in the same earthen huts as the regular dwelling pits. They were soon overflowing with Jews, weakened, depleted, and completely exhausted physically and spiritually. And there was not even any basic medicines or medical arrangements.

At this opportunity it is worthwhile mentioning that the camp Jews had great allegations against people from the central sick ward, like Dr. Zacharin, a former Jewish doctor from Kovno. True, he had neither an easy, nor a thankful job as the person responsible for the sick ward. However, it is a fact that he was responsible for the selections of candidates for Auschwitz or for the "protected camps." In addition, his relationship with the sick was so harsh and inhumane that he was justifiably hated in the camp world.

After liberation, in the beginning of May 1945, he disappeared from the view of former campmates as fast as possible, to avoid any recrimination against him. It ended fatally.

Those people who, according to their character traits were skilled at adapting to various difficult situations, kept a longer plane of life. The more placid people who were not able to push their elbows out in front, quickly became "*Musselmen*," that means physically and spiritually exhausted people. They were the first candidates for all kinds of selections.

[Page 250]

At first, selections would take place every month, whereby those very sick and weakened campmates would be sent to the death-factories to be exterminated. Such larger selections took place in the labor camps in August, September, and October 1944.

Later, the approaching catastrophe for Hitler's Germany shook up the internal certainty of many Himmlers, and other horrific mass-murderers of the Third Reich, so they stopped the extermination of Jews by gassing and burning. For the weakened and sick people who were unable to work, they set up "protection-camps" where the people would truly not have to work, but received even less than the usual camp rations, so actually, they would die of hunger.

To get an idea about how the people from the "protection camps" were considered already more dead than alive, can be judged by the fact that they would take away their camp clothing and they would lie naked in the barracks, four or five people under one blanket. Such "protection camps" were around Landsberg and were numbered IV, and for a while, also camp number VII. In camp IV, where there was space for about 2,000 people, there would be more than double that number.

Thousands of people who had to go into the "protection camps" knew very well that this was their last road in life and from there they would never return. Day in and day out, they would die by the hundreds, and they would then be thrown into mass graves, often still with signs of life.

According to the decree from the camp administration, they would take the dead from these places to bury them, and every day Jewish dentists would come to pull gold teeth out of the dead.

As we know from the ghetto times, various Jewish "people in power" displayed little tolerance for the simple folk-people. In the concentration camp however, this specific situation was much worse. The simple Jew would spend these years very much wanting to be "more religious than the Pope," so they would be even more charming to their S.S. bosses, and to the various Jewish "titleholders" in the camp, for example, the Kapos, foremen, block elders, kitchen personnel, and other slaves created by the S.S.

[Page 251]

Some Jewish criminal types were murderously sadistic. For example, the Kapos Burshtein, Grinfeld, Volpert, Shpegel, Isserlis, and others, gave Jews murderous beatings for various "sins" at work, like while walking in columns, while standing at the roll call place, or for asking for another portion of "soup," etc. Their murderousness would be especially great when they would hit someone in the presence of a camp administrator. At that moment, they would do it with special "enthusiasm."

After liberation, these criminals wanted to disappear from the deserved revenge of the campmates. A few of them fell into the hands of Jews who delivered them to the American military powers, which incarcerated them with S.S. men and tried them in court.

Aside from the Kovno Jews who were mainly concentrated in camp numbers I and III in the other camps around Landsberg, Lithuanian Jews and Jews from the Shavl Ghetto were placed together with Jews from other countries. Hungarian Jews, for example, were already in those camps before the Kovno and the Shavl Jews got there. Later, due to the Soviet offensive that began in 1945, when the Germans evacuated Auschwitz, Polish, Czech, Hungarian, and other Jews, who worked in various work commandos in Auschwitz, were transported to the camps around Landsberg.

Despite the excruciatingly difficult living conditions and the strict camp regime, socially active persons from the home group would, from time to time, organize themselves in the barracks in groups to chat about the happenings on the fronts, about the international situation, about general or Jewish problems etc. The goal of these home group discussions was to raise the morale of the camp inmates and to strengthen their hope in the continuous downfall of the Nazis. Jews searched for various ways to learn about the situation on the fronts and find out what was going on in the world.

[Page 252]

It is necessary to note the persons who conducted these chats: Engineer, T. Blumental about the Strategic situation at the fronts; Michael Burshtein, Polish-Jewish typesetter, about the camp inmates; Advocate, L. Garfunkel about problems in Jewish society; Dr. S. Grinhoiz about political happenings; Dr. L. Goldshtein about popular medical chats; M. Bramson about Kovno Ghetto issues; Aronovski about questions on the Land of Israel, etc.

The camp inmates would enjoy listening to these chats, mainly to the commentaries about the situation on the fronts, and many of them became active in the discussions.

Jews also knew when the Jewish holidays would fall. Hanukah, Purim, and the like, so the mood in the hall was higher than other days. The historical parallels from greatly experienced Jewish folk tradition would have an encouraging effect. Religious Jews would take pains to pray in a minyan in secret, etc.

Meanwhile, the war was moving forward with huge steps to its long-awaited end. On the eve of Spring, 1945, the huge joint offensive by the Soviets in the east and from the Anglo-Saxons in the west finally began. The hope to survive to liberation by the bunch of surviving camp Jews became greater from day to day. Everyone felt that soon, soon Hitler's Germany would completely fall apart.

As the march of the British-American military divisions came through with full steam during the second half of April 1945, it became clear to the rest of the Jews in the labor camps that they are coming closer to the distinctly fated days for the remaining Jews in the labor camps.

The socially conscious elements started to prepare themselves to organize their followers, both from the left wing, as well as from the Zionist-oriented camp Jews, to come out with active events for when things in the camps will reach a critical moment.

[Page 253]

Spearhead scouts from the American army units moved in the direction of Dachau at a colossal speed just before the final blow to the Hitler machine. On the 24th of April 1945, there suddenly came an order to evacuate the camps belonging to the Dachau camp. Other camps had already gotten the order to evacuate earlier.

The official version from the Nazis was that the goal of the evacuation was to bring the camp inmates to the Swiss border where, due to the mediation by the International Red Cross, they would be exchanged for German prisoners of war, who were under the authority of the Allied powers.

Of course, the camp world had no reason to believe the official declaration, but there was no other choice but to allow themselves to go on this unfamiliar evacuation march. Resisting the evacuation was not possible.

According to the decree, only the healthier persons would go on the march. The sick and weak ones from the sick ward and from the "protection camps" were concentrated in camp I, which was liberated because the people were already out on the march. Many weakened people tried to join on foot because they believed that all the sick and weak ones would probably be killed.

As was mentioned, at first there was an order to collect all the sick in one barrack and set it on fire together with the people. However, because of the head-spinning speed of the offensive, no one from that S.S. wanted to take upon themselves such a job. Therefore, the sick ones were evacuated toward Dachau. A portion of the sick managed to make it through, but the majority remained at the site and were freed in the beginning of May.

Physically and spiritually exhausted from camp life, many Jews couldn't maintain the tempo of the march and they had to stop on the way. The murderous S.S. guards accompanying the camp inmates, killed many people at this opportunity, by shooting those who stopped along the way.

[Page 254]

Seeing the murderous attitude of the guards toward the marching camp inmates, each one, with the last of his strength, strained so as not to stop on the march and continued with everyone. The stronger people helped their weaker acquaintances, who did not have the strength to walk alone.

It was later clarified that the Nazis had planned for the healthy people to evacuate to the Tyrol mountains, where, after losing their positions in Germany, Hitler's Third Reich hoped to set up the battle against the Allies. In this case, the camp inmates would be turned into a work force for the fortification work.

However, the road to Tyrol was already cut off by the Allied army divisions. The S.S. conducting the march tried taking the evacuees here and there, searching for a way out of the situation.

Many Jews also suffered from the heavy bombardments by the Allied Air Force on the downtrodden German forces. For example, at the train station in Shafhaussen[d] more than 100 inmates were killed and quite a few were wounded from that air attack on a German military train which stood near an inmate column. Many people were also shot by the S.S. guards who opened fire on them when they ran into nearby woods to hide from the bombings. The Germans would purposefully cover their military transports with evacuated inmates. Thus, the Allied pilots, while fulfilling their military jobs, indirectly caused the death of hundreds of Jews.

From hour to hour, the ring of fire around the remainder of the completely beaten German military became narrower, until the frontrunners of the American army finally reached the marching camp inmates and freed them.

Not all the camps were together on this evacuation march, rather they were taken in many groups, separated from each other. Therefore, their liberation did not take place in the same place, nor on the same day.

[Page 255]

So, for example, the people near Landsberg were freed on the 28th of April; near Dachau, on the 29th of April; near Alach[e] on the 30th of April; in Buchberg[f] on the 1st of May; in Bad-Telz[g] on the 2nd of May, etc.

Due to the horrific experiences in the camps, the inmates' senses became strongly atrophied, so their happiness and surprise about surviving to liberation was extraordinarily large. People fell on each other kissing, crying from happiness, and said *Shehechiyanu* [prayer for celebrating special events]. Everything seemed as if in a dream, as if it was not really happening. They still didn't believe that this was true. It looked as if each one would want a repeat, to convince himself that he actually belonged to the chosen ones who had finally survived the realization of the years-long dream – liberation from the horrific Hitler hell.

In this elevated moment, which was full of incomprehensible happiness, everyone's thoughts moved to their nearest and dearest, who had not been allowed to survive to this moment of redemption. Feelings of happiness were mixed with grief, so at that moment, it was difficult to say which feeling was stronger.

The attitude of the American troops toward the freed people was a real humanistic one. Even the liberators were strongly moved by the dramatic moment of liberation of the camp inmates. They expressed their shared happiness of having saved the people from death by distributing gifts of food right and left, like cigarettes, chocolate, etc.

Overwhelmingly, in their concern for the freed camp inmates they did everything so that the surviving people should revive themselves as quickly as possible. They especially devoted themselves heavily to the sick and weak, for whom they organized hospitals with all needed medical facilities.

The starving people grabbed the food, thus, many of them were harmed and became sick from it; many even died as a result. Not recovered from all the evil and afflictions from the camps, many people died right after liberation. However, with time, the majority of those liberated did manage to recuperate from all the difficult experiences that they endured during the horrific Hitler years, especially in the hell of the concentration camp.

[Page 256]

In the Stutthof Concentration Camp after the selection of mothers with children and of the elderly and weak women, over 3,000 younger and healthier women remained and were sent out to work in the various work camps in Prussia.

Approximately 1,000 women from Stutthof were taken to the small village of Truntz, near Elbing, where they spent a few weeks. From there they were later moved toward Loibitch, near Torun.

In Loibitch, the Jewish women were quartered in a building of a large mill, which was located a few kilometers from the city. After settling into the women's camp, the associated camp regime took them daily to do fortification work which mainly included digging protection pits.

In comparison with the extremely strict regime, which the men had in the Dachau work camps, the women had it easier. Not just the actual work but also their conditions with the guards was not as horrible and unbearable as in the work camp for the men.

In order to quiet their hunger, the women would sneak out of the workplace, and would run to the surrounding peasants to beg for a few potatoes, a piece of bread, etc. True, the guards would beat them murderously after catching a woman committing such a "crime", but the urge to ease the hunger with anything was so strong that the sadistic punishments could not stop the women from running to beg for a piece of bread. Therefore, for the women in the Loibitch camp such physical exhaustion from hunger and slave labor was not as noticeable as in the Dachau work camps.

But the situation for the women was still quite dark and bitter. Like in the men's camps, the women's camp had terrible congestion and filth, and a shortage of clothes and shoes predominated. There was an insulting relationship between the hooligan S.S. guards and the "chosen" Jewish women who were appointed by the Germans to be the overseers of work in the camp, in the kitchen, etc.

[Page 257]

In addition, the women were also full of lice, which caused the spread of epidemic illnesses. In the camps there was no possibility of receiving even basic medical help, so it became clear why many women left this world very quickly, as many had worn out their last bit of health.

The weakened women would be sent to Stutthof, "on recovery," as they called it. In fact, they would kill them there and burn them in the crematoria.

At this point it is worth mentioning that once, while they were sending a larger party of weakened women to Stutthof "to rest," a few dozen healthier women also requested to be allowed to accompany them to Stutthof for a few days' rest. Their request, of course, was satisfied by the camp administrators. Both the weak, as well as the less-weakened women were killed in Stutthof.

On the 14th of January 1945, during the Winter offensive when the Soviet forces started to get closer to Torun, this women's camp quickly started to evacuate from Loibitch. They took the women from Loibitch toward Torun and from Torun, in the direction of Bromberg.

Like on the men's evacuation march, many women could not keep up the tempo of the march on the road, and the S.S. men shot a large number on the spot. Barefoot, naked, and starving, the women dragged themselves through the great frost of the month of January. During the march, many women froze feet, hands, limbs, etc.

Seeing that the Russians were very close, the S.S. guards quickly disappeared, leaving the women behind somewhere in a forsaken forest which was located off the road between Torun and Bromberg, some 20 kilometers from Torun.

Before this time, other Soviet army divisions occupied Bromberg. Learning that a Jewish women's camp was marching between Torun and Bromberg, the Soviet intelligence divisions went out searching to free the Jewish women.

[Page 258]

Because the women were dragged to a forest off the road, the Russians could hardly find them. These women were liberated on the 23rd of January 1945.

Aside from the Kovno women, who were dragged to Loibitch, a large party of Kovno women from Stutthof were sent to Derbek, a small village near Elbing.

At that time, more large women's camps existed in Derbek, where they worked digging protection pits - fortification work. In these camps, aside from the Kovno and Shavl women, there were also Jewish women from Hungary.

After finishing work in Derbek, for approximately 5-6 weeks, about 700-800 Kovno women were then sent over to Malkin, a small settlement not far from Strasburg in Western-Prussia.

In Malkin, the women were also employed in various front-line construction works, and they suffered there just like in all the other Nazi concentration camps.

A month later after their arrival in Malkin, a selection of the weaker women was conducted. A few hundred women were then sent from Malkin to Stutthof, where they had the same ending as all the other women transported to Stutthof extermination camp.

At the second selection, which took place a few weeks after the first one, 100 women were caught who were also sent to Stutthof.

Not more than 500 women were taken out on the evacuation march, which started in Malkin on the 18th of January 1945. From there, the women marched for over two weeks to Praust where they found many other women, among them also Kovno women, from other evacuated camps.

From Praust they marched further until Chinov [Chynowie], near Lauenberg, where they remained from the 20th of February until the 10th of March 1945, when they were liberated by the Red Army.

[Page 259]

In Chinov, there were over 1000 women cramped into a barn in an open field. Because of the extraordinary crowding, filth, hunger and cold, a terrible typhus epidemic broke out, from which hundreds of women died in three weeks. The sick actually laid around under the feet of the healthy ones, who, in a short time, also become sick. There was not even a divider between the healthy, the sick and the dead. All were knotted together, and one could not imagine what kind of horrible scenes were to be seen. They later took the dead and threw them into pits, which were located near the barn. The pits were sprinkled only when they became full of dead bodies.

At this opportunity it is worth mentioning that the former Jewish camp elder of Malkin, Dora Arbeter, who was a true underworld type and strongly bullied the women, was taken to court by the Soviet powers after liberation and received 15 years hard labor.

A few hundred Kovno women from Derbek transferred to Gutau. In this camp there were, excluding the Kovno women, 500 or 600 Jewish women from Hungary and a few hundred women from the Shavl Ghetto. In total, there were close to a thousand Jewish women in this women's camp.

These women also worked at digging protection pits, and they lived through all seven stages of hell in a Hitlerite concentration camp. A larger number of weak women were also there and were sent to Stutthof for extermination.

Due to the Soviet Winter offensive, the camp started to evacuate. There were approximately 800 women, of which 500 could keep up with the evacuation march and the rest were so weakened that they could not be taken on the march.

According to a decree from the higher ups, or according to their own initiative, the camp administration injected these weakened women with a poison serum with the goal of killing them.

[Page 260]

Perhaps it was due to their great haste for evacuation, or injecting intravenously instead of injecting intramuscularly, or, because of some unclarified reason, the injections did not work. As it turned out, luckily there were no deaths from these injections. Excluding a small number of women, who died from blood poisoning or another complication, almost all the other women remained alive. A few days later, they were liberated by the Red Army which occupied this area.

Also, after a two-day march, the healthy women were liberated by the Russians on the 22nd of January, not far from Neimark.

A few hundred women were brought from Stutthof to Riberg, near Elbing, where they were held for a month. From Riberg they were transferred to Shtoboi, not far from Riberg. There they were held for a month and a half, and they were dragged to Nidervarben. In Nidervarben a selection took place by which a few dozen women were sent to Stutthof to be exterminated.

In a few weeks, the women from Nidervarben were transferred to Hohegek, near Neimark. This was already in December 1944. In Hohenek a new selection took place. The selected women, who were supposed to be sent to Stuttoff, were sent to Malkin, because at that time a typhus epidemic was spreading in Stutthof, and the Stutthof concentration camp was closed.

In January 1945, the healthy women from the Hohenek camp were supposed to evacuate to Danzig. Due to the Soviet offensive, the direct road to Danzig was blocked. Therefore, the women were brough to Praust from where they were sent to Chinov together with other women. They stayed there a few weeks and they got through all the horrors in that tragically infamous barn. They were liberated by the Russians on the 10th of March.

[Page 261]

A few dozen Kovno women were put together with the Shavl women and other Jewish women and sent to Sofienvald near Berent. They remained there from the end of August until the beginning of February 1945, when they started to evacuate the camp. After a six- day march, the camp arrived at Gottenhof, which was a collection camp for evacuated concentration camp inmates. They arrived at this camp on the 12th of February, and they stayed until the 9th of March when they left for Chinov. On the same day of their arrival in Chinov, that is, the 10th of March, they were liberated by the Soviets.

A small number of Kovno women, together with a few hundred women from the Shavl Ghetto and from Hungary, were sent over to the Dachau camps for men. This same women's camp built a type of island in the sea of that men's camp, and, by comparison, didn't have it so bad. At the same time, while the men had extraordinarily horrible conditions, the camp administration for the women was not as strict, and they had it much better than in the other women's camps.

Among the Hungarian women who were brought in, there were some pregnant women who gave birth there. The camp administration did not kill the newborn children[h] and the mothers, together with the children, were liberated at the end of April 1945, by the American army divisions.

While most of the healthier women were sent out from Stutthof to various labor camps, a few hundred women from the Kovno Ghetto remained working in Stutthof itself. A portion of these women worked in those sick wards and the rest worked in various workshops.

In October,1944, a larger party of women were sent out to work in the surrounding agricultural fields. They worked there for a few months and were then brought back to the Stutthof camp. Although, the Jewish women slaved very hard in agricultural work, they had it much better with respect to food, than in Stutthof.

[Page 262]

As mentioned, in addition to the working women in Stutthof, there were many old and weak women who were exterminated in stages in those crematoria. Almost every day, selections of the older and sick women would take place and those selected for death were killed. These extermination actions continued until December 1944.

At the end of 1944 in Stutthof, a typhus epidemic broke out which continued until the evacuation of the camp in April 1945. Of these few thousand women who were there, many died of typhus. During the typhus plague "life" in the Stutthof concentration camp was true hell. The conditions, both for the sick, as well as for the healthy, were horrible and therefore the total number of deaths was very high.

On the 26th of April 1945, the evacuation of Stutthof began. A portion of camp prisoners were taken by train and the rest with a freight steamer. On the 28th of April the S.S. guards threw many sick women, who were laying on the deck of the steamer, into the sea. Every day, the S.S. murderers would search for the sick and they would throw them into the sea. Hundreds of women were killed in this cruel way. In addition, there were many deaths of sick women who were evacuated by train.

On May 2nd, the steamer with the evacuees was bombed by an English airplane. A portion of the steamer was damaged by the bombing and therefore, many people were killed. However, while the engine of the steamer had problems, it was still functioning and could travel on.

A passing ship picked up a few hundred persons from the steamer. The rest had to remain on the damaged steamer, which arrived, with great difficulty, in Ekernferde, near Kiel [Germany]. The people arrived in the port of Kiel on the 4th of May.

Kiel was already occupied by the British. The happiness of the new survivors was tremendous. The people were immediately transferred to a camp where there were Czechs and other trailing persons. After recuperating from all the horrific experiences, most of the women headed out in various directions seeking family members.

Original footnotes:

    a. The only child of the Polish-Jewish acquaintance of printer Michael Burshtein, who was caught up in the Kovno Ghetto.
    b. From the beginning they worked in two work shifts of 12 hours from start to finish. Later 3 shifts of 8 hours each were established.
    c. A de-lousing facility for the camp inmates was organized only in the middle of January 1945.
    d. Not far from Kaufering.
    e. Near Dachau
    f. Near Fernvald
    g. South of Munich, not far from the Austrian border
    h. There were 7.

CHAPTER XXVIII

After Liberation

-New problems and worries for the liberated men and women-The life of the surviving Lithuanian Jews during the first years of the "surviving-remnants"

[Page 264]

After recuperating from the first impressions and experiences related to the liberation, a whole series of new problems and worries stood before these liberated people. The situation, however, was entirely different between the women who were liberated by the Russians, and the situation for the men, liberated by the Americans.

When the women from the labor camps in Prussia were freed by the Red Army in the beginning of 1945, the sick and weak immediately were transported to hospitals for medical attention. The healthier women, however, were quickly mobilized for various work details for the army, because the war with Germany had not yet ended.

The work of the mobilized women varied: they worked in military hospitals, in military economic organizations, etc. A larger number of liberated women were also employed in herding animals, which the Soviets were taking to Russia from the occupied German areas.

However, truth be told, most of the liberated women were not very glad to do such physically exhausting work, like chasing animals on foot for many months. They were not happy for the following reasons:

[Page 265]

First, most women were mainly interested in finding their husbands or other members of their families, who were taken away in the deportations.

Second, many women left their children with Christians in Lithuania, and they wanted to get there as soon as possible to recover the children.

Third, after all the horrible experiences in the Ghetto and in the concentration camps, the women wanted to recuperate and not start all over again being shackled to work, especially under a military regime.

A small number of more energetic women avoided the work mobilization and tried to strike through all military barriers to get themselves out to Lithuania. Already in March 1945, a few Jewish women who were liberated from the German concentration camps started arriving in Vilna, Kovno and Shavl.

The appearance of the liberated women was an extraordinary surprise, especially among the former ghetto Jews, because everyone believed that no trace remained of those Jews deported to Germany. So, for example, one day a notice circulated in Kovno that a Kovno liberated woman had arrived in Vilna. Not waiting for her arrival in Kovno, many Jews immediately left for Vilna to look at her and hear authentic accounts from her about the fate of the deported Jews.

Furthermore, in the Spring of 1945, even more individuals and groups of liberated women started returning to Lithuania. No one in Lithuania knew anything about the fate of the deported men until the end of the war.

At this opportunity we must add that the liberated Jewish women received a very cold reception from the official Lithuanian institutions. If not for the little help organized by Jews themselves, many of them would not have had anywhere to lay their head or anything to eat. Most of them lay on the floors of the former Kovno Choir Synagogue and in other community places for weeks until they got work and started having a "normal" life.

[Page 266]

So very fortunate were those liberated mothers who found their little children in Jewish children's homes, which were established in Kovno right after liberation through the initiative of a group of former ghetto Jews.[a] They started collecting the little Jewish children who were given away to Christians during the ghetto times, and whose parents were not found. In the establishment and existence of the Children's Home, particular recognition should be given to the Russian Jew Colonel Professor Rebelski, a psychiatrist by profession, who was chief of the large military sanitorium office, located in Kovno in those days. Thanks to his active interest in the fate of the little children during those difficult years, he was successful in creating very basic tangible opportunities for the Children's Home. By the way, he was quite an interesting personality and a good person with a very warm heart.

A Jewish elementary school with a kindergarten was also established in Kovno[b] at the same time as the children's home.

Many mothers found their little children still in the homes of the Christians. Aside from the older children, the Christians did not want to give the children back. A larger number of Christians didn't return any Jewish children whose parents were killed, and none of the surviving Jews knew where or by whom the children were to be found. Because of this, there are Jewish children who remained with the Christians to this day.

At the end of June 1945 about 500-600 liberated Jewish women returned to Kovno.

The case of the liberated men was different. In general, the greatest portion of men were in far worse physical condition than the women. To recuperate a bit, they needed immediate medical help and recovery. In addition, like the women, many men became sick with various typhus illnesses right after liberation, which they contracted on the evacuation marches, or a short time beforehand. Being so very weak and exhausted from all the concentration camp horrors, many of them could not get through their illnesses and died. Only the younger and healthier were able to recuperate.

[Page 267]

Almost all the women who were liberated by the Russians had one clear goal after the liberation –to get to Lithuania as soon as possible. But, among the largest portion of men, there were large differences of opinion right from the beginning.

A smaller number of the left-leaning ones, started to agitate for the men to go back to Lithuania.

The Zionist-leaning elements, on the contrary, decided never to go back to Lithuania. After all the horrific experiences that Jews went through in the Hitler years, every Jew should, irrespective of his past political circumstances, strive to settle in Eretz-Israel.

The non-political Jews, who, by the way, were the majority, were neutral and waited to receive more exact information about what was happening there before traveling to Lithuania. Men who received word that their liberated wives had returned to Lithuania, left for Poland, to find a way to connect with their wives once there.

As we know, in the beginning of Summer 1945, a voluntary repatriation of established national minorities started between Soviet Russia and Poland. Those Kovno Jews who did not want to remain where there were mass graves of their murdered family members, strove to join their relatives in Eretz Israel, America and other lands. They took advantage of this stream of repatriation and got through to Poland. From there, they came to Germany, Austria, Italy, etc., from where they sought a way to get in touch with their foreign friends.

Those who arrived from Lithuania did not deliver warm regards about Jewish life there. The very fact that they left Lithuania and brought unfavorable news about the situation of that Jewish population, strengthened the position of those "not-returning." Furthermore, many Jews who were prepared to go back to Lithuania, refused at the last moment.

[Page 268]

Liberated Jews who managed to return to Lithuania, and who discovered that their family members were in Poland or Germany, sought ways to get there.

Meanwhile, the Jewish mass escape from east to west became even greater from month to month. This escape stream tore the Lithuanian Jews apart even more – both those who were in the Ghetto, as well as those who escaped to Russia.

A portion of those Lithuanian Jews, especially the younger ones, succeeded in various ways to immigrate to Eretz-Israel. Some individuals left to go to relatives in the United States and other lands across the sea.

For a variety of reasons, the overwhelming majority of Lithuanian Jews remained sitting in the Jewish DP camps in the American Zone in Germany, or in Italy, where they shared the fate of the entire "surviving remnant." These camps were in Landsberg, Munich, Feldafing, Sankt- Ottillian, and other settlements in Germany, as well as in Rome, Milan, Bari, and other points in Italy. Many Kovno Jews took up positions of responsibility in local Jewish social life.

After a while the liberated Lithuanian Jews in Germany and Italy organized themselves and connected with the Lithuanian Jewish organizations and "countrymen organizations" in Eretz Israel, U.S.A., South Africa, Canada, etc.

A Union of Lithuanian Jews was established in Landsberg, at the end of 1946, in the American Zone in Germany. On the 28th of October 1946, at the 5th year commemoration of the Big Action in the Kovno Ghetto, they arranged a large mourning commemoration. Almost all the Lithuanian Jews from the "remaining remnant" in the American Zone took part.

The first Conference of Lithuanian Survivors of the Diaspora in Germany took place in Munich, on the 14th and 15th of April 1947.

At this important conference it was decided to put forth a resolution about "the guilt of the Lithuanian people in the murder of Lithuanian Jewry."

[Page 269]

This resolution affirmed, as follows: "The conference confirms that:

    a. All levels of Lithuanian people (academics, officials, peasants, skilled workers, workers, etc.) together with the Nazi murderers, took an active role in the murder of Lithuanian Jewry, especially in the provinces.
    b. A large portion of these Lithuanian murderers are in the American, English and French Zones in Germany and Austria where they are counted as "deportees" and enjoy "UNRRA support."

"The conference gives latitude to the newly elected management of the Union to publicly inform them about the deceptive acts of the large numbers of Lithuanians who, before and during the Nazi occupation, conducted mass-murders of their Jewish citizens."

"We, the few remaining from the prior 160 thousand total of Lithuanian Jewry, are living witnesses to the horrible cruelties which were committed by the Lithuanians on their Jewish neighbors. Each one of us can tell numerous facts illustrating the horrible murders by the Lithuanian people toward the unprotected and helpless Jewish population during the occupation years. Despite our huge pain, we must declare that the smaller Jewish settlements in the Lithuanian provinces were exterminated exclusively by Lithuanians, and in the larger Jewish settlements, with their most active participation. As is generally known, the bestial murders of Jews in Kovno, like for example, in the various garages during the horrific Slabodka pogrom, and at the time of the huge massacre at the 7th Fort, where more than 9,000 Kovno Jews were killed during the early occupation weeks, were conducted by Lithuanians."

"Furthermore, it is also known about the active participation of the Lithuanians in the extermination of the Jewish ghettos and camps outside the borders of Lithuania, such as Majdanek, Warsaw, and the like. The Union of Lithuanian Jews in the Diaspora in Germany considers it our Jewish and human duty to bring these facts to the awareness of the Jewish and non-Jewish public."

Original footnotes:

    a. Those active on the committee to help the Children's Home were Benjamin Freidman, Engineer Faivush Goldshmidt, Hirsh Levin, Engineer Mayer Yellin, Engineer Kolodny, David Tepper, Madam Dr. Golvitch, Advocate Diner, Yosef Gar, and others.

    b. Rafael Levin was the administrator of the children's home and the elementary school. Teachers in the elementary school and kindergarten were: Berel Cohen, Mrs. Levin-Abramovich, Mrs. Yellin, Frida Strashon, Sonia Garber. After her return from Russia Helene Chatzkels worked in the school as a teacher. Later, Mrs. Solomin took over the running of the children's home. The businessman, Moshe Sherman, also did a lot for the children's home.

CHAPTER XXIX

Cruel Blood Reckoning

-Over 90% of the Kovno Jews, who lived in Hitler's hell perished for being Jews

[Page 270]

In an effort to emphasize the bloody total of the deported Kovno Jews, we must come to the following tragic conclusion:

The difficulty in calculating an exact statistical number is self-explanatory. Thus, we must accept that of the approximately 8,000 Jews deported from the Ghetto and from the surrounding labor camps, 3,000 were men and 5,000 were women and children.

The men taken to the Dachau labor camps near Landsberg, suffered for more than nine months, that means, from the middle of July 1944 to the beginning of May 1945. Of these men, over 2,000 men died from hard labor, hunger, cold, lice, epidemic illnesses, murderous camp regime, shootings during evacuation marches, etc. Approximately seven to eight hundred men survived to liberation. As mentioned, a great number of men and women died of epidemic illnesses just after liberation.

Of the approximate 5,000 women and children who were brought to Stutthof, one thousand mothers with their little children were sent to Auschwitz for extermination, after the selection which was conducted immediately after their arrival.

During the later selections in Stutthof, there were seven to eight hundred elderly or weak women who were not sent to work in the camps but were killed in stages in those crematoria.

[Page 271]

Over 3,000 younger and healthier women were sent out to labor in the Prussian camps in inhumane living conditions, but hundreds of these women became weakened, and were sent from the camps to Stutthof for extermination. During the evacuation marches in the beginning of 1945 there were, once again, hundreds of women who died on the way by being shot, from sicknesses, and other afflictions.

Calculating the women who died of various sicknesses right after the liberation, we can say with great certainty, that half of the over 3,000 women who were sent from Stutthof for work, another 500 women got through all the troubles and finally scrambled out from under the nails of the Hitler's angels of death.

So, we can see that from the 8,000 deported Kovno Jews exactly three quarters died in various ways, and just a little more than one-quarter, that is, approximately 2.5 thousand men and women, succeeded in surviving the Nazi extermination.

In comparing a total of close to 40,000 Kovno Jews, who had the misfortune of falling under the Hitler occupation, with a total of 3,000 surviving Jewish souls[a], we arrive at this conclusion which screams to the high heavens:

More than 90% of Kovno Jews who languished in Hitler's hell, had their lives sacrificed for being Jews.

In this huge blood reckoning, our six million martyrs were killed in horrific ways by the Nazi mass murderers and their various collaborators. Such strange deaths were not even mentioned in *Tocheichah* [Chapter 26, Leviticus] in the Bible. The tens of thousands of Kovno martyrs who were killed by burning, by killing, by choking, and other strange deaths, occupy a prominent place.

Together with the memory of all our innocent martyrs whose lives were sacrificed on the altar for the thousands of years old "sanctification of the name of God," the memory of the martyrs of the community of Kovno will remain holy in the annals of Jewish history for generations.

[Page 272]

Generations will go and generations will come, but the biggest stain of guilt in world history, the murderous Hitlerism, will forever illustrate the cannibalistic cruelty of the German "superman" and their "devotees," among other people, and their downward spiral in the middle of the 20th century. Until the end of time, our fiercest curses will remain hanging on the heads of the wicked nations of the world, whose sons and daughters conducted such bestial mass murders on us Jews.

It is our deepest human conviction that there must come - and there will yet come - an historical judgment day over the malicious government of the Christian sodomite world which collaborated with the bloodthirsty Hitlerites. A judgment day will fulfill the last desire of our martyrs, who, at the same moment as their last "Hear O Israel" [prayer] on their lips, begged God to take revenge for the innocent spilling of blood of the people of Israel.

On the seventh day of mourning, we bow our heads in great awe to the scattered holy ashes of our murdered and burned men and women, from elderly to babies, we whisper the ancient Jewish prayer: "That their souls should be wrapped in bundles of life."

Original footnote:

a. In addition to the 2.5 thousand surviving Jews in the concentration camps, about five to six hundred Jews were saved in the partisan camps, by individual Christians, during the deportations from the Ghetto, etc.

[Page 273]

After the liberation

Jewish escapees smuggle across borders through the mountains and through valleys on the way to Eretz-Israel

Recently liberated Jews in Kovno kiss each other in the streets

Jewish escapees smuggle across borders through the mountains and through valleys on the way to Eretz-Israel

Reuven Rubinstein opens the mourning academy in Landsberg for the 6th annual commemoration of the Big Action in the Kovno Ghetto

First conference of surviving Lithuanian Jews in the diaspora in Germany

MONOGRAPH

Jewish Institutions in the Kovno Ghetto

Jewish Institutions in the Kovno Ghetto

(Monograph)

[Page 277]

Introductory Remarks

It was already mentioned in the Prologue to this book that the goal of this Monograph is to describe the activities of the Jewish institutions in the Kovno Ghetto, and to finally clarify the kind of influence the Jewish institutions had on the formation of the inner life of the Ghetto. Therefore, it is not possible to create an exact description of life in the Ghetto, which ignores the work of the Jewish administration.

As is known, the role of Jewish "autonomy" in the ghettos during Nazi sovereignty has been discussed very passionately. Most of these rebukes were of a negative character, and they very sharply condemned the handling of the Jewish population by the "Jewish Councils" and other Jewish ghetto leaders.

To our shame we must admit that in those reproaches there was much truth. Alas, many Jews who were standing at the head of the ghetto settlements did not uphold humane Jewish practice. Some ghetto witnesses recounted the shameful events of their morally corrupt "leaders."

However, the responsibility for historical truth demands that we differentiate between the efforts by Jews to somehow control their lifelines, so to speak, even in the inhumane ghetto conditions, and the criminal handling by the despicable Jews for whom the Ghetto was an arena to reveal their personal ambitions and power-lust. That's why we should not approach this painful problem too lightly from our nightmarish ghetto reality.

[Page 278]

At this opportunity the editor wishes to underscore that with this monographic work he is not, G-d forbid, trying to respond to the very serious, main question. The question about whether Jews, under the Hitler occupation, should, or should not have engaged with the Nazis in matters related to the life interests of the Jewish population. Since this was not a localized issue of the Kovno Ghetto alone, but a general Jewish question, it is understandable that such a judgment can only be carried out by recognized Jewish social authorities.

The editor would be very pleased if this monograph, aside from its actual task of describing the Kovno Jewish ghetto institutions, would indirectly also serve as a stimulus for an objective critical review of the Jewish ghetto administration in the horrible Hitler years.

J.G. [Joseph Gar]

CHAPTER I

The Elder's Council

- Establishment of the Jewish Committee in the first weeks of the occupation and its further development- Some main elements about the activity of the Elders Council as the highest representatives of the ghetto settlement- About the Jewish ghetto administration in general and the politics of the Elders Council, specifically- Leading persons of the Elders Council

[Page 279]

A few weeks after the Nazi occupation, when the mass-excesses against the Kovno Jewish population had partially subsided, the Gestapo decided to organize a Jewish committee in Kovno with whom the occupation regime would be in contact on issues relating to the Jewish population.

At first, the Gestapo approached the Kovno Rabbi Shapiro, wanting to designate him to be the representative of Jewish Kovno. He refused giving the reason that he is old and sick. At this opportunity he gave the names of a few Jewish community leaders, like Advocate, I. Goldberg, Advocate L. Garfunkel, Dr. Yefis Rabinowitz, and others, who the regime could contact regarding Jewish issues.

On the 4th of July 1941 the aforementioned three persons, as well as Rabbi Snieg and Rabbi Shmukler were also brought to the Gestapo where the Chief of the Gestapo, S.A. Colonel Jaeger and a certain General Paul had the following chat:[a]

"Since all Jews are Communists" – the Nazis claimed– "therefore, the Lithuanians cannot live together with the Jews, so the Jews will have to go over to live in a ghetto. As for the ghetto area, the suburb of Slabodka was the prospective site. If the Jewish representatives were prepared to help organize the relocation into the Ghetto, the regime, on their part, was prepared to give all Slabodka to the Jews for the ghetto area and, if necessary, also the smaller villages near Slabodka. They were given one month's time to transfer the Jews to the Ghetto."

[Page 280]

"The German regime," the Gestapo higher-ups continued, "is against the outbreak of a pogrom on the Jewish population by the Lithuanians. The only effective means to stop this "outbreak of the Lithuanian popular wrath" is for the Jews to go over to live in the Ghetto. Then the regime hopes that the Jews in the Ghetto will be able to live in tranquility. By the way, if the Jews demonstrate "good will" the regime is prepared to immediately free the arrested Jewish women and children who were located at the 9th Fort."[b]

Hearing such talk by the Gestapo leaders, the Jewish representatives relayed the following wishes:

    a. They should designate the ghetto area in the Old City, not in Slabodka where, for hundreds of years Jews have already been living in closely packed masses, and second, because all Jewish public institutions are already there, like the Jewish hospital, the Jewish children's homes, the study houses, etc. All the institutions which they would need in Slabodka would have to be built from scratch. In addition, the Jews contended, Slabodka does not have water purification, no canal system, or other basic sanitary hygienic facilities. For this reason, it poses a serious danger for an epidemic to break out among the tens of thousands Jewish souls who would have to transfer into the Ghetto.

    b.   Since the Jews don't have any means of transportation, the relocation would take longer than the month that is being anticipated.

    c.   They should give the messengers a day's time to sit with other Jewish businessmen about these issues.

[Page 281]

The Gestapo higher-ups responded that the Lithuanian magistrate would have the final decision about whether to designate the ghetto area to be in Slabodka or in the Old City. Regarding the lengthening of the time frame for the relocation, they would take it into account, if there really would be a need. The Gestapo men reiterated that the main thing is that by their actions the Jews will demonstrate that they are helping the regime carry out its objectives.

On the same day after this meeting, a broader social meeting took place in the house of Rabbi Shapira. Aside from the aforementioned people who were at the Gestapo meeting, a long list of other people, like Dr. Grigory Wolf, Kopelman, Engineer Roginski, Gemelitzski, Dr. Berman, Arloik, Ch. Kagan, Shtreichman, and others also took part. This consultation announced that we should ensure that the regime not set the ghetto area in Slabodka but rather in the Old City. And in addition, they should intervene for a longer time frame for the relocation to the Ghetto.

No real resolution came from the Jewish stubbornness to force this issue from the official German and Lithuanian authorities. Furthermore, the Kovno Lithuanian magistrate was disposed to be "more religious than the Pope" and the Lithuanians did everything not to fulfill the Jewish requests.

In the first half of July 1941, the newly established Jewish Committee quartered themselves in one of the rooms of the Kovno Council Building. From that time on, there started to be frequent activities on the Jewish streets.

As was previously mentioned about this issue[c] at that time, one of the most important jobs of the Jewish Committee was to help locate temporary shelter for those Jews who, after the outbreak of war, tried to evacuate, but were arrested along the way and turned back to Kovno, where they found their homes taken over by Christians. The Committee would take pains to regulate these issues with the help of the Lithuanian offices which the magistrate delegated to the Committee. Secondly, and this was the main point, the Jewish Committee had to organize the relocation into the Ghetto.

After lengthy dealings with the regime, they forced the size of the ghetto area. It became clear on which Slabodka streets Jews were to live. The Jewish Committee worked out a plan, according to which the relocation would take place. Jews from the suburbs and from the newer city quarters were to be relocated first, and lastly, came the turn of the Old City Jews.

[Page 282]

Organizing the relocation was not only about a rational distribution of available living space in the ghetto area, but another serious problem was the issue of means of transportation. Wagon drivers had their horses taken away, and to get a Christian wagoneer was very difficult for many Jews. And additionally, during those days, Jews themselves had to rapidly build a barbed wire fence around the ghetto quarter, build the hanging bridge on Paneriu Street, dig a tunnel on Jurborker Street, etc. It already became clear why in those first days of the existence of the Jewish Committee, it was bogged down with a lot of work.

To take care of all their issues, the Committee had to put together quite an operation. So, it created special committees which took care of questions about accommodation, transportation, legal help, social support, etc. These committees were the origin of the later standing Jewish ghetto institutions of the Elders Council.

The Jewish Committee didn't remain in the building of the Rathaus very long. Already in the second half of July they transferred their quarters to a local former Elementary School on Daukshos (Yatkever) Street number 24.

At the end of July, the relocation into the Ghetto was moving forward at full speed. Large portions of the Jewish population, mainly those with material means, the well-to-do, as was mentioned, had the means to acquire an apartment for themselves in the Ghetto and thereafter get an apartment from the Housing Office of the Committee. Jews without means did not have any other option but to wait for a shelter designated by the Jewish Housing Office. Because of the hundreds of interested people who besieged the Committee daily, they mainly had to deal with apartment issues. All other matters for the Jewish population were then moved to the shadows because some Jews, before everyone else, wanted to ensure themselves a little corner in the Ghetto to lay their head and a bit of their baggage.

[Page 283]

At the end of July, the Jewish Committee selected a "Jewish Elders Committee" from among its members and announced this to the regime. As can be imagined, there were no volunteers for such a position because none of the committee members had any motivation to take upon himself such a difficult and responsible duty. After a long committee meeting, which was filled with tragic and dramatic moments, Dr. Elchanan Elkes[d] agreed to take over this office, according to the will of all the participants.

At the beginning of August 1941, when the largest portion of the Jewish population moved into the Ghetto, the Jewish Committee transferred itself to the Ghetto. At first it had its quarters on Krisciukaicio Street 107, where there was also one of the largest reserves of community buildings for the ghetto poor. In a few weeks it moved across to Varniu Street 49, where it remained until the end of 1943. The S.D. workshops which were run by the Gestapo were set up in this building in the city. The Jewish representatives then went over to Margiu Street 32, where it remained until the arrest and liquidation of the Elders Council.

During the 2.5 months[e] which included the locking up of the Ghetto for the Big Action, the Jewish Committee succeeded in creating the most important ghetto institutions: the Jewish Ghetto Police, the Jewish Labor Office, the Offices for Social Care, Workshops, Housing, etc.

Indeed, the Jewish Committee, which later was officially called the "Elders Council," was not able to complain or even partially mitigate the extermination Action, which at that time passed through like a storm over the Ghetto and swallowed up about 13-14 thousand Jewish victims. The occupation regime, particularly the Gestapo, which conducted the Jewish extermination, would carry out its Actions according to their own plan. The Elders Council, as well as the entire ghetto population, were powerless to change or do anything about it.

[Page 284]

Life in the Ghetto became "normalized" in stages after the Big Action. That's when the Elders Council activated its activities. At that time, work was more or less, stabilized at the Jewish ghetto institutions and the Large Ghetto Workshops were also set up. As we saw, these played an important role in the life of the ghetto population.

The growing activity of the Elders Council aligned with the partial normalization of the general situation in the Ghetto. This is the period which started at the beginning of Spring, 1942 and ended at the end of Summer, 1943, when the Ghetto was converted into a concentration camp. There are many topics to describe what happened during this same half year, but it is opportune to mention that no extermination Actions took place in the Ghetto. At this same time, a period of relative improvement of economic well-being arrived.

In the Summer, 1942, the City Commissar reduced the status of the Elders Council to four persons. However, unofficially, from time to time, other persons would take part in the Elders Council meetings, specifically those who, from the start, belonged to the Elders Council, or who later played a visible role in the activity of the illegal social groupings.

Aside from the forced labor issues which were overseen by the German Work Office in the Ghetto,[f] the Elders Council would receive directives for their work from the City Commissar, mainly through their representatives on ghetto issues. Members of the Elders Council would be in the City Commissariat almost daily, taking care of various ghetto matters. Very often, the Nazi ghetto bosses would also come personally to the Elders Council. These souls would come to the Ghetto on purpose as often as possible because they knew very well that they would not return home with empty hands. The Elders Council would systematically give them fat "gifts."

[Page 285]

As representatives for ghetto issues of the City Commissariat there were:

-Kaminskas, the Lithuanian "hero" of the Intellectuals Action and other decrees, right after the lock-up of the Ghetto. After Lithuania was liberated, he, like many other Lithuanian Jew murderers, attached himself into the camps for "displaced persons" in Germany.

Jordan – from the beginning of Autumn 1941 until before Spring 1942. He was a fearsome Jew murderer. One of the head leaders of the extermination Action in the first months of the Ghetto's existence. For carrying out excesses by stealing valuable items for himself from robbed Jewish possessions, he was removed from his post and sent to the Soviet front where he was killed in August 1942 near Rezhev.

Videman – a bitter Nazi, he took up this post during the months March-May 1942

Von Kepen – a young S.A. man from the German aristocracy. Was in this office during the summer months of 1942 and managed to create quite a bit of problems for the Ghetto.

Miller – from Autumn, 1942 to Autumn, 1943. Really crazy. Because of his strange speech and actions, the ghetto Jews considered him out of his mind. In general, however, he was comparatively more moderate than his predecessors.

Every month, the Elders Council would send the City Commissariat detailed reports about the activity of the most important ghetto institutions. In addition, the Jewish Labor Office[g] had to submit exact reports to the City Commissariat every 10 days about the total number of Jewish workdays according to the individual workplaces.

There were a few shocks which took place in the Ghetto during this period. For example, the two relocation Actions to Riga (February and October 1942), the Mek incident, the arrest of the Elders Council (November 1942), the "Stalingrad Action" (February 1943) etc. The Elders Council, as the highest representative in the ghetto collective, had to withstand many difficult days and nights. Every ghetto commotion needed to be calmed all over again so that the Elders Council could continue with its work as before.

[Page 286]

A fundamental change for the worse in the activity of the Elders Council came at the end of Summer, 1943 when the Ghetto was converted into a concentration camp and went over to the authority of the S.S. Lt. Colonel, Goecke.[h]

Taking over the leadership of the ghetto administration, Goecke transferred the most important functions of the Elders Council and their institutions to the camp management which was trained by the Camp Commander. From that moment, the decline of the Elders Council and its institutions began.

As previously mentioned, after the arrest of the Elders Council and its liquidation at the beginning of April 1944, the only person connecting the ghetto collective and the Camp Commander on the part of Goecke, became the appointed Dr. Elkes, who, as the "Elder Jew" came out to represent the Jewish community in the last couple of months of the dying Ghetto.

Imagine a separate chapter with attempts by certain persons and social associations in the Ghetto to exercise influence on the activity of the Elders Council. In the first tier we must mention each individually: Caspi-Serebrovitz and Liptzer, about whom we should take the opportunity to give more details.[i]

In Spring, 1942 "Matzok"[j] was established, in which there were resentful representatives from the Zionist streams. One of the tasks of "Matzok" was to influence the activities of the Elders Council and their institutions. "Matzok regularly participated in the most important decisions and orders of the Elders Council and its institutions. It was truly not difficult to achieve because most of the members of the Elders Council belonged to the Zionist groups.

[Page 287]

Also, in the Kazernirungs Commission, one of the most important institutions of the Elders Council, we know that there were representatives from among the social directors in the ghetto who were resentful.

At the end of 1943 and beginning of 1944, a movement caught on with the youth groups in the Ghetto, to get themselves out to the partisans in the forest. Also, the Partisan Committee strongly attempted to use the work of the Elders Council and its institutions.

In the authority of the Elders Council there were the following ghetto offices: 1) Jewish Ghetto Police, 2) Labor Office, 3) Workshop Office, 4) Social Care Office, 5) Housing Office, 6) Health Office, 7) Social Office, 8) Statistics Office, 9) Education Office, 10) Ghetto Court[k], 11) Ghetto Firefighters. For a specific time, the Elders Council also led[1] the large Ghetto Workshops which were later transferred to the direct authority of the City Commissariat and, finally, to the camp management by the Camp Command.

The Elders Council would appoint a leader as head of a few offices. The general guidelines for the work of the ghetto offices would be established by the Elders Council. The leaders of the institutions, from time to time, had to give an activity report to the Elders Council so it was always oriented about what was going on in the Offices.

The Elders Council would publish general laws and orders from the regime to the ghetto population through public acquaintances in German, but mostly in Yiddish. Some publications from the Elders Council or from a ghetto office would not only be read carefully, but also strongly commented upon, in an effort to read between the lines about what was often not said…

Confirmations and denouncements of the appointees to the ghetto institutions were also heard, regarding the competence of the Elders Council. At first, the ghetto operation was active with a larger number of employees and workers. When, over time, the demand for Jewish work forces was increased by the regime, the Elders Council was forced to reduce the number of associates from the employees.

[Page 288]

According to other ghetto Jews, since the employees of the "Magistrate," as the Jews of the ghetto administration called it, enjoyed an entire list of privileges, it is understandable why any reductions would create a panic among the employees. Those who were lined up to be removed from their posts, would search in every possible way to apply pressure from the Jewish influencers of the Ghetto, to remain working in the ghetto operation. Those reduced colleagues would be transported to work in the city work places or in a ghetto workshop.

The employees would receive no rewards for their work. Like all working ghetto Jews, they would receive a ration of a couple of kilograms of bread per week, etc., aside from the normal ghetto distribution. However, the higher office workers would receive larger rations of food products and other items from the resources which were found in the authority of the ghetto offices.

Aside from this, the colleagues of the institutions had a comparatively easier time than most ghetto Jews, who took on the hard burden of forced labor. So, the Jews doing hard labor looked at the administrative employees like parasitic elements. This same antagonism, which would often take on harsh expressive forms, was reduced with the downfall of the Elders Council and their institutions, starting at the end of 1943.

To receive a somewhat objectively critical picture about the activities of the Elders Council and its institutions, it would be appropriate at this time to bring forth the general arguments for and against the existence of the Jewish ghetto administration.

As previously mentioned in the introduction to this Monograph, this work does not pretend to give an exhaustive answer to the complex problem which is connected to the Jewish "Ghetto autonomy". The raising of both types of arguments is only intended to touch upon this responsible theme, as much as possible.

[Page 289]

The comparative complaints from the supporters of a Jewish ghetto administration are summarized as follows: witnesses reported that the defenseless Jews absolutely could not hope for help from the neighboring Christian world during the horrific murders by the Lithuanian population in the first chaotic days, even before the Nazis managed to warm their feet in occupied Lithuania. Jews were likened to an animal which fell into a trap, from where there was no way to tear himself out. In such a case, Jewish interests dictated accepting the requirement by the occupation powers to create Jewish representation with which it could come in contact about Jewish issues.

By the way, we should not forget that at that time no one could even vaguely imagine the thought that the Hitlerite murderers had created a devilish plan to annihilate the Jewish population in the occupied areas. Logically thinking, it was then actually desirable not to be locked out of the possibility of affirming contact with the Nazi rulers in whose hands lay the fate of the Jewish prisoners.

By having Jewish representation, they hoped to be updated and informed about understanding the decrees. They believed that thanks to Jewish advocacy they succeeded in canceling this or that decree, and if not entirely, at least lightening it somewhat.

If, in principle, we rejected this collaboration with the Nazis, they would be forced to organize Jewish life by themselves. They then thought that such a situation would surely increase the murders and suffering of the Jewish population, because then there would not be any possibility to intervene.

Going on these basic assumptions at that time, there was no other way out but to take advantage of the one and only chance to save as many people as they could. The only hope at that time was securing their aspiration to win as much time as possible, and that stimulated the search for how to adapt to their tragic fate.

[Page 290]

They purposefully did not want to give the evil ones any opportunity to bad mouth and pitch the Jews as if they were parasites and useless people, an argument which was then used to bring fatal results for the entire Jewish collective. Taking that into account, there was no other choice but to request that the Jews work on various forced heavy labor jobs, no matter how costly it should be for a Jew to toil in drudgery. They also had to require that he carry out the regime's order to give up his possessions. They had to make it clear for the people that in all these persecutions and insults about us as Jews and as a people, no one should lose their patience, because reacting against the scoundrels, even if they actually deserved it, would only serve as provocation for new murderous evil acts.

There was no other way but to agree to build a Jewish organization which should, on the one hand, be a mediation authority between the regime and the Jewish population, and on the other hand, help organize the public needs of the ghetto Jews. They had to cooperate as much as possible on all these issues of life and death.

Speaking objectively, of all the preventable and unpreventable defects of the Jewish ghetto administration, they were more helpful for the general Jewish public than it would have been with the "best" of the Nazi ghetto higher-ups. Somehow, the Jewish ghetto administration always remembered that it represented the Jewish public, and it had to deal in their interests. Confirmation of this can be found in the following facts:

First, the Jewish ghetto representatives tried, in various ways, to personally interest the Nazi ghetto governors in the long-term existence of the ghetto settlement through hefty bribes, gifts, etc. This helped a lot for those upon whom the existence of the ghetto was dependent and perhaps defended our aspirations not to liquidate the ghetto collective, contrary to their Nazi "principles."

Second, the intention to establish ghetto institutions was a social-positive: to ensure fairness in equalizing the heavy loads of ghetto slavery and bringing some order to the areas of forced labor, food products, workshops, health, housing questions, social help, etc.

Third, when it was time for groups of youth to escape with arms in their hands to the forest, to get to the partisans to fight the Nazi enemy, or when in the Ghetto they started building hideouts where they could hide themselves in a moment of distress – the ghetto administration, especially the Ghetto Police unofficially helped these life-saving ghetto movements.

[Page 291]

Fourth, the smuggling of dozens of Jewish children out of the Ghetto, to give them away to Christian families, was possible thanks to the help of the Jewish ghetto organization, mainly with help from the Jewish functionaries at the Ghetto Gate.

Fifth, according to their possibilities, the Jewish administration took care of the intellectuals, for whom it was much more difficult than for the general public, to adjust to the inhumane ghetto conditions.

Sixth, it is an unquestionable fact, that the politics conducted by the Jewish ghetto representatives played a large role in the Kovno ghetto settlement. They were one of the "last Mohicans" of the ghettos in "the East," existing for three years and continuing up until the liberation of Lithuania. On the day of the ghetto liquidation, more than 10,000 Jewish souls remained alive. If the Soviet offensive, which started on the 22 of June 1944 near Vitebsk, would have continued its tempo all the way from the start toward Kovno, a larger portion of the ghetto collective and the surrounding labor camps would have, without a doubt, survived to liberation. The Nazis would never have managed to deport the Jews to Germany, which was indeed the case when they had the Ghetto under their authority for a few extra weeks.

And above all, we must establish the fact that after Dachau, where the men were taken, and after Stutthof, where the women were located, a few thousand Kovno Jewish men and women remained alive. This was an absolute gain in the final political account of Jewish ghetto leadership.

The opponents of a Jewish ghetto organization put forth the following motives against this thesis:

[Page 292]

First, Jews should in no way have ever dared work together with the most bitter murderers of the Jewish people, because a few collaborations with the Nazis (no matter how good and honest the Jewish intentions were) were in essence against Jewish life-interests. Already from their first bestial acts toward the Jewish population, before the establishment of the Ghetto, as well as in the first months of the Ghetto's existence, it was clear to see that, sooner or later, the evildoers would annihilate us all, and every illusion to this detail was unfounded. So why would a ghetto Jew dare take upon himself such a violation and stain of shame, like laying his hand out to confirm the fate of another ghetto Jew? Every Jew, who wore the same yellow patch as another Jew, always had to remember that no matter how miserable it was, his direct or indirect participation in Hitler's murders against the Jews was his fault. This is not in comparison to the greater one, like the Nazi murders, because they, the evil doers, "are allowed" to do it, and Jews – should absolutely not.

Second, the agreement by Jews to create a Jewish ghetto organization, under the "protection" of the Nazis, in a certain sense helped the mass murderers reach a state that Jews themselves should do a portion of their annihilation work. Examples were, chasing the people to do forced labor, relocating Jews from the Ghetto to the labor camps where the regime and the living conditions were much harder than in the Ghetto itself. In addition, aside from the fact that the Jewish ghetto administration was itself actively involved in the relocation Actions outside the borders of Lithuania, like, for example, to Riga and specifically to Estonia, where the relocated people were placed in conditions of destruction and extermination. The "contribution" of the Jewish ghetto governors became clear to all of them seeing what Jews had to withstand during the horrible Hitler years.

Third, a few honest and objective-thinking ghetto people would have to recognize that all the "community leaders" of the Jewish ghetto power holders were really nothing more than a means to protect their own skin and create for themselves a privileged and lighter living situation on the backs of their other brothers. The so-called argument about gaining time for the community, for these specific people, meant first, to protect themselves and their families. During various larger and smaller ghetto decrees, the Jewish ghetto managers, before anything else, attempted to get themselves out of the general troubles.

[Page 293]

Fourth, during these three years of ghetto existence, those responsible within the Jewish ghetto administration undertook no noticeable, serious steps to curb the protectionism, corruption, and other anti-social and immoral acts by specific office people of the ghetto institutions. The Elders Council, as the highest representative of the ghetto settlement, allowed the rampage to go undisturbed by the various Arnshtam's (Ghetto Police), Lurie's, Margolis' (Labor Office), and other ghetto tyrants, who were at the top of the ghetto population. This created a situation where the simple, helpless ghetto Jews had to withstand double pressure: both by the Nazi murderers, as well as, by the Jewish "ghetto-government."

Fifth, all the better and easier workplaces in the city and in the Ghetto were controlled by the protected members. Because of this, the simple-Jew was actively worked to death at the Aerodrome and in the heavy city brigades, where extreme heavy labor would batter the Jews and, aside from this, they did not have any opportunity to purchase even a small amount of foodstuffs.

Sixth, the Kazernirungs Commission was supposed to order the quartering from the ghetto settlement in an equitable manner. However, they exclusively sent those people to the labor camps who didn't have access to any of the Jewish ghetto rulers who could take on their grievance.

Seventh, the Elders Council allowed all the ring leaders of the social groupings to protect their "activities" on the backs of the ghetto community. Therefore, it was an entirely "normal" phenomenon in ghetto life that a young and healthy person from whichever "party" would have an easier workplace, and an older and weaker, simple-Jew would be torn apart by punitive work.

Eighth, although the Elders Council and its institutions could not be blamed for co-responsibility in the annihilation Actions, the blame remains on the conscience of certain leading persons from the Jewish ghetto administration for the following:

[Page 294]

A) Right on the eve of the "test Action" which took place in September 1941, the Elders Council agreed to distribute 5000 "Jordan-certificates" among the ghetto population, when in the Ghetto there were then close to 30,000 Jewish souls. There was no doubt that the owner of a "Jordan certificate" would, in this way or another, be more privileged than others who did not get a certificate. And truly it was just like that: both during the "test Action" and, also during the Action in the Small Ghetto in October 1941, the Jordan certificates were "life certificates" in the literal sense of the word. The Elders Council should have handled the question with more seriousness and responsibility about whether to accept the "Jordan certificates," or not.

B) Without a doubt, on the eve before the Big Action, the Elders Council was in the picture, based on a talk with the murderer, Rauca, the Gestapo in charge of Jewish issues. They knew that the Ghetto was on the eve of an Action, but it was not openly announced to the ghetto population in a way that they could understand the upcoming danger. On the contrary, their announcement to the ghetto population about the order from the powers to appear at Democracy Square, did not indicate the purpose of the assembly. It contributed to the assembly of all the 26,000 ghetto Jews at the selection place, from which over 10,000 men, women and children were sent away for annihilation. The sin of the Elders Council cannot even be minimized by a hair because it received approval by Rabbi Shapira to publish the order in the version in which it was announced.

C) Many ghetto Jews started to hide themselves at the time of the relocation Action to Estonia in October 1943, when at lunch time in the Ghetto it became clear that the assembled people were not being deported to the work camp Ezheretshai, near Kovno, as was at first "promised" by Goecke, but rather to somewhere else. So, the Kazernirung Committee of the Elders Council started putting together new lists of Jews for relocation. This was done without considering something which had serious cause for suspicion - that perhaps the people were being taken somewhere to be killed.

These were the basic reasons of those who believed that, in the final balance, the existence of a Jewish ghetto administration served the interests of the Nazi murderers more than those of the general ghetto population.

Dr. Elhanan Elkes was Chairman of the Elders Council the entire time during the existence of the Ghetto

[Page 295]

Until the Nazi occupation of Lithuania, Dr. Elkes was one of the most well-known Kovno internists at the Internal Department in the Kovno Jewish hospital "Bikur Holim." He was also the house doctor of the Lithuanian Prime Minister Tuvialis, and for a few foreigner legations (among them, also from the German legation) in the Lithuanian residence.

Ideologically, Dr. Elkes was close to Zionism, but he did not actively mix in Jewish social life. He was renown as an independent person, and he had gained large popularity as an honest doctor.

Since it was expected that due to his non-political past, the Nazis would not be able to reject him, and in addition, he had connections with responsible persons of the previous German agents in Kovno, so he was nominated by the Jews to stand at the head of the Jewish representation on the Elders Council. The occupation powers accepted his candidacy as the Chairman of the Elders Council without objection.

At this opportunity it is worthwhile adding that the Nazi ghetto governors behaved toward him with great respect (as much as one can talk about respect by the Nazis to a Jew). He especially had good fortune with the S.S. Lt. Colonel Goecke, who after converting the Ghetto into a concentration camp, became the Camp Commander. This high-level S.S. functionary would very often call on him to confer on various ghetto issues and would, by contrast, treat him as an equal.

Because of this relationship between Dr. Elkes and Goecke, just before the liquidation of the Ghetto, when the Red army was already standing near Vilna, Dr. Elkes dared to make the following proposal: If he, Goecke, would cooperate so that the Ghetto should peacefully fall into the hands of the Soviets, he would receive a large gift of money from the Jews, and in addition he would help him rehabilitate himself in the eyes of the Soviet powers. True, Goecke, after certain deliberation rejected the proposal, and as we know, a short time later he liquidated the Ghetto in the cruelest way. But the very fact that Dr. Elkes made such a proposal bears witness to the level of their relationship.

[Page 296]

Dr. Elkes was not very interested in the daily work of the ghetto institutions, which stood under the authority of the Elders Council. This happened not only because of his weak health condition, but also because he gave free rein to the people of the individual ghetto offices. Therefore, it would very often happen that high "influencers" in the Jewish Ghetto Police, or from the Labor Office would often not consider his wishes and they would do whatever they wanted. This relationship of Dr. Elkes to the daily ghetto issues indirectly helped create chaos, lawlessness, and other negative phenomena in the public life of the Ghetto. Mainly, he would become active when they would need to engage with the powers to condemn or soften a decree for the Ghetto.

Thanks to his restrained and honest private life, Dr. Elkes gleaned the attention of the ghetto population. The ghetto Jews believed that Dr. Elkes had good intentions in every case regarding the Ghetto. And whatever he could do for the benefit of the ghetto collective, he certainly did.

At the liquidation of the Ghetto, he was taken to the Dachau labor camps near Landsberg together with all the men. There he was active as a doctor in the sick ward in the concentration camp. As a sick and weaker person, Dr. Elkes could not survive the camp tortures and he died in the camp on the 17th of October 1944.[m]

The entire time that Dr. Elkes was Chairman of the Elders Council, his Vice Chairman was Adv. Leib Garfunkel.

In pre-war Jewish social life in Lithuania, Adv. Garfunkel had an important position. His active leadership in Lithuania started after the First World War, when independent Lithuania laid the basis for Jewish national autonomy, but he was later ostracized by the Lithuanian Jew-haters. For a certain time, he was also the Jewish deputy in the Lithuanian Parliament. He belonged to the leaders of the Zionist-Socialist movement in Lithuania.

[Page 297]

A few weeks after the Red Army marched into Lithuania on the 15th of June 1940, he together with a few active leaders of the liquidated Zionist organizations were arrested and sat the Kovno jail. A few days later, after the outbreak of the German-Soviet war he was freed from jail, because the Soviets didn't manage to evacuate the prisoners, so the arrested freed themselves. Without a doubt, the fact that he was persecuted by the Soviets, contributed to his confirmation by the Nazi powers as the Vice Chairman of the highest Jewish ghetto authority.

In the Elders Council, Adv. Garfunkel dedicated himself mainly to the activities of the Ghetto Police and other ghetto institutions. He was infrequently in contact with the Nazi ghetto authorities because Dr. Elkes, and sometimes also other members of the Elders Council, occupied themselves with this.

In the Ghetto, when the Zionist groups started reviving their social activities, Adv. Garfunkel demonstrated full interest in this issue, especially in the work of the Zionist-Socialist group. He also demonstrated an understanding of the youth movement that prepared to go out into the forests to the partisans. As previously mentioned, when the Elders Council was arrested during the liquidation of the Jewish Ghetto Police, he was arrested by the Gestapo and was at the 9th Fort longer than other members of the Elders Council; he was badly tortured.

Like Dr. Elkes, Adv. Garfunkel also conducted a modest and restrained private life and he, together with Dr. Elkes, were showered with respect and trust by the ghetto population. In his personal life there were a few that rejected him because he also did very little to curb the anti-social phenomena in the Jewish ghetto organization.

After the liquidation of the Ghetto, he was taken to the labor camp near Landsberg, where he survived to the liberation at the end of April 1945. After liberation he was active with the "remaining remnant" in Italy, where he was the chairman of the Zionist Committee of the Jewish refugees.

Adv. Yakov Goldberg was one of the most distinguished members of the Elders Council during its existence.

[Page 298]

As a former officer of the Lithuanian army, he stood at the head of the Jewish Front-Fighters-Union in Lithuania. Because of that, he was arrested during the time of Soviet sovereignty in Lithuania, and when the Germans marched into Kovno he was freed from jail. Also, like Adv. Garfunkel, because of the persecution he endured by the Soviet regime, he was accepted by the occupation powers as a leading person in the ghetto settlement.

Aside from his office as a member of the Elders Council, Adv. Goldberg was active as a high-level person of the Jewish Labor Office in the ghetto, from Autumn of 1941 to Summer 1943.

As mentioned, Adv. Goldberg was also at the 9th Fort during the arrest of the Elders Council and suffered terribly from the Gestapo.

He was freed from the Dachau labor camp where he was taken together with the men of the Kovno Ghetto. After liberation he did not get involved in social activities.

We should mention the other people who were members of the Elders Council from the beginning:

Hirsh Levin – was one of the most important speakers in the Elders Council, especially in the first period of the ghetto's existence.[n]

Rabbi Snieg – a former army Rabbi in Lithuania. Freed in Dachau concentration camp. Later he became the Head Rabbi of the "remaining remnant" in Bayern.

Rabbi Smuckler – a former Rabbi of Shantz. Died in the Ghetto.

Dr. Grigory Wolf – a familiar Jewish Social Worker in Kovno. Died in the Ghetto.

Dr. Chaim-Nachman Shapiro – mainly dedicated himself to cultural issues and Zionist activities in the Ghetto.[o]

The following were active as Secretaries of the Elders Council: Adv. Israel Bernstein – took over this office until Spring 1942, when he was arrested in association with the fallout of the illegal mail links between Kovno and other ghettos.[p] After being freed from arrest, he worked in other ghetto institutions. Died in a *malina* [hideout] during the liquidation of the Ghetto.

[Page 299]

Adv. Avraham Golub – at first was a helper to Adv. Bernstein. Later, after Bernstein's arrest, he became Secretary of the Elders Council. Wrought a very strong influence on the activities of the highest divisions of the Jewish ghetto administration and, as they said, was the uncrowned dictator. As a man with a strongly developed ambition for power, he was always disposed to pushing through his opinions in all the most important decisions of the Elders Council.

In addition to the ghetto organization, Adv. Golub was also one of the head speakers for Zionist life in the Ghetto, especially in the grouping of the general right-wing Zionists.

After the relocation Action to Estonia, in Autumn 1943, he went away from the Ghetto and hid out with a Christian in the countryside. Later, after liberation, he wound up in Italy where a court case took place about his activity during the ghetto times.

Adv. I. Shinberg – worked a long time in the Secretariat of the Elders Council. Thereafter he went over to work in the food base in the Social Welfare Office. During the days of the liquidation of the Ghetto he went out into the city and saved himself. He died after an operation, Passover, 1945, in Kovno.

The following also worked together in the bureau of the Elders Council:

Rostovsky – professional of German correspondence. An older Jew from Memel. Escaped during the Action of the children, old and sick, at the end of March 1944.

Miss Elstein – typewriter technician. During the arrest of the Elders Council in April 1944, she also was taken to the 9th Fort. Was taken to Stutthof. After liberation she wound up in Sweden.

Shmuckler – (son of Rabbi Shmuckler) courier of the Elders Council. As a gate keeper, he had the opportunity to see and listen to everyone and knew what took place in the "Holy of Holies" in the Ghetto. He really listened in to the best-informed people in the Ghetto. Many Jews would often be jealous of this boy, who was always updated on the most important ghetto happenings. Died somewhere in a *malina* [hideout] during the liquidation of the Ghetto.

Original footnotes:

a. As told to the editor by Advocate, Goldberg
b. They were brought there from the 7th Fort, where, as we know, about 7-8,000 Jewish men were killed.
c. See "Establishment of the Slabodka Ghetto."
d. Details about him – see "Leading Persons in the Elders Council."
e. From the 15th of August to the 28th of October 1941.
f. The Jewish Labor office would have to carry out the orders.
g. Until the establishment of the German labor office in the Ghetto.
h. After the deportation from the Ghetto to Germany, he was sent away to the Italian front where he died at the end of 1944 in a "heroes-death" for his service to the Third Reich, and after his death he received the high rank of Colonel in the S.S.
i. See "Battle between Caspi-Serebrovitz and Liptzer because of the influence over the leadership of on ghetto life."
j. "The Zionist center in Viliampole, Kovno" See Zionist Activity in the Ghetto"
k. The last two institutions existed only for a short time.
l. Through the Jewish people appointed by the Elders Council
m. Hebrew date: Chaf'Tet Tishrei, Tashad
n. See "Persons who were involved with the partisan movement.
o. About his tragic fate and that of his family – see "School-Office."
p. See "Statistics Office."

CHAPTER II

Jewish Ghetto Police

-Founding of the Jewish Ghetto Police and its basic tasks-The role of the police in ghetto life-The Ghetto Police and the "Service Order"-The separate units of the police-The Police Orchestra

[Page 301]

Right after the locking of the Ghetto in the middle of August 1941, the Jewish Committee slowly started to regulate public life in the Ghetto. The powers ordered the set-up of the Jewish Ghetto Police. It was said that the Jewish Police would have to supervise the public peace and order in the Ghetto and, additionally, stand in service to the Jewish institutions.

To recruit young people for the Ghetto Police, the Jewish Committee put out a request to those who served in the military to come forth for police service. We must say, however, that they were then dealing with a total of about 50 people, but not more than a few dozen young people responded voluntarily. The additional ones had to be recruited on the way from the gathering.

At the start, the composition of the Jewish Ghetto Police, aside from military servicemen, also included athletes from "Makabi" [Jewish sports club] who stepped up, and a certain number of intellectuals. The simple people kept themselves back from police issues. The founders of the police therefore decided to mobilize a few young people from the levels of the simple folk, to create trust in the activities of the police by all strata of the ghetto population.

After the Ghetto was locked up, the newly created Ghetto Police had a lot of work regulating the housing issues. Hundreds of Jews still did not have any roof over their heads. Many people didn't even have a corner in which to house themselves. Every day the Housing Office would become besieged by hundreds of interested people and the Ghetto Police had to help the Housing Office carry out their functions.

[Page 302]

Later, when the other ghetto institutions became involved in more intensive activity, it was necessary to get the help of the Ghetto Police once again. So, for example, the Ghetto Police was used by the Labor Office to recruit the necessary number of Jews for various forced labor; Ghetto Police had to keep order at the food distribution shops, where there were long lines to pick up the ghetto rations; they also had to protect the communal ghetto gardens which were stormed by hungry ghetto Jews.

The duties of the Ghetto Police were increased, as they were needed to complete the operation, understand, and coordinate the functions of the various police agencies.

At the head of the Ghetto Police there were people who ran all the police issues. The Central Police was made up of a police chief and his helpers, a police inspector, people from the various police resources, a bureau person with an entire staff of colleagues, etc.

The agreement with the Elders Council established the guidelines for the police's activities in the Ghetto. The Central Police dealt with the following issues: to help the ghetto institutions carry out their duties, instruct the other police precincts, manage the ghetto jail, and the like.

To be able to properly carry on with the police issues, the Ghetto was divided into a few police areas, and in each area there was a police precinct. At the founding of the Ghetto, there were in total four police precincts. After the liquidation of the Small Ghetto, in October 1941, there remained three police precincts. When in December 1943, the area of the old ghetto was reduced, that police precinct was also liquidated. From then on, there remained only two police precincts in the Ghetto until the liquidation.

Each police precinct had a precinct chief, bureau office worker and a certain number of police, depending on the size of the area. In addition to the police functions, as mentioned, the Ghetto Police were very active in helping the Labor Office in the issues of work duty. Therefore, in a few police precincts there was also an active labor inspector who was the mediator between the Labor Office and the Ghetto Police.

[Page 303]

From the start, a police reserve was active at the police center, which, among other duties, also organized the division of the Jewish Police which guarded the Ghetto Gate. Later, the police reserve was liquidated and the Jewish policemen at the gate were trained for a separate division of the Ghetto Police.

At the end of 1941, a criminal police force was set up, whose role was the punishment of criminals. The number of criminal violations increased after the big Action, when over ten thousand Jews were taken out of the Ghetto. Various people were caught with property belonging to the Jews who were taken away.

The Criminal Police also had to deal with uncovering the guilty in robberies of private persons, and of the ghetto institutions. Thank goodness, in the Ghetto, there was no shortage of private and social hoaxes and the Criminal Police had to clarify all these issues. To conduct their work, the Criminal Police had in its authority special agents who would provide confidential reports, which were important to uncover various crimes.

There was also a Police Court in the Ghetto, which was an inheritance from the liquidated general Ghetto Court.[a] Like the Ghetto Court, the Police Court would handle various civil and criminal issues of the ghetto population. Court judgments were harshly carried out.

Under the authority of the Ghetto Police there were also a few ghetto jails, where those convicted for jail would suffer their punishment. In addition, the Ghetto Jail served as a collection point for recruiting people for the labor camps. The so-called labor deserters were also held there, until they were sent to work in such workplaces where there was always a shortage of people.

[Page 304]

There was also a Sanitary Division which was active in the Ghetto Police, which supervised the sanitary hygienic situation. The shortage in sanitary facilities necessitated active measures to maintain the sanitary conditions in the Ghetto, at least at a minimal level. The police would, therefore, systematically go out to control the cleanliness in and around the houses. In this detail there was collaboration between the Sanitary Division of the Police and the Health Office.

The telephone exchange in the Ghetto also belonged to the Ghetto Police, which organized and had available what might pass for a telephone network. It was made up of dozens of telephone units. When the Ghetto belonged to the City Commissariat, the telephone exchange was linked to the outside world by the Ghetto Guard, and, in Goecke's time, it was linked through the Camp Commander.

In the second half of 1942, the situation in the Ghetto became more-or- less stabilized and the regime organizations had a shortage of German guards to accompany the Jewish work brigades to the city. For a certain time, the Jewish Ghetto Police was attached to the guards of the Jews in the city workplaces. By the way, it is worthwhile adding that at that time the City Commissariat mobilized ghetto policemen a few times, by applying police tactics to the non-Jewish population in the city.

This is being presented as an evaluation of the activities of the Ghetto Police in "normal" times. The Ghetto Police played a very important role when the Ghetto received unexpected decrees, like for example, to quickly recruit a certain number of people for a labor camp outside the Ghetto, or when the Ghetto had to collect people somewhere for a foreign place (relocation Actions to Riga and Estonia).

Since the Jewish Ghetto Police, in essence, was not more than an executor for the decisions of the Elders Council and its institutions, we must admit that it was not very popular among the ghetto Jews.

[Page 304a]

Surviving young Jewish children from Kovno right after liberation
Photo by G. Kadisch

[Page 304b]

Jewish Ghetto Orchestra

From left to right: M. Borstein; B. Kariski; Abramson M, Goldstein Director, M. Hofmekler and violinist A. Stupel

[Page 305]

The Jewish Police were disliked by the wide ghetto world for the following reasons:

First, it had to conduct various thankless jobs, for example, chasing people for work duty to forced labor, collecting the designated screaming people for the labor camp; forcing Jews to suffer punishment in the Ghetto Jail, etc.

Second, there were plenty of young men in the police who, with their strong and frequently brutal interactions with people, increased the gap even more between the Police and the vast majority of the ghetto population.

In addition, we must not forget that the simple ghetto Jew was not indifferent to, nor did he ignore the fact that the Jewish policeman and his family belonged to the protected element in the Ghetto. True, people from the other ghetto institutions were also drenched in quite a bit of privilege, but these protections were mainly of an internal Jewish character.

The Jewish Police was the only ghetto institution protected not only by the Jewish organization, but also by the regime organization, under whose authority the Ghetto existed. So, for example, the Nazi ghetto bosses, starting at the Big Action in October 1941 until the liquidation of the Jewish Police in March 1944 placed the police in a protected position in various critical situations for the Ghetto.

During these 3.5 years, being a ghetto policeman meant relative assurance that his family would be less affected by community troubles. During this period, belonging to the police organization was real protection from all kinds of decrees in ghetto life. Because of this, there was an understood, and a justified antagonism between the Ghetto Police and the ghetto population.

However, truth be told, we must highlight a few activities of the Jewish Police during its existence:

a. during the selection at the Big Action, when it was possible for the Ghetto Police to move around the assembly place freely, the policemen helped many Jews get out of the selection or switched from the bad to the good side. Thanks to them, many ghetto Jews were saved from extermination.

b. in the Ghetto, when it became unsafe for the youth movement to leave for the partisans in the forest, the police helped smuggle arms into the Ghetto. They also helped with secret military training of the candidates for the partisans, when they went out of the Ghetto to the forest, etc.

[Page 306]

The Police Chief and his assistants took an active part in the Secret Committee leading the partisan movement. For this activity, he, together with another 40 ghetto policemen were arrested and paid with their lives.

Just these enumerated facts speak positively of the Jewish Ghetto Police, who, to a certain extent, rehabilitated themselves, at least partially, for past injustices done to large portions of the ghetto population.

As previously described,[b] the Jewish Police was liquidated in a cruel manner and the "Service-Order" was created.

Making a small parallel between the Ghetto Police and the "Service-Order," it was established that with all its shortcomings, the Jewish Police was an institution whose activities were conducted with the approval of the Elders Council. The "Service-Order," by contrast, was organized by the Nazis, and it was hypothetically inclined to comply with the requirements of the regime organization, without regard for how these requirements subjected the ghetto settlement to the bloodiest life events. As roughly described, there were also problems which the "Service-Order" imposed on the ghetto collective just before the liquidation of the Ghetto.

Because of this, the Jewish Police were left with a comparatively good name, and the "Service-Order" remained in the memories of the ghetto Jews like an anti-Jewish authority, which only caused harm to the Ghetto. These strongly negative opinions were even strengthened because of the painful fact that among the ranks of the "Service-Order" there were betrayers and revealers who quite often betrayed the Ghetto. And Jews were deathly afraid of them, not less than of the Gestapo itself.

[Page 307]

But even here, truth be told, we must say that not all members of the "Service-Order" were as corrupt as this group of criminals. More honest people from the liquidated Ghetto Police, who didn't want to go to the "Service Order" were forced by Liptzer, the all-powerful of the "Service-Order." These honest people, however, were not able to influence the activity of the "Service-Order, and, as we say, they became insignificant. The reputation of the "Service Order" was created by the immoral and asocial elements.

Aside from the general Jewish Police in the Ghetto, an autonomous police institution in the Large Ghetto Workshops and in the Service Order workshops was also active. These separate police units stood in service only for the relevant institutions and they had very little to do with the general Ghetto Police.

The police at the Large Ghetto Workshops became trained in 1942, and its main task was, first, to guard the workshops, where, as we know, a few thousand Jews worked in various appointments from the German Wehrmacht. In these workshops, there were always large quantities of various materials, as well as, finished products, which were worth hundreds of thousands of Marks. Since the Jewish leaders of the workshops were responsible for all the workers, they needed a special police guard.

In addition, at the exit from the workshop at midday, or after the end of work, police were stationed to check the Jewish workers at the exit gate, so that they couldn't carry any stolen items or materials out of the workshops. If they caught someone violating the commandment "thou shall not steal," he was strongly punished. In more serious cases of guilt, one would not only get punished, but they would kick him out of the workshop and transfer him to a job in a harder workplace outside the Ghetto. Nevertheless, dozens of Jews, day in and day out, ignored these controls and took things out of the workshop and somehow got through with the vital items.

[Page 308]

Three or four dozen men were active in the Ghetto Workshop Police. At the head of the police was a chief who conducted his work with approval of the Jewish leaders of the workshops.

At this opportunity it is worth mentioning that during the arrest of the Jewish Police, at the end of March 1944, the Gestapo freed all the Workshop Policemen from the 9th Fort. This liberation happened because the Gestapo dismissed any collaboration between these policemen and the partisan movement in the Ghetto.

The Chief of Police in the Large Ghetto Workshops was Melamdovich (killed in a *malina* [hideout] during the ghetto liquidation). We must mention some of the other higher police officers: Weiner (shot during the evacuation march from Dachau); Kalvariski (killed by Gestapo because of a betrayal by a Christian as he was looking to buy arms for the Ghetto); Takatsh (liberated in Dachau); etc.

Also, the Service Order workshops had their own police force of a dozen people who oversaw close to a hundred Jewish artisans who worked in appointments by the Gestapo. Their duties were like the duties of the police in the Large Ghetto Workshops, which was to protect the property of the workshops, etc. During the arrest of the Jewish Police, none of these policemen suffered.

As we know, a police orchestra existed in the Ghetto since Summer, 1942. From time to time, it gave concerts for the ghetto population. In addition to playing in the orchestra, the police orchestra also had to carry out various duties for the general police or for the police of the workshops to which they belonged.

During Goecke's time no concerts took place for the ghetto population. But very often, the orchestra gave concerts for the Camp Commander and for invited Nazi higher-ups from the city.

[Page 309]

At this opportunity it would be of interest to submit the following characteristic episode:

As was already mentioned, a heavy battle was going on between the Kovno City Commissar, Kramer, who belonged to the S.A., and Goecke, who belonged to the S.S., over the leadership of the Ghetto. Since this battle finally ended with a victory for Goecke, Kramer looked for an opportunity to compromise Goecke.

After one concert, where Goecke invited guests from the city, the City Commissar, Kramer, sent a report to Berlin, in which he described Goecke's great "sins;" that he and other invited Germans listened to music conducted by a Jewish orchestra.

Right after this, a harsh inquiry arrived for Goecke from Berlin, demanding an immediate clarification about this issue. Despite these difficulties, he never succeeded in smoothing over this issue, and he continued to remain in disfavor among those in the high Nazi sphere in Berlin. It could be that after liquidating the Ghetto, this incident contributed to his being sent away to the Italian front, where he was killed.

Goecke strongly favored the Police Orchestra, and it was demonstrated by the fact that during the arrest of the Police, none of the orchestra policemen were ever arrested.

In the labor camps of Dachau, where the orchestra musicians were grouped together with other Kovno Jews, the orchestra - from time to time - gave concerts for the S.S. leaders of the camps, and on occasion, also for the camp inmates.

After liberation this "camp orchestra" became active in the American Zone in Germany where it gave concerts for the "surviving remnant" of Jews.

The director of the orchestra was Misha Hofmekler. The following orchestra participants should also be remembered: Abrasha Stopel, the brothers Borshtein, Pomerantz, Percy Hayir, Volfberg, Frau Dukshtolski, Levitan, Frau Gladstein, Rozmarin (all survived to the liberation); Yellin, Finkel, Dariski, Frau Shor, Lint (all died), and others.

[Page 310]

The vocal numbers in the ghetto concerts would be carried out by: Yakov Zaks, Mrs. Ratshka, Mrs. Dr. Shmuckler, Miss Nechmod (all were killed); Mrs. Bar Kupritz (freed in concentration camp). Most recitals were given by the artist Kupritz (died in Dachau).

The size and composition of the Jewish Police varied at various periods of ghetto life. At first the police had 50 people, later – a couple of hundred persons. During the various reductions of colleagues in the Jewish organizations, there were concomitant reductions in the composition of the Police.

Not only did the ghetto settlement have a Jewish Police, but also there was a Jewish Police in the labor camps, which helped administer the labor camp and was subject to the Jewish camp Elders.

In 1942, the Jewish Police distributed special ghetto passes to the entire ghetto population. From then on, those few ghetto Jews always had to have their ghetto pass with them. Each pass had to be reported to the relevant police precinct.

It is certainly unnecessary to mention that the Jewish Ghetto Police was not armed with either hot or cold arms. It didn't even have any rubber sticks or other "effective" police features. The only symbols of "police power" they had was this dark blue uniform hat with the metal police emblem, and the white and blue police band (on the left arm) with "Jewish Ghetto Police Viliampole" written in German.

For the defeated ghetto Jew, who found himself under double pressure – non-Jewish and Jewish – these innocent symbols were enough (more than enough!) to obediently carry out the orders of the Police. The plagued and broken ghetto Jew, willingly or unwillingly, had to make peace with the idea that there is a Jewish "power" present in the Ghetto, and one must be subjected to it…

[Page 311]

The following leaders were active in the Jewish Ghetto Police:

 a. Kopelman (Police Chief from August 1941 until Autumn 1943. After liberation in Kovno was sentenced and sent to jail by the Soviet power organization); Moshe Levin (police chief from end of 1943 until the liquidation of the Ghetto Police, was shot at the 9th Fort); M. Bromson (killed in Dachau); Adv. Yakov Abramovitch (liberated in Dachau camp); Yudel Zhopovitch (shot at the 9th Fort), and others.

 b. From the other high police functionaries, we must recognize: Grinberg, Panemonski, Aronovski, Zeltzer, Bukantz, Rubinson, Adv. Zilberkvayt, Adv. Zak, Chvoles, Koretchenski (all shot at the 9th Fort); Padison (liberated as a partisan); Berger (liberated in Dachau) and others

 c. As "Service Order" leaders: B. Liptzer[c], Arnshtam[d] Grossman (liberated in Dachau), and others.

Original footnotes:

 a. See "Ghetto Court".
 b. See "Unexpected Transfer of the Jewish Police to the 9th Fort" and "Liquidation of the Ghetto Police and founding of the "Service-Order."
 c. See "Comment about Liptzer's role in the life of the ghetto settlement."
 d. See "founding of "Service-Order."

CHAPTER III

Labor Office

- The significance of labor in the life of the ghetto population- Early forms of forced labor for the ghetto Jews- Gradual formation of stable Jewish workplaces in town- First concrete steps to regulate the problems of forced labor- The organizational structure and basic activity of the special labor offices sections- Important periods in the history of the Jewish Labor Office

[Page 312]

In public ghetto life, the Jewish Labor Office occupied a place of honor among the Jewish ghetto institutions. The specific importance of this ghetto office developed because of the problem of work – more correctly stated - forced labor. It was also due to a few issues which were some of the most painful problems during the three-year existence of the Ghetto.

During the descriptions of the general ghetto occurrences, we opportunely saw that for the ghetto Jew, work often meant that you did or did you not survive a selection connected to an extermination action. Did you remain in the Ghetto where there were comparatively favorable living conditions, or were you "relocated" somewhere to a labor camp belonging to a concentration camp regime? Did you have a source of somehow living through – or being dependent on the official starvation rations distributed by the regime? Did you work in the open field at hard punitive labor, or have lighter work in a factory, or in the Ghetto itself? Did you work in the neighborhoods of the Ghetto, or did you have to withstand a daily march of 10-12 kilometers to get to work and back, etc.?

[Page 313]

So, why did the activity of the Labor Office have such a decisive influence on the fate of the ghetto Jew? And why were the existential questions of the ghetto population dependent on many of these fair or unfair dealings?

Before we step closer to familiarize ourselves with the structure of the Jewish Labor Office and its activities, it is necessary to provide at least a quick basic story about the development of forced labor in the Ghetto.

Already in the first weeks of the Nazi occupation in Kovno, when the huge wave of mass excesses against the Jewish population was over, they started capturing Jews for various jobs for the German military units or for the Lithuanian "partisans." The work was random then, and it would mainly consist of loading merchandise on the train, clearing up military casements, and the like.

The attitude toward the Jews by the Germans, and even more by the Lithuanian partisans, was then very brutal: they would beat the Jews murderously, ordering them to do the most difficult work, not allowing them to catch their breath and, above all, there was no shortage of rude obscenities and humiliation relating to Jews and Communists, which, for these murderers, was one and the same. At work the Jews would be guarded by military guards and after ending work, the Jews were allowed to go home.

The Jews could not free themselves for very long from the specter of being captured by the mass arrests and pogroms. These were in evidence at the same time as the Nazi occupation, so most Jewish men remained hidden in their homes. Only those Jews who went out on the street to do various urgent errands would be caught. This arbitrary manner of capturing Jews for work continued until the founding of the Ghetto.

At the end of July and beginning of August 1941, Jews themselves had to fence in the entire ghetto area with barbed wire, build the hanging bridge over Paneriu Street, and dig the tunnel on Yorburker Street, etc. So, every day, the Jewish Committee mobilized the needed number of Jews for these jobs from among their employees.

[Page 314]

As we know, the Ghetto was locked up on the 15th of August 1941. German military service sites, which needed Jewish workers, would come to the Ghetto Gate demanding the necessary number of Jews from the Ghetto.

At first, from time to time, the newly established Jewish Ghetto Police collected the required number of workers from among the ghetto population. Later, when in the Jewish Committee started to organize the structure of the Jewish Labor Office, each skilled laborer, through the Ghetto Police, would be requested to come on scheduled days of the week to the Ghetto Gate to be ready for work wherever they were needed. In cases when the resultant number of Jews at the Ghetto Gate would be too small to fill the demand for Jewish laborers, the Jewish Police would go through Jewish houses to capture the missing number of Jews.

However, the demand for Jewish forced labor rose even more from day to day. And hundreds of new ghetto Jews were dragged into the process of hard punitive work.

The random, disorganized capturing of people for work couldn't be maintained. The need to quickly regulate this question became frightening. The first test of the self-established Jewish Labor Office was to bring some order to the sector of forced labor.

At that time, many German military workplaces needed continuous Jewish labor and they started requesting that the same Jews come to work for them every day. Now, this workplace was a favorable one. That meant, the attitude toward the Jews was not so cruel, since they would not beat them, relocate them, etc. So, the Jews themselves wouldn't let any other Jew get this work. Not to mention, that at work they would throw out a bit of bread to the Jews or give them a bit of soup. Then, the permanent workers had to do battle with people on the sidelines who also wanted to get into to this workplace.

[Page 315]

Because of hunger and semi-hunger in hundreds of ghetto homes, such a workplace invoked envy from thousands of half-hungry Jews who couldn't acquire such "luck."

It was difficult to recruit the needed number of Jews for workplaces where the work was terribly difficult physically, and there were various humiliations and insults. In such workplaces they had to capture people each day by force, and each one would take pains not to fall into such an unfavorable workplace.

At this moment it is necessary to add that at this workplace, the various Jewish artisans like carpenters, locksmiths, electricians, and others, had a much easier fate than the unqualified workers. The Germans related to the artisans with a greater attitude of respect than to the unqualified workers. By the way, there were many Germans who were surprised about the fact that there were authentic Jewish artisans available, and they watched the work of the Jewish skilled workers with curiosity. The more decent Germans would state that they now see how incorrect was the generally accepted opinion that Jews do not know how to work.

Many Jews who had the right to work at a workplace where they were treated less harshly, started to work on the security guards. With the help of bribes, they allowed them to buy some food products from the neighboring Christians. Carrying it back home, the Jews somehow smuggled the food products into the Ghetto. Due to the catastrophic nutritional status in the Ghetto at that time, this was an issue of greatest importance and significance.

When the guards from this workplace came to the assembly point at the Ghetto Gate to pick up the Jewish workers, there was terrible chaos because everyone wanted to break into the "good" work brigade.

To reinstate order, the guards at the Ghetto Gate would start beating the Jews brutally. Blackjacks, loaded guns, and the like, started flying over Jewish heads. Frequently there would also be shocking gunfire, and various other strategies to "calm" the Jews.

[Page 316]

However, hunger never frightened anyone away, and no one would step away from the Ghetto Gate or give up the effort to go to work. These were painful scenes, which illustrated the low and lawless Jewish situation. The "cultured" Germans from the Ghetto Guard would, at each opportunity, continue to reject the Jews because of their "inadequacy."

In the Ghetto, getting into such a workplace, from where they could bring home some food, was a very painful question. It is demonstrated by the fact that many higher officials from the Jewish ghetto administration voluntarily gave up their privileged posts in ghetto institutions to go to work in the city, especially in the good brigades of the engineer Mil.[a]

As was previously mentioned,[b] in mid-September 1941, the Germans started carrying out a large reconstruction project at the Kovno Aerodrome. They started requesting Jewish labor forces for construction work from the Ghetto. In the early days, it only amounted to about a hundred or two hundred Jews per day. Later, the demand for Jewish workers rose to a few thousand people per day.

As mentioned, the work at the Aerodrome carried on day and night, and work conditions there were extremely difficult. The attitude of the German masters toward the Jews was terrible. Furthermore, the actual work at the Aerodrome was horribly exhausting and they would beat the Jews dreadfully without any reason. Aside from that, there was no possibility of bringing any food products home from the Aerodrome. Therefore, getting such a relatively large number of Jews to work at the Aerodrome every day became a very difficult and painful problem for the Ghetto.

[Page 317]

On the first day of Rosh Hashana [Jewish New Year] 1941, the Elders Council called the entire skilled ghetto population of workers together in an open place, with the aim of clarifying to those in attendance about the urgent importance of collecting the needed number of Jews for work at the Aerodrome. A few Jewish skilled workers demanded to understand the importance of this issue for the ghetto's existence and saw to it to get themselves out of work duty at the Aerodrome.

At first, these appeals from the Elders Council had some effect. From day to day however, the collection of the needed number of Aerodrome workers created even more difficulties. The efforts of the Jewish Labor Office to establish a bit of order and a certain schedule for going to work at the Aerodrome, did not help much.

Issuing special work certificates, validated by the German front-construction-people, labor armbands, etc., for Aerodrome workers, did not have much impact on recruiting the needed number of people for Aerodrome work either.

For the ghetto Jew, working at the Aerodrome became a real scourge, and they could not get rid of it. On the other hand, the regime organization started giving even greater importance to this front construction work. Therefore, this created an extraordinarily difficult situation in the Ghetto.

For the ghetto Jew, the problem of work was not only a question of fulfilling the duty of forced labor, but at the same time it was also a question of having an opportunity to bring home some foodstuffs – or not. So, the Jewish ghetto leadership, especially the Jewish Labor Office, had to quickly start bringing in a bit of order and a bit of justice to this serious and important issue.

The Jewish Labor Office was then approached to carry out a detailed registration of all the skilled workers among the ghetto population. In addition, they also had to make other preparations which were needed for the activity of the Labor Office. But all the attempts and preparations came to naught after the mass extermination Actions, which took place in the Ghetto in the Autumn of 1941.

The Big Action cost the Ghetto a huge number of victims, and the small remnant of the surviving ghetto Jews were physically and spiritually shaken up to the core. Because of the depression and apathy which predominated in the Ghetto right after that catastrophe, no one even contemplated "organizing" the lives of those already on a death sentence…

[Page 318]

Related to this fact was that during the Big Action, as mentioned, thousands of skilled Jewish men and women workers were killed, among them hundreds of artisans. For the ghetto Jews, the illusion that work is a little piece of salvation allowing the Jews to live, was completely overturned. No one in the Ghetto was able or wanted to believe that the question of working- or not - had a significant influence on the fate of the Jews. During such a generally depressed atmosphere among the ghetto population, this Labor Office then let everything go with the flow, so to speak.

Weeks passed. The surviving ghetto Jews, willingly or unwillingly, had to continue carrying the heavy yoke of forced labor, and the Jewish Labor Office started to organize the issue of forced labor once again.

In the second half of November 1941, the Jewish Labor Office distributed special work passes, i.e., work duty cards to all the skilled working men and women. The age limits for men were established from 14-60 years old. For women, it was, at first, from 16 to 45 years old and later, from 15 to 55 years old. Women who had little children up to 8 years old (later up to 4 years old) were completely freed from work duty.[c]

For healthy men, a full work week of 6 and even 7 days per week was established. At the workplace they would demand Jewish workers also on Sunday. For women, at first it was decided that work duty would be only 3 days per week. Later, when the demand for Jewish labor rose strongly, younger women had to work 5 days per week, and older women, 3 or 4 days per week. The number of weekly work duty days for those with weaker health conditions would be established through the Jewish Doctors Commission of the Labor Office.[d]

[Page 319]

During the distribution of the work duty cards to the skilled-worker ghetto population, the Labor Office succeeded in establishing available contingent work duties for men and women. In addition, over time, they also set up certain controls over how Jews had to fulfill their work duty obligation for forced labor.

Before the distribution of the work duty cards, it was possible for a skilled worker to avoid going to work. Now this ended. A few skilled workers, men, and women, had to punctually fulfill their work duty in the workplace to which they were attached. If not, they would have heavy sanctions placed on them by the Jewish ghetto administration.

If the work duty person didn't have any permanent workplace in a city work brigade, or in the ghetto itself, he would have to go to work at the Aerodrome, where all Jews had to work at that time. The construction people from the Aerodrome would demand such large numbers of Jewish work forces from the Ghetto, that they would have to pull people away from other workplaces to fill the required number of Jewish workers for the Aerodrome work - every day.

At the end of 1941 and beginning of 1942, the general situation in the Ghetto started to become relatively stable. As a result, the Jewish ghetto institutions started normalizing their activities. Thus, the Labor Office also managed set up an entire system to regulate the issues of forced labor.

The Labor Office consisted of a specific dozen divisions, and a few divisions had a full list of functions to carry out. Within each division there were lead division people, under whose authority there were special personnel to carry out the needed work.

At the head of the Labor Office was a person who had oversight over the activities of all the Labor Office divisions. This person in the Labor Office would be in contact with the Elders Council, where they, among others, would decide the general guidelines for the various ghetto institutions.

[page 320]

During the existence of the Labor Office, that means from August 1941 until April-May 1944, the following persons worked in this office: Engineer Frenkel – the first few weeks since the founding of the Ghetto (died in Dachau); Advocate Yakov Goldberg- from Autumn 1941 until Summer 1943 (liberated in Dachau); Herman Frenkel – from Summer 1943 until the liquidation of the Jewish Labor Office in Spring 1944 (died a few weeks after the liberation from Dachau); General Secretary and later Vice-Chair of the Labor Office, was Dr. Shmuel Grinhaus (liberated in Dachau); for a short time Engineer Bargman was also Vice-Chair of the Labor Office (died in a Dachau labor camp).

Print machinists who were active in the Secretariat of the Labor Office were: Ms. Krakinovski (died in a labor camp in Germany) and Ms. Sukenik (was taken to Estonia and died there).

To present the activities of the Jewish Labor Office, it is necessary, at least schematically, to become familiar with the structure and most important functions of each separate Labor Office division.

A. The Registry Division

The Registry Division had 2 main functions:

    1. Always having a precise set up with all the needed information about the entire ghetto population, in general, and of the labor duty men and women specifically, and
    2. having all necessary notices about where and who is working, and how the labor duty person is fulfilling their work duty. Aside from the basic functions, the Registry Division, as we will see, also engaged itself in other issues which had direct and indirect connection to the complex work problems.

As was previously mentioned, each work duty man or woman received a work duty card from the Labor Office. The number on the work duty card was permanent and the work duty person would have to remember this number, no less than their given and family names… this was the most important designation of personal information for those on work duty.

[Page 321]

For the Registry Division to have control over how the work duty people did their work at each workplace, a Jewish Brigadier or Colonel was designated.[e] Aside from carrying out their direct duties with the work group and mediating between the Jewish workers and the workplace, each Brigadier and Column person had to submit a report to the Registry every day[f] about the relevant men and women who worked at their workplace that day.

After signing off on the received reports in the work control logs at the Registry, they would immediately establish who on this particular day, did, or did not, fulfill their work duty.

When a worker on duty became ill and was not able to go to work, he would have to turn to the Medical Division which would give him a permit for the time of his illness.

If, for a specific reason, a work duty person had to remain in the house for a day, he would have to get a permit from the work inspector[g] of his area.

The list of persons authorized for leave due to illness or other reasons was immediately sent to the Registry to be signed off in the work control books. In this way the Registry would be able to establish exactly who was without a justification on that specific day and did not work. The person without justification who avoided work duty was transferred to the Mobilization and Punishment division to be punished.

For the Registry to know to which work place the worker was sent, the other divisions of the Labor Office sent over a list of all those working at the Aerodrome, in the city brigades, as well as in the Ghetto Workshops, and in the ghetto institutions. Every workplace had its specific code and every work card from a workplace in the city or in the Ghetto had to have a stamp of the Registry. Without such a stamp on a work card, it was invalid.

[Page 322]

Through separate divisions of the Labor Office, all permanent and even temporary modifications in individual workplaces about the workers would immediately have to be reported to the Registry so that they were informed where the work duty person was supposed to work.

There were better and worse work jobs and people from the worse workplaces would take pains to selfishly jump across to the better workplace. So, the Registry provided daily reports to the Brigadiers and Column people so that they would also know each day the exact behavior of these defectors, who for such a "sin" became motivated by their responsibility.

For older women on work duty who had children up to 8 years old (later up to 4 years old), the Registry would give out special exemptions from work duty. This was done so that during the time of a work review by the Jewish Ghetto Police, this relevant woman would not be arrested as a work deserter and be sent to the police district or to the Ghetto Jail.

It was also established from the start that a work duty woman who served and conducted housework for at least 3 work duty persons, who worked not less than 6 days per week (if at home there were no other non-workers, like older women, and the like, who could do the household chores), would be freed from work duty. Later, this very decision was cancelled.

When the work duty women worked only 3 times per week, half of the women would work Monday-Wednesday-Friday, and the other half, Tuesday-Thursday-Saturday. Such a division of work duties relieved the women from exhaustion from work. In addition, on their free days, they could prepare food and organize their home economics on the days when they did not have to go to work.

On the women's work card, in large, highlighted letters it would show which work cycle she belonged to. That meant, which day of the week she had work-duty. If it was not her workday, a woman could peacefully walk around in the Ghetto and not be afraid of a labor patrol. The Jewish Police would systematically carry out these patrols in the streets and in the homes, with the aim of catching and punishing the work deserters.

[Page 323]

So that the file folders and other materials from Registry would always be in order, the Registry systematically collected all the notices about the changes in the condition of the ghetto population. For example, they noted communications about deaths, newborns, relocations from the Ghetto to other labor camps, etc.

After an Action, when the Registry didn't have any idea which persons were pulled out of the Ghetto, a new registration of the ghetto population was carried out.

So, this was the way the Registry of the Labor Office was able to receive continuous information about a work duty person – about his previous or current workplace, how this person fills the work duty, when and how long the worker was authorized because of illness, or other reasons, etc.

The heads of the Registry Division were: Zundelevich (saved himself during the liquidation of the Ghetto); as colleagues: A. Daitch (was shot in Ghetto during the deportation); R. Levin (jumped off a train during the transport to Germany and was thereafter freed); Vinik (died in a labor camp in Estonia); Griliches (was burned in a hideout in the Ghetto); Ogov (left during the Action of Children, Elders and Ill); Beregovski (died in Ghetto during the deportations); Mrs. Davidovich (liberated in Liubitsher labor camp where she was a Camp Elder), and others.

B. Mobilization and Punishment Division

The task of the Mobilization and Punishment Division was, firstly, to mobilize the needed number of workers for the various labor places. These were mainly for the difficult and bad work positions, where no volunteers ever wanted to go. They had to force the people to go there. In addition, the functions of these divisions were to tie together the responsibility of those work duty persons who would violate the determinations of the work duty.

[Page 324]

For the Mobilization & Punishment Division to be able to carry out its functions properly, it maintained close contact with the Jewish Police. To this aim, in each police precinct there was an active work inspector whose task was to supervise how the work duty people from the relevant police areas fulfilled their work duty. There were three or four such work inspectors, based on the number of police precincts in the Ghetto. The activity of the various work inspectors would be coordinated by one higher work inspector.

Receiving the presentation from the Registry about those persons who, on that respective day violated the determinations of their work duty, so the Jewish Police were brought to the work inspectors, who, after establishing the "guilt," carried out their verdict against the work deserters.[h]

In most cases the "violators" would immediately be transferred to the Ghetto Jail where they would be held overnight. In the morning, as a punishment, they were sent to work at the Aerodrome or to another hard workplace, where they would always have to send people by force. When they were dealing with a person who frequently did not fulfill his work duty, he would receive a similar punishment, not for just one day, but for a much longer term.

It would frequently happen, that right after the work duty person left for work, the Labor Office would get a sudden request that the Ghetto should immediately send a determined number of workers for urgent work. In such cases, the Mobilization and Punishment Division, with the help of the Jewish Police, went all around the Ghetto catching the needed number of people. Understandably, they would not consider whether the other had a legal permit, or not, etc. The main thing would be to carry out the regime's request as fast as possible.

[Page 325]

Until the creation of the Quarterings Commission at the end of Summer, 1943, it was also the job of the Mobilization and Punishment Division to recruit for the labor camps.[i]

The people from the Mobilization and Punishment Division, as well as the labor inspectors, had the right to give permits to the work duty people for a day or two for important family issues. Because of patronage and influence only the more privileged layers of the Ghetto could enjoy this right. The simple helpless folk-people were seldom able to attain such a permit. A determination for this can be found in the ghetto folk creations[j] where these injustices were very often portrayed.

In addition to these functions, the work inspectors, along with the heads of the people from the Mobilization Division would also be involved at the Ghetto Gate when they would let people out for work.[k]

The Mobilization and Punishment Division had to carry out the requests of the regime regarding forced labor. Understandably, the ghetto Jew could not call out any other feelings other than hate or contempt. And that is how it really was. Because of its thankless duty, this specific division of the Labor Office was the demon of the working ghetto population.

At this opportunity we must add that the person from the Mobilization and Punishment Division, P. Margolis, who excelled with his harsh and brutal relationship with the workers, was tried and sentenced for hard jail time after the liberation of Kovno by the Soviet regime.

The work inspectors were deported to the Dachau labor camps together with the other ghetto Jews. There, they were so harshly persecuted that not one of them survived to liberation. Such was the great bitterness of the ghetto Jews toward the leaders from this division of the Labor Office.

[Page 326]

Aside from Margolis, more important members of the division were: Zaks, Mendelson, Kaptchevski, Prisman (all were work inspectors and died in Dachau); Melamedovitch, Secretary of the Division (was burned in a hideout); Markovski, technician colleague (saved himself by leaving the Ghetto), and others.

C. Aerodrome Division

The Aerodrome Division had to establish the necessary numbers of Jewish labor forces for the Aerodrome. This was one of the most difficult, and, by the way, the largest workplace of the ghetto settlement. From Autumn 1941 until Spring 1942, there were 3-4 thousand Jewish workers working daily at the Aerodrome. This division was the most important division of the Labor Office.

The Aerodrome workers were mostly recruited from the lower social levels of the Ghetto population. The hard yoke of the real punitive forced labor was carried on the shoulders of these simple ghetto Jews.

Aside from the punitive slave labor under the open sky throughout a long workday, there were persecutions and insults by the murderous masters during the exhaustion of walking, the long distance to work and back, day in and day out. The aerodrome worker at this workplace, did not have any opportunity to acquire a little sustenance, like those who worked in the city brigade.

True, at the Aerodrome there were also a small number of workplaces that were not so bad. The overwhelming majority of Aerodrome workers however worked in inhuman work conditions. A few aerodrome workers had one wish: to get out of this slave labor and get work in a city brigade, where the type of work and the relations with the Jewish workers – and above all – the chance to acquire a bit of foodstuffs was relatively better than at the Aerodrome.

There was talk about all sorts of bonuses that the Aerodrome Division organized for the punctual aerodrome worker, with the aim of improving their material situation. However, the harsh material situation of the "aerodrome-worker" was not improved and the bonuses did not have much significance to win over the ghetto Jews for aerodrome work.

[Page 327]

Relating to the increase in the number of workers for the city workplaces, in Spring of 1942 many aerodrome workers went over to work in the city. This meant a radical change for the better for them economically.

The demand for aerodrome workers was always increasing, and this created huge stress. Thus, it was decided that people who worked in the city brigades would also have to work at the Aerodrome a few times per week. This principle did not only apply to men, but also to women on the city brigades. For example, it was established that women, who worked three times per week in the city brigade, in addition must also work at the Aerodrome one or two days a week.

It must be said, however, that because most of the more privileged men and women of the Ghetto worked in the better city brigades, a large portion of them already found a legal "foundation" to free themselves from that work at the Aerodrome. Due to all these reasons, strong antagonism developed in the Ghetto between the "aerodrome workers" and the workers at the better work brigades. On this very terrain, unique social relations would play out.

Those working at the Aerodrome were divided into a few dozen work columns. At the head of each work column stood a Jewish Column Leader, appointed by the Aerodrome Division. The various construction companies from the Aerodrome would through the construction workers demand the needed number of Jewish artisans and physical laborers every day from the Jewish Labor Office. And the Aerodrome Division would take pains to follow the request from the construction people.

To mediate between the construction workers and the Aerodrome Division, there were specially chosen Jewish functionaries who were called "Shift Leaders." A few shift leaders at the Aerodrome had their shift people. The column leaders had to mediate between the workplace and the work column, put together the reports for the Labor Office, etc.

[Page 328]

Aside from the workplaces at the Aerodrome itself, the Aerodrome Division dealt with a few out of city workplaces which had a connection to the aerodrome work, like for example, in Gayzhon, Keidan, etc. The work in the Gayzhon swampy forests was very hard, and the people became sick with rheumatism and other illnesses very quickly.

When many Jewish workers worked at the Aerodrome, they believed that the aerodrome work had great significance for the existence of the Ghetto. However, the extermination Actions, especially the Big Action, completely crushed this supposition.

The ghetto population always needed some sort of anchor which gave the illusion that this Ghetto had some right to live. So, for the Ghetto, the prior importance of the aerodrome work was now ascribed to the Big Ghetto Workshops.

Because of that, this division now had to carry out such ungrateful tasks that it was also not very loved by the ghetto population. This negative relationship from the ghetto world continued its nourishment not only from the very difficult work relations at the Aerodrome, but also partially because at the head of this division from the Winter of 1942[l] stood a specific young Jewish man, Adv. Wolf Lurie (a former court investigator in the time of Smetana). He was a very energetic and very strong man, from whom the ghetto Jews would shudder like from a real despot. Not a single ghetto Jew, in general, and no aerodrome worker specifically, would dare come in a conflict with him. While relating with people he was like a court investigator with criminals. The Ghetto created a special folk song about his conduct.

During the liquidation of the Ghetto, he decided not to cooperate in the deportation. He poisoned his child, himself, and his wife. The poison however only worked on the child and he and his wife remained alive. Then he asked an S.S. guard to come to his home and shoot them both. As was told at the time, the S.S. man was not skittish, and he shot them both.

[Page 329]

In the Aerodrome Division the following people were also active: Flier (died during the ghetto liquidation); engineer Goldman (a Warsaw Jew liberated in Dachau); Fritz Bernstein (a German Jew, who because of his bad behavior as a Kapo in the Alexotas labor camp, and in Dachau Concentration Camp, he was punished after liberation by the Allied regime organizations); Davidovich (liberated in Dachau), and others.

D. City Brigades Divisions

The task of the City Brigade Division consisted of recruiting the male and female workers for the city work places, distributing work cards, confirming Brigadiers, etc.

At first, a total of a few hundred Jews worked in 10-15 city workplaces. Over time[m] approximately 50 larger and smaller city work brigades were created where over 5,000 men and women worked. The growth in this number of city brigades continued from Spring 1942 until Autumn 1943, when Goecke started liquidating the largest portion of the city brigades with an urgent tempo. This was to prepare the conditions for the conversion of the Ghetto into a concentration camp.[n]

As mentioned, working in a better city brigade was considered a great privilege, which only a small portion of the ghetto population could acquire. True, not all city brigades had the same value. There were good brigades where they were able to "make a good package", that meant, they could create a livelihood for favorable prices. However, there were also many brigades which were far from good, and in addition, had very difficult work conditions or minimal possibilities to arrange for food products.

[Page 330]

Mainly, those privileged ghetto Jews who had good connections with the leading persons from the ghetto hierarchy, got work in the better work brigades, or they would bring them products at city prices. For the simple ghetto Jew, it was almost impossible to get access to a good brigade. Most ghetto Jews would therefore work in the ordinary city brigades, where there was almost no difference between these and the workplaces at the Aerodrome.

It has already been stated many times that corruption, protectionism, etc. dominated in the ghetto institutions. The Labor Office sinned greatly in this domain, as well. It was no secret that with the help of bribery in this or another form, the leading functionaries of the Labor Office were able to achieve a lot. Therefore, the ghetto Jew without resources would never be able to attain a workplace in a good brigade.

Camps of men and women which had worked in bad workplaces the entire time, would in the afternoon hours besiege the Labor office, searching to get a better workplace. But this Jew did not have any "Vitamin P,"[o] so he would rarely be able to achieve his plea.

The City Brigades Division wanted to offer those who worked in a bad work brigade to, at least once, get into a better brigade to buy some food products there. So, they gave out a one-time permit so they could join this or another better brigade. To get one of these certificates was not the easiest thing. By the way, from time to time, such permits were also given to those who worked in the ghetto workshops, or in the ghetto hierarchy. It was the only way to make a living for lower prices.

[Page 331]

For a certain time there existed in the Labor Office a Shift Commission, which had as its task transporting workers from the Aerodrome to the city brigades and back. They wanted to compensate those ghetto Jews who worked at the Aerodrome for a long time with a workplace in a better brigade. But since most people from the better city brigades would be protected by one or another "Yales,"[p] so this shift had no practical meaning, because the better work brigades were monopolized by the protected elements.

In families where there were multiple work duty persons, the Labor Office would strive to set it up so that a portion of them would work in better workplaces and the others, in worse ones. But even this attempt at equalizing would very often be violated by the privileged strata.

Aside from offering possibilities to acquire food products, there were various city brigades which were better or worse because they had easier or harder work-relations, proximity, or distance from the Ghetto, etc. But the kind of work the Jews would be doing was also very important. If it was a job which had to do with food or with factory-production, the Jews would already see it as something "to cultivate" how much and what it could lead to. By the way, it is interesting to note that, in general, women in the brigades were more skilled than the men and in many ghetto families the women were the only breadwinners.

As mentioned, the City Brigade Division would both give out work cards for the workers in the brigades and decide on the brigades.

The work cards would be distributed for a period of a few months. A few workplaces would be designated with a running number, which would be stamped with many stamps on the work card so that at the Ghetto Gate they would easily be able to recognize where the owner of the work card works. The entire procedure of finalizing the work cards[q] being signed by the Registry, taken to the respective files, and so forth, would take a lot of technical work.

We must say that the Brigadiers, especially in the better work brigades, had an opportunity to be well situated materially. The Brigadiers, the majority energetic young people, would consider the brigades as a source of grabbing as much personal use out of it, and as a means for making a good living. The Brigadiers would strongly exploit the brigade members from whom they would get a portion of their business in the brigade, or they would be paid well by those who wanted privileges at work, etc.

[Page 332]

If the Brigadier was a quiet and honest person, the brigade would not function, and he would sooner or later have to leave his post. A brigade worker would seldom win by complaining to the Labor Office against various dealings by a Brigadier. Typically, for such a "chutzpa" the Brigadiers would find various ways to sideline him from the brigade. However, there were also a few Brigadiers and Column leaders who would strive to be helpful to the people of their work commands, only when it was possible.

The Brigadiers and the Column Leaders who led larger work commands were: Idelson, Berkman, Braz, Blatt, Engineer Blumental, Engineer Goldberg, Glickman, Dr. Grinberg, Nordau, Vinik, Yasvon, Engineer Yellin, Charashtshenishok, Lubetzki, Lurie, Lipshitz, Leybzon, Mizrach, Engineer Mil, Nachumson, Ginsboim, Engineer Slonimski, Pikert, the brothers Friedman, Tzitzes, Tzipkin, Tzipin, Koniuchovski, Karpus, engineer Reiness, Shabashevitch, engineer Shachnovski, Engineer Shachat (all survived to liberation); Altman, Aylberg, Aks, Blumental, Hirsh, Yeshorin, Lint, Naftal, Srolovitch, Frenkel, Friedman, Kagan, Klompus, Shtein, Shafranski (all died), and others.

At first, the head of the City Brigade Division was Advocate Makovski (died during the ghetto deportation), then Advocate Zak[r] and later – Advocate N. Gershovitch (liberated in Dachau concentration camp). As colleagues: B. Oretshkin (well-known Russian-Jewish journalist; was killed during the "Stalingrad Action"); J. Gar (editor of this book. Jumped from a train during the deportation to Germany and was later liberated); Dr. Wolf (a German Jew. Died in Dachau); A. Staravolski, D. Tamshe, S. Bloch (all died in Dachau concentration camp); Ms. Rein (caught tuberculosis during the Action of the Children, Elderly and Sick); Ms. Lipshitz (liberated in a labor camp), and others.

[Page 333]

Also in that Division was Amtirt Yatzkan (liberated in Dachau concentration camp), who was commissioned by Liptzer to oversee the activities of the Labor Office, especially for the City Brigades Division.

E. Vocation Division

The Recruiting Division had to organize the recruitment of craftsman for the various workplaces in the city and in the Ghetto.

There was no independent division which had the right to distribute work cards in the Recruiting Division. Their task consisted only of collecting the needed artisans for all the workplaces and transferring the relevant artisan lists to the other divisions of the Labor Office. This included, for example, the City Brigade Division (when the skilled workers were needed in a city brigade), in Aerodrome Division (when they needed the skilled workers at the Aerodrome), in the Large Ghetto Workshops, in the Small Ghetto Workshops, etc.

These divisions would already give out the duty cards to the professionals.

The Recruiting Division owned specific set ups of various craftsmen and their recommended workers would be considered dependable for all the other Labor Office divisions as well as for the workshops. Even here protectionism and other unforgivable dealings would take place because this "system" was characteristic for almost all the ghetto institutions.

Aside from the genuine artisans from pre-war times, there arose a level of "ghetto artisans" in the Ghetto. That meant, people who got their history changed to artisans. This inconsistency mainly took place in this way: after a short time working with genuinely skilled workers, the former shopkeepers, businessmen, people of the liberal occupations, very often equated themselves to the genuine artisans at the workplaces.

[Page 334]

Aside from this, the Vocation Division also dealt with the vocational school where children learned a trade. In the end of Summer 1942, when the general schools were liquidated, students would unofficially also receive a bit of general education in the trade school. The trade school played an important role in ghetto life after the Children's Action, when the hidden children, aged 8 to 12 found shelter there and in this way could legalize their existence.[s]

Those who oversaw the Vocation Division were Agronomist I. Oleiski (liberated in Dachau); as colleagues: Engineer S. Ratner[t], S. Frenkel, Grinberg (both died in Dachau concentration camp), and others.

Active in the trade school were: Engineer Sadovski (liberated in Dachau); Felman (died during the ghetto liquidation), and others.

F. Division for Ghetto Labor

There were work duty men and women who, because of their condition, were not skilled to work either in the city work places, nor in the large or small ghetto workshops. So, the Medical Committee would give them a lighter workload in the Ghetto itself, for example, serving the institutions, keeping cleanliness in the open places, etc. This category of work was called "ghetto workers."

The ghetto workers would work 4-5 hours per day and the very sick would not work more than a few days a week. At work they would not be given any regimen that was too difficult, and the work would not strain them too much. In addition, they would get Medical Commission permits very easily. They didn't have anything to complain about, as they were not sent to forced labor.

Aside from the Jewish institutions, during Goecke's time, the ghetto workers also had to serve the Camp Commandant, which had its quarters just near the Ghetto.

We must admit that by enabling the very sick ones to be employed in lighter work in the ghetto itself, the Jewish Labor Office did a good thing. First, these unfortunates could get through the yoke of forced labor easier, and second, for such people the work card would be a source of encouragement, indicating that also they, the sick ones, were not just "useless" Jews – usually the first victims of various decrees and afflictions.

[Page 335]

The leader of the ghetto workers was B. Rabinovitz (died in Ghetto during the liquidation). We must mention the colleagues: Davidovitch (an invalid. Died during the ghetto deportation); Tzindler (during the Children's Action in the Palemon labor camp, he, together with his wife voluntarily went away with their children), and others.

G. Medical Division

The Medical Division of the Labor Office was actually a medical commission which had the following functions: first, to give the work duty persons medical help and permits when they were sick; second, to establish who among the work duty people could not work a full work week due to their weakened health condition. They must not do very heavy physical work in a city workplace and must therefore work only lighter work in the Ghetto itself; third, to completely free those who are very sick and suffering from serious chronic illness from work duty.

Because of the inhumane living conditions and hard punitive labor, the number of illnesses was extraordinarily large, and the Medical Commission had much to do. It was specially beleaguered with work during the Winter of 1941-42 when, because of hunger, cold and hard labor at the Aerodrome, the health condition of the ghetto population worsened.

In general, the Medical Commission had a difficult and unthankful task. On the one hand, it had to defend the interests of the Labor Office to which it belonged, and therefore it was stingy with permits for the sick when many sick were not freed from work duty, etc. On the other hand, in the Ghetto there were many people whose strength was destroyed by the inhumane forced labor. From the medical standpoint, these commissions had to guard the victims from punitive work and ease their fate, as much as possible.

[page 336]

Since the Medical Commission would strive to represent the interests of the Labor Office more than of the working people, it was not much loved by the working ghetto population. Most work duty ghetto Jews would relate to the Medical Commission with the same critical attitude, as for example, towards the Mobilization and Punishment Division, because the sick and physically weak ghetto Jew could not always find the needed understanding for his health condition there.

When a work duty person, due to his weakened health condition, would not be able to work a full work week, the Medical Commission would note how many days per week the sick person can do his work duty. On the work card of said person the day of the week he is on work duty would be visible. For the remaining days of the week, he would remain at home.

For everyone, the most bitter and difficult of all the jobs at which the ghetto Jews worked was at the Aerodrome. The city brigades had comparatively lighter work conditions. Thus, the Medical Commission decided whether the work duty person who was suffering from a chronic illness, could continue working at the Aerodrome, or should be transferred to work in a lighter city brigade.

The Medical Commission determined whether the very sick could work in the Ghetto itself as a ghetto worker.

As was seen, with respect to the work, this was a very big relief.

The incurably sick people would be freed completely from work duty by the Medical Commission. However, those very sick persons who could work did not want to be counted among the invalids of the Ghetto and thereafter be in danger of being captured during an extermination Action, as "ballast" for the Ghetto. Most of these sick people would rather agree to go to work in the Ghetto itself, just to have the work card of a ghetto worker on him.

[Page 336a]

The building of the Elders Council and others. Important Jewish ghetto institution on Varniu Street 49. On the fence around the house – orders and announcements to the ghetto population.

[Page 336b]

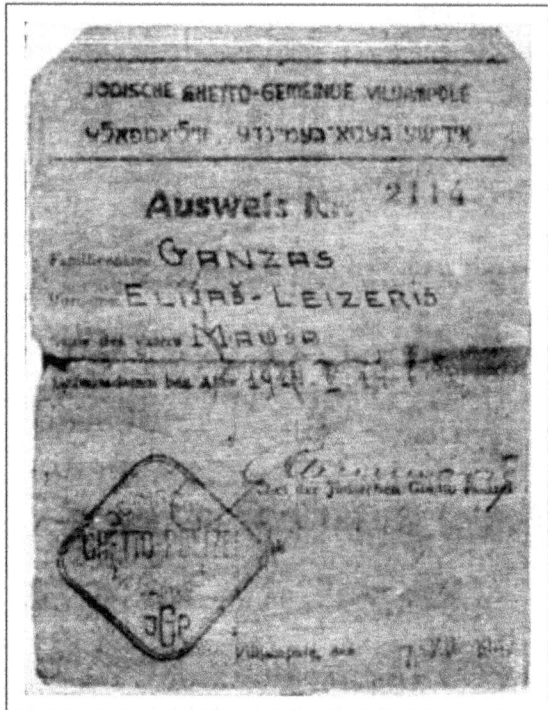 

A ghetto pass, distributed through the Jewish Ghetto Police
On the back side: Police registrations and other marks

[Page 337]

All the determinations by the Medical Commission, like for example, permits, changes in the weekly number workdays for work duties, etc., were transferred to the Registry Division, so that these determinations would be noted in the Registry books.

Disregarding all the negative moments in the activity of the Medical Commission, it did carry out a fairly positive role in the realm of protecting the health of the working ghetto population. Forced labor destroyed their physical strength.

Those doctors active in the Medical Commission were Dr. Nachumovski, Dr. Vindsberg (both liberated in Dachau); Dr. Gilde, Dr. Friedman, Dr. Levitan (all died during the liquidation of the Ghetto), and others.

In addition to the Medical Commission, the Labor Office also had an active Sanitary Service which would be engaged in organizing medical stations at the workplaces, like for example, at the Aerodrome, and in the larger work brigades in the city. In such a large workplace, they would place a doctor, together with the permanent workers, to give medical help during unfortunate situations. The heads of the Sanitary Service were Dr. Goldberg (liberated after leaving the Ghetto); Dr. Ch. Finkelshtein (liberated in Dachau), and others.

H. Division for Social Welfare

There was a Social Office in the Ghetto which organized the question of social help for the needy. But there was also, a special division for social help at the Labor Office. During this time when the Social Office helped all destitute ghetto Jews, independent of whether they worked or not, the Social Division at the Labor Office only took care of the destitute, specifically for the needy aerodrome workers.

It was also lamented at various other times, that it was mainly the destitute ghetto Jews who worked at the Aerodrome. In addition, they were engaged in heavy work and their material situation was dismal. For these people the Social Division at the Labor Office would see to getting them a piece of clothing, a pair of wooden shoes, some food products, a bundle of wood, etc.

[Page 338]

The Social Division did not demonstrate any greater tangible accomplishments because its resources were limited. These divisions would also deal with giving support to the needy workers through the general Social Office, whose possibilities for social help were much greater than their own.

The economic situation in the Ghetto became more stabilized with relation to the growth of the number of Jewish workers for the city brigades versus the Jewish work for the Aerodrome. Thus, the relevance of social help in ghetto life dropped. The possibilities for battling out a livelihood increased. This was the cause for a decrease in the number of people noted for support. When they started transporting Jews to the labor camps, the question of social support for the needy camp Jews was revisited, once again.

All appointments by the Social Division of the Labor Office were completed in the Small Ghetto Workshops which exclusively worked for the population in the Ghetto and in the camps.

Leaders in the Division of Social Help were Engineer Bargman (former Vice-Chair of the Labor Office) and G. Markovski (formerly in another Labor Office Division, later transported to the Large Ghetto Workshops).

I. Ghetto Gates

Traffic between the Ghetto and the outside world would take place through the specially built Ghetto Gates. At first there were two Ghetto Gates: one in the area of the old section of Slabodka (on the corner of Krisciukaicio and Ayregoler streets), and the second, in the new area of the Slabodka suburb (on the of corner Varniu and Paneriu streets). However, the main traffic would take place through the first Ghetto Gate. From December 1943, after which Jews had to leave the area of old Slabodka, then the traffic between the Ghetto and the city took place only through the gate on Varniu street.

[Page 339]

In addition to the large Ghetto Gates, in the early years, the Ghetto also had a pair of smaller exits to the "free" world. These "little gates" were used by the guards of the Ghetto Guards, and a few Jewish work brigades, which worked in the vicinity of that small exit. In the general, these little gates occupied no distinguishable position in the traffic between the Ghetto and the city.

Security guards would always stand at the Ghetto Gates. The following held watch around the Ghetto Fence and by the Ghetto Gates during the three-year ghetto existence: German Police, G.S.K.K people,

Lithuanian Partisans and Police, Hungarian S.S. people, and at the very end, during the ghetto liquidation, Latvian S.S. men together with Gestapo people. A few ghetto guards had their "work methods" which had huge significance in the daily life of the ghetto Jew.

At the Ghetto Gates, together with the guards from the Ghetto Guard,[u] there would also be functionaries represented by the Jewish Ghetto Police and from the Labor Office. Officially, the duty of the Jewish Police and of the Labor Office employees was to be helpful at the exit in the morning when the Jewish workers in the city went to work, and at night at their return from the city to the Ghetto. However, aside from that, as we will see, they actually carried out entirely different functions.

Approximately 6-7 thousand Jewish men and women worked at the Aerodrome and in the various City Brigades. At around 5 am, the city workers would start getting ready at the assembly place near the Ghetto Gate, grouped according to the individual brigades in the city, and according to the columns for the Aerodrome. In these hours inspectors would start arriving at the Ghetto Gate from the workplaces, together with military guards, to transport the Jews to work.

The eventual march out of the workers, who had worked in dozens of different workplaces, would take about one hour. The Jewish functionaries at the Ghetto Gate required much organizational work: lining the people up in rows, grouping the people according to their workplace, and counting the people or the passage through the Ghetto Gate. This was done to give the regime organization a daily registration of the number of working ghetto Jews and – above all – to ensure, on the spot, the recruitment of the daily missing number of people for the Aerodrome and other heavy workplaces. All of this had to be organized by the Jewish officials at the Ghetto Gate.

[Page 340]

Like real slaves, the Jews would have to go through the Ghetto Gate with great speed and with uncovered heads. Nearby, the Nazis would address them not only with curse words and insulting expressions from the Hitlerite lexicon, but not infrequently they would let loose with their rubber sticks, their loaded guns, etc.

But not only the Nazis themselves were at the Ghetto Gate demonstrating their cruel relationship with the Jews. To our great shame we must state that also some higher Jewish ghetto officers, like for example the chief of the Jewish Police at the Ghetto Gate, T. Arnshtam, the people from the Mobilization and Punishment Division, P. Margolis, the people from the Aerodrome Division, V. Lurie, and others would very often show the Germans that they, too, can be harsh with the Jews…

This contemptible handling by the Jewish "ghetto powers" was much more painful to the Jews than the brutal behavior towards them by the Nazis. Shameful scenes, like how one Jew with yellow patches beats or curses another Jew also with yellow patches, would create a shattering and painful impression and would remain to illustrate the extraordinary situation of the simple ghetto Jew.

At night, when the Jewish workers from the city would start returning to the Ghetto, the real festival at the Ghetto Gate would begin again. First, they would have to count the Jews returning from work, to see if anyone remained in the city; second, a control took place to see if Jews were carrying any rationed food products which they illegally acquired at work into the Ghetto. The controllers would mainly be German guards from the Ghetto Security[v] and the confiscated products would be transferred to their authority.

The Jewish functionaries at the Ghetto Gate were very energetic young people. Despite the strongest controls, they set up such commercial relationships that for the price of a bribe, Jews could peacefully bring in their purchased products. A similar situation also took place in the morning when going to work. Jews would carry out of the Ghetto various items to exchange in the city with Christians. Also, it would then be necessary for the guards at the Ghetto Gate to check the Jews, who were "unkosher."

[Page 341]

The Jewish officers who negotiated with the guards at the Ghetto Gate made a thriving business just from these unique "transactions." A few of them actually became rich from this and lived in material prosperity that they never dreamed of. However, this was a mediation activity for the Ghetto that was a very necessary. Thanks to this work with the guards at the gate, thousands of Jews brought food products into the Ghetto daily. Thus, the Ghetto was not condemned to hunger rations from the official welfare for the Jewish population.

True, a huge amount of food product was confiscated at the Ghetto Gate each day, but according to the number of products which were brought in, it was relatively small. It would be bad in those cases during the search at the Ghetto Gate, when an inspector from the City Commissariat or from the Gestapo would suddenly arrive, and the controllers would have to show their strength. Then they would not only confiscate the products but also the guilty would be punished with lashes, with jail, etc. This did not frighten anyone from bringing purchased sustenance into the Ghetto again the next day.

When the movement of the youth to leave to the partisans arose, the Jewish functionaries at the Ghetto Gate helped very much by getting these people out of the Ghetto, by bringing arms into the Ghetto, etc. Through various schemes, they would turn the heads of the guards, and in this respect they never failed. Also, carrying children out of the Ghetto to give them to Christian families in the city or in the villages would almost not have been possible without the intervention of the Jews who worked at the Ghetto Gate.

[Page 342]

Therefore, it is understandable why the Ghetto Gate played such an important role in the life of the ghetto Jew and why it took up such a distinguished position in the folkloric creations of the Ghetto. And that's why the folk songs and sayings about the Ghetto Gate were very popular for the ghetto population.

From the Labor Office, the work at the Ghetto Gate was carried out by: Natkin (a German Jew liberated in Dachau) and Yankl Verbovski (he was the "inspiration" of the Jewish functionaries at the Ghetto Gate and he played the most important role in all the aforementioned issues. Saved himself in a *malina* in the days of the deportation). In addition to the above, the following were also active: I. Tarko (a Polish Jew liberated in Dachau); S. Shvartz (killed during the ghetto liquidation); Z. Shalitan (liberated in Dachau); I. Lurie (killed in the Ghetto during the liquidation), and others.

The Chief of the Jewish Police at the Ghetto Gates was Arnshtam[w]. All the other higher police functionaries at the Ghetto Gates like Aranovski, Chvales, Zhopovitch, and others were shot at the 9th Fort during the arrest of the Ghetto Police. Policemen who were active for a longer time at the Ghetto Gates were: Alexandrovitch (liberated in Dachau); Perkol (liberated by leaving the Ghetto); Isserlis (killed by a Christian in the countryside); Levenshtein (liberated in Dachau; as a Kapo he had a bad time with the inmates in the camp); Slonimski (liberated in Dachau), and many others.

After carrying out a cross section of the structure and foundation activity of the individual Labor Office Divisions, it is necessary to add that in the developing history of the Jewish Labor Office[x] we must differentiate the following stages:

A. Since the founding of the Ghetto in August 1941, until the eve of Spring 1942, the Jewish Labor Office carried out and provided Jewish work forces. These forces were received by the German Labor Office in Kovno through the intervention of the one responsible for ghetto issues in the City Commissariat.

[Page 343]

B. Thereafter, an affiliate of the German Labor Office in Kovno was founded in the Spring of 1942. So, the Jewish Labor Office would receive orders for Jewish labor forces directly from the German Labor Office in the Ghetto.

The German Labor Office in the Ghetto would give the Jewish Labor Office only the general request to put together work forces. The official determination and the distribution of work cards was the job of the Jewish Labor Office. Such a situation continued until Autumn 1943 when the Ghetto was taken out of the jurisdiction of the City Commissariat and was transferred to Goecke's authority.

During the year and a half between Spring 1942 and Autumn 1943, at the head of the German Labor Office stood S.A. Captain Herman, who, as noted,[y] didn't give the Ghetto too many big problems. On the contrary, for the price of frequent and nice gifts, he would attempt to comply as much as possible with Jewish wishes. His tenure was connected to the peaceful period in ghetto life, specifically free from Actions and other decrees, as well as with the "ghetto prosperity," when the economic situation was tolerable.

C. When the Ghetto was converted into a concentration camp in November 1943, Goecke appointed S.S. Unit Leader, Ouer[z] as leader of the German Labor Office. The functions of the Jewish Labor Office then shrank even more than in the time of Hermann.

D. After the liquidation of the Elders Council and of the Jewish "Ghetto autonomy" almost all the Jewish ghetto institutions were closed, and among them also the Jewish Labor Office. The leading functionaries were then transported as technical workers to the German Labor Office in the Ghetto. Such a situation continued until the liquidation of the Ghetto.

[Page 344]

As already mentioned, Dr. Itchak Rabinovich was appointed by the Elders Council to be a Jewish advisor to the German Labor Office. During the days of Hermann, he contributed a lot for the benefit of the Ghetto. During the Goecke period he manifested complete obedience to Goecke's plans which, in general, stood like a complete slap to Jewish life-interests and, personally, he committed quite a few sins.

In addition to Dr. Rabinovitch (liberated in Dachau) in the German Labor Office, there were: Yotkowski (during the Kinder Action he went together with his child); Melamedovich (killed in a *malina* during the ghetto liquidation); Meris, Dr. Shlapoverski (both liberated in Dachau); Ms. Tchernow (killed in Ghetto during the deportation); Mrs. Sh. Rabinowitz (liberated in a labor camp in Germany), and others.

Original footnotes:

    a. At the construction of a garage on Kestuchia Street
    b. See "Problems of Applying the Jewish Labor Forces"
    c. After the Action of the children, elderly, and sick, each person in the Ghetto was on work duty and had to have a workplace.
    d. See in this same chapter: "Medical Divisions."

e. At the Aerodrome the Jewish workers were divided in columns and the Jewish leaders were called Column-people or Column-leaders. At the head of the Jewish work Brigade in the city were the Brigadiers.

f. The reports would contain the performances of the numbers of the work duty cards of the people who were working on that day.

g. See in the same chapter: "Mobilization and Punishment Division."

h. Aside from their work pass, a few duty people also had a work card that the Brigadier, or Column Leader would have to sign every day. This signature would confirm that the owner of the work card worked on that day. For example, if someone didn't work on one day, in his work card there would be a blank and a review by the Jewish Police or the work inspector would immediately establish this work sin.

i. See "Recruitment for the first small labor camps in the provinces."

j. See "Motifs from Ghetto Folklore."

k. See in the same chapter: "Ghetto Gates"

l. Until then, the person from the Aerodrome Division was Dr. Valsonok.

m. See "Problem of applying the Jewish Labor Forces."

n. See "Preparations for converting the Ghetto into a concentration camp from separate labor camps."

o. In the Ghetto, this is how they called protectionism. See Ghetto Folklore.

p. This means the higher functionaries from the Jewish ghetto administration.

q. All would have to be done by hand in a primitive way.

r. See" Ghetto Court"

s. About the Trade-School – see "School Office.

t. See "Persons who were involved with the Partisan movement."

u. Aside from the period of the deportations and liquidation of the Ghetto.

v. For a longer time, Lithuanian policemen or partisans were also employed.

w. See "Founding of "Service-Order"

x. Officially called: Judische Arbeitsensatnstelle Gheto-Gemeinde Viliampole- Jewish Labor Places in Ghetto Viliampole.

y. See "Problems of registering the Jewish workforces."

z. After liberation he was tried by the American military court in Dachau and sentence to death for his actions in labor camp Mildorf, which belonged to the Dachau concentration camp, and because of his participation in carrying out of the Kinder Action in the Kovno Ghetto.

CHAPTER IV

Economics Office

-Founding of the Economics Office-Appointments and activities of the Economics Office and its functions at organizing economic life

[Page 345]

It would be worthwhile to say at least a few words about some ghetto offices which not only have their story, but also their "history."

Already in July 1941, the newly created Jewish Committee started organizing the relocation into the Ghetto. As we know, the Committee created various commissions which had to deal with housing, transportation, judicial and social help, etc. In addition to all the other problems after the lock-up of the Ghetto, a long list of issues of an economic nature developed.

From the beginning, Jews had to build and organize everything in the Ghetto. Thanks to Jewish initiative it only took a short time to create various economic institutions which had important significance for public life of the ghetto population. It was necessary to coordinate the activities of the newly established economic institutions very quickly. To this end, a special office was established in the Elders Council which was tasked with organizing economic issues.

This Economic Office, like every other ghetto office, went through quite a huge path of development, until it became a self-sustaining, broadly branched ghetto institution. To carry out its economic functions, the Economics Office oversaw the following appointments and activities:

[Page 346]

- a. Small Ghetto Workshops,
- b. Transportation Office,
- c. Electric Office,
- d. Ghetto Bath,
- e. Pharmacy and Laboratories,
- f. Ghetto Laundry,
- g. Ghetto Gardens,
- h. Cemetery,
- i. Burial Society.

The leader of the Economics Office during the first few months was Gemelitzki.[a] Later on, from the end of 1941 until Summer 1943, Potroch (died in the Ghetto), and last was Advocate Bernstein.[b] For a specific time, Hirsh Levin was Vice-Leader.[c] The actual leader of the Economics Office was I. Yochelson (liberated in Dachau).

A. Small Ghetto Workshops

The Small Ghetto Workshops belonged to the oldest ghetto institutions. They were founded earlier than the Large Ghetto Workshops.

Because of the shortage in housing during the period of relocation to the Ghetto, the destitute ghetto population was set up in communal dormitories, that meant, in larger community buildings. Thus, there arose the need to create a division to carry out small renovations in the communal dormitories.

After a while, the sphere of activity of these small renovation workshops grew mainly because they also had to carry out renovations in private apartments. The first most important work of this renovation workshop was to bring order to the clean-up of the Large Ghetto Workshops.

After the Big Action, large quantities of clothes from the transported Jews were sent over to the authority of the Social Office. There they were distributed to the distressed Aerodrome workers. The renovation workshop was then requested to set up workshops for tailoring, shoemaking, furrier, etc. In subsequent stages, a combination of smaller workshops was set up, in which they worked for the needs of the ghetto population.

To get the needed material for the Small Ghetto Workshops, like leather, fabric, etc., from time to time, the City Commissariat would throw random goods out to the Jews, which were designated for the civilian population in the city. The problem, however, was that most of the better materials were claimed by the higher Jewish ghetto officers for their own aims, and thus, only the crumbs remained for the rest of the Jews. Large swaths of the ghetto population had strong and justified complaints about this "custom."

[Page 347]

When the Ghetto was converted into a concentration camp, the Small Ghetto Workshops were transferred to the authority of the Camp Command. But even then, they mainly worked for the needs of the Ghetto and the neighboring labor camps, and partially also for the orders of the command itself.

At the head of the Small Ghetto Workshops was Lurie (died in Dachau); his colleagues were D. Treger (liberated in Dachau); Varantz (died in Dachau); Srebnitzki (died going out into the city); and others.

The renovation workshops were led by: Bonim, Engineer F. Goldschmidt (both survived in a ghetto hideout); Segalovski (died in Dachau), and others.

B. Transportation Division

The Transportation Division had under its authority 10-15 horses and served the transport needs of the various institutions, enterprises, and workshops.

The people in the Ghetto looked dark and sorrowful. Even the horses didn't give, so to speak, a better impression of the entire transportation capability. It was difficult to imagine how such skinny shapes carried fully laden wagons with their last energies over the unpaved sandy little streets. In this same ghetto image, we saw how the fearfully degraded level of the ghetto Jews' lives played out.

The Transportation Office would also carry out sanitation works. Since movement was forbidden at night, they would carry out this work during the day. This work would pollute the air even more in the already tight and thickly populated ghetto streets.

[page 348]

The wagon drivers of the Transportation Division played a certain role in helping smuggle food products into the Ghetto. When the movement started to give the children away to Christians, many children were transported out of the Ghetto with the help of the Jewish wagon drivers.

Active in the Transport Division were: Neividl (liberated in Dachau); Rabinovich (liberated in Dachau); M. Bromson (died in Dachau), and others.

C. Electric Division

The Electric Division organized the use of the flow of electricity. The Jewish population could only use electric lights during approved hours of the day, at night, and in the morning.

Since there was always a shortage of wood in the Ghetto, and in addition, many families lived in one room, not everyone could use the electricity at the same time, as there was only one lead oven or plate on which to cook a little bit of food. People were therefore forced to use the electric current for cooking.

As we know, all electric appliances were confiscated during the robbery of Jewish possessions. Ghetto Jews figured out that in lime pots they could install simple iron nails or metal teaspoons, forks to which they could tie up an electric current and they would get a full electric "appliance." True, from such "ghetto cookers" the tea or the food would be full of iron rust and other poisons from the metal items, which would slowly dissolve off the electric current. However, the ghetto population didn't have any other option.

Due to the use of such primitively made electric equipment, the strong current soon became overloaded. Therefore, the light from electric bulbs would shine so weakly that very often they couldn't even see the lamp itself. In addition, the transformers were spoiled, and entire quarters would remain in darkness for a long time until they could fix the electric network.

In the battle against the overload of the electric current, the Electric Division would come to check the homes and confiscate the electric cooking utensils. In ghetto life, even rulings on this topic did not have any integrity. After a while, the privileged strata would freely use the electric current, but the simple ghetto Jew had their "cookers" confiscated, thus taking away the possibility of enjoying the comfort of cooking.

[Page 349]

Those active in the Electric Division were Dr. Razin (died in Dachau); as a worker there were: R. Segal (liberated in Dachau); Balkin (died in Ghetto during the liquidation); Indursky (liberated in Dachau); Milshtein (taken to Estonia and from there to Dachau, where he was liberated), and others.

D. Ghetto Bath

At the start, in July-August 1941, approximately 30,000 Kovno Jews went over to live in the Ghetto. At that time, there was no bath, nor any other public sanitary facilities, like water supply, plumbing, etc. The extreme crowding in the apartments and, in addition, the fact that Jews were forced to work not only the most arduous, but also the dirtiest work, raised the important question of building a public bath and a delousing facility[d] in the Ghetto.

On the eve of Spring, 1942, with great effort, the Jews themselves built a bath, which the ghetto population could use a few days per week. The bath fully contributed to maintaining the sanitary hygienic condition in the Ghetto - at least at a minimum level.

At this opportunity it is worth mentioning that when all the ghetto houses were blown up and burned during the liquidation, for some unexplained reason, the building with the ghetto bath remained undisturbed and a few Jews survived in a hideout which was set up in the bath house.

The bath house was managed by: Epstein (saved himself during the ghetto deportation) and others.

[Page 350]

E. Pharmacy and Laboratory

Thanks to Jewish efforts, a pharmacy was established where- for money- you could get various medicines.

From time to time, the Pharmacy would receive a portion of more simple medicines in the city at official prices. The expensive ones would have to be purchased at speculators' prices in an illegal way.

Through the intervention of the Social Office, the poor ghetto Jews would receive medicines for free.

Also, on the topic of receiving medicines, this is when the "principle" of protectionism started: the better medicines would be accessible mainly for the ghetto big shots, but for an ordinary human it was not easy to get foreign medicines.

Aside from a pharmacy, there also existed a laboratory to conduct various medical analyses. This Laboratory was used both by the hospital, as well as by the general ghetto population.

The Pharmacy was run by: Srebnitzki (killed by the Gestapo as he was hiding in the city); the laboratory by Dr. Schmidt (liberated in Dachau). Those working in the Pharmacy were: Levin (killed during the ghetto deportation); Segalson (freed in Dachau); Mrs. Kadushin (saved herself in the country), and others.

F. Ghetto Laundry

The Ghetto Laundry was established with the aim of serving the population in washing laundry. In this laundry a few dozen Jewish women were employed.

It was declared, formally, that the ghetto population could freely make use of this laundry. However, this ghetto facility was mainly used by the higher office functionaries of the Jewish ghetto administration.

It would take four or five weeks until an ordinary ghetto Jew could pick up the little bit of laundry that he gave in to wash. The fact was that these Jews did not have many clothes, therefore, they couldn't afford such a long wait. Therefore, the laundry had no practical value for most of the ghetto Jews.

Later, when a larger number of Jews were relocated to work camps where there was great difficulty to wash clothing, the camp Jews started to use the Ghetto Laundry. Seletzky (died during the ghetto liquidation) and others were involved in the Laundry.

[Page 351]

G. Ghetto Gardens

In order to raise some vegetables for the ghetto population, the Economics Office acquired about 25 hectares for gardens under its authority. The gardens were located inside the domain of the Ghetto and were worked by skilled women.

The Ghetto Gardens were worked very carefully. The City Commissariat, under whose authority the Ghetto found itself until Autumn, 1943, even found it necessary to organize modern inspections in the Ghetto Gardens. This was to ensure that the higher officials of the City Commissariat would have vegetables from the Ghetto Greenhouse for a full year.

Once again, during the distribution of vegetables from the garden, the higher ups in the offices of the ghetto unit were the privileged ones. The simple Jews would have little benefit from the gardens.

Aside from the communal gardens, some ghetto Jews made individual efforts to use the empty pieces of land around their home to plant some vegetables. A well-supervised garden would have great significance from the perspective of nutrition. By the way, it is necessary to remember that in the beginning, the planting of private gardens was deemed obligatory by the Jewish ghetto administration to ease the problem of food.

So that no one would steal vegetables from the gardens during the summertime, a special Jewish guard would protect the gardens around the clock. Later, they organized a youth organization in the Ghetto called "ESHL,"[e] to protect the gardens.

The Ghetto Gardens were overseen by: Agronomist Kelzon[f]; Agronomist Gershovitch (liberated in Dachau); Krom (saved himself with Christian friends in the country); Mudrik (liberated in Dachau); Vilenski (died in a concentration camp in Estonia), and others.

[Page 352]

H. Cemetery and Burial Society

Between the end of July and the beginning of August 1941, after the largest portion of Kovno Jews transferred over to the Ghetto, the question arose of creating a place in the ghetto domain for a cemetery, and at the same time, founding a Burial Society.

Except for the normal cases of death, at that time many Jews fell victim to the Nazi murderers or the Lithuanian partisans who would shoot people without any motive, day in and day out. The number of Jewish dead was especially high during the robbery of Jewish property. Thus, the Burial Society had plenty of work.

At the end of 1941, the huge wave of extermination Actions passed, after which more than half of the ghetto population was killed, mainly the old and physically weak people. At that time, a younger and healthier element remained in the Ghetto. In addition, as we know, material life became comparatively easier than in the earlier times. Because of that, the death count was comparatively low.

By the way, it is necessary to add that thanks to Jewish efforts, no large-scale epidemic illnesses came to the Ghetto. Jews knew very well that an outbreak of an epidemic would be an existential danger to the life of the Ghetto. In such cases, the Nazis were skilled at exterminating both the sick as well as the healthy people.

During the three-year existence of the Ghetto there were about 700-800 Jews interred to their eternal rest in the Cemetery. According to a decree by the regime after the liberation of Kovno by the Red Army, German POW's dug open a few larger mass graves in the Ghetto cemetery where bones of those holy souls killed during the liquidation of the Ghetto were buried. The largest portion of dead people, however, remained lying under the ruins of the blown up and burned ghetto houses.

[Page 353]

The Burial Society didn't have in its authority any cart to transport the dead to their grave. Therefore, they would have to carry the dead in the coffin themselves from the house to the Cemetery. Jewish "life" looked lonely and dejected in the Ghetto, and the look of a Jewish funeral the Ghetto was even more pitiful.

At this opportunity it is worth mentioning that in Kovno, just before Spring, 1946 there was an extraordinarily large flood where many people died. The Vilya River, which flooded huge areas of Slabodka also completely disturbed the former Ghetto Cemetery. The flood at that time also inundated a children's home in Slabodka and many Christian children died. Since this happened on the 28th of March, the Catholic priests in their churches declared that the flood was a punishment from God for the murdered Jewish children.

Those active in the Burial Society were: Dvoretsky (died in a ghetto hideout); Kantorovich (died in Dachau); Kaplan (liberated in Dachau), and others.

Original footnotes:

    a. See "Large Ghetto Workshops"
    b. See "Leading Persons of the Elders Council"
    c. See "Persons who dealt with the Partisan Movement"
    d. See "Health Office"
    e. See, "Zionist activities in the Ghetto"
    f. See "Large Ghetto Workshops"

CHAPTER V

Provisions Office

-Official provisions for the ghetto population-Institutions of the Provisions Office

[Page 354]

The job of the Provisions Office was to organize the distribution of the official provisions that were rationed for the ghetto population by the occupation regime.

To give an idea about the hunger-nourishment which the Nazi regime established for the ghetto Jews, we submit the following numbers referring to ghetto rations, decided upon by the Kovno City Commissariat in the Summer of 1942:

Amount of food products per person per week:

1. Bread	700 grams
2. Meat	125 grams
3. Flour	122.5 grams
4. Coffee/tea/substitutes	75 grams
5. Salt	50 grams

For the working population additional food was also anticipated, which consisted of the following amounts of products (also per person per week)

1. Bread	700 grams
2. Meat	125 grams
3. Fat/oil	20 grams

Aside from that, they would, sometimes, distribute a few kilograms of potatoes, mostly rotten, and in the wintertime, frozen ones to each ghetto resident.

[Page 355]

These numbers speak a language which clearly demonstrates the "generosity" of the Hitlerites, specifically for Jewish provisions. And for this, there is no need for further commentary.

But even for this insignificant amount of food, the full amount would not even be delivered to the Jewish population. The City Commissariat would make some deals so that some of the food products would always remain undelivered, ostensibly, like a debt. These "debts" would never be covered by the regime; for the officials of the City Commissariat, it was a source of enrichment, on the ghetto's account.

Therefore, it was understandable why the ghetto Jews had to find other ways to acquire food for themselves in order to stay alive. Practically, there was only one way: to smuggle food products into the Ghetto illegally.

Through various schemes[a] the unique ways and means to which a ghetto Jew would be forced to supply a piece of bread for himself and his family have been described. To survive the horrors of the Nazi regime, this battle against hunger remained one of the most heroic acts of daily life of the ghetto Jews.

As crazy as this must sound, we must add that there was a partial improvement regarding the Official Provisions. This took place just after in Autumn of 1943, when the Ghetto was removed from the authority of the City Commissariat and was converted into a concentration camp under the supervision of the S.S.

As previously mentioned, the Camp Commandant, Goecke, wanted to gain the trust of the ghetto Jews and at the same time hide his evil plans regarding the Ghetto. He decided on enlarging and partially improving provisions for the ghetto residents.

According to his orders, they started to give the Jews not only the full food rations which they officially deserved, but from time to time he even gave the ghetto population certain amounts of butter, marmalade, sugar, etc. The Jews, however, understood very well that the improved provisions were not more than a maneuver to create the impression that the new ghetto bosses were not so badly disposed regarding the Ghetto.

[Page 356]

Goecke would typically improve the provisions especially on the evening of a significant decree for the Ghetto. This went so far as after distributing the butter or sugar to the Jews, they would start looking around for a new bashing and calamity for the ghetto Jews. Therefore, the Jews couldn't care less about Goecke and his "generosity" on the topic of food products.

To properly carry out its work, the Provisions Office had in its authority: a) a station for food products, b) distribution centers, and c) meat markets.

At the head of the Provisions Office for almost the entire time was Rapaport (died in Dachau); his colleagues were: Bernstein (died in Estonia); Ullman, Lapidus (both died during the ghetto liquidation), and others.

A. Station for food products

The food products were stored at a station, and the food was received by the regime to distribute to the ghetto population. The products were transferred from the station to separate distribution stores.

With the help of the wagon drivers from the Transportation Division, the station would pick up the products from the food distribution centers in the city. Having few means of transportation, it was not one of the easiest things to bring the products into the Ghetto.

Aside from the main station, there was also a potato station which would be open only when potatoes arrived for the Ghetto. As mentioned, they gave potatoes to the Ghetto – only sometimes. Afterwards the City Commissariat distributed the same genuine potatoes - but for the Jews, simply the trash. The effects of the rotten potatoes would often be heard throughout the Ghetto.

From the end of 1941 to the beginning of 1942, when the issue of nutrition became catastrophic, the ghetto Jews would even be happy with the frozen potatoes, as if they were gems. For hours, the Jews would stand in line to get the little bit of potatoes even though it was more garbage than potatoes.

First, with the general improvement of the economic situation, most ghetto Jews were less focused on the shortage of official food products, especially of potatoes.

[Page 357]

Those working in the main station were: Kovarski (died in ghetto); Baicovitz (liberated in Dachau); Fin (saved himself by going into the city); Advocate Shinberg,[b] and others.

Those working in the potato station were L. Gurvitch (died in Dachau); Steinberg (died during the ghetto liquidation), and others.

B. Distribution Centers

To distribute the official food rations to the population, there were distribution centers in the various ghetto areas.[c]

Since there were few distribution centers in the Ghetto, they would have to stand in line for hours to pick up that little bit of food. One would mainly see children in the lines, and not any work duty people. To maintain order in the lines, the Gestapo restored the Jewish Ghetto Police. It wasn't so easy for the ghetto Jew to be able to pick up even these hunger-rations.

In the beginning, they would have to pay a certain monetary payment for food products. At the end of Summer, 1942, a "money-less economy" was introduced in the Ghetto, so they would receive the food products for free.

The distribution centers were run by: Joels (died after jumping from a train during the deportation); Rochelson (died in Dachau); Edelstein (died in Estonia); Fentster (died during the ghetto liquidation), and others.

[Page 358]

C. Meat Markets

In general, it was decided that the ghetto population would get only horse meat. Rarely, however, was the meat in any condition to be eaten. It would often happen that the horsemeat which they brought for the Ghetto, would have to be buried immediately to avoid an outbreak of an epidemic.

The guys who were employed as butchers in the markets were: the brothers Telzak, Resnik (all died in Dachau); Bliacher (liberated in Dachau); Lipman (saved himself in a ghetto hideout) and others. As employees: L. Yellin[d], Shalit (died in Dachau) and others.

Also, in the institutions of the Provisions Office, as in all the other ghetto institutions, there was no shortage of abuses or other awful acts.

Both in the stations, as well as in the distribution centers there were certain criminal elements who made various deals on the backs of the community. It was no secret in the Ghetto that responsible functionaries from the Provisions Office had a hand in these "operations".

Original footnotes:

    a. See "Problems of Nutrition in the Ghetto," "Smuggling of Food."
    b. See "Elders Council"
    c. The ghetto population would call the distribution centers "Parama", the same name as the distribution centers in the city.
    d. See "Liquidation and Deportation from the Ghetto"

CHAPTER VI

Housing Office

-Painful question about living space in the Ghetto-Extermination Action "to clear out" needed apartments-Greater reduction of the ghetto areas- Activities of the Housing Office

[Page 359]

By July of 1941, the occupation regime published an order to the Kovno Jewish population to relocate to a newly established ghetto in Slabodka. It became clear to everyone that the settling of approximately 30,000 Jewish souls in the demarcated ghetto area would be an extraordinarily difficult problem. Whatever Jewish efforts that were mustered to enlarge the area of the Ghetto never reached actual resolution because of the anti-Jewish attitude of the Kovno Lithuanian Magistrate.

Also, as we know, the Jewish Committee was mainly occupied with organizing the issue of relocation into the Ghetto. Large portions of the Jewish population, mainly those with material means, started searching for apartments in the ghetto area without waiting for the Committee. In this way hundreds of families managed to get an apartment in the Ghetto on their own. But most Jews had to wait for the Jewish Committee to distribute a residence.

Already at that time, the Housing Office[a] tried to introduce a bit of order to the painful question of apartments in the Ghetto. First, they had to record the entire living area of ghetto houses so that they could somewhat logically divide the available living spaces.

In the ghetto area, aside from private houses, there were a few large blocks and a few dozen smaller blocks, which were built in later years for the Kovno working population. Immediately from the start, these large and small blocks, which were in much better condition than most little private houses, were grabbed by the "higher ups," who had access to the Jewish Committee, in general, and to the Housing Office, specifically.

[Page 360]

Also, the Jews with less access tried to arrange for an apartment somehow. Those families which were not able to acquire a room for themselves, did it together with another family. The poorer Jews were quartered in the communal dormitories. Thereafter, there were still hundreds of Jewish families which remained without shelter.

That is why the Housing Office at that time was laden with work to find a resting place for Jews without shelter. In cases when someone got more living space than was established by the Jewish ghetto administration, they would have to take in more people. If, however, he did not want to carry out the instructions of the Housing Office willingly, the Ghetto Police would carry it out by force.

There were great difficulties in acquiring a piece of living space for all ghetto Jews. The crowding in most houses was huge. During the day this issue was somehow bearable. However, problems started in the evening when they had to set up a bed for everyone to sleep.

It is certainly unnecessary to describe the way the communal dormitories looked, where hundreds of people were lying on the floors in crowding and dirt. In such a place, the cry of children would mix with the groans of the sick and elderly. The fighting and motion in such a human beehive would continue for a full 24 hours around the clock.

But very quickly the ghetto Jew had to deal with problems more serious than apartments. The extermination Actions which took place in the early period of the ghetto's existence, put all the daily worries and plagues on the back burner. Also, they had not yet properly understood the planning and systematization of Hitler's extermination project. At that time, things such as crowding and discomfort in the residence didn't enter anyone's head. More space in Jewish homes was the result of Jews removed for extermination.

[Page 361]

However, the high point of thinning out the ghetto population was achieved through the Big Action, after which there remained in the Ghetto only a bit more than half of the Jewish population that entered at the start. After three and a half months, only 16,000 souls remained of the 30,000 Jews. The problem of living space disappeared with the indirect help of the Gestapo, which, in a short time, managed to kill 13-14 thousand Jews, not counting the victims up to the entry into the Ghetto.

After the Big Action, the Housing Office, along with all the other ghetto institutions, gradually started stabilizing their activities. At that time, this Office still didn't have much work. As previously mentioned, this was because the extermination Actions reduced the ghetto population almost to half, and they already arranged shelter for some ghetto Jews.

From time to time, the Housing Office would, once again, become stationed in the center of ghetto life. This happened when the regime organization gave out unjust decrees to reduce entire ghetto sectors.

The Nazi plans for Jewish extermination included, among others, the continuous moving around, here and there, of large groups of Jews. This was done so that their ability to resist against the regime of terror would be undermined. Also, these frequent relocations from one ghetto area to another caused these people the loss of much of their, as they say, acquired comforts, like a bed, a bit of provisions, and the like.

These relocations typically happened in a great hurry. After such relocations, the relocated Jew had to streamline his "living standard" in his new resting place and give up much of what he had in his former place. Furthermore, after each reduction of a ghetto quarter, the new modest living space became even smaller, and it became evident why such an event meant real punishment for the Ghetto.

[Page 362]

During the three years of the existence of the Ghetto, the following ghetto areas were reduced: [b]

a. Liquidation of the Small Ghetto - During this Action in October 1941, as we know, 1,500 Jews who survived this selection were chased out to the remaining portions of the Ghetto with just the shirts on their backs. That was, by the way, the only clear-out of a ghetto area which took place in such a murderous manner. A small portion of the Jews from the former Small Ghetto settled down with friends. All those remaining had to go through the Housing Office on the same day to get a small corner somewhere, otherwise they remained lying on the street.

b. Reduction of the Vienozhinskiu area - This reduction [b] which took place in January 1942, was carried out over a few hours, and created many problems for the Ghetto. Also, the Housing Office had many worries at that time about creating small living spaces for people. Later, this area was again transferred back to the Ghetto and then again cleared out, until it was finally transferred over to the authority of the Christian population.

c. Reduction of a portion of Paneriu and other streets - The only "advantage" of this reduction, which happened in May 1942, was that a bit more time was given to carry it out, and it was possible to get organized without great haste.

d. Reduction of the large blocks - This reduction in October 1943 had to be carried out in a short time, and it caused huge anguish. By the way, it gave the impression that, Goecke, the new ghetto boss, aside from all the other intentions of this decree, was partially diverting the attention of the confused ghetto Jews before an upcoming relocation Action to Estonia.

e. Reduction of the first sector in December 1943 - This was the biggest reduction of a ghetto area and thousands of souls were moved. The crowding in the remaining ghetto boundary reached its culmination point and this embittered an already bleak ghetto life.

[Page 363]

Aside from these larger reductions, during the ghetto's existence there were also smaller reductions of ghetto quarters. Such reductions meant a harsh decree for the Ghetto, and they had to go along with it, willingly, or unwillingly.

As was noted, the Housing Office had a huge bit of work in the early period of the ghetto's existence and during the reductions of entire ghetto areas.

Also, we cannot deny that this ghetto agency had no easy task satisfying everyone's demands, specifically regarding housing. It never happened that a simple ghetto Jew could come upon a better residence in a normal way. All the claims and responses from such ordinary Jews were useless because the Housing Office conducted its activity in such a way that it made the "Yales," happy by fulfilling their requirements first; that meant, the important people of the Ghetto. In addition to that, there was no shortage of corruption, etc.

At the same time when the Ghetto was dominated by horrible crowding, and people really didn't have a place to lay their head, there were quite a few families who lived in comparatively large spaces. That meant that all these hard restrictions on living space never applied to the various higher-ups of the ghetto hierarchy and their friends. Like for many other details of the ghetto reality, this detail mirrored the unique social differentiation which ruled all aspects of ghetto life. It was therefore understandable why the Housing Office did not enjoy any sympathy from most of the ghetto Jews.

In Spring, 1944, when the Jewish ghetto institutions were liquidated, and their functions were transferred to the authority of the German Camp management, the Housing Office remained in existence until the liquidation of the Ghetto. This Office, however, did not carry out any important work because there were other worries and problems greater than apartments at that time. Some Jews at that time dreamed about getting themselves out of the Ghetto, as the soil under their feet was becoming hotter from hour to hour.

[Page 364]

Working in the Housing Office from the early ghetto months were: Advocate Gershovich.[c] Later, Meshkotz was appointed (died during the ghetto liquidation) and served in this Office until the end of the Ghetto. As leading colleagues there were: Katz (died in Dachau); Weintraub (liberated after he left the Ghetto); Svirsky (died during the ghetto deportation), and others.

Original footnotes:

    a. Not counting the reduction of a row of streets, like Jurborker, Raudondvarer, Dagtuku and others during the lock up of the Ghetto in August 1941.
    b. See "Reduction of the Ghetto Quarters"
    c. See "Labor Office"

CHAPTER VII

Health Office

-Problems of the state of health in the early months of the ghetto's existence-Medical institutions in the Health Office and their significance in ghetto life

[Page 365]

The problem of the health of the Jews became evident from the first days of the outbreak of the war in Kovno. During their first acts of terror on the defenseless Jewish population, the Lithuanian Hitlerites, among others, also threw Jewish patients out of the hospitals. The sick people who were not killed on the spot were forced to lie in their home without clinical attention. The sick didn't have any possibility of getting private medical attention because a Jew would be in danger of death if he showed up on the street in the early occupation weeks.

A long list of medical issues became evident after the relocation to the Ghetto. Before anything else, they had to organize hospitals for the seriously ill. In August 1941, two hospitals were set up in the Small Ghetto: one for infectious diseases and a second one for surgery and internal illnesses. The horrible details of the tragic fate of this hospital, especially the one for infectious diseases, were already described,[a] when the patients were burned alive, along with the medical personnel.

After this unprecedented Nazi barbarism, they were afraid to create new hospitals in the Ghetto because it was logical to be suspicious that the Nazis were apt, once again, to repeat similar murders of Jewish patients. Therefore, the Ghetto remained without a hospital for a certain time.

[Page 366]

After the Big Action, the strain in the Ghetto was slowly reduced and the Jewish ghetto institutions started their intense activity. By then the Health Office was established and also started addressing the medical problems of the ghetto population.

Like all the other ghetto offices the Health Office had at its disposal numerous institutions in order to support its work. The following institutions belonged to the Health Office:
a) Hospital, b) Ambulatory, c) Medical branches in other ghetto institutions, d) Publications Institution, and, e) Crazy House [Mental Clinic].

A. Hospital

In the last months of 1941, the Health Office first addressed the creation of a hospital. The number of patients grew, and the founding of a hospital became an extremely urgent issue. Waiting any longer was impossible. The most important medical instruments and facilities for the hospital were collected from Jewish doctors who had hidden a portion of their medical instruments during the time of the robbery of Jewish possessions, in August-September 1941.

The Ghetto Hospital had divisions for internal, surgery and other illnesses. Until May 1942, the hospital also had a maternity division. Thereafter, when the decree was announced by the regime about forbidding pregnancy in the Ghetto,[b] this division was liquidated.

No division for infectious diseases existed in the hospital because, as mentioned, they had a basic fear that the Nazi governors would kill these patients. Therefore, in the reports given to the regime organization, there were no infectious diseases in the Ghetto. The patients with infectious diseases would have to be kept at home, or they would be brought into the hospital under another formal diagnosis.

The Jewish doctors had a hard job which they carried out with success. Despite such inhuman conditions, there were no epidemics during the ghetto's existence. In this regard, the Sanitation Commission supported the Health Office which coordinated its work with the tasks of the Sanitation Division of the Jewish Ghetto Police.

[Page 367]

The Hospital also had (with certain disruptions) their own X-ray cabinet which greatly contributed to the success of the medical activity.

Also, the Pharmacy and Laboratory, which formally belonged to the Provisions Office, stood at the disposal of the Hospital and other medical institutions of the Health Office.

Thereafter, because a large portion of Jews were transported to the labor camps near Kovno and in the provinces, they organized sick rooms in the camps for the slightly ill. The seriously ill would be brought to the Ghetto Hospital for attention.

The hospital which only had a few dozen beds and had to serve 15,000 souls, was one of the most needed ghetto institutions. The hospital fulfilled a very important function as it offered clinical attention to seriously sick Jewish patients.

B. Outpatient Clinic

Aside from the Hospital, the Health Office also had a well-established Outpatient Clinic, with divisions for various illnesses (internal, surgery, eyes, nose and throat, women, children, etc.). A dental branch was also active. All these divisions were visited daily by dozens of patients who received necessary medical help there.

In 1942, when the area of the Ghetto was relatively large, medical branches were organized in a few sections of the Ghetto, which were affiliated with the central clinic. These medical positions made it easier for the ghetto population to get medical attention. During Goecke's time, these medical institutions were liquidated because the area of the Ghetto was eliminated.

[Page 368]

C. Medical branches in other ghetto institutions

Aside from these medical institutions that belonged to the Health Office, the Ghetto also had a few other active medical facilities. They functioned under the authority of other ghetto institutions but were in contact with the Health Office.

As was seen, there was a Medical Division in the Labor Office which took care of medical issues of the labor duty population.

Aside from the Medical Division of the Labor Office, as previously mentioned, there were a few larger labor positions at the Aerodrome and in the city. A sanitation post was active there, which gave medical help to the working Jews in case of a misfortune during work.

Also, the Large Ghetto Workshops had a separate medical branch, which served the few thousand men and women who worked in the workshops. These branches were subject to Jewish oversight by the ghetto workshops.

Both the Medical Division at the Labor office, as well as the medical branches in the ghetto workshops together served almost two thirds of the general number of ghetto Jews. These played an important role in the state of health of the Ghetto.

D. Delousing Facility

There was also a delousing facility in the Health Office, which greatly helped maintain the cleanliness of the ghetto population. In this ghetto institution, which was built thanks to a Jewish initiative, a Jew would be able to wash himself well, and finally clean his clothes of lice and other parasites. From time to time, during their work duty, workers could receive passes from the ghetto administration for this purpose.

E. Crazy [sic] House [Mental Clinic]

There was also a Crazy [sic] Clinic under the authority of the Health Office, where a few dozen mentally ill men and women were supported. During the Action on the children, elderly and sick, these sick people were transported to be exterminated. Among the victims was also Professor Shimon Belatzkin.[c]

[Page 369]

The Health Office organized courses for medical nurses to prepare a cadre of doomed nurses. A few dozen women studied in these courses and afterward became active in their occupation in the hospital and in other medical institutions.

Despite not being free of crippling protectionism, the accomplishments of the Health Office for the benefit of the ghetto population must be highlighted. Within the framework of their very limited ghetto possibilities, the institutions of the Health Office did very important work. The fact that the ghetto Jew could receive medical help relatively easily, was of great significance.

Dr. Zacharin was the Head of the Health Office. More details were described earlier[d] about his shameful role as a leader of the sick bay in the labor camps of Dachau Concentration Camp. He was also a leader of the Ghetto Hospital.

After the liquidation of the "autonomous" Jewish ghetto institutions, the activity of the Health Office also was minimized. At that time, the designated S.S. Commissar of the Hospital was the one in charge of "ordering" the state of health of the population in the Ghetto and in the labor camps.

Those active in the hospital, in the clinics and other medical institutions (aside from those already mentioned) were the following doctors:

Dentist Akabas, Dr. Berman, Dr. Braunz, Mrs. Dr. Bar-Vishtagetzky, Dr. Goldstein, Dentist Griliches, Ms. Dr. Yochelson, Dentist Dr. Lurie, Dr. Blumberg, Dr. Segal, Dr. G. Elkes, Mrs. Dr. Gurvitch-Eliashkevitz, Dr. Pertzikovitch, Dr. Kaufman, Dr. Katz, Mrs. Dr. Kaplan, Dr. Klibanski, Dr. Klebanov, Dr. Kagan, Dentist Ms. Kagan, Mrs. Dr. Rosenblum (all liberated in the concentration camps in Germany); Dr. Gershtein, Dentist Dr. Glickman, Professor Lazerson (all died in Dachau); Dr. Blumberg (died in Estonia); Mrs. Dr. Kamber (were taken to Estonia and committed suicide in a camp); Dr. Orlianski, Mrs. Dr. Golach, Dr. Gurvitch, Mrs. Dr. Tankel, Dr. Zaltzberg, Dr. Mattis[5] Dr. Yakin, Dr. Feldstein, Dr. Tzeitel, Dentist Mrs. Stein (all died during the deportations); Dr. Eizenstadt (died in a Christian's hideout); Dr. Abramovich, Dr. Ipp, Dentist Mrs. Olitzky, Dr. Blasberg, Dentist Mrs. Leibovich-Goldschmidt, Dr. Vidutchinsky, Dentist Mrs. Margolis, Dentist Mrs. Nementchik, Dr. Richman (all saved themselves before and during the ghetto liquidation), and others.

[Page 370]

It is necessary to mention the nurses in the medical institutions:

Mrs. Levin (killed in Stutthof); D. Igdalski (died after liberation); R. Glagovski, R. Lipschitz, B. Lipshitz-Weiner, Mrs. Gotz, R. Slove, Ingel, D. Shapiro, Mrs. Sudak-Katz (all freed in the camps in Germany); R. Epstein, A. Strelitz, Z. Tint (all were in the partisans and survived to liberation); Ch. Leibovitz, Shevtz, Flink-Yoselevich, Krok (all saved themselves during the ghetto deportation), and others.

At this opportunity it is worth mentioning that immediately after the Big Action at the end of 1941, two Kovno doctors, Dr. Nabriski and Dr. Voshtshin, escaped into the city where they were hidden in a hole by a Christian. In the Summer of 1943, during a Gestapo inspection in another section, they were found, arrested, and were to be killed. Thanks to the efforts of Dr. Elkes, Liptzer, and others, they finally succeeded in saving them from death and they were brought back to the Ghetto. The "reason" why the Gestapo needed just these doctors in the Ghetto, among others, was because they were both gynecologists and were very necessary and needed in the Ghetto since the regime decreed that all pregnant Jewish women must have abortions. Dr. Nabriski was liberated in Dachau and Dr. Voshtshin saved himself by leaving the Ghetto a short while before the deportations.

Original footnotes:

a. a. See "Action and Liquidation of the Small Ghetto"
b. See "New Decrees and Little Decrees."
c. See "Ghetto Court"
d. See "Fate of the Deported Jews."
e. His father, Dr. Moshe Mattis died in the Ghetto, Summer, 1941

CHAPTER VIII

Social Welfare Office

*-Necessary resources for large portions of the ghetto population-
Establishment of the Social Welfare Office and its activities*

[Page 371]

The Jewish population had the misfortune of falling under the Nazi authority. At the passing of the first wave of mass murders against the helpless Jews, it became evident to them that what stood before them were also large material profits. The various Lithuanian knife-wielding heroes couldn't imagine, even in their wildest dreams, such a "lucky" time, when they could directly and freely murder Jews and rob their possessions. In the early chaotic days, they took advantage of this opportune moment as much as possible.

The efforts of many years of Jewish toil fell into the hands of the Lithuanian Jew-murderers in the blink of an eye. Those horrific days meant life and death for every Jew. So, understandably, the question of losing or not losing their property wasn't on their mind. The one and only worry at that moment was how to survive this extermination storm.

Thousands of destitute Jews, who had made a very fine living until the outbreak of war, were added to the community dormitories after the thorough robbery of Jewish possessions in August-September 1941. Over time, the professional beggars didn't restrain themselves and reminded the Jewish Committee about their need for social support, however, the impoverished upstanding Jewish families suffered in silence.

After the thorough robbery of Jewish possessions, the unceasing mass Actions halted complaints about worries of livelihood. How was it possible to think about the fact that not a penny was earned for months, at a time when, week in and week out, thousands of Jews were ripped out of the Ghetto for extermination?!!!

[Page 372]

The Big Action, which stands as the high point of the mass slaughter in the Ghetto, left the surviving Jews so strongly depressed that for a certain time after the huge blood bath no one could imagine worrying about their material existence. Various ghetto Jews started thinking about whether they would become candidates for a new Action which would come today or tomorrow.

The first series of mass exterminations was concluded after the Big Action, and then came a period of relative quiet. The exhausting forced labor at the Aerodrome, where thousands of Jews worked day and night; the hunger in all ghetto homes; the lack of clothing and footwear and other material problems for many ghetto Jews, made for the founding of a special institution which would at least lighten the material troubles of the destitute. The newly established Social Welfare Office was to help with these scarcities in ghetto life.

The Social Welfare Office was established after the Big Action, and the following reason was attributed to its foundation:

As mentioned, many ghetto Jews tried to grab clothing from completely unknown people who were taken away during the Action. With the agreement of Jordan, the designee of ghetto issues of the City Commissariat, the Elders Council decided that the clothing of the transported Jews, who did not leave behind any close relatives in the Ghetto, were to be given over to the authority of the ghetto administration. They were to be distributed to the destitute entities. The first in line were many needy Aerodrome workers who had to carry the heavy yoke of slave labor. Organizing the issues of social support was given over to the established Social Welfare Office.

[Page 373]

With the help of the Jewish Ghetto Police, huge amounts of bedding, clothes, underwear, footwear, and household utensils, which belonged to the exterminated Jews were collected in the storehouses of the Social Welfare Office. Afterwards, the better items were chosen as "gifts" for the Nazi ghetto bosses and other needs of the Elders Council, and the remaining items were slowly divided among the needy Jews based on individual requests.

Aside from the support in clothing, the Social Welfare Office would distribute some food products to the destitute Jews from time to time, which was received by the Provisions Office and other economic ghetto institutions for this purpose. On occasion, the Social Welfare Office would throw in some products which were confiscated from Jews during the searches at the Ghetto Gate. For a certain time, workers from the better city work brigades systematically contributed charitable cash or food products to benefit the Social Welfare Office.

In the Summer of 1942, the Social Welfare Office established a kitchen where the destitute could eat lunch. The food consisted mainly of a vegetable soup without fat or meat. Sometimes the cooking would include the bones of horsemeat. For lunch, each one had to bring bread from their own bread rations. It is certainly unnecessary to talk about this satisfying and appetizing "lunch."

For a certain time, the Social Welfare Office had its own bakery. The earnings from the baked bread would be applied to the support of the Office. The Social Welfare Office would also give out "little notes" for the Pharmacy, Clinics, Small Ghetto Workshops, and other ghetto institutions which would unofficially take cash payment so that they could take care of the needs of the needy Jews for free. In the summertime, the needy would receive some vegetables from the Ghetto Gardens and in winter, occasionally, a bundle of wood.

In summarizing the role of the Social Welfare Office in ghetto life, we must conclude that, in general, its accomplishments were varied. This institution, which was supposed to alleviate the social needs in the Ghetto, fulfilled its task in very limited measure. This is explained, not only by the lack of wider resources, but also because the better confiscated clothes and belongings, the material basis of the Social Welfare Office, were designated to completely different purposes. And the poor ghetto Jew received almost rags. It should be added that, like in all the other ghetto institutions, there was also a ruling bureaucracy and even certain abuse. It became clear just how minimal the activity of the Social Welfare Office was. And, therefore in this needy world, this ghetto institution, did not have a very good reputation.

[Page 374]

Once the material situation of the ghetto population improved, after the Summer of 1942, so the significance of the Social Welfare Office became narrower. Many Aerodrome workers who deserved social help were transferred to work in the city brigades and the problem of "making a living" was partially alleviated for them. The main clients of the Social Office were then only the older and non-working entities of the ghetto poor.

Once again, the problem of social help became relevant with regard to the transfer of large numbers of Jews to labor camps, where life was fairly similar to the Ghetto itself. At that time, as with the Social Welfare Office (with the help of the Labor Office) collections of clothes, underwear, footwear etc. were conducted for the benefit of the needy in the labor camps.

During the liquidation of the ghetto institutions in the last months of the Goecke period, the Social Welfare Office was trashed even further. Practically, its activity didn't have any significance. Also, on the eve of the upcoming ghetto crisis, the destitute ghetto Jew was by then completely interested in other problems.

In the beginning, the head of the Social Welfare Office was Dr. Segal;[a] later, it was Shauchet (liberated in Dachau); positions of responsibility were held by: Yeglin (liberated in Dachau); S. Goldstein (hid out with a Christian in the countryside), and others.

In the early period of the Social Welfare Office, the following also worked there: Adv. Gershovitch,[b] Adv. Koziol (died in Estonia), D. Treger,[c] S. Glatt (liberated in Dachau), Schmerkovitch (died during the ghetto liquidation), and others.

Original footnotes:

a. See "Health Office"
b. See "Labor Office"
c. See "Small Ghetto Workshops"
d.

CHAPTER IX

Statistics Office

-Representation in the Statistics Office and Address Bureau-Establishment of the "Estates Office"-Attempt at creating an illegal mail connection between Kovno and other ghettos-Use of the materials of the Statistics Office

[Page 375]

The Statistics Office also occupied a prominent position in the unique structure of the Jewish ghetto administration. Like most ghetto institutions, this office was also established in the early period of the existence of the Ghetto, at the end of Summer, 1941.

The Counselor for Jewish issues in the City Commissariat, in the first half of September 1941 was the tragically famous Lithuanian, Kaminskas. He ordered a general registration of the ghetto population. The completed registration established that there were in total close to 30,000 souls in the Ghetto. The leading people from this census set up the seed for the subsequently established Statistics Office.

When the Jewish Police started organizing its operation of police issues, it was first necessary to have an exact file of all the ghetto residents. In October 1941 the task of putting together the file was transferred to the Statistics Office.

In Autumn of 1941, out of the Statistics Office, a special Addresses Bureau, named the "Subsequent Residents Office" became visible and was subject to the leaders of the Ghetto Police. Since the Addresses Bureau was a semi-autonomous ghetto institution, it was tightly connected to the Statistics Office.

[Page 376]

The extermination Actions which raged unceasingly during the first months of the Ghetto's existence also erased all the toil, effort and material of the Statistics Office and Addresses Bureau. Specifically, all the statistical information and numbers were found to be very valuable in relation to the Big Action, when in one day, over 10,000 Jews were taken away for extermination.

Therefore, one of the most urgent jobs of the Statistics Office and Addresses Bureau after the Big Action, was to carry out a new registry of the ghetto population. This registration, which took place in November 1941, established that a total of 16,000 souls remained in the Ghetto. Based on just this registration a new dossier of the general population was set up.

For the Addresses Bureau to always be in the picture regarding changes of address of the ghetto residents, the Ghetto Police published a duty order about signing in and signing out of the Police Precincts, in cases of apartment changes. Later, when the population received ghetto-passes, the police would sign in with a stamp on the other side of the ghetto-pass.[a]

Within the Addresses Bureau, an "Estates Office" was established in 1942 to register the demographic changes of the ghetto population, like births, deaths, marriages, etc.

In the Ghetto at that time, quite a few weddings took place. There was a trend to marry, especially among younger women whose husbands were taken away in the Actions. This took place during the establishment of the Ghetto or later. These women were afraid to be without a man because during the Actions many of these remaining single women would be sent away for extermination. By the way, young men and women without families were the first candidates the Jewish ghetto administration sent for general relocation to labor camps outside the Ghetto. Everything together motivated many young people to get married. These "ghetto weddings" were considered "protection." Having a workplace somewhere in a stable and good brigade, a position in the ghetto administration, or other similar "guarantees" were protection and security for the poor ghetto people.

[Page 377]

In the early period of the existence of the Ghetto, many births were noticeable. This specific phenomenon is explained herein, because many women became pregnant before the outbreak of the war and gave birth while being in the Ghetto. Thereafter, the number of births dropped even more until the prohibition of pregnancy (Summer, 1942), which was the reason that no births took place in the Ghetto.

Regarding mortality in the Ghetto, it was already emphasized that during the extermination Action mainly older and weaker people were caught. Thus, most people remaining in the Ghetto were younger and healthier entities. Aside from cases of natural deaths, the mortality among the ghetto Jews was relatively low.

The following episode also belongs to the history of the Statistics Office:

A certain time after the Big Action, the Ghetto succeeded in establishing an illegal mail connection between the Kovno Ghetto and the ghettos in Vilna, Shavl, and later, also in Riga. Understandably, the possibility of corresponding with family members in those ghetto settlements had great significance for the ghetto Jews. This mail exchange was made possible thanks to the help of a few reliable Christians, who received a material reward for it. Involved in this illegal "Ghetto Post" were a few people from the Statistics Office and the Secretary of the Elders Council. However, in the beginning of February 1942, five hundred Kovno Jews were caught.

In the Spring of 1942, a package letter fell into the hands of a Kovno Gestapo person, by chance. After an investigation, the Secretary of the Elders Council, Adv. Bernstein, a colleague from the Statistics Office, Adv. Chaykin and A. Zilberman, a worker from the Jewish brigade near the train, were arrested. They sat for a few weeks in the Gestapo jail but succeeded in getting released. The entire issue was erased with the help of a few Jews who were influential in the Gestapo, as well as some heavy bribery gifts.

[Page 378]

Through this failure, the illegal "postal service" in the Ghetto was liquidated. From this point on it was difficult to ever send out a letter to the other ghetto settlements.

For the Elders Council and its institutions, the finished products of the Statistics Office in certain measure served as support for establishing the guidelines of their activity. Such materials were important for the Jewish Labor Office in regulating the painful problem of forced labor. Having accurate statistical information, the Labor Office was able to orient itself and control the labor duty, especially for the women who made up 60% of the general ghetto population. The information from the Statistics Office was also used by the Elders Council for their monthly activity report to the Kovno City Commissar, under whose authority the Ghetto existed from its founding, until Goecke's time.

The Addresses Bureau also had much to do with giving out the ghetto passes to the population. True, distribution of the passes formally belonged to the Ghetto Police, but, in this way, the Addresses Bureau carried out the most important preparation work.

Also, the Statistics Office belonged to the small ghetto institutions, so as noted, it carried out a certain positive role in public ghetto life. This ghetto institution was mainly a support institution for other facilities of the ghetto administration.

The Statistics Office did not come in frequent contact with the ghetto Jews. Also, at the "Estate Office" they would not have to stand in line for hours, thank goodness, as was the case for most of the ghetto institutions. Because of that, the ghetto population noted a neutral attitude towards these institutions, which meant, not good, not bad.

[Page 379]

The Statistics Office, as well as, the Addresses Bureau, had a longer existence among the most important Jewish ghetto institutions. When the Elders Council was liquidated and Dr. Elkes was designated as "preeminent," these institutions were transferred over to the authority of Dr. Elkes. Nothing remained except the former signboards,

Leaders of the Statistics Office included at first, Ch. Kagan.[b] Later I. Leibenzon became leader (saved himself through a Christian in the countryside). For a certain time, the office was led by Dr. Valsonok.[c]

Colleagues in this office were: Polish-Jewish typesetter, Michael Burstein. At first, he worked in the Jewish Labor Office. Thereafter, went over to the Statistics Office, where he, together with Dr. Valsonok, worked on material for the Elders Council and its institutions. At that time, he also was engaged with collecting ghetto folklore. Both his fictional ghetto writings (novellas and a larger novel, "The Yellow Patch"), as well as his collections of folklore material, which he hid somewhere in the Ghetto, were lost. Later, he worked in the Ghetto Workshops. During the liquidation of the Ghetto, he was taken to the labor camp of Dachau concentration camp (Camp 1 near Landsberg/Kaufering) together with the other men, where, on the 27th of March 1945, he died of pneumonia, just one month before liberation. F. Berniker (liberated in Dachau); Adv. Chaykin (died in Dachau); Volpe (died during the ghetto deportation), and others.

Original footnotes:

a. See Reproduction of a Ghetto-pass.
b. See "Large Ghetto Workshops"
c. See "People Involved with the Partisan movement"

CHAPTER X

School Office

-Educational issues in the early ghetto months-founding and character of the children's schools-Liquidation of the schools and the School Office- Activity of the Vocational School-Attempts to alleviate the cultural needs of the ghetto population

[Page 380]

The sudden cessation of Jewish children's studies was an additional tragic repercussion to Jewish life caused by the Nazis, from the first days of the occupation. Understandably, Jews didn't think about what their children were studying during those horrific days when bestial mass abuses against the helpless Jewish population were going on. The heads of the Jews were occupied with existential questions that were more important than education. By the way, most of the school children were starting their summer holidays when the war broke out at the end of June 1941.

In the first few months of the Ghetto's existence, during this bloody period of extermination Actions, the ghetto Jews certainly could not think about education for their children. But quite a few parents searched for something to do so that their children should have some opportunity to study, even in those horrible days. The only way was through private instruction. These parents would discuss private instruction for their children with teachers. The teachers at the former high schools, elementary schools and other Yiddish-Hebrew learning facilities collected their students in smaller groups and studied together with them.

For a certain time after the Big Action the ghetto Jews slowly started to calm down from the mass killings. While various public Jewish ghetto institutions were emerging, the time came to establish an institution which would take on pedagogical issues. Indeed, at the end of 1941 the Elders Council established the School Office for this purpose.

[Page 381]

The first job of the newly founded School Office was to carry out a registration of available children of elementary school age, that meant from 7-8 years old to 12-13 years old.[a] For the almost 16,000 souls who were then in the Ghetto, the number of school children was relatively small, because during the mass slaughters, especially during the Big Action, many families with small children were sent away for extermination.

It was already mentioned that at first, those mothers who had children up to 8 years old and, later, only up to 4 years old, were freed from labor duty. There were, therefore, many families where all the adults would have to go to work and the older children would have to remain at home to take care of the household or the younger brothers and sisters. To convince more parents to register their children to study, the Elders Council published an order about forced education.

Thereafter, the School Office finished all the necessary preparations and founded two schools: one in the old ghetto area, in one of the former Yeshiva buildings on Yeshiva Street 16, and the other on Raminoler Street 4.[b] In each school there were about 200 students.

The Ghetto School presented itself with a mix of students who had earlier studied in schools from the various streams, like, Zionist-Hebrew, Yiddish-secular, religious etc. True, during the Soviet period in Lithuania, all the previous school streams were liquidated. Only one type of Soviet school was open for Jewish children in Yiddish language education. However, the one year of Soviet school-life did not result in a loss of influence on the students from the various types of schools from the former years. The teachers in the Ghetto Schools, therefore, had quite a task for themselves, to meld together the students from the separate school streams into one school collective.

[Page 382]

The Ghetto School had to satisfy the needs of those children who already finished a 4-year elementary school. Thus, the school program was broadened, and students studied there starting from elementary school and ending with the first four grades of a middle school. The language of instruction was mainly Hebrew. The older children also studied Yiddish literature. The learning of religion was also included in the school program. The ideological spirit of the school was Zionist-Hebrew.

It was not easy for the schools to acquire the necessary books, notebooks, and study tools. Whatever the students had, they collected themselves. The rest was collected in various ways, with difficulty. As a result, studies would take place in two shifts: before noon and after noon.

It was self-explanatory that with the difficult ghetto conditions, the school's achievements were very limited, but the significance of the school was entirely apparent, as the teachers tried to maintain a satisfactory pedagogical level for the schools. In the short period of the schools' existence, the few school holiday celebrations left behind a touching impression.

In Spring, 1942 the youth organization "Eshel"[c] was founded. Most of the older school students found social expression in the Zionist spirit.

Aside from the elementary schools, two kindergartens were also established where children up to school age could enjoy themselves a few hours per day. They took in many little children and carried out an important function in education.

Even during the school days in the Ghetto, there was also private teaching. The more prominent Jews and those who could afford it and didn't want their children to study in the same facilities with the rest of the people, got lessons for their children from private teachers. This would take place especially for children of preschool age.

[Page 383]

As was already mentioned,[d] on the 26th of August 1942, the regime published an order to close the children's schools. This order came unexpectedly and liquidated the schools which had existed for 7-8 months. It played an important role in the field of education.

The School Office was also liquidated in parallel to the closing of the children's schools. This ghetto institution, as we will see, was also engaged in various cultural events, as had been their activities for the schools.

The younger children had the opportunity to continue their studies, as little as there were. They were organized into smaller groups of students who were taught by teachers from the closed schools. This illegal education would take place in private apartments for a few hours per day, and they always had to be protected so that the regime should not find out about it.

The largest portion of older school children went over to study in the Vocational School, which was founded in June 1942 in the Ghetto. In the Vocational School the boys studied painting, locksmith, sheet metal work, carpentry, etc. The girls studied ladies tailoring and other occupations.

From Spring, 1942, when the City Commissariat started taking Jewish craftsman into the city factories and into the military service positions[e], the issue arose about educating new handwork forces among the growing youth. There was great demand for Jews to carry out various artisan occupations in the city workplaces.

In a short time, the vocational students acquired the same elementary knowledge in their occupation, and they were later taken in as assistants in the city workplaces where Jewish craftsmen worked. A portion of the young artisans went out to work in the Ghetto Workshops.

[Page 384]

Aside from educating for knowledge about practical and theoretical occupations, the Vocational School unofficially also taught Jewish studies, like Jewish history, Hebrew, knowledge of Eretz Israel, etc. The Vocational Schools in this way tried to fill in the pedagogical gap created due to the liquidation of the schools. The Zionist youth organizations also introduced Zionist topics to the vocational student circles.

The importance of the Vocational School grew just before and after the Action of the children, elders and sick. A work card from the Vocational School was actually a matter of life or death for dozens of ghetto children. At that time, the Vocational School was relocated to the Large Ghetto Workshops where it was not considered a formal school but was called vocational training workshops for youth.

Regarding the subject of schools, it is still necessary to add that the former teachers from the Kovno Yiddish Comertz High School, S. Rozenthal and his wife, A. Frebelistin, ran a private school where, for a certain time, they illegally taught a few dozen children from the left-leaning streams. In this school the language of instruction was Yiddish, and the spirit of the studies was proletariat radical. By the way, from time to time, secret discussions on various political and social themes also took place there for the people who belonged to the left learning circles.

As mentioned, aside from pedagogical issues, the School Office also unofficially occupied itself with other cultural activities. For example, the Public Library, which was established at the end of 1941,[f] belonged to this ghetto institution. In this Library, which had a few thousand books in Yiddish, Hebrew and other languages, ghetto Jews would be able to get a book to read and, in this manner, chase away some of their difficult thoughts. This Library was located in one of the smaller blocks on Varniu Street, with Rabbi Oshry and Gershtein as librarians.

[Page 385]

From time to time, they would also organize lectures, conferences, celebrations etc. These illegal cultural presentations would be arranged mainly for the people who were close to these social groupings. In the lost cultural life of the Ghetto, these had general educational significance. The Chet Tamuz Academy of 1943 must be mentioned, as it attracted a large audience and left a strong impression. Also, the celebrations which took place in June 1943, connected to the one-year anniversary of the Vocational School, were very impressive. During the school holiday, an exhibition of the work of the vocational school students was organized.

The orchestra of the Jewish Police offered the ghetto population musical vocal concerts a few times a week. These concerts were very successful for all. The ghetto Jew found artistic outlet in these concerts.

Dr. Chaim Nachman Shapira was a leader in the School Office. He was the son of the Kovno Rabbi, Abraham Duberkahana Shapira, who died in the Ghetto in March 1943. As we know, Dr. Shapira was a private lecturer of Semitic Studies at the Kovno University and the editor of the seminal work "History of the New Hebrew Literature."

Already in the first months of the ghetto's existence, the Elders Council assigned Dr. Shapira to collect and at the same time, perfect the documents and materials for the History of the Kovno Ghetto. For this purpose, the Elders Council ordered a secret archive. Later, the archive was taken over by the Secretary of the Elders Council, Advocate Golob. Regarding the fate of the archive, it was said that after the liberation, Adv. Golob should have had the entire archive, or he gave a portion of it over to the authority of the Soviet regime organization.

Also, the Ghetto Police secretly engaged in writing about ghetto events. A portion of these writings fell into the hands of a certain ghetto Jew, Lipman, and what became of it was unknown. Valuable writings about ghetto life were also conducted by the known Kovno Businessman Abba Balosher[g]. For a certain time, the former General-Secretary of the Rabbi's Union in Lithuania, David Itzikovitch (both died in Dachau), also wrote about the ghetto happenings.

[Page 386]

When the School Office was founded, Dr. Shapira took over the leadership of the Office and devoted himself very much to pedagogical problems. After the liquidation of the School, he became the leader of the Center for Vocational Education of the Jewish Labor Office.[h]

Dr. Shapira also took up a distinguished place in Zionist life in the Ghetto. His collaboration was also great in the organizing of the cultural arrangements, where he was always one of the head speakers.

In the beginning of December 1943, entirely unexpectedly, Dr. Shapira, was arrested by the Gestapo together with his family. The arrest had to do with the fact that there was an inquiry lodged through the International Red Cross in Berlin about the fate of Rabbi Shapira's family. The inquiry was in the name of relatives or from a Jewish organization in the USA. Dr. Shapira, his wife, child, and his mother – the Kovno Rebetzin – were all shot at the Ninth Fort. Right after the execution they burned all of them on the same pyres upon which, at that time, were burning the excavated dead, to erase the spores of the Nazi horrors.

The aforementioned Itzikovitch was Deputy Head of the School Office for a certain time, and Mrs. Snieg was Secretary (died in a labor camp in Germany).

The teachers who worked in the children's schools were Kapit, Kizel, Zhopovich, Stokol, Norvitch, Volfovich, (all died during the ghetto liquidation or in the Dachau labor camps); Mrs. Tzarfat (died in the Ghetto Summer, 1943); Rosenblat (taken to Estonia), and others.

Those who were active as kindergarten teachers were Mrs. Dr. Segal, Mrs. Sobolevich, Mrs. Levin (all liberated in labor camps in Germany), and others.

In addition to the teachers at the shuttered children's school, the teachers of general studies in the Vocational School were A. Melamed (liberated in Dachau); I. Shapira (died during the ghetto liquidation), and others.

Original footnotes:

    a. The work duty for boys started in the age of 15 years and later – from 14 years, for girls – from 16 and thereafter from 15 years old.
    b. Later this school was transferred to Democratiu Street 28.
    c. See "Zionist Activity in the Ghetto"
    d. See "New decrees and little decrees"
    e. See "Problem of applying the Jewish labor frces"
    f. The library was liquidated during the Book "Action" in February 1942.
    g. He hid his writings somewhere in the city with Christian friends.
    h. The Vocational School was founded under the authority of the Vocational Division of the Jewish Labor Office

CHAPTER XI

Ghetto Court

-Origins of the Jewish court entity in the Ghetto-Activity of the Ghetto Court and its liquidation-Police Court

[Page 387]

Already in the early days of the establishment of the Ghetto Police, in August 1941, they started conducting various administrative punishments on the population. For example, the Police started punishing violations of labor duty decisions, for not carrying out the orders of the self-formed ghetto institutions, for not following the rules of public order, etc.

In the stormy beginning of the Ghetto's existence, when fear for the future was especially great among the ghetto population, it was rare that serious conflicts would be resolved by themselves without the intervention of the newly established Jewish ghetto administration. Only in cases where the sides could not find a compromise between themselves did their claims come to the Elders Council. They then applied to the Legal Commission for clarification of the issue.

The Legal Commission was active in the Elders Council from the first days of the existence of the Ghetto. It also occupied itself with issues such as, establishing competencies for the newly established ghetto institutions, handling complaints from the population against unlawful dealings by the ghetto institutions, etc. The Ghetto Court originated from this Legal Commission.

Since the occupation regime started demanding more workers each day from the Jewish work forces in the Ghetto, they started actively pursuing labor deserters, especially for the Aerodrome. The people who systematically got themselves out of labor duty were taken to a special quick court. The quick court would carry out a court hearing procedure, and then carried out judgment against the accused.

[Page 388]

Most of the judges on the quick court, were higher officials from the Labor Office and from the Ghetto Police. These were the two most important ghetto institutions which had to take care of the demands of the regime organizations, especially for forced labor. As punishment, the convicted had to work in a heavy labor post for longer periods of time as there were no eager volunteers for these positions.

So that the punishments would have a greater impact on the labor duty population, the judgment against the work deserters was published in the form of public announcements in the streets. Later, as mentioned, such types of punishments were transferred over to the capacity of the Mobilization and Punishment Office of the Jewish Labor Office.

A short time after the Big Action, the widely advanced network of Jewish ghetto institutions was established in stages, and the idea developed of creating a stable Jewish Ghetto Court. Such a court was created at the end of 1941.

The jurisdiction of the Ghetto Court was comparatively the same as that which was applied to the Lithuanian Republic until the entry of the Soviets into Lithuania in 1940. In its capacity, civil and criminal issues belonged to the Ghetto Court. Appeals against the judgment of the Ghetto Court were carried out in the name of the Elders Council, the highest "government established" institution of the ghetto settlement.

Most court issues were due to various monetary conflicts, stealing, swindling, attacks, etc. As was mentioned many times, the possessions of those Jews who were taken away during the Big Action and who didn't leave behind any close relatives, had to be transferred to the authority of the Social Office to distribute to the poorer sectors. But if there were relatives, conflicts often arose among them due to inheritance of the possessions of the murdered ones. These "inheritance" processes instructed and became the backbone of the Court's activities in the Ghetto.

[Page 389]

However, the Ghetto Court also came out to handle other issues, like for example, when one Jew gave a second Jew some item or clothes to exchange for something in the city at work and, thereafter, a conflict arose because of this business deal. Material claims also arose when during the inspection at the Ghetto Gate, or in the city itself, when they would confiscate an item from a Jew which he took from someone to sell for him. There were also those who faked a confiscation and, in this way, made a few rubles on his account. Many conflicts also arose from various partner "handling-operations" in the Ghetto or at the workplace in the city.

A few times, the Ghetto Court had to also judge community violators, that meant immoral participants in the ghetto system. These uninformed souls conducted various illegal activities in fulfilling their duties. For example, when there was an issue against Jewish butchers who were employed to distribute meat to the ghetto population and committed big swindles in the process. There were also judgments for stealing from the clothing shops of the Social Office, for requests from the food distribution shops, etc.

The Ghetto Court would remain in close contact with the Jewish Ghetto Police so that it could appropriately carry out its functions. The Criminal Police mainly occupied itself with uncovering violations. Therefore, among their duties, the Ghetto Police also heard the carriage of judgments of the Ghetto Court. If a guilty party was judged to go to jail, his punishment was carried out in one of the two ghetto jails, which were in police authority.

In August 1942, when the School Office was liquidated and other ghetto decrees were given out, these were also concluded by the Ghetto Court. This institution existed semi-officially, meaning that the regime organization knew little about the activity of the Ghetto Court.

At one time, the Elders Council received an order to reduce the number of its institutions and, in addition, to strongly lower the number of participants in the ghetto hierarchy. This decree was related to the aspiration of the City Commissariat to enlarge the number of Jewish workers in the city workplaces. They formally kept the older and physically weaker people working in the ghetto offices. This Ghetto Court was then dissolved as an "unnecessary" ghetto institution.

[Page 390]

The functions of the liquidated Ghetto Court then went over to the authority of the court of the Jewish Ghetto Police. This same Police Court took over as its functions everything that originally belonged to the Ghetto Court.

The Chairman of the Ghetto Court was Professor S. Belatzkin, who in pre-war Lithuania was a famous lawyer and was, in addition, a professor at the Faculty of Law in the Lithuanian University. Thereafter, since his son died during the Action of the academics, right after the closing of the Ghetto, he remained alone, poor and without family. Due to the difficult ghetto conditions, he went out of his mind and thereafter was moved to the Crazy House [sic]. During the Action of the children, elderly and sick he, together with all the sick in the Crazy House, was transported for extermination.

The Deputy Chairman of the Ghetto Court was Adv. I. Abramovitch[a]. Later he became Deputy Chief of the Jewish Ghetto Police and aside from that had in his purview the Police Court. Lastly, he left the Police and transferred to the Large Ghetto Workshops.

The Prosecutor of the Ghetto Court was Adv. Buch. Thereafter, he moved to the Police Court. When the Jewish labor camp in Shantz was created, he was Camp Elder there for a certain time. During the Children's Action he fought to accompany his child and was thrown into a truck together with the captured children, in a horrible way.

On the court were also active: Adv. Rutenberg, Defender (died in Dachau); Adv. Zak[b] Judge; Mrs. Adv. Luntz, Court Secretary (saved herself in a ghetto bunker); Adv. Shinberg[c] and others.

Original footnotes:

   a. See "Jewish Ghetto Police"
   b. See "Jewish Ghetto Police"
   c. See "Elders Council"

CHAPTER XII

Ghetto Firefighters

-Firefighters Commando and its additional duties

[Page 391]

During the inception period for most of the ghetto institutions, i.e., the beginning of Autumn, 1941, a Firefighter Commando was also established, which had to protect the Ghetto from fires.

While the area of the Ghetto was comparatively large, three firefighter points were organized: a) near the Old Ghetto, on Linkever Street, b) around the blocks on Viteniu Street, and c) in the Large Ghetto Workshops. After the reduction of the area of the Old Ghetto only two last firefighter points remained active. The "inventory" of the firefighters consisted of a few wagons to carry ropes, water, and a pair of hand hoses and other firefighters' tools.

During the three years of the ghetto existence, the Ghetto Firefighters did not have much work because the Ghetto did not have any large fires. To put out the few fires that did break out at the time, it was necessary to call the city firefighters, because if not, the fire would spread to a larger number of ghetto houses.

At this opportunity it is necessary to mention that the ghetto population guarded itself from fires. Individually, they had to be very careful of the "ghetto *plitkes*," that means, the little tin sheet metal ovens which were manufactured in the Ghetto, which both heated and cooked a few pots at the same time. Because of the shortage of wood and because even more families lived in one apartment, these little *plitkes* ovens were very commonplace.

At first, there were about 50 ghetto firefighters. In parallel to the frequent reductions of the ghetto system, in the end there remained in total some 15-20 firefighters. Like the Ghetto Police and other higher functionaries of the ghetto institutions, the Firefighters also wore uniform hats and armbands – the symbol of "kingdom" in Ghetto.

[Page 392]

Aside from their direct duties, the firefighters also carried out the following auxiliary functions:

First, they helped the Ghetto Police and the Labor Office mobilize people to work, during the early ghetto period. Whenever it would be necessary to collect a certain number of Jews for forced labor, mainly for the Aerodrome, the Firefighters participated in these jobs. They also helped the Ghetto Police in their other jobs. In essence, they were a type of police assistant.

Second, their duty was to guard and maintain the Ghetto Fence. When someone tried to smuggle food products in through the Ghetto Fence, it would be necessary to fix the disturbed barbed wire of the fence around the Ghetto almost every day. By the way, this was a good chance for the Firefighters themselves to do business at the Ghetto Fence in the time of the "repair work."

For a certain time, the Firefighters also maintained a bakery which was very popular with the ghetto Jews during the hunger months in the Ghetto, from Autumn, 1941 until Spring, 1942. Even though their bread was almost always an unbaked, squashed dough, the hungry ghetto population never rejected such bread, which contained more water than flour…

During the liquidation of the Jewish ghetto institutions, during Goecke's time, the German camp management did not disband the Firefighters Commando and it remained in existence until the deportation from the Ghetto.

Those participating as Ghetto Firefighters were: Abramovich (liberated after leaving the Ghetto); Engineer Oshinsky, Finkelstein, Lipshitz (all were liberated in Dachau), and others.

CHAPTER XIII

Drawing and Painting Workshop

-Completion of various graphics works

[Page 393]

To complete the schematic picture of the ghetto institutions, it is necessary to also say a few words about the Drawing and Painting Workshop which was established at the end of 1941 and existed until the liquidation of the Ghetto.

The activity of the Drawing and Painting Workshop consisted of completing posters for public orders, compliances, and notices, which the Elders Council or other Jewish institutions needed to publicize to the population. They would also prepare the various symbols for the ghetto institutions, and the writing on the armbands for the Jewish Police, Firemen, Brigadiers and Column Leaders, higher officials, etc.

In the Painting Workshops they would also draw various diagrams about the activities of the ghetto institutions, especially for the Elders Council and from the Jewish Labor Office. A portion of the graphic work, together with the reports, would be sent over to the official regime divisions which had to do with the Ghetto. There they would also finish designs for work cards and other printed items, later to be duplicated, in a primitive manner, in the necessary number of copies.

But very quickly the Germans enjoyed the workmanship skill of the painting workshop, and they began to make orders for their institutions. The Nazi ghetto-rulers often observed the Drawing and Painting Workshop, not only during the period when the Ghetto was under the authority of the City Commissariat, but also during Goecke's time. So, for example, very often Goecke would sit there for hours and chat with the people of the workshop about painting, and similar topics.

[Page 394]

In the Large Ghetto Workshops, as we know, a division existed to produce dolls and other children's toys. These products were shipped to the Nazi's children in Germany. The models for these toy products would be finished under the supervision of craftsmen from the Painting Workshop.

Leading the Drawing and Painting Workshop was the gifted graphic artist Gadiel (liberated in Dachau); his assistants were: Engineer Mishelski, Mrs. Kagan, Mrs. Gurevitch (all survived to liberation); Schmidt, Rozenbaum, Rozin (all died), and others.

ADDENDUM – NOTES

1. Zionist Activity in the Ghetto
2. Samples of Ghetto Folklore

1. Zionist Activity in the Ghetto

[Page 397]

The Zionist stream took up a very distinguished position and developed an active role among the individual social groupings in the Ghetto.

As we know, after the Soviets marched into Lithuania in June 1940, all the Zionist organizations were liquidated, and the majority of the Zionist party leaders were deported to the Asiatic areas of Russia. The deportations took place just before the outbreak of war between Germany and the Soviet Union. However, the Zionist activities carried on under illegal conditions during the Soviet times. In the confined space of the Ghetto, it had "unrestrained" possibilities for development.

In the Ghetto, in November 1941, they started forming the first and most significant Zionist youth organization, "A.B. Z." (Organization of Alliance of Zion). Ideologically it stood between the general Zionists and Z.S. Leaders of the "A.B.Z." were: Itzhak Shapira, Arieh Cohen, Abraham Melamed, Shlomo Frenkel, Rozenberg, and others.

At the same time, tests were made to renew the Hebrew newsletter "*Nitzotz*" [spark] which started to appear illegally in Kovno, even during the Soviet period. Aside from this pair of volumes of "*Nitzotz*" a few volumes from the newsletter "*Shalhevet*" [flame] also appeared in the Ghetto with an edition dedicated to resistance issues. These editions did not get out to a large readership.

In April 1942, "*Matzok*" (Zionist Center Viliampole, Kovno) was founded. Involved in this center, aside from the Chairman and Deputy-Chairman of the Elders Council, Dr. Elkes and Adv. Garfunkel, were also Chairmen of the General Zionists – A' (Dr. Ch. G. Shapira), General Zionists B' (A. Golub), Revisionists (Hirsh Levin), and Z.S. (Srebnitzki). The Chairmen of "*Matzok*" was Dr. Shapira.

[Page 398]

Already at the establishment of "*Matzok*," the Zionist businessmen who had positions of responsibility in the ghetto hierarchy, tended to protect their former party members. This was evidenced in various ways, for example, by receiving "Jordan certificates," better work positions, etc.

As was already mentioned, "*Matzok*" maintained an influence also on the activity of the Elders Council and its institutions. So, for example, all the most important decisions of the Elders Council in carrying out the orders of the regime, and by deciding and dismissing the officials of the ghetto hierarchy, went through the filter of "*Matzok*."

In May 1942, "*Eshel*" (Organization for the Protection of Saplings) was established. The purpose of "*Eshel*" was a double one: guarding the Ghetto Gardens and organizing the Zionist youth. At the head of this youth organization were Dr. Shapira (from the Zionist side) and Dr. Yefim Rabinovitch (from the Economic Office). From those among the leaders of the youth leadership, we must mention: Itzhak Shapira ("A.B. Z.") and Leib Ipp (Revisionists). "A.B. Z." had the influence. "*Eshel*" had 300-400 youth from ages 14-18.

Aside from "A.B.Z." which was the most distinguished Zionist youth group, there were also other active Zionist youth streams, like "*Hashomer Hatzair*" (leading members: Rauzuk, Vaskoboynik;) "*Beitar*" (Ipp, Neishtot, Barishnik); "*Hachalutz-Hazair*;" "*Dror*" (Kaptshevski, and others).

The number of members in the youth organizations was comparatively small. So, for example in Summer, 1943 the largest youth organization "A.B.Z." had about 150 active members and a few hundred in its periphery. "*Beitar*" mainly had active members. Its periphery was small.

"A.B.Z." emphasized cultural educational activities for its members. For this purpose, they organized seminars for youth (led by Rozenberg) and for adults (Dr. Shapira). "*Beitar*," by comparison, was engaged in social help for its members, taking up important positions in the ghetto hierarchy, especially in the Police. "The Young Guard, *Hashomer Hazair*" and "The Young Pioneer, *Hechalutz Hazair*" founded the only Kibbutz in the Ghetto.

[Page 399]

The older Zionists gathered around the following Zionist streams: a) Z.S. (Meshkotz, Srebnitzki, Engineer Sadovski, B. Cohen, S. Goldshtein, A. Cohen); b) Revisionists (H. Levin, M. Levin, Bukanz, Gotstein); c) Jewish statesmen (Chaitin, Sherkovitch, Engineer Goldberg); d) "*Mizrachi*" (Melamed, Shuv); General Zionists A' (Dr. Shapira, Ch. Kagan, Dr. Levitan, Alexandrovitch); General Zionist B' (Golob, Dr. Katz, B. Takatsh, Klotz). The last four Zionist streams educated toward a type of unified front, i.e., "Coordination."

The leading persons of the "Coordination" were Ch. Kagan, and A. Golob. In the Summer of 1943, under the influence of the General Zionist A' and "*Hapoel HaMizrachi*," they established the organization "B.Z." (Zionist Union). The chairman of the "B.Z." was Dr. Shapira. After his death this office was taken up by Ch. Kagan.

"B.Z." postured to become the "United Zionist Organization" also after liberation. At this opportunity it is interesting to mention that even then, in the programs of these organizations, they predicted proclamations about a Jewish state in Eretz Israel (understandably, not knowing at all about similar decisions taken at the Biltmore Conference).

Also, "A.B.Z." was ideologically close to "B.Z.", and "A.B.Z." was much more progressive. Its program was not strongly Socialist, but it had a distinct social color. A. Cohen published a brochure about the ideological essence of the "A.B.Z". Thereafter, in February 1943, a platform was worked out from the "A.B.Z." that on the 10th and 11th of April 1943, a special Board meeting would be convened which confirmed this platform.

In July 1943 the "A.B.Z." and "The Young Guard" created the "Organizational Association of Zionist Youth." "*Beitar*" did not join this "union."

After the closing of the children's schools, they succeeded in creating Zionist youth circles near the Vocational School. Besides teaching various crafts, unofficially they were also learning general studies. From time to time, the youth groupings also organized cultural events and a large audience would attend.

At the end of 1942, many members of the former student organization became active, especially those from the civic groups.

[Page 400]

Aside from the cultural-social activity, the youth groups interested themselves in getting better workplaces for their members in the city brigades, in the ghetto workshops, and in the ghetto administration. During the time of recruitment for labor camps they would try to protect the interests of their own members.

Whatever was related to the conspiracy of the Zionist activity, we must say, that at first, they were very careful. Starting in the Summer of 1942, when the situation in the Ghetto became somewhat stabilized, the conspiracy returned to its earlier strong character.

In the Ghetto, whenever life was shaken-up, like for example, due to an Action or another decree, then social activities were temporarily paralyzed.

Also, as we know, in the movement to leave for the woods to join the partisans, the Zionist youth groups played an important role.

Zionist work was conducted not only in the ghetto settlement but also in the labor camps. For objective reasons, the work there was carried out on a much more restricted scale than in the Ghetto itself.

After the Children's Action, the "*Matzok*" itself became dissolved, but the youth groups did not halt their work. After the liquidation of the Elders Council, Dr. Elkes became nominated as "Elder Jew." Once again, contact was re-established between him and the Zionist groups. These connections were held until the deportations from the Ghetto.

The Jewish Police was liquidated and those leading the writings about ghetto events were killed at the 9th Fort. Thus, A. Cohen, on assignment from the Zionist groups, took over this work and did it during the final months of the Ghetto's existence.

Almost all leaders in the Zionist youth groups hid in the social-group hideouts during the deportation. But the largest portion died in the flames of the bombed and burned houses during the liquidation of the Ghetto.[a]

Original footnote:

    a.   Most of the information for these notes was received from colleague, Sh. Frenkel.

[Page 401]

2. Samples of Ghetto Folklore

During the three-year existence of the Kovno Ghetto creations of folklore emerged, like folksongs, witticisms, and jokes, just like in every other ghetto settlement. These creations mirrored the various aspects of the relationship between the tragic ghetto reality and the Jewish people.

Occupying a place of honor in this folklore were the Ghetto songs which were created by poets with the intention of "memorializing" the most important phenomena in ghetto life. Many of these songs quickly became the property of the entire ghetto collective.

With simple, but heartfelt and touching words, the ghetto poet complained about the murderous measures of the occupation regime, about the helpless Jewish population, mass slaughters, relocations, forced labor, physical and moral humiliations, etc.

Very popular ghetto creations were those which criticized or "parodied" public ghetto life in a satirical or humoristic manner. For example, they referred to corruption, protectionism and other wail-provoking evils and inequities of the Jewish ghetto administration toward most ghetto Jews, the unique social differentiation in ghetto life, and the like. Because of that, we can often glean much more from a folk song or witticism than from lengthy writings in understanding the pain and "happiness" of the ghetto person.

The purpose of this information is not to give a judgement or evaluation about the folklore of the Kovno Ghetto. Rather, it is only to submit a few characteristic samples of its folkloric creation and show how well it complements the material which is included in this book.

[Pages 402-403]

A. Folk Songs:

Song: A year has already passed...

Author unknown. Created in 1942; it was one of the numerous original Holocaust songs, where the bloody fate of the ghetto Jew under the Nazi death-regime was lamented. The anonymous author ends his Lamentations-Song with words of comfort which call for perseverance and hope for better times.

    a)
A year has already passed
In days of pain and in days of fear
Soon another comes
And tells us that nothing better is coming
With coiled barbed wire
The patches are tightly sewn on us
So, they recognize you immediately
You are a Jew! You are a Jew!

    b)
They came from far
With sharp swords at their side
With hearts thirsty for blood
With murder, with fury

They soon mowed us down
Cut down young, cut down old
From women to children - no difference
You are a Jew! You will die!

c)
The animal became satisfied
The swords sharpened and smooth
The world is in shambles from the huge catastrophe
The rest is worthless, entirely a horror
Separating us from people in the city
In chains, enslaved, pursued by all
Life abandoned and plagued…

d)
A short time has indeed passed
They take people without end
They pull them by night, here and there
The 9th Fort is not far
They pluck and tear us apart limb by limb
The animal never gets tired
When will it ever end?
Thinking about it terrorizes us!…

e)
We have no more strength
It is so difficult for us each hour
There should have already been time enough
To be freed from the Ghetto
Only bravery, brothers, not thoughts
This night will disappear
And the sun will shine for us
And call us: "come on, already, come on!" …

[Page 404]

Song: Jewish Brigades…

Lyrics – Abraham Axelrod. Melody by Pilsodski-Marsh: "We the First Brigade." Created at the end of 1941. This folklore creation described the humble Jewish "life" in the Ghetto and declared that the murderous Hitlerites must soon disappear.

A new time for us has come
A time of lament, need and pain
Away from us the sun and flowers
Remaining only a work-certificate.

Jewish brigades dressed up in patches
Marching, day in and day out
And hold back the sorrows - be bold!

You have created ghettos for us
And conducted many Actions
You made slaves and servants of us
And annihilating us is your goal.

Jewish brigades dressed up in patches
Marching, day in and day out
And hold back the sorrows - be bold!

We work for you and build
And you pay us with beatings
Strongly guarded by enemy convoys
We have no right to protest.

Jewish brigades dressed up in patches,
Marching, day in and day out
And hold back the sorrows - be bold!

We don't ask you for mercy
Not your pity, you hold no word
We know your hounds very well
The "nice events" at the 9th Fort.

Jewish brigades dressed up in patches
Marching, day in and day out
And hold back the sorrows - be bold!

We don't complain and cry to you,
Even when you hit and whip us
Therefore, you shouldn't think
That you will break our spirit.

Jewish brigades dressed up in patches,
Marching, day in and day out
And hold back the sorrows - be bold!

We will survive it, brothers
Our spring, our victory
Then we will straighten out our limbs,
And sing a new freedom song.

Jewish brigades, dressed up in patches,
Marching, the time is near.
The Spring is coming, it is not far!

[Page 405]

Song: The Aerodrome Worker

Lyrics – Abraham Tzipkin. Created in 1942. The Aerodrome worker, the "slave" of the Kovno Ghetto settlement, was described many times in his book "The Aerodrome Worker," which illustrated the inhumane conditions of this slave labor, through which thousands of Jews worked day and night.

Friends, I want to sing a song for you,
A song which cries out from my heart,
Telling you everything, like I see it,
Telling, telling the entire thing…

The early morning is gray, it is dark and wet,
Our bones are broken from yesterday,
The clothes are torn; they are hanging, still wet,
Soaked from the terrible weather.

Soft little hands knead the lime
Pure souls are suffering
Enough of this hell, we want to go home
This calamity cuts like knives…
Little boys carry gravel
Their strength is already disappearing

The master gives another swipe with his rod
And even adds a curse to the devil.

And food? – what food, when do they give food?
Water with cabbage, only to sip,
And searching hard for a grain pellet in the middle
We need to call it out of the pot…
Hands already thinned out and bodies already tired.

Life has already become ugly,
We don't want and can no longer sing any song,
It seems that everything is lost.
Just hold yourself, just strengthen yourself, you eternal Jew,
Don't lose hope and belief
It won't be bad forever, nor will the slavery last forever.
You will not be in pain forever!

[Page 406]

Song: At the Little Ghetto Gate

Lyrics– A. Axelrod. Melody "Oifn Pripitchok Brent a Fayerl" [A little fire is burning on the hearth]

This little song depicts the checkpoint at the Ghetto Gate, while Jews were returning from work in the city.

At the little ghetto gate
A fire is burning,
And the terror is great.
Jews are coming
From the brigades
And they are dripping with sweat.

Should I continue forward?
Or should I remain in place?
I don't know when or where.
The little commandant
In the little green coat
Takes everything away.

A chunk of wood,
Money from the little purse
Oy, horror, he's taking it:
Milk from the saucepan
Bacon from the scoop,
Jews, we're burned!

Hey, pal with the armband[a]
I am completely "illegal"

Help me get through the check point
For this, I will give you
A kilogram of bacon today
And tomorrow – more again.

Stand confidently.
You stay right near me.
Don't run to the side!
Go to the non-Jew on the right.
"This guy is already O.K." [In Lithuanian]
He gets a loaf of bread…

[Page 407]

Song: The Committee Guy

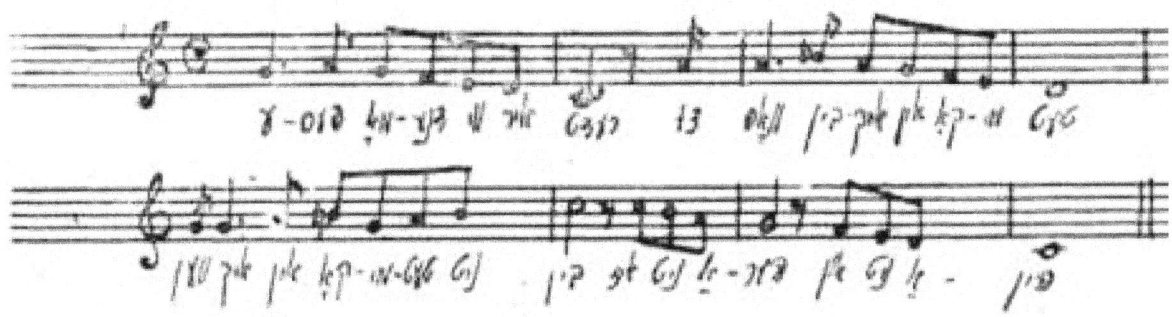

Lyrics – Natan Markovski. Created in 1942. A list of privileges flowed for the colleagues from the Jewish administration. This caused social antagonism between the "Committee guys" and most of the ghetto-Jews. The reader can get a picture of this situation from this song.

Something strange about how you speak.
Why am I in the Committee?
If I weren't in the Committee-
I would not be here or there…

Here, for example, there is a queue.
At the "bread bakery" they stand for hours.
That, however, is not for me,
They take me through the back door…

Potatoes are given, alas and alack
Wet, rotten, and full of straw.
However, I am not an idiot,
They give me from a different sack…

Or, wood is distributed by the river,
Wet and few – this is for you.

For me it is a different thing,
For me it is dry, and a lot…

To the Aerodrome we must go.
This you understand, yourself.
When you mention the fact,
That you are not in the Committee

One would be lucky to be in the brigade
Where they work at the "green bridge,"[b]
This is however only for "them."
For me it is the "Service-Police."[c]

Six persons in a kitchen.
At least they are sleeping crowded near a cooking stove.
For me it does not happen.
For me the room is just for one.

Now you will finally understand
What was mine was mine.
"If I were not in the Committee,
I would be neither here nor there" …

Indeed, I am telling you the truth.
In the Committee it is also not equitable.
One gets whatever he wants,
The other – remains a Don Quixote…

[Page 408]

Song: Big Shots

Lyrics– A. Axelrod. Created in 1942. This folk song is also a social critique about the same privileged elements in the Ghetto – the Big Shots [*Yales*]

    Tell me, tell me you little ghetto Jew,
    Who plays the first fiddle in the Ghetto?
    Who among the big shots, some more, some less,
    Wants to rule here just like a king.

    Cymbals, cymbals, play little ghetto-Jew,
    Play a little song about the Jewish big shots-

    About all the "chiefs" and "inspectors"
    Who became important people in the Ghetto…
    Who from among the big shots can give out a work card,
    And a certificate to remain alive?
    And how much does one have to pay,
    To get into a good brigade?

    Cymbals, cymbals, play little ghetto-Jew.
    Play a little song about the Jewish big shots-

    Why do the big shots eat white baked goods,
    Warm little bagels, rolls and biscuits?

And enjoy music and playing cards,
And celebrate "holidays" with real cakes?

Cymbals, cymbals, play little ghetto-Jew
Play a little song about the Jewish big shots.

Have the big shots ever worked at the Aerodrome
With an ax, with a shovel, or with a disability?
Maybe our big shots would have understood
Why the poor masses are asking such questions.

Cymbals, cymbals, play little ghetto-Jew.
Play a little song about the Jewish big shots.

Who needs the concerts amid great sadness,
And the hunger wails in the poor man's home?
Better get them a bowl of "pig swill"
And stop celebrating at the big shots' parties…

Cymbals, cymbals, play little ghetto-Jew.
Play a little song about the Jewish big shots.

[Pages 409 - 410]

Song: Not your luck…

Lyrics and music – Shaul Shenker. A fragment from a song about "equity" among the Jewish officials and how they distributed passes to a working woman, the so-called ghetto-madam…

> Little Deborah goes in to see the doctor.
> Her nose is covered with a lovely little handkerchief.
> My dear Sir Doctor, give me a day's pass.
> That guy with the little white hat[d] - he should go to hell
> I rested a little while on the grass,
> So, he came running and broke my nose…"

> "Not your luck to be free,
> We must do forced labor, guys, we must go.
> There is no pass, don't delude yourself.
> Tomorrow there must be the full demanded number."[e]

> To the same little table, a madam comes by.
> She has no idea about working at the Aerodrome.
> Her eyes are shining, her lips – like blood,

She courageously speaks to the inspector in Russian.
"Today I demand of you again, give me a pass for 25 days."

"You are lucky, you are free,
You'll receive a new pass again
With such eyes, lips, and teeth
Of course, you won't go to the Aerodrome…"

[Page 411]

Song: Tall Man!

Lyrics- N. Markowski. Created in 1942. V. Lurie described the brutal attitude towards the ghetto-people by the people from the Aerodrome-division of the Jewish Labor Office. In his folk song (this is only a fragment from the song) the writer depicts the "dictatorial" manner of this angry Jewish ghetto ruler.

In the Ghetto there was
A really big man
Who became a tyrant here.
Every early morning
He chased people, like livestock
Thinking that he will live forever.
Always wild, screaming and cursing
At the people with a wild animal roar.

Tall man, big man, give a smile.
Don't make yourself out to be a hero in the Ghetto.
Tall man, big man, be smart.
Know that there will yet be a different world.

I don't understand what he thinks
That brought him to this.
What did it take that he alone would have the power?
Screams, like he is the only honest one.
Except for him – no one else.
Only we know indeed, that to be honest is difficult.
One is brought salt,
One is brought fat,
But for him, they indeed bring him everything.

Tall man, big man, give a smile.
Here there is no place for dictators.
Tall man, big man, be smart.
Know that this is not the last word…

[Pages 412-413]

Song: Yiddish Tango

Lyrics by Reuven Tzarfat. In pre-war Jewish Lithuania this author was a familiar writer, who received notoriety with his fourteen successful pamphlets. "Jewish Tango" which was much more than an ordinary folklore-creation and was very popular far beyond the borders of the Jewish Kovno settlement. The writer was killed in the Dachau labor camps.

>Play a tango for me in Yiddish.
>It could be Misnagdish or Chasidish.
>So that grandmother herself
>Should be able to understand it.
>And, indeed, dance to it a while!
>
>   Chorus:
>Play, play orchestra, play.
>Like a Jewish heart with feelings
>Play, with soul, with feeling, I beg you,
>Play a little dance for me, oh, play.

Play me a tango about refugees.
About people separated and dispersed.
So that big and small children
Should be able to understand it,
And, indeed, dance to it a while!

Chorus
Play, play orchestra, play.
Like a Jewish heart with feelings
Play, I beg you, with soul, with feeling.
Play a little dance for me, oh, play!

Play for me a tango, not at all Aryan.
It shouldn't be Aryan, nor barbarian.
So, the enemies should see
That I can still dance
A little dance, still with fire!

Chorus
Play, play orchestra, play!
Like a Jewish heart with feelings
Play, I beg you, with soul, with feeling.
Play for me a little dance, oh, play!

Play for me a tango about peace.
It should be peace, not a dream,
That Hitler with his Reich,
Oy, the direct atonement
Oh, will that be a little dance for you!

Chorus
Play, play orchestra, play!
Like a Jewish heart with feelings.
Play, I beg you, with soul, with feeling.
Play for me a little dance, oh, play!

[Page 414]

B. Folk Sayings, Jokes, etc.

YALEH: the following is the "story" about this ghetto word: In Autumn, 1941, thousands of Jews were engaged in forced labor at the Kovno Aerodrome. The relations of the masters and guards to the Jewish workers was quite harsh. When a guard or a master stepped away from the workplace for a while, the Jews could catch their breath and not work. However, they would have to watch carefully in case a supervisor returned unexpectedly. They would get deathly beatings for such "violations." One day, during a moment of rest among the workers, the Carmelite Rabbi Broude,[1] saw a German guard approaching. He started shouting: "*Yaleh v'yavo.*" [from a Hebrew blessing]. With that he meant to warn the Jews that a German is coming. From then on, the word "*Yaleh*" became a code word at the workplace, signifying that a supervisor is approaching. Later the word "*Yaleh*" became a synonym not only for a non-Jewish tyrant, but also for a

Jewish ghetto "official." The word "Yales" referred to the higher functionaries of the Jewish ghetto administration.

VITAMIN "P": the plague of protectionism, among other plagues, which ensnared all areas of public ghetto life, was touched upon in the description of the activities of the Jewish ghetto institutions. Efforts by the simple Jews to get something from a ghetto institution was almost always unsuccessful if they didn't have any acquaintances or introduction to someone from the leading Jewish ghetto officials. In ghetto life, the ruling "principle" was, take care of me and I will take care of you. That meant, you do me a favor and I will serve you with something. This protectionism reigned especially in the Jewish Labor Office, which would distribute the better workplaces mainly to persons who were protected by a "*Yaleh*." In such a case it was said that the Jew has Vitamin "P" (a vitamin of Protectionism). For short, they would call it "vitamin." For example, "he has a vitamin from this one or that one"; "he is a person with vitamins;" "there is a spot for those who have vitamins," and the like.

[Page 415]

NOT YOUR LUCK: if a common Jew wanted to aspire to some better workplace or get something which was accessible only to the "higher" classes in the Ghetto, and his efforts did not bring any positive results, it would be said: "not your luck to get it"; "it is not your luck to access it," etc.

MAKING A PACKAGE: one of the most painful issues in ghetto life (aside from extermination Actions, captures, and other decrees) was the question of something to eat. The Jew had to risk his life and often also the lives of his family members to acquire a bit of bread and something along with it for the family. The Gestapo would punish them very harshly for this illegal buying of food products, oftentimes also with death. However, the drive to quell their hunger did not hold anyone back from getting a bit of food through work. "Making a package" meant buying food products from Christians at affordable prices and thereafter smuggling it into the Ghetto.

COMPRESS: to illegally smuggle purchased food products in through the checkpoint at the Ghetto Gate, they would have to hide the food in various ways. One of the numerous types of disguises was "making a compress." This meant binding up the little bit of flour, the piece of meat, butter, etc. on the body around oneself like a compress. Mainly women would do this. The checkpoint guards did not always manage to check every Jew so thoroughly each time. In this way, the majority would succeed in fooling the gate officials with a compress.

[Page 416]

BURNED UP: if the gatekeepers did find some food product on a Jew, they would confiscate it and, in addition, often punish him with a slap or a beating. In the case of confiscation, it was said that they were "burned up" at the gate. During a very strict control, the Jews would warn each other at the gate with the codeword: "we're burning!"

ORGANIZING: this meant simply swiping something from one's workplace, like for example, grain, vegetables, factory products, and the like. Several ghetto Jews paid with their lives for unsuccessful attempts at "organizing" something. For such sins they were transferred to the Gestapo. It must be said that the inhumane living conditions in the Ghetto and especially in the concentration camps would loosen people's moral inhibitions. So, with a light heart they would allow themselves various "permissions" …

MALINA: this little word had many meanings: a) a bunker or a hiding place where one could hide himself until the fury passed during an Action, or some other ghetto calamity;   b) a good workplace, where work conditions were favorable, and c) a place where one could buy food at inexpensive prices. In such cases they might say: I caught a real *malina*;" "this is a one-time *malina*," and the like.

YOSHNIK: a cooked dish without meat or fat. A soup which consisted of water with some cabbage leaves and a few potatoes. The Jews would receive such "soup" at lunch at the Aerodrome and other labor sites as well as in the kitchen of the Social Office. The very word "yoshnik" means feed which is given to pigs.

[Page 417]

MALACH: someone who has a good workplace, could also be assigned to work at the Aerodrome or at another hard labor site for one or two days. A materially enabled Jew could rent a non-duty youth or older person to substitute for him. Such a substitute was called a "*malach*." [angel]

STEPPING, BOTHERING: this meant working, carrying the heavy yoke of forced labor, or hard labor at the Aerodrome, or in a difficult city brigade.

WITH THE NOURISHMENT COMES THE MOTION: the Nazis, as we know, designated hunger-based nourishment for the Jews and, in parallel, required that the Jews do the most difficult forced labor. When a German master or guard started to force the Jews to work harder and screamed: "move!" So, the Jews, more to themselves than to the Germans, murmured: "with the nourishment comes the motion..."

EVERY BIG SHOT HAS HIS BRIDE: it was already pointed out that certain higher functionaries in the Jewish ghetto hierarchy, from time to time, allowed themselves to have "parties" and other forms of entertainment for "their own people." Aside from that, these elements would strongly violate the [commandment] Thou Shalt Not Covet and, also other prohibitions. Many of them had "lovers" who would exercise strong influence on their "admirers". These "festivities in the time of an epidemic" and other outbreaks of lawlessness reached such lengths that the ghetto people responded in its fashion with a witticism, or with a little folk song: "Every *Yaleh* has his bride, and the police… have two."

[Page 418]

THE BROWN HOUSE: the building on Varniu Street 49, where the Elders Council, the Jewish Labor Office, and other important ghetto institutions were located, happened to be painted brown. Bolstered by the Jewish ghetto "kingdom," Jews would sarcastically call the quarters of the Elders Council "the brown house" – a reference to Hitler's brown house…

JEWS ARE FORT PEOPLE: various German commissions and inspectors often came into the Ghetto and held conferences about the fate of the ghetto population. Understandably, Jews would truly gobble up even the smallest sound regarding decisions of the commission. In Spring 1944, when the Ghetto was already on the eve of liquidation, a commission of high Nazis came to the Ghetto. The rumor that spread among the Jews about the commission's decision regarding the Ghetto, was the following: the Commission realized that the Jews are Fort People. That meant, people who must be killed at the Fort… (the opposite possible interpretation, in this sense, was that Jews are "obviously" people).

THE MEANING OF 'SOMETHING ELSE': one ghetto Jew asks the other: "Tell me, what is the meaning of the term "something else?" The second Jew answers: "as a matter of fact, the term "something else" has more meanings; but the best meaning is a pig."

SALVATION ON THE NOSE, SLAUGHTER KNIFE ON THE NECK: in July 1944, with the approach of the front line, deportation and liquidation of the Ghetto became likely. The Jews characterized that situation with a sharp minded witticism: "salvation lies on the nose, and the slaughter-knife, on the neck." That meant, on the one hand, liberation was very close, and on the other, the danger that the Nazis would kill the rest of the surviving Jews still remained.

Original footnotes:

    a.   a Jewish functionary at the Gate.
    b.   A very difficult workplace where the simple Jews worked renovating the Kovno railroad bridge.
    c.   One of the best city brigades where the "aristocratic" men and women of the Ghetto. worked.
    d.   A German Aerodrome supervisor who would beat the Jews.
    e.   Means the demanded number of Jewish workers for forced labor.
    f.   He was taken to Riga during the first relocation Action in February 1942 and was killed in a labor camp.

[Pages 419-423].

INDEX OF NAMES
[Page numbers from the original text]

A

Abramovich, Adv. Yakov, 311, 390
Abramovich, Dr., 369
Abramovich, 392
Acabas, Dentist, 369
Alexandrovich, 342, 399
Aloiz, Monach, 170
Altman, 332
Aranovski, 252, 311, 342
Arbeter, Dora, 259
Arliock, 281
Arnshtam, T., 218, 293, 311, 340, 342
Auer, S. S. Staff Sergeant, 346
Axelrod, Abraham, 404, 406, 408
Aylberg, 332

B

Baal-Machshavot, 21
Baicovitz, 357
Bargman, Engineers, 319, 338
Bar-Kupritz, 310
Bar-Vishtanetzki, Dr., 369
Barishnik, 398
Belatzkin, Prof. Shimon, 368, 390
Bentzko, Camp leader, 178, 224, 240
Beregovski, 323
Berger, 311
Berkman, 332
Berman, R., 143, 191
Berman, Dr., 281, 369
Berniker, F., 379
Bernstein, Adv. Israel, 298, 346, 377
Bernstein Fritz, 329
Bernstein, 356
Blasberg, Dr. 369
Blatt, 332
Bliacher, 358
Bloch, Sh., 352
Blumberg, Dr., 369
Blumental, Eng., T., 252, 332
Bonim, 347
Borstein, brothers, 309
Bobialis, Polkovnik, 34, 41
Borochovitz, Alte, 193
Braunz, Dr., 369
Braz, 332
Brakaytiteh, Ana, Monachin, 170
Bramson, M., 193, 252, 311, 348
Brick, H., 110
Broude, Rabbi, 414
Buch, Adv., 390
Bukantz, 311, 319
Burstein, Michael, 252, 379

Burstein, Daniel, 247
Burstein, 251

C

Caspi-Serebrovitch, 113, 114, 286
Chatzkels, Helene, 266
Charashtenishok, 332
Chaykin, Adv., 377, 379
Chaitin, 399
Chvales, 311, 342
Cohen, Arieh, 397, 399, 400
Cohen, Berl, 266, 399

D

Daitsch, A., 323
Davidovich, Mrs., 323
Davidovich, 329
Davidovich, 335
Diner, Adv., 266
Dukshtolski, Mrs., 309

E

Edelshtein, 357
Eizenshtat, Dr., 369
Elkes, Dr., Elchanan, 47, 53, 73, 80, 106, 131, 158, 166, 202, 218, 219, 233, 283, 284, 286, 294, 295 296, 297, 370, 397, 400
Elkes, Dr., G., 369
Elshtein, 299
Epshtein, 349,
Epshtein, R., 370

F

Feldshtein, Dr., 369
Felman, 334
Fentzter, 357
Fin, 357
Finkel, 309
Finkelshtein, Dr., Ch., 337
Finkelshtein, 392
Fleishmann, Chef from Ghetto guard, 132
Flink-Yoselevich, 370
Flier, 329
Friedman, B., 110
Friedman, Benyamin, 269
Freidman, brothers, 332
Friedman, Dr., 337
Freidman, 332
Frenkel, Engineer, 320
Frenkel, Herman, 320
Frenkel, Shlomo, 397
Frenkel, V., 332
Frenkel, Sh., 334

G

Gadiel, 394
Gar, Yosef, 266, 332
Garber, Sonia, 266
Garfunkel, Av. Leib, 47, 219, 252, 279, 284, 296, 297, 397
Gemelitzki, 110, 281, 346
Gempel, 90
Gerber, Dr., 90
Gerstein, Dr., 369
Gerstein, 384
Gershovitch, Adv., N., 332, 364, 374,
Gershovitch, Agronomist, 351
Glagovski, R., 370
Gladstein, 309
Glazman, Yosef, 114
Glatt, Sh., 374
Glickman, 332
Glickman, Dentist, 369
Goecke, S.S, Lt. Colonel, 100, 116, 150, 151, 152, 153, 155, 157, 158, 161, 166, 173, 180, 181, 185, 186, 187, 189, 200, 201, 203, 204, 205, 212, 213, 218, 219, 221, 222, 223, 224, 225, 228, 232, 233, 234, 237, 238, 241, 286, 294, 295, 309, 344, 355, 356,
Golach, Professor, Dr., 369
Goldberg, Adv. Yakov, 47, 219, 279, 284, 297, 298, 319
Goldman, Eng., 329
Goldstein, Sh., 374, 399
Goldschmidt, Engineer, F., 266, 347
Golub, Adv. Abraham, 284, 299, 385, 397, 399
Gordon, 332
Gottstein, 399
Gotz, Mrs., 370
Grossman, 311
Griliches, 323
Griliches, Dentist, 369
Grinberg, Dr., 332, 369
Grinberg, 334
Grinberg, Yitzhak, 99, 192, 206, 311
Grinhoiz, Dr., Shmuel, 252, 319
Grinfeld, 251
Gurevitch, L., 357
Gurevitch-Eliashkevitch, Dr., 369
Gurevitch, Dr., 369
Gurevitch, Mrs. Dr., 266
Gurevitch, 386
Gurevitch, Miss., 394
Gutman, 100

H

Halpern, Dima, 190
Hauer, George, 111
Hayir, Percy, 309

Herman, S.A. Captain, 105, 106, 141, 343, 344
Hirsh, 332
Hofmekler, Misha, 309

I

Idelson, 332
Indurski, 349
Ingel, 370
Ipp, Dr., 369
Ipp, Leib, 398
Irena, 146
Isserlis, 251, 342
Itzikovich, David, 385

J

Joels, 357
Jordan, Ghetto spokesperson, 46, 56, 59, 61, 62, 76, 78, 84, 94, 95, 96, 107, 121, 285

K

Kadushin, Mrs., 350
Kagan, Ch., 110, 281, 379, 399
Kagan, Dr., 369
Kagan, Dentist, Mrs., 369
Kagan, Elchanan, 193
Kagan, 394,
Kagan, 332
Kalvariski, 308v Kamber, Mrs., Dr., 369
Kaminskas Ghetto spokesperson, 45, 54, 61, 285, 375
Kantorovich, 353
Kaptshevski, 326, 398
Kapit, 386
Kaplan, Mrs. Dr., 369
Kaplan, 353
Kariski, 304
Karpus, 332
Katz, Dr., 369, 399
Katz, 364
Kaufman, Dr., 369
Kelzon, Agronomist, 110, 351
[von] Kepen, Ghetto spokesperson, 124, 285
Kittel, Jewish spokesperson in Gestapo, 117, 161, 192, 196, 205, 211, 216, 218, 222, 227, 228
Kirkila, Lithuanian Officer, 42
Kizel, 100, 386
Klebanov, Dr., 369
Klibanski, Dr., 369
Klompus, 332
Klotz, 399
Koniuchovski, 332
Kopelman, 281, 311
Koretchinski, 311
Kovarski, 357
Koziol, Adv., 374

Kozlovski, Chef of Ghetto guard, 64, 131,
Krakinovski, Pine, 182
Krakinovski, 320
Kramer, Hans, Kovno City Commissar, 45, 68, 70, 94, 149, 309
Kreve-Mitzkevicius, Professor, 24
Krok, 370
Krom, 351
Kubilionas, General, 34
Kupritz, 310

L
Lapidus, 356
Lazerson, Professor, 369
Leibowich-Goldshmidt, Dentist, Mrs., 370
Leibowich, Ch., 369
Leibzon, 332
Leibenzon, I., 379
Lemchen, 100
Levin, Hirsh, 192, 266, 298, 346, 398, 399
Levin, Money, 196
Levin, 205
Levin, Moshe, 155, 192, 206, 311, 399,
Levin, Rafael, 266, 323
Levin, 350
Levin, Mrs. 370
Levin-Abramovitch, 266
Levin, 386,
Levin, Mrs. Dr., 386
Levitan, 309
Levitan, Dr., 337, 399
Levner, 205
Levenshtein, 342
Lint, 309, 332
Lipman, 385
Liptzer, Benno, 89, 114, 115, 116, 117, 143, 211, 216, 286, 311
Lipshitz, 332, 334
Lipshitz, R., 370
Lipshitz-Veiner, 370
Lipshitz, 392
Lubetzki, 332
Luntz, Mrs. Adv., 390
Lurieh, Adv., Volf, 293, 328, 340
Lurieh, 332
Lurieh, I., 342
Lurieh, 347
Lurieh, Dentist, 369

M
Makovski, Av., 332
Mapu, Abraham, 21
Margolis, P., 156, 293, 325, 340
Margolis, Dentist, Mrs. 370
Markovski, N., 155, 338, 326, 340, 411
Markovski, 326

Matematik, Chaim, 117
Mattis, Dr., Moshe, 369
Mattis, Dr. (son), 369
Matz, Dr., Shmuel, 36
Meizel, Olia, 193
Melamed, Abraham, 386, 397, 399
Melamdovich, 308, 326, 344
Mendelson, 326
Mek, 130, 132, 133
Meris, 344
Meshkotz, 364, 399
Miya, Camp Commander, 176, 177
Mizrach, 332
Michles, brothers, 110
Mil, Engineer, 316, 332
Miller, Ghetto Spokesperson, 133, 285
Milshtein, 349
Mishelski, Engineer, 394
Mudrik, 351

N
Nabriski, Dr., 370
Nachumovski, Dr., 337
Nachumzon, 332
Naftal, 332
Nakan, Dr., 369
Natkin, 342
Neividel, 348
Neishtot, 398
Nechmod, 310
Nementshik, Dentist, Mrs., 370
Nissenboim, 332

O
Ogov, 323
Oleiski, Agronomist, Yakov, 334
Olitzki, Dentist, 369
Oretshkin, Boris, 136, 332
Orlianski, Dr., 369
Oshry, Rabbi, 384
Osovski, Rabbi, 38
Oshinsky, Eng., 392

P
Padison, 311
Paletzskis, Justas, 25
Panemunski, 311
Paukshtis, Galach, 170
Paul, General, 279
Pertzikovich, Dr., 369
Perkol, 342
Pilovnik, Aydl, 193
Pilovnik, Tuvia, 193
Pilgram, S.S. Staff Sergeant, 198, 234, 244

Pikert, 332
Pomerantz, 309
Portnoy, Dr., 182
Potroch, 346
Prisman, 326

R
Rabinovich, Dr., Yefim, 47, 279, 398
Rabinovich, Dr., Itzhak, 106, 344
Rabinovich, Mrs., 344
Rabinovich, B., 335
Rabinovich, 348
Rapaport, 356
Ratner, Engineer, Sh., 156, 190, 334
Ratner, David, 156, 191
Ratnikas, Lithuanian Police officer, 135
Rauca, Gestapo-official, 55, 72, 73, 76, 77, 78, 84, 163, 294
Rauzuk, 398
Razin, Dr., 349
Razin, 394
Rebelski, Professor, 266
Rein, 333
Reiness, Engineer, 332
Reznik, 358
Richman, Dr., 369
Ring, S.S. Captain, 110
Rochelzon, 357
Roginski, Engineer, 281
Rostowski, 299
Rozmarin, 309
Rozenberg, Alfred, Reich person, 100
Rozenberg, 397-398
Rozental, Sh, 384
Rozenblat, 386
Rozenbaum, 394
Rozenblum, Mrs. Dr., 369
Rubinson, 311
Rutenberg, Adv., 390

S
Sadovski, Engineer, 334, 399
Sapozshnikov, Menashe, 191
Segal, Dr., 369, 374
Segal, Mrs. Dr., 386
Segal, R., 349
Segalovski, 347
Segalson, M., 110
Segalson, Prov., 350
Seletzki, 350
Senior, Leah, 193
Shabashevich, 332
Shachnovski, Engineer, 332
Shafranski, 332

Shalit, 358
Shalitan, Z., 342
Shapiro, Rabbi, 73, 279, 294, 385,
Shapiro, Dr., Chaim-Nachman, 298, 385, 386, 397, 398, 399
Shapiro, D., 370
Shapiro, Itzchak, 386,397, 398
Shauchet, 374
Shevtz, 370
Shenker, Shaul, 410
Sherman, Moshe, 191, 266
Shinberg, Adv., 299, 357, 390
Shtitz, Jewish spokesperson in Gestapo, 115, 117, 128, 136
Shtein, 332
Shtein, Dentist Mrs., 370
Steinberg, 357
Shuv, 399
Shvartz, Y., 110
Shvartz, Sh., 342
Shlopoverski, Dr., 344
Shmerkovich, 374, 399
Shmidt, Dr. 350
Shmidt, 394
Shmuckler, Rabbi, 47, 279, 298
Shmuckler, Mrs. Dr., 310
Shmuckler, 299
Shor, 309
Shpegel, 251
Shtreichman, 281
Skirpa, Polkovnik, 34
Slonimski, Engineer, 332
Slonimski, 342
Slove, R., 370
Smetana, Antanas, 19, 24, 46
Snieg, Rabbi, 47, 279, 298
Snieg, Mrs., 386
Sobolevich, Mrs., 386
Solomin, 269
Srebnitzki, Prov., 350, 398, 399
Srebnitzki, 347
Srolovich, 332
Staravolski, A., 332
Stokol, 386
Stopel, Abrasha, 309
Strashon, Frida, 266
Strelitz, A., 370
Sudak-Katz, 370 Sukenik, 320
Svirsky, 364

T
Tamshe, Dr., 332
Tankel, Mrs. Dr., 369
Tarko, I., 342
Tchatch, B., 308, 399

Telzak, brothers, 358
Tepper, David, 266
Tint, Z., 370
Tornbaum, Police Chief, 57, 76,
Treger, D., 347, 374
Tubialis, Lithuaian Prime Minister, 295

TZ
Tzarfat, Mrs., 386
Tzarfat, Reuven, 413
Tzeitel, Dr., 369
Tzindler, 335
Tzipin, 332
Tzipkin, Abraham, 332, 405
Tzitzes, 332

U
Ullman, 356

V
Valsonok, Dr., Rudolf, 191, 328, 379
Varantz, 347
Verbovski, Yankel, 171, 342
Videman, Ghetto spokesperson, 285
Viduchinski, Dr., 369
Vilenski, 351
Vindsberg, Dr., 337
Vinik, 323, 332
Volf, Dr., Gregory, 47, 281, 298
Volf, Dr., 332
Volfberg, 309
Volfe, 379
Volfovich, 386
Volpert, 251
Voskoboynik, 398
Voshtshin, Dr., 370

W
Weiner, 308
Weintraub, 364

Y
Yasvon, 332
Yatkonski, Mordechai, 37
Yatkonski, Dentist, Mrs., 38
Yatzkan, 333
Yeglin, 374
Yeger, S.A.-Shtandartnfurer, 279,
Yellin, Chaim, 145, 190, 225, 226 227, 228
Yellin, L., 234, 358
Yellin, Engineer, 266, 332
Yellin, 309
Yellin, Mrs., 266
Yeshorin, 332

Yitzhak-Elhanan, Head Rabbi, 21, 106
Yochelson, I., 346
Yochelson, Mrs. Dr., 369
Yotkovski, 344

Z
Zacharin, Dr., 249, 369
Zak, Adv., 311, 332, 390
Zaks, Yakov, 310
Zaks, 326
Zaltsberg, Dr., 369
Zeltzer, 311
Zhopovich, 342, 386
Zhopovich, Yudel, 206, 311
Zieman, H., 229
Zilberkveit, Adv., 205, 311
Zilberman, 377
Zundelevich, 323

Name Index
For the English Translation

A

Abetz, 64
Abramovich, 241, 255
Abramovitch, 204, 253
Abramson, 200
Akabas, 241
Aks, 216
Alexandrovitch, 223, 257
Altman, 216
Aranovski, 223
Arbeter, 170
Arenshtam, 145
Arloik, 184
Arnshtam, 191, 204, 222, 223
Aronovski, 165, 204
Axelrod, 261, 264, 267
Aylberg, 216

B

Baicovitz, 233
Balkin, 228
Balosher, 250
Bargman, 209, 221
Barishnik, 257
Bar-Vishtagetzky, 241
Belatzkin, 240, 253
Ben-Eliezer, 115
Beregovski, 211
Berger, 204
Berkman, 216
Berman, 92, 116, 126, 184, 241
Berniker, 247
Bernstein, 195, 214, 226, 233, 246
Blasberg, 241
Blatt, 216
Bliacher, 234
Bloch, 216
Blumberg, 241
Blumental, 165, 216
Bobelias, 20
Bobelis, 25
Bonim, 227
Borochovitz, 127
Borshtein, 203
Borstein, 200
Bramson, 127, 165
Braunz, 241
Braz, 216
Brick, 70
Brokaitite, 110
Bromson, 204, 227
Broude, 273
Buch, 253
Bukantz, 204
Bukanz, 257
Burshtein, 30, 162, 165, 172
Burstein, 139, 246

C

Caspi-Serebrovitch, 75, 76
Caspi-Serebrovitz, 187, 196
Chaitin, 257
Charashtshenishok, 216
Chatzkels, 176
Chaykin, 246, 247
Chvales, 223
Chvoles, 204
Cohen, 176, 256, 257, 258

D

Daitch, 211
Dariski, 203
Davidovich, 211, 214
Davidovitch, 218
Defender, 253
Diner, 176
Dukshtolski, 203
Dvoretsky, 231

E

Edelstein, 234
Eizenstadt, 241
Elkes, 27, 33, 44, 49, 67, 86, 103, 108, 133, 139, 145, 146, 154, 161, 185, 187, 192, 193, 194, 241, 246, 256, 258
Elstein, 195
Epstein, 228, 241

F

Feldstein, 241
Felman, 217
Fentster, 234
Fin, 233
Finkel, 203
Finkelshtein, 220
Finkelstein, 255
Fleishmann, 86
Flier, 214
Flink-Yoselevich, 241
Frebelistin, 249
Freidman, 176
Frenkel, 209, 216, 217, 256, 259

Friedman, 5, 70, 216, 220

G

Gadiel, 256
Gar, 1, 3, 4, 5, 7, 176, 182, 216
Garber, 176
Garfunkel, 27, 145, 146, 165, 183, 193, 194, 256
Gemelitzki, 70, 226
Gemelitzski, 184
Gempel, 57
Gerber, 58
Gershovich, 237
Gershovitch, 216, 230, 244
Gershtein, 241, 250
Gilde, 220
Ginsboim, 216
Gladstein, 203
Glagovski, 241
Glatt, 244
Glazman, 75
Glickman, 216, 241
Goecke, 70, 76, 77, 83, 99, 100, 101, 102, 103, 105, 108, 112, 119, 120, 122, 123, 124, 132, 133, 134, 135, 142, 145, 146, 147, 148, 149, 151, 154, 155, 157, 158, 159, 161, 187, 192, 193, 198, 202, 203, 214, 217, 224, 232, 236, 239, 244, 246, 255
Golach, 241
Goldberg, 27, 145, 183, 194, 196, 209, 216, 220, 257
Goldman, 214
Goldschmidt, 227
Goldshmidt, 8, 176
Goldshtein, 165, 257
Goldstein, 200, 241, 244
Golob, 250, 257
Golub, 195, 256
Golvitch, 176
Gotstein, 257
Gotz, 241
Griliches, 211, 241
Grinberg, 64, 127, 135, 204, 216, 217
Grinfeld, 165
Grinhaus, 209
Grinhoiz, 165
Grossman, 204
Gurevitch, 256
Gurvitch, 233, 241
Gurvitch-Eliashkevitz, 241
Gutman, 64

H

Halpern, 125
Hart, 158
Hauer, 71
Hayir, 203
Herman, 67, 91, 224
Hermann, 224

Himmler, 164
Hirsh, 216
Hitler, 6, 7, 14, 17, 20, 32, 55, 56, 60, 75, 88, 113, 137, 161, 163, 164, 166, 167, 168, 174, 176, 177, 182, 190, 191, 235, 273, 275
Hofmekler, 200, 203

I

Idelson, 216
Igdalski, 241
Indursky, 228
Ingel, 241
Ipp, 241, 257
Isserlis, 165, 223
Itzikovitch, 250, 251

J

Jaeger, 183
Joels, 234
Jordan, 27, 34, 36, 37, 38, 46, 47, 54, 60, 61, 68, 80, 186, 242, 257

K

Kadisch, 199
Kadushin, 229
Kagan, 70, 127, 184, 216, 241, 246, 256, 257
Kalvariski, 202
Kamber, 241
Kaminskas, 27, 33, 34, 37, 186, 244
Kantorovich, 231
Kapit, 251
Kaplan, 231, 241
Kaptchevski, 212
Kaptshevski, 257
Kariski, 200
Karpus, 216
Kaspi-Serebrowitz, 63
Katz, 237, 241, 257
Kaufman, 241
Kelzon, 70, 230
Kirkila, 25
Kittel, 77, 125, 126, 129, 131, 135, 141, 144, 145, 147, 150, 151
Kizel, 64, 251
Klebanov, 241
Klibanski, 241
Klompus, 216
Klotz, 257
Kobiliunas, 20
Kolodny, 176
Koniuchovski, 216
Kopelman, 184, 204
Koretchenski, 204
Kovarski, 233
Koziol, 244

Kozlovski, 39, 86
Krakinovski, 120, 209
Kramer, 27, 41, 42, 60, 74, 98, 202
Kreve-Mizkevicius, 15
Krok, 241
Krom, 230
Kupritz, 203

L

Lapidus, 233
Lazerson, 241
Leibenzon, 246
Leibovich-Goldschmidt, 241
Leibovitz, 241
Lemchen, 64
Levenshtein, 223
Levin, 102, 126, 129, 135, 161, 176, 194, 204, 211, 226, 229, 241, 251, 256, 257
Levin-Abramovich, 176
Levitan, 203, 220, 257
Levner, 135
Leybzon, 216
Lint, 203, 216
Lipman, 234, 250
Lipschitz, 241
Lipshitz, 216, 255
Lipshitz-Weiner, 241
Liptzer, 57, 63, 73, 75, 76, 77, 92, 126, 141, 144, 187, 196, 201, 204, 216, 241
Lubetzki, 216
Luntz, 253
Lurie, 191, 214, 216, 222, 223, 227, 241, 270

M

Makovski, 216
Mapu, 13
Margolis, 102, 191, 212, 222, 241
Markovski, 102, 212, 221, 265
Markowski, 270
Matematik, 77
Mattis, 241
Matz, 21
Matzok, 97
Meizel, 127
Mek, 85, 86, 87, 187
Melamdovich, 202
Melamed, 251, 256, 257
Melamedovich, 224
Melamedovitch, 212
Mendelson, 212
Meris, 224
Meshkotz, 237, 257
Michles, 70
Mil, 207, 216
Miller, 87, 186
Milshtein, 228

Mishelski, 256
Miya, 114, 118
Mizrach, 216
Mudrik, 230

N

Nabriski, 241
Nachumovski, 220
Nachumson, 216
Naftal, 216
Natkin, 223
Nechmod, 203
Neishtot, 257
Neividl, 227
Nementchik, 241
Nordau, 216
Norvitch, 251

O

Ogov, 211
Oleiski, 217
Olitzky, 241
Oretshkin, 89, 216
Orlianski, 241
Oshinsky, 255
Oshry, 250
Osofsky, 22

P

Padison, 204
Paletzkis, 15
Panemonski, 204
Paul, 183
Peretzman, 50
Perkol, 223
Pertzikovitch, 241
Pikert, 216
Pilgram, 130, 155
Pilovnik, 127
Pilsodski-Marsh, 261
Pomerantz, 203
Portnoy, 120
Potroch, 226
Prisman, 212

R

Rabinovich, 224, 227
Rabinovitch, 224, 257
Rabinovitz, 68, 218
Rabinowitz, 27, 183, 224
Rapaport, 233
Ratgeber, 20
Ratger, 102
Ratner, 102, 125, 126, 217

Ratnikas, 88
Ratshka, 203
Rauca, 34, 44, 46, 47, 54, 106, 126, 192
Rauzuk, 257
Razin, 228
Rebelski, 173
Rein, 216
Reiness, 216
Resnik, 234
Richman, 241
Ring, 70
Rochelson, 234
Roginski, 184
Rosenblat, 251
Rosenblum, 241
Rostovsky, 195
Rozenbaum, 256
Rozenberg, 64, 256, 257
Rozenburg, 64
Rozenthal, 249
Rozin, 256
Rozmarin, 203
Rubenstein, 8
Rubinson, 204
Rubinstein, 3, 180
Rutenberg, 253

S

Sadovski, 217, 257
Sapoznikov, 126
Schmerkovitch, 244
Schmidt, 229, 256
Schmonovitz, 4
Segal, 228, 241, 244, 251
Segalovich, 91
Segalovski, 227
Segalson, 70, 229
Seletzky, 229
Senior, 127
Shabashevitch, 216
Shachat, 216
Shachnovski, 216
Shafranski, 216
Shalit, 234
Shalitan, 223
Shapira, 44, 184, 192, 250, 251, 256, 257
Shapiro, 183, 195, 241
Shauchet, 244
Sheinzohn, 8
Shenker, 269
Sherkovitch, 257
Sherman, 126, 176
Shevtz, 241
Shinberg, 195, 233, 253
Shlapoverski, 224
Shmuckler, 195, 203
Shmukler, 27, 183

Shor, 203
Shpegel, 165
Shtein, 216
Shtitz, 76, 77, 85
Shtreichman, 184
Shuster, 8
Shuv, 257
Shvartz, 223
Shwartz, 70
Skirpa, 20
Slonimski, 216, 223
Slove, 241
Smetana, 12, 14, 15, 27, 214
Smuckler, 195
Snieg, 27, 183, 195, 251
Sobolevich, 251
Solomin, 176
Srebnitzki, 227, 229, 256, 257
Srolovitch, 216
Staravolski, 216
Stein, 241
Steinberg, 233
Stitch, 89
Stokol, 251
Stopel, 203
Strashon, 176
Strelitz, 241
Stupel, 200
Sudak-Katz, 241
Sukenik, 209
Svirsky, 237

T

Takatsh, 202, 257
Tamshe, 216
Tankel, 241
Tarko, 223
Tchernow, 224
Telzak, 234
Tepper, 176
Tint, 241
Todt, 91, 97
Torenbaum, 35
Torenboim, 46
Treger, 227, 244
Tuvialis, 192
Tzarfat, 251, 272
Tzeitel, 241
Tzindler, 218
Tzipin, 216
Tzipkin, 216, 263
Tzitzes, 216

U

Ullman, 233

V

Valsonok, 102, 126, 225, 246
Varantz, 227
Vaskoboynik, 257
Verbovski, 133, 223
Verbovsky, 111
Videman, 186
Vidutchinsky, 241
Vilenski, 230
Vindsberg, 220
Vinik, 211, 216
Volfberg, 203
Volfovich, 251
Volpert, 165
Von Kepen, 81, 186
Voshtshin, 241

W

Weiner, 202
Weintraub, 237
Wolf, 27, 184, 195, 216

Y

Yakin, 241
Yasvon, 216
Yatkonski, 22
Yatzkan, 216
Yeglin, 244
Yellin, 96, 97, 125, 133, 144, 149, 150, 151, 152, 155, 176, 203, 216, 234
Yeshorin, 216
Yochelson, 226, 241
Yotkowski, 224

Z

Zacharin, 164, 240
Zak, 204, 216, 253
Zaks, 203, 212
Zaltzberg, 241
Zeltzer, 204
Zhopovich, 251
Zhopovitch, 204, 223
Zieman, 152
Zilber, 1
Zilberkvayt, 204
Zilberkweit, 135
Zilberman, 246
Zitchl, 13
Zundelevich, 211
Zupovich, 135

www.ingramcontent.com/pod-product-compliance
Lightning Source LLC
Chambersburg PA
CBHW081420160426
42814CB00039B/217